외투기업의 No.1 노무법인
KangNam Labor Law Firm
Second Edition

Practical Manual
on Labor Law (6/20)

Manual on Working Hours, Holidays and Leaves

근로시간, 휴일, 휴가 매뉴얼

Dr. Bongsoo Jung
Ph.D. in Law / Labor Attorney
법학박사/공인노무사 정 봉 수

- Labor Law Practical Manuals
① Work Force Restructuring
② Foreign Employment and Immigration
③ Lawful Dismissal
④ Labor Union
⑤ Wage
⑥ Working Hours, Holidays and Leave
⑦ Irregular Employment and 'Employee' Status
⑧ Employment Contract
⑨ Industrial Accident Compensation
⑩ Preventing Workplace & Sexual Harassment
⑪ Labor Inspection Preparation
⑫ Rules of Employment

실무자를 위한 노동법 실무 매뉴얼 시리즈
① 구조조정 매뉴얼
② 외국인 고용과 비자 매뉴얼
③ 해고 매뉴얼
④ 노동조합 매뉴얼
⑤ 임금 매뉴얼
⑥ 근로시간, 휴일, 휴가 매뉴얼
⑦ 비정규직과 근로자성 판단 매뉴얼
⑧ 근로계약 매뉴얼
⑨ 산재보상 매뉴얼
⑩ 직장 내 괴롭힘과 성희롱 예방 매뉴얼
⑪ 근로감독 준비 매뉴얼
⑫ 취업규칙 매뉴얼

강남노무법인

Preface

The current Moon Jae-in government, since his inauguration on May 10, 2017, has been pushing labor-friendly policies, reflected in the increased minimum wage, shortened working hours, additional vacation time and holidays, expanded coverage of industrial accident insurance, and stronger labor supervision. The most significant changes to the working environment are the reduced working hours and the increase in holidays and leaves.

In terms of working hours, the 52-hour workweek has been introduced and settled. By introducing the concept that 7 days equal one week, including a weekly holiday, the maximum weekly working hours were reduced from 68 to 52 (amended on March 20, 2018). In recent legal cases, it has been stated that the limit for working hours is 52 hours per week, and there is no limit to daily overtime work (as of December 7, 2023). In annual leave regulations, the number of days for employees working less than two years had been limited to 15 over that two-year period. The related law was amended to allow for an additional 11 days in the first year, and 15 days in the second (amended November 18, 2017). In addition, national holidays were introduced as statutory holidays (amended March 20, 2018).

In this business environment, where working hours have been shortened and more holidays and vacation days added, there is no possibility for companies to remain externally competitive and internally more productive. Instead, they must design their working hours to suit their own company characteristics. This manual explains various types of working hour schedules so that flexibility can be designed. It also introduces related regulations, agreements between labor and management, and detailed methods of introduction necessary so that this manual can be used well in practice.

It is my hope that this manual will be of assistance to HR managers, giving them an opportunity to better understand the legal concepts of working hours, holidays, and leaves and see how working hour-related matters in labor law apply in practice.

I would like to thank Instructor Hyun-jin Lee, and Publisher Young-cheol Jung who edited and published the book so that it might see the light. In particular, I thank my longtime friend and proofreading editor, Dave Crofton. This manual, which has been made possible by the efforts of many people, is a collaborative work and not a product of the author alone.

February 10, 2024
Bongsoo Jung
Labor Attorney, PhD in Law

머리말

2017년 5월 10일 문재인 정부가 들어서면서 노동친화 정책을 추진해 오고 있다. 최저임금 인상, 근로시간 단축, 휴가와 휴일 추가 부여, 산업재해보상 확대적용, 근로감독 강화 등이 그것이다. 이 가운데 근로시간 단축, 휴일과 휴가의 증가는 장시간 노동시간의 노동현장을 되흔드는 노동환경의 가장 큰 변화로 꼽힌다. 근로시간에 있어서 주52시간제를 도입하여 정착하고 있다. 1주의 개념을 휴일을 포함하여 7일의 개념으로 법제화함으로써, 1주 최대의 근로시간이 기존에 68시간에서 52시간으로 단축되었다(2018.3.20.). 최근 판례에서 근로시간은 한도는 1주 52시간이고, 1일의 연장근로 한도는 없다고 판시하였다(2023.12.7.). 연차휴가 규정에 있어서도 2년 미만 근로자의 휴가가 15일로 제한된 휴가 규정이었다. 이에 대해 최초 1년에 대해 추가적으로 11일의 휴가를 사용할 수 있도록 관련법을 가정하였다(2017.11.18). 또한 국가 공휴일(현재 15개)를 모두 법정 휴일로 도입하였다(2018.3.20.).

근로시간 단축과 휴일이나 휴가가 증가되는 경영환경에서 기업이 대외적 경쟁력과 대내적 생산성 확보를 위해서는 기존의 근로형태로는 가능성이 없다. 기업에서는 기업의 특성에 맞는 근로시간 설계가 절실하다고 할 수 있다. 이러한 현실에서「근로시간, 휴일, 휴가 매뉴얼」은 탄력적인 근로시간제를 기업에 맞게 설계할 수 있도록 다양한 형태의 유연근로시간제를 설명하고 있으며 실무에서 활용할 수 있도록 관련 규정, 노사간의 합의서, 도입 방식 등에 대해 자세히 기술하고 있다.

이번 매뉴얼을 통해 실무자들은 노동법에서의 근로시간, 휴일, 휴가에 대한 내용을 이해하고, 다양한 근로시간 제도를 기업에 맞추어 도입하여 기업의 생산성 향상에 기여할 수 있는 기회가 되기를 바란다.

본서 출간에 있어 문맥 교정과 더불어 전반적으로 내용을 감수해 주신 이정애 노무사님, 장정화 노무사님, 이현진 원장님, 그리고 이 책이 빛을 볼 수 있도록 편집과 출판을 해 주신 정영철 사장님께 감사드린다. 특히 나의 오랜 친구이자 영문교정을 맡고 있는 Dave Crofton에게도 감사드린다. 여러 사람의 노력이 배어있는 본 매뉴얼은 공동의 작업이지 결코 저자 혼자만의 산물이 아니라고 생각한다.

2024년 2월 10일
정봉수 (공인노무사, 법학박사)

Contents

Chapter 1 — Working Hours

I. Determining Working Hours ········ 6
II. Recess Periods ········ 10
<Case Study 1-1> Disputes around Working Hours ········ 17
<Case Study 1-2> Whether Union Activities by Union Officials is Company Work ···· 18
<Case Study 1-3> Whether a Study Room Manager's Working Hours can be recognized as Full-time Work ········ 23

Chapter 2 — Working Hours and Extended Working Hours

I. Legal Standard Working Hours ········ 30
II. Contractual Working Hours and Inclusive Wage Systems ········ 32
III. Overtime, Nighttime and Holiday Work ········ 39
<Case Study 2-1> Driver of Director Paid Less than Statutory Allowances ········ 47

Chapter 3 — Exceptions from Application of Working Hours

I. Surveillance · Intermittent Employees ········ 55
II. Managerial and Supervisory Positions ········ 60
III. Workplaces Ordinarily Employing Fewer than Five People ········ 62
IV. Part-time Workers ········ 68
V. Working Conditions for Minors ········ 71
<Case Study 3-1> Whether a Managing Director is Considered to Hold a Managerial and Supervisory Position ········ 72

차 례

제1장 근로시간의 이해

Ⅰ. 근로시간의 판단기준 ··· 6
Ⅱ. 휴게시간 ·· 10
　　<실무사례 1-1> 근로시간 분쟁 ·· 17
　　<실무사례 1-2> 노조간부의 조합활동이 업무인지 여부 ······ 18
　　<실무사례 1-3> 독서실 총무의 근로시간 인정여부 ··········· 23

제2장 근로시간과 연장근로수당

Ⅰ. 법정근로시간 ·· 30
Ⅱ. 소정근로시간과 포괄임금제 ·· 32
Ⅲ. 연장근로, 야간근로와 휴일근로 ······································ 39
　　<실무사례 2-1> 임원기사의 법정수당 미지급 사건 ··········· 47

제3장 근로시간 적용의 제외와 특례

Ⅰ. 감시 단속적 근로자 ··· 55
Ⅱ. 관리 감독자 ·· 60
Ⅲ. 5인 미만의 사업장 ··· 62
Ⅳ. 단시간 근로자 ·· 68
Ⅴ. 연소근로자 ·· 71
　　<실무사례 3-1> 외국기업의 상무 관리감독자 여부 판단 ······ 72

Chapter 4: Flexible Working Hours

I. Requirement Before Introducing Flexible Working Hours ········· 77
II. Flexible Working Hour System ········· 85
    <Table 4-1> Rules of Employment on Flexible Working Hours for 2-Week Units ········· 92
    <Table 4-2> Labor-Management Agreement on Flexible Working Hours for 3-Month Units ········· 93
III. Selective Working Hour System ········· 94
    <Table 4-3> Selective Working Time Policy ········· 98
    <Table 4-4> Labor-Management Agreement on Selective Working Hour System ········· 100
IV. Deemed Working Hour System ········· 101
    <Table 4-5> Labor-Management Agreement on Deemed Working Hours for Outside Work ········· 103
V. Discretionary Work System ········· 104
    <Table 4-6> Rules of Employment for Discretionary Working Hour System ········· 107
    <Table 4-7> Labor-Management Agreement on Discretionary Working Hour System> ········· 107
VI. Compensatory Leave System ········· 109
    <Table 4-8> Labor-Management Agreement regarding the Compensatory Leave System ········· 111
VII. Work-from-Home Systems ········· 112
    <Table 4-9> Working from Home in the Rules of Employment ········· 116
    <Table 4-10> Regulation Example: Work-from-Home Service Regulations ········· 117
    <Table 4-11> Example Working from Home Policy ········· 119
    <Table 4-12> Working from Home Checklist ········· 123
    <Table 4-13> Agreement to Protect Security while Working from Home ········· 124
VIII. Work-from-Home Systems ········· 125
    <Table 4-14> Sample Labor-Management Agreement to Introduce a Vacation Savings Account System for Working Hours ········· 127
    <Table 4-15> Introduction through the Rules of Employment ········· 128

Chapter 5: Statutory and Contractual Holidays

I. Statutory Holidays ········· 130
II. Contractual Holidays ········· 135

제4장 유연 근로시간제도

Ⅰ. 도입요건: 근로자대표 선정 ·· 77
Ⅱ. 탄력적 근로시간제 ·· 85
　〈표4-1〉 2주 이내 탄력적 근로시간제 취업규칙 ················ 92
　〈표4-2〉 3개월 이내 탄력적 근로시간제 노사합의서 ········ 93
Ⅲ. 선택적 근로시간제 ·· 94
　〈표4-3〉 선택적 근로시간제 규정- 시차 출근 ···················· 98
　〈표4-4〉 선택적 근로시간제 노사합의서 ···························· 100
Ⅳ. 간주 근로시간제 ·· 101
　〈표4-5〉 사업장 밖 간주근로시간제 노사합의서 ·············· 103
Ⅴ. 재량근로시간제 ·· 104
　〈표4-6〉 재량근로시간제 취업규칙 ···································· 107
　〈표4-7〉 재량근로시간제 노사합의서 ································ 107
Ⅵ. 보상휴가제 ·· 109
　〈표4-8〉 보상휴가제 노사합의서 ·· 111
Ⅶ. 재택근로제 ·· 112
　〈표4-9〉 취업규칙 규정 ·· 116
　〈표4-10〉 취업규칙 중 재택근무제 복무규정 ·················· 117
　〈표4-11〉 재택근무 규정 ·· 119
　〈표4-12〉 재택근무 체크리스트 ·· 123
　〈표4-13〉 재택근무 보안서약서 ·· 124
Ⅷ. 연차유급휴가를 이용한 저축휴가제도 ···························· 125
　〈표4-14〉 근로시간 저축휴가제 노사합의서 ······················ 127
　〈표4-15〉 취업규칙을 통한 도입 내용 ······························ 128

제5장 법정휴일과 약정휴일

Ⅰ. 법정휴일 ·· 130
Ⅱ. 약정휴일 ·· 135

<Case Study 5-1> Petition for Unpaid Weekly Holiday Allowance ········ 136
<Case Study 5-2> Unpaid Wages for Temporary Workers ················ 138

Chapter 6 Statutory Leave and Contractual Leave

Ⅰ. Annual Paid Leave ·· 143
    <Reference> Annual Paid Leave – Questions and Answers ············· 151
Ⅱ. Granting Annual Paid Leave ··· 159
Ⅲ. Protective Leave (Maternity, Paternity, Menstruation Leave, Nursing Hours) ···· 167
    <Case Study 6-1> Whether Unused Annual Leave should be Compensated ········ 170
    <Table 6-1> Promoting the Use of Annual Leave & Application
        for Use of Annual Leave ·· 172
Ⅳ. Substitution of Annual Paid Leave ·· 173
Ⅴ. Contractual Leave ·· 173
    <Table 6-2> Sick Leave-related Cases in the Rules of Employment ·········· 177
    <Table 6-3> Congratulatory or Condolence Leave-related Cases in the Rules of
        Employment ··· 179

Chapter 7 Protection of Motherhood

Ⅰ. Protection of Maternal Employees ·· 182
Ⅱ. Protection leave for maternal employees ······································ 183
Ⅲ. Childcare Leave and Reduced Working Hours for the
    Childcare Period ·· 190
Ⅳ. Menstruation Leave ·· 194

Chapter 8 Other Related References

Ⅰ. Rules of Employment regarding Working Hours, Holidays,
    and Leaves (Standard Sample) ·· 196
    <Table 8-1> Form: Application for Leave ·· 207

<실무사례 5-1> 주휴수당 미지급 진정사건 ·· 136
<실무사례 5-2> 지방의회의 일급직 사무보조자(위촉직)의 임금체불 사례 ·········· 138

제6장 법정휴가와 약정휴가

Ⅰ. 연차유급휴가 ··· 143
   <참고> 실무자를 위한 연차유급휴가 Q&A ·· 151
Ⅱ. 연차휴가 부여방식 ·· 159
Ⅲ. 연차유급휴가 사용촉진제도 ··· 167
   <실무사례 6-1> 미사용 연차수당 지급 진정사건 ································· 170
   <표 6-1> 연차 사용 촉진 안내 및 휴가 사용계획 신청서 ···················· 172
Ⅳ. 연차유급휴가의 대체 ··· 173
Ⅴ. 약정휴가 ··· 173
   <표 6-2> 병가 관련 취업규칙 사례 ·· 177
   <표 6-3> 경조사 관련 취업규칙 사례 ·· 179

제7장 모성보호

Ⅰ. 임산부 보호 ·· 182
Ⅱ. 임산부의 보호휴가 ·· 183
Ⅲ. 육아휴직과 육아기 근로시간 단축 ··· 190
Ⅳ. 생리휴가 ··· 194

제8장 기타 근로시간 관련 참고자료

Ⅰ. 근로시간, 휴일, 휴가에 대한 취업규칙 (표준샘플) ································· 196
   <표8-1> 휴가신청서 서식 ·· 207

Chapter 1 Working Hours

I. Determining Working Hours
II. Recess Periods

⟨Case Study 1-1⟩ Disputes around Working Hours

⟨Case Study 1-2⟩ Whether Union Activities by Union Officials is Company Work

⟨Case Study 1-3⟩ Whether a Study Room Manager's Working Hours can be recognized as Full-time Work

제1장 　근로시간의 이해

Ⅰ. 근로시간의 판단기준

Ⅱ. 휴게시간

　　〈실무사례 1-1〉 근로시간 분쟁

　　〈실무사례 1-2〉 노조간부의 조합활동이 업무인지 여부

　　〈실무사례 1-3〉 독서실 총무의 근로시간 인정여부

Chapter 1 Working Hours

I. Determining Working Hours

> Working hours refer to the actual hours during which the employee provides labor service prescribed by the employment contract under the employer's direction and supervision. Article 50 of the Labor Standards Act regulates that working hours shall not exceed 8 hours per day and 40 hours per week, excluding recess hours. The employer shall pay an additional fifty percent (50%) of the ordinary wage for extended working hours exceeding the legal standard working hours. Working hours are usually implemented within contractual working hours that the employer and the employee have agreed upon, but there have been some disputes in recognizing working hours in cases where the employee conducted work before or after contractual working hours, or in cases of waiting time for work, training hours, traveling hours, company events, etc.

1. Understanding Working Hours

(1) Working hours shall be stipulated in the labor contract, rules of employment, or the collective agreement.

Working hours shall be the total hours from when the employee starts to provide contractual work to the employer to when the employee finishes his/her work, excluding recess hours. The Labor Standards Act regulates that the employment contract shall include the starting and finishing times for work, and that the rules of employment shall contain statutory items.

(2) Working hours shall be under the employer's direction and supervision.

Working hours mean the time during which the employee provides labor service described by the employment contract under the employer's direction and supervision. Even though waiting time or recess and sleeping time are times that the employee is not engaged in actual work in the middle of working hours, if these times are not allowed to be used freely by employees, but are, in practice, under the employer's direction and supervision, those times belong to working hours.[1]

---

[1] Supreme Court ruling on May 27, 1993, 92Da24509.

I. 근로시간의 판단기준

> 근로시간이란 근로자가 사용자의 지휘·감독 아래 근로계약상의 근로를 제공하는 시간, 실 근로시간을 말한다. 법정 근로시간은 휴게시간을 제하고 1일에 8시간 1주일에 40시간을 초과할 수 없다고 규정하고 있다 (근기법 제50조). 이 법정근로시간을 초과하는 근로시간에 대해 통상임금의 50%를 가산하여 지급하여야 한다. 근로시간은 대개 당사자 간에 근로하기로 합의한 소정근로시간 이내에 이루어지지만, 근로자가 사업주의 지시에 의해 시업시간 전 또는 종업시간 후에 업무를 수행한 경우, 또는 그 외 대기시간, 교육시간, 출장시간, 행사시간 등에 대해 근로시간 인정 여부에 대한 다툼이 생기는 경우가 많다. 이에 대해 근로시간에 대한 판단 기준을 명확히 하고, 그 구체적 사례에 대해 검토해보고자 한다.

1. 근로시간의 이해

(1) 근로시간은 근로계약, 취업규칙, 단체협약 등에 규정되어 있어야 한다.

근로시간의 계산은 근로자가 사용자에게 소정의 근로를 제공하기 시작한 시간부터 그 제공을 종료한 시각까지의 총 시간에서 휴게시간을 공제한 시간으로 산출하는데, 근로기준법에서는 시업과 종업시간을 근로계약에 명시하도록 하고 취업규칙에서 반드시 기재하여야 할 필요적 기재사항으로 정하고 있다 (근기법 제17조, 제93조).

(2) 근로시간은 사용자의 지휘·감독 하에 있어야 한다.

근로시간이라 함은 사용자의 지휘·감독 아래 근로계약상의 근로를 제공하는 시간을 말한다. 작업시간 도중에 현실로 작업에 종사하지 않은 대기시간이나 휴식·수면시간이라 하더라도 그것이 휴게시간으로서 근로자에게 자유로운 이용이 보장된 것이 아니고 실질적으로 사용자의 지휘·감독 아래 놓여있는

Chapter 1   Working Hours

Whether the subsidiary time required in actual working hours belongs to working hours or not shall be judged by whether those times are implemented under the employer's direction and supervision. Such subsidiary times include the time needed to change into the work uniform and gather necessary tools, waiting time, conferences prior to work, shift-changes, wash-up time after finishing the work day, organizing things for the next day's work after finishing the workday, travel time during business trips, etc.[2]

(3) Working hours shall be related to work characteristics under the employment contract.

The type of work described under the employment contract is not limited to the work tasks themselves, but actual working hours shall include those times essential to preparing for work and to arranging things after finishing the work day in relation to actual work performance. It is regarded as working hours in cases where those activities besides actual working hours are stipulated as the employee's mandatory duties according to related laws, collective agreements, rules of employment, labor practices, and employment contracts, or in cases where non-implementation charges disadvantage the employees concerned.

2. Concrete Judgments on Working Hours

(1) Time worked before the workday begins
① **In cases where the employee arrives at the workplace earlier than the official starting hour**

Whether the company shall pay wages for working hours when the employee comes earlier to the workplace to ensure normal operations shall be dependent upon the following: If the employee did not come to work earlier than the official starting hour, his wages could be reduced or he might be punished for violating the service regulations. If this situation does not exist, then the time before the official starting hour does not belong to working hours.[3]

② **Conferences held before working hours**

Conferences held before working hours to deal with safety training for underground mine workers, work directions, and organization of working groups. These meetings shall be held essentially for the purpose of underground shift work and be implemented under the employer's direction and supervision. Therefore, these meetings shall be included in actual working hours.[4]

---

[2] Supreme Court ruling on Mar. 9, 1993, 92Da22770.
[3] MOEL Guidelines: Kungi 01254-13305, on Aug. 30, 1988.
[4] Supreme Court ruling on Sept. 28, 1993, 93Da3363.

시간이라면 당연히 근로시간에 포함된다.[1]
　작업복을 갈아입는 시간, 작업도구 준비시간, 대기시간, 작업 전 회의, 교대시간, 작업 후 목욕시간, 작업종료 후 정돈 시간, 출장 중 이동시간 등 실제근로에 부속되는 시간이 근로시간 인지 여부도 사용자의 지휘·명령 아래에서 이루어지는지에 따라 판단된다.[2]

(3) 근로시간은 근로계약상 업무성이 있어야 한다.
　근로계약에서 정하여진 근로의 종류는 반드시 그 근로 자체만을 뜻하지 않고 그 근로에서 실제 작업에 필수 불가결한 준비행위나 작업종료 후 뒷정리를 위한 시간도 근로시간에 포함된다. 근로시간외의 활동을 법령, 단체협약, 취업규칙, 노사관행 또는 근로계약에서 근로자의 의무로 명백히 정하거나 그 불이행에 대해 일정한 불이익이 있는 경우도 근로시간에 포함한다.

2. 근로시간 인지 여부 판단

(1) 시업 전 시간
① 조기 출근한 경우
　시업시간 이전에 조기 출근토록 하여 시업에 지장이 없도록 하는 것을 근로시간으로 인정하여 임금이 지급되어야 할 것인가 여부는 조기출근을 하지 않을 경우 임금을 감액하거나 복무 위반으로 제재를 가하는 권리의 무관계라면 근로시간에 해당될 것이나 그렇지 않다면 근로시간에 해당되지 않는다.[3]

② 작업시간 전 취업회의 시간
　작업시간 전에 갖는 취업회의 내용인 갱내 근무자에 대한 보안교육이나 작업지시 및 작업조 편성은 갱내 교대근무를 위한 필요불가결한 것으로서 사용자의 지휘 감독에 의한 구속 하에 행하여질 수밖에 없으므로 실근로시간에 포함시키는 것이 타당하다.[4]

---

[1] 대법원 1993.5.27 선고 92다24509 판결.
[2] 대법원 1993.3.9 선고 92다22770 판결.
[3] 행정해석: 근기 01254-13305 1988.08.30.
[4] 대법원 1993.9.28 선고 93다3363 판결.

(2) Time worked after the workday is over

The end of the workday is the time for the employee to be free from the employer's direction and supervision. When the employee continues to be under the employer's direction and supervision after he finishes his regular work time, actual working hours end when the employee is actually free from the employer's direction and supervision. Such examples of the end of the workday not being the end of actual working hours are time when workplace repairs, examinations, organization, and cleaning are performed after completing work under the employer's direction and supervision.[5]

(3) Waiting time

> The Labor Standards Act: Article 50 (Working Hours) ③ ~ waiting hours the worker spends while under the employer's direction and supervision for work shall be regarded as working hours.

Waiting hours are working hours but recess hours are not. Recess hours under the Labor Standards Act refer to time that employees can use freely, away from the employer's direction and supervision, regardless of the name given for such times, such as waiting time, etc. In this case, unlike the working structure stipulated by the rules of employment, under the employer's implied agreement, the employees work every two hours in repeated practice and off-time employees take recess hours, playing chess or baduk, or watching TV. There is a clear division of waiting time and working hours. The employees cannot go out of the workplace during this waiting time, but they can use it freely, away from the employer's direction and supervision. In this case, the waiting time shall be recognized as recess hours.[6]

In cases where an employee drives a company car as necessary from time to time, just like a regular driver of a company car, if the employee cannot use the waiting time freely, this shall be regarded as working hours; but, if such time is free for the employee to use as he/she wishes, it is considered part of recess hours and cannot be included in working hours.[7]

---

[5] Supreme Court ruling on Mar. 9, 1993, 92Da2270.
[6] MOEL Guidelines: Kungi 68207-3298, on Oct. 25, 2000.
[7] Supreme Court ruling on July 28, 1992, 92Da14007.

(2) 종업 후 시간

근로시간이 끝나는 종업시각은 근로자가 사용자의 지휘 감독으로부터 벗어났다고 인정되는 작업종료 시각이다. 그러나 작업이 끝나도 계속하여 사용자의 지휘 감독아래 있을 때는 시업시각의 경우처럼 그 구속으로부터 벗어난 시각이 종업시각이 된다. 사용자의 지휘 감독아래 하는 작업 후 기계 기구의 정비 점검 정돈과 사업장의 청소 등 이에 속한다.[5]

(3) 대기시간

> 근로기준법 제50조(근로시간) ③ ~ 근로시간을 산정함에 있어 작업을 위하여 근로자가 사용자의 지휘·감독 아래에 있는 대기시간 등은 근로시간으로 본다.

대기시간은 근로시간이고 휴게시간은 근로시간이 아니다. 휴게시간이란 휴게·대기시간 등 명칭 여하에 불구하고 근로자가 사용자의 지휘·감독으로부터 벗어나 자유로이 사용할 수 있는 시간을 말한다. 따라서 취업규칙상 근로형태는 아니지만 사업주의 묵시적인 동의하에 관례적으로 근로자들 스스로 2시간 단위로 작업을 하고 작업을 하지 않는 근로자들은 대기실에서 장기, 바둑, TV시청 등을 하는 형태로, 대기시간과 근무시간의 구분이 명백하고, 근로자가 사전에 대기시간을 알고 있으며, 그 대기시간 중에는 사업장 밖으로 나갈 수는 없지만 사용자의 지휘·감독을 벗어나 시간을 자유로이 이용할 수 있다면 이는 휴게시간으로 인정할 수 있다고 판단된다.[6]

업무용 자동차 운전자와 같이, 필요할 때마다 간헐적으로 운전업무를 하는 경우 다음 운전업무까지 대기하는 시간은 그 시간을 자유롭게 이용할 수 없는 한 이를 근로시간으로 보는 것이 원칙이나 자유로운 시간 이용이 보장된다면 이를 휴게시간으로 보며 근로시간에 포함하지 않는다.[7]

---

[5] 대법원 1993.3.9 선고 92다2270 판결.
[6] 행정해석: 근기 68207-3298 2000.10.25.
[7] 대법원 1992.7.28 선고 92다14007 판결.

Chapter 1 Working Hours

(4) Education and training time

Training time is working hours. It is working hours when the employer implements job training during working hours in relation to work, concerning work safety and work efficiency to improve productivity, and it is also working hours when the employer gives compulsory training outside of working hours or during a holiday. However, it is not working hours when the employee attends compulsory individual training like driver's education, regardless of the company's business, or when ethical or safety training etc. is recommended for employees and provided by the nation due to major national policies outside of working hours or during a holiday.[8]

(5) Company picnics or events

In cases where the company hosts a picnic, athletic event, etc., if the employee needs to attend the picnic, athletic event, etc., the participating time shall be deemed working hours. Conversely, if the employer hosts a picnic, athletic event, etc. for the purpose of welfare, and if employees are free to participate in the event at their own discretion, it shall not be deemed as working hours even though employees attend such an event.[9]

If the company hosts a picnic on a working day in accordance with the company's operation rules, the wages for that day shall be paid accordingly. If the picnic was held on a holiday, the wages payable on that holiday and ordinary wages to compensate for holiday work (i.e. the picnic party) shall be paid.[10]

(6) Business travel

① **Travel time between employee accommodations and the appointed workplace**

In calculating working hours for business travel, travel time to the workplace shall be included in working hours in principle, but when the workplace is on the way to the regular office, such travel time can be excluded from working hours. However, for long-distance business trips, travel time from the company workplace to the workplace on business travel shall be included in the working hours.[11]

---

[8] MOEL Guidelines: Kungi 01254-14835, on Sept. 29, 1988.
[9] MOEL Guidelines: Kungi 01254-554, on Jan. 10, 1989.
[10] MOEL Guidelines: Kungi 1455-7105, on July 12, 1979.
[11] MOEL Guidelines: Kungi 68207-1909, on June 14, 2001.

(4) 교육시간

교육시간은 근로시간이다. 사용자가 근로시간 중에 작업안전, 작업능률 등 생산성 향상 즉 업무와 관련하여 실시하는 직무교육과 근로시간 종료 후 또는 휴일에 근로자를 의무적으로 소집하여 실시하는 교육은 근로시간에 포함되어야 할 것이다. 그러나 근로자가 회사와는 관계없는 운전면허증 소지자에 대한 소양교육과 같은 법적 이행 개인의무사항 교육이나 국가기관 등의 시책사업으로 사용자에게 협조를 요구하여 근무시간 외 또는 휴일에 회사에서 단체로 근로자에게 의무사항이 아닌 권고사항으로 시행하는 국민정신교육, 안전관계교육 등은 근로시간에 포함된다고 볼 수 없다.[8]

(5) 야유회 등의 행사

일반적으로 사용자가 근로자의 야유회, 체육대회 등의 행사를 행하는 경우 그 야유회, 체육대회 등의 참가자가 근로자의 의무로 동원되는 경우에는 그 참가시간은 근로시간으로 보아야 할 것이고, 반대로 이러한 야유회, 체육대회 등을 사용자가 복리 후생 차원에서 행하고 근로자의 참가 여부가 그 스스로의 자유에 맡겨진 때에는 근로자가 이에 참가하더라도 그 시간은 근로시간이 아니다.[9]

회사운영방침에 따라 근로하여야 할 날에 야유회를 실시하는 경우라면 임금은 당연히 지급되어야 하며, 유급 휴일에 야유회를 실시하는 경우라면 휴일에 당연히 지급되는 임금과 당해 유급 휴일의 근로(야유회)에 대한 소정의 통상임금을 지급해야 한다.[10]

(6) 출 장

① 출장업무 수행을 위해 이동하는 시간

출장에 통상 필요한 시간을 산정할 경우 출장지로의 이동에 필요한 시간은 근로시간에 포함시키는 것이 원칙이나 출퇴근에 갈음하여 출장지로 출근 또는 출장지에서 퇴근하는 경우는 제외할 수 있을 것이다. 다만, 장거리 출장의 경우 사업장이 소재하는 지역에서 출장지가 소재하는

---

[8] 행정해석: 근기 01254-14835 1988.09.29.
[9] 행정해석: 근기 01254-554 1989.1.10.
[10] 행정해석: 근기 1455-7105 1979.07.12.

② **When the employee is required to engage in business travel at night or during a holiday by order of the employer, such time shall be regarded as night or holiday work.**

In cases where the employee carries out his duties in whole or in part outside the workplace for business travel or for other reasons, the calculation of working hours shall follow exceptional rules[12]. In consideration of the concept of the same Article, if it is evident that the employee conducts business travel at night or during holidays by order of the employer, the night work and holiday work shall be considered working hours. However, if the employee only travels to the workplace during the night or holiday and does not engage in any business, it is difficult to deem such travel time night work or holiday work.[13]

II. Recess Periods

The purpose of a recess is to relieve worker fatigue and reduce the boredom caused by continual work, thereby enabling them to continue to work feeling refreshed and willing to work.[14] A 'recess period' is the period of time during which a worker is free to rest without being directed or supervised by an employer.[15]

The Labor Standards Act states, "Working hours per week shall not exceed 40 hours excluding recess hours. Working hours per day shall not exceed 8 hours excluding recess hours. In calculating working hours, waiting hours the worker spends while under the employer's direction and supervision for work shall be regarded as working hours." (Article 50 of the Labor Standards Act). The recess period in the Labor Standards Act is excluded from working time, but time waiting for work is determined to be working time, not a recess period. Although the relationship between working time and recess period is clear, there is a vague distinction between 'waiting time' and

---

[12] Paragraphs 1 and 2 of Article 58 of the Labor Standards Act
[13] MOEL Guidelines: Kungi 68207-2650, on Aug. 5, 2002.
[14] Ha, Kaprae, The Labor Standards Act 28th ed., 2016, p. 323; Lim Jongyul, Labor Act 17th ed., 2019, p. 460.

지역까지의 이동시간은 근로시간에 포함시키는 것이 타당하다.[11]

② 사용자의 지시에 의해 야간 또는 휴일에 출장 업무의 이동이 명확한 때에는 야간·휴일근로로 볼 수 있다.

출장근무 등 사업장 밖에서 근로하는 경우에 있어서의 근로시간 산정에 관하여는 특례를 규정하고 있다.[12] 동조의 취지로 볼 때 사용자의 지시에 의해 야간 또는 휴일에 출장업무를 수행하는 것이 명확한 때에는 야간, 휴일근로로 볼 수 있으나 단순히 야간 또는 휴일에 이동하는 때에는 야간, 휴일근로를 한 것으로 보기 어렵다.[13]

Ⅱ. 휴게시간

휴게제도는 근로자가 계속해서 근로할 경우 육체적·정신적 피로가 쌓이게 되므로 근로자의 피로를 회복시키고 권태감을 감소시켜 노동력의 재생산과 작업 의욕을 확보 유지하는 데 그 목적이 있다.[14] 휴게시간은 근로시간 중간에 사용자의 지휘와 감독을 받지 않고 근로자가 자유로이 휴식을 가지는 시간을 말한다.[15]

근로기준법에서는 1주 근로시간은 휴게시간을 제외하고 40시간을 초과할 수 없고, 1일의 근로시간은 휴게시간을 제외하고 8시간을 초과할 수 없다고 기술하고 있다. 근로를 제공하지는 않지만 작업을 위하여 근로자가 사용자의 지휘와 감독 아래에 있는 대기시간은 근로시간으로 보고 있다(법 제50조). 근로기준법상 휴게시간은 근로시간에서 제외되지만, 근로를 위해 대기하는 시간은 휴게시간이 아닌 근로시간으로 판단하고 있다. 이 경우 근로시간과 휴게시간의 관계가 명확하지만 대기시간과 휴게시간은 구분이 모호한 면이 있다. 근로시간을 설계함에

---

11) 행정해석: 근기 68207-1909 2001.06.14.
12) 근로기준법 제58조 제1항 및 제2항
13) 행정해석: 근기 68207-2650 2002.08.05.

Chapter 1 Working Hours

> 'recess period'. In designating working hours, it is possible to secure optimal working hours even within statutory working hours if the proper recess period is used in consideration of the characteristics of the work. In order to design a suitable working time system, the concept of recess periods, and the criteria for distinguishing between 'waiting time' and 'recess period' is explained, along with examples of some working time systems using relevant recess periods.

1. The Concept of a Recess Period and its Practical Use

Recess hours are free hours exempted from working hours and occur after a certain number of working hours. According to the Labor Standards Act, "An employer shall allow a recess period of 30 minutes or more for every 4 working hours and at least 1 hour for every 8 working hours during working hours" (Article 54 of the Labor Standards Act). "Any person who violates the provision of 'recess period' shall be punished with imprisonment of up to 2 years or a fine not exceeding 20 million won" (Article 110). "Working hours per week shall not exceed 40 hours excluding recess hours, and working hours per day shall not exceed 8 hours excluding recess hours. Waiting hours that the worker spends while under the employer's direction and supervision for work shall be regarded as working hours" (Article 50).

(1) Free use of recess periods

'Recess period' means time which a worker is free to use away from the supervision and command of an employer during working hours.[16] Here, the term 'working hours' refers to the time when a worker provides work in a labor contract under the direction and supervision of an employer. Even if a worker is not actively working (i.e. waiting time, rest time, sleeping time, etc.), if it is a period of time when that free use is not guaranteed to the worker and is actually time under the control and supervision of an employer, this time is included in working hours.[17]

---

[15] Government Guide: Bubmoo 811-28682, issued on May 15, 1980.
[16] Supreme Court ruling on Apr. 14, 1992: 91da20548.
[17] Supreme Court ruling on Nov. 23, 2006: 2006da41990; Supreme Court ruling on Dec. 5, 2017: 2014da74254.

> 있어서 업무의 특성을 고려하여 적절한 휴게시간을 잘 이용한다면, 법정 근로시간 내에도 최적의 근로시간 확보가 가능하다. 이하에서는 적합한 근로시간제도의 설계를 위하여 휴게시간의 개념, 대기시간과 휴게시간을 구분하는 기준을 이해하고, 휴게시간을 이용한 근로시간제도 사례를 검토해 보고자 한다.

1. 휴게시간의 개념과 사용

휴게시간은 일을 하고 다음 일을 원활히 하기 위해 근로의무가 면제된 쉬는 시간이다. 근로기준법에서 근로시간이 4시간인 경우에는 30분 이상, 8시간인 경우에는 1시간 이상의 휴게시간을 근로시간 도중에 주어야 한다(근기법 제54조). 이 휴게규정을 위반한 자는 2년 이하의 징역 또는 1천만 원 이하의 벌금에 처한다(법 제110조). 또한 법정근로시간은 휴게시간을 제외하고 주 40시간, 1일 8시간으로 제한하고, 작업을 위한 대기시간은 휴게시간이 아닌 근로시간으로 규정하고 있다(법 제50조).

(1) 휴게시간의 자유이용

휴게시간이란 근로자가 근로시간 도중에 사용자의 지휘·명령으로부터 완전히 벗어나 자유로운 이용이 보장된 시간을 의미한다.[16] 여기서 근로시간이라 함은 근로자가 사용자의 지휘·감독 아래 근로계약상의 근로를 제공하는 시간을 말한다. 근로자가 작업시간 도중에 실제로 작업에 종사하지 않은 대기시간이나 휴식·수면시간 등이라 하더라도 그것이 휴게시간으로서 근로자에게 자유로운 이용이 보장된 것이 아니고 실질적으로 사용자의 지휘·감독하에 놓여있는 시간이라면 이는 근로시간에 포함된다.[17]

휴게시간은 작업의 시작으로부터 종료 시까지로 제한된 시간 중의 일부

---

14) 하갑례, 「근로기준법」 제28판, 2016년, 323면; 임종률, 「노동법」 제17판, 2019년, 460면.
15) 법무 811-28682, 선고일자 : 1980-05-15
16) 대법원 1992.4.14. 선고 91다20548 판결
17) 대법원 2006.11.23. 선고 2006다41990 판결; 대법원 2017.12.5. 선고 2014다74254 판결

Chapter 1 Working Hours

A recess period is part of the working hours from the start to the end of work, so even during a recess period it is unavoidable that a worker may still be subject to a certain level of restriction, such as the command and supervision of an employer to continue to carry out work. In other words, workers can be given free breaks, but at the same time there may be some restricted recess periods, depending on the nature of the work, when it is necessary to maintain continuity of work and efficiently respond to emergency situations. In this case, if workers are free to use the recess period beyond the command and supervision of the employer, even though they are restricted within the workplace or are not allowed to leave the workplace during the break without permission, these limitations, which may be required in order to meet objective criteria recognized in advance, can be accepted as a reasonable limitation as to where and how breaks are used.[18]

(2) Scope and use of recess periods
1) Principle: Article 54 (1) of the Labor Standards Act stipulates that an employer shall provide a recess period of 30 minutes or more for 4-hour periods of work, or 1 hour or more for 8-hour periods of work. This is the minimum standard for recess periods that employers must provide for workers who work continuously for specific periods of time.[19] Even if the recess period is provided and given in divided portions distinct from working hours, as long as such recess periods are reasonable in view of the nature of the work and the working conditions, this cannot be regarded as a violation of the recess regulation.[20]
2) Working hours of less than 8 hours: Employers shall provide 30 minutes or more of recess period during the working hours to workers whose working time is more than 4 hours and fewer than 8 hours.[21] However, since this is the lowest standard, it is not a problem to provide more recess time.
3) Divided recess periods: The Labor Standards Act does not provide any provision for dividing a recess period into 10 minutes for every hour or 20 minutes for every two hours. A breakdown of subdivided hours is not permitted, as the purpose of a recess period is to provide relief from fatigue, promote work efficiency, prevent work accidents, provide eating time and meet other socio-cultural requirements.[22]

---

[18] Government Guide: The Legislative Office 16-0239, issued on Aug. 19, 2016.
[19] Government Guide: The Legislative Office 15-0847, issued on Dec. 24, 2015.
[20] Government Guide: Gungi 68207-3307, Dec. 2, 2002.
[21] Government Guide: The Legislative Office 15-0847, issued on Dec. 24, 2015.
[22] Government Guide: Gungi 0125-884, June 25, 1992.

이므로, 휴게시간 중이라고 하더라도 다음 작업의 계속을 위하여 사용자의 지휘·감독 등 일정 수준의 제약을 받는 것은 부득이하다. 즉, 근로자에게 그 종사하는 업무의 특성에 따라 자유로운 휴게시간을 부여하면서도 업무의 연속성을 유지하고 업무와 관련한 긴급 상황에 효율적으로 대응할 수 있도록 하는 등 최소한의 질서유지를 위하여 휴게시간의 이용에 관한 제한이 이루어질 수 있다. 이 경우 근로자로 하여금 사용자의 지휘·감독을 벗어나 휴게시간을 자유롭게 이용할 수 있도록 하고 그 장소를 사업장 안으로 제한하거나 휴게시간에 사업장 밖에 나갈 수 있도록 하면서도 이를 사전에 마련된 객관적 기준에 합치되는 경우에만 허가하는 등의 제한은 휴게시간의 이용 장소와 방법에 관한 합리적인 제한이다.[18]

(2) 휴게시간의 범위와 부여방법

1) 원칙 : 사용자는 근로시간이 4시간인 경우에는 30분 이상, 8시간인 경우에는 1시간 이상의 휴게시간을 근로시간 도중에 주어야 한다고 규정하고 있다(근기법 제54조 제1항). 이는 문헌상 일정 시간 동안 계속적으로 근로하는 근로자에게 사업주가 부여하여야 하는 휴게시간의 최저기준을 정한 것이다.[19] 근무시간과 명백히 구분하여 휴게시간을 분할하여 부여하더라도 작업의 성질, 근로여건 등에 비추어 사회통념상 합리성이 있고 휴게제도의 취지를 벗어나지 않는 한 이를 법 위반으로 보기 어렵다.[20]

2) 8시간 미만의 근로시간 : 사용자는 근로시간이 4시간 이상 8시간 미만인 근로자에게 30분 이상의 휴게시간을 근로시간 도중에 주어야 한다.[21] 다만, 이는 최저 기준이므로 더 많은 시간을 주는 것은 문제가 없다.

3) 분할부여 : 휴게시간을 분할해 1시간마다 10분, 2시간마다 20분 등과 같이 세분화해 부여할 수 있는지에 대해 근로기준법에는 이에 관한 규정이 없으나 피로해소, 작업능률증진, 재해발생예방, 식사 기타 및 사회적-문화적 욕구의 실현 등이 휴게의 목적인 만큼 지나치게 세분화된 휴게시간은 인정되지 않을 수 있다.[22]

---

[18] 법제처 16-0239, 회시일자 : 2016-08-19
[19] 법제처 15-0847, 회시일자 : 2015-12-24
[20] 근기 68207-3307, 회시일자 : 2002-12-02
[21] 법제처 15-0847, 회시일자 : 2015-12-24
[22] 근기 0125-884, 1992.6.25

Chapter 1 Working Hours

4) Working hours exceeding 8 hours: When working more than 8 hours per day, a recess period of 30 minutes or more per 4 hours of overtime and 1 hour or more for 8 hours of overtime or more shall be provided pursuant to Article 54 of the Labor Standards Act.[23]

2. Classification of Waiting Time and Recess Period

(1) Standard for Determination

'Working time' refers to the time during which an employee provides work under the direction and supervision of an employer. Any waiting time is under the direction and supervision of the employer, and so shall be regarded as working time (Article 53 (3) of the Labor Standards Act). On the other hand, 'recess period' refers to the time which a worker is free to use away from the command and supervision of an employer during working hours.[24]

Both 'waiting time' and 'recess period' are common, in terms of occurrence during working hours. The difference is that 'waiting time' is the time preparatory to engaging in work as soon as the employer instructs and is therefore under the direction and supervision of the employer. 'Recess period' on the other hand, is time which workers are free to use separate from the direction and supervision of an employer. Therefore, distinction between the two is made according to whether the worker can freely use the time available.[25] If the worker can clearly distinguish the recess period before starting work, and can freely use it with no direction or supervision of an employer, it must be regarded as a recess period, but if it is not known when there will be work-related instruction from the employer while the worker is waiting, the time cannot be considered a recess period, but as working time.[26]

1) Drivers for transportation companies

When transportation company workers, such as tour bus drivers, go to work and are certain of the time they will be dispatched for work, and freely wait at

---

[23] Government Guide: Working condition guide team-722, Feb. 6, 2009.
[24] Guidelines on Working Hours and Recess Period for Surveillance or Intermittent Work, Oct. 2016.
[25] Lee, Seonggil. "Recess Periods According to Labor Law", Labor Law, Apr. 2004, Vol. 155, Joongang Kyungjae.
[26] Government Guide: Gungi 01254-12495, Aug. 5, 1987.

4) 8시간을 초과하는 근로시간: 하루 8시간을 초과하여 연장 근로를 하는 경우, 연장 근로 4시간에 대하여 30분 이상, 8시간 이상 근로 시 1시간 이상의 휴게 시간을 근로기준법 제54조에 의거하여 부여할 법적 의무가 있다.[23]

2. 대기시간과 휴게시간의 구분

(1) 판단기준

근로시간은 근로자가 사용자의 지휘·감독 아래 근로계약상의 근로를 제공하는 시간을 말한다. 그 명칭 여하를 불문하고 근로자가 그 노동력을 사용자의 처분 아래에 두고 있는 경우에는 근로시간으로 인정한다. 작업을 위하여 근로자가 사용자의 지휘·감독 아래에 있는 대기시간 등은 근로시간으로 본다(근기법 제53조제3항). 이에 반해 휴게시간은 근로자가 근로시간의 도중에 사용자의 지휘·명령으로부터 완전히 벗어나 자유로운 이용이 보장된 시간을 말한다.[24]

대기시간과 휴게시간은 모두 출근한 상태에서 근로시간 중간에 부여한다는 공통점이 있다. 그러나 대기시간은 사용자의 지시가 있으면 바로 작업에 종사해야 하는 시간으로 작업상 지휘·감독 하에 놓여 있다. 반면에 휴게시간은 사용자의 지휘·감독에서 이탈하여 근로자가 자유로이 이용할 수 있는 시간이다. 따라서 양자의 구별은 그 시간을 근로자가 자유롭게 이용할 수 있는지의 여부에 따라 판단한다.[25] 작업의 진행 상황에 따라 근로자가 미리 작업개시 전에 휴게시간을 명백히 구분할 수 있는 상황에 있고, 그 시간 중에 사용자의 지휘·감독을 벗어나 자유로이 시간을 활용할 수 있다면 휴게시간으로 보아야 할 것이다. 다만 사용자로부터 언제 업무지시가 있을지 불분명한 상태에서 대기하는 시간은 휴게시간으로 볼 수 없고 근로시간으로 본다.[26]

1) 운수회사의 버스기사

관광버스 운수회사의 근로자가 출근 시간에 출근하여 퇴근 시까지 어느

---

[23] 근로조건지도과-722, 회시일자 : 2009-02-06
[24] (2016.10) 감시, 단속적 근로자의 근로시간과 휴게시간 구분에 대한 가이드라인
[25] 이승길, "노동법상의 휴게시간", 월간 노동법률, 2004년 4월호, Vol. 155. 중앙경제.
[26] 근기 01254-12495, 회시일자 : 1987-08-05

the workplace, that waiting time is considered a recess period. However, when workers wait without knowing when they will be requested to work for the employer, such waiting time is not considered a recess period. However if, due to the nature of the work, it is not possible to uniformly set a certain recess period in advance, if the dispatch time of the day is clearly defined so that the distinction between dispatch time (vehicle operation time) and waiting time is clear before work or on the day of work, and if the worker knows the waiting time in advance and if such waiting time is available freely beyond the direction and supervision of the employer, this is a recess period.[27]

2) Apartment security guards

In this instance, apartment security guards worked 24 hours from 07:00 to 07:00 the next day, and then rested. Of these 24 hours of duty, the recess period consisted of 6 hours, and was divided into 1 hour for lunch, 1 hour for dinner, and 4 hours for a night break (from 24:00 to 04:00). They were required to respond immediately if something urgent happened, even if it occurred during the night recess period. Although guards were wearing their work uniforms and allowed to take a nap during the night recess period, they were ready to react immediately in case of emergency, and therefore such night rest periods shall be regarded as working time.[28]

3) Goshiwon (long-stay inn) receptionists

Goshiwon receptionists do not have predetermined times set aside for recess periods. As visitors or new tenants do not have fixed arrival times, the receptionists must remain in place without leaving the Goshiwon house. The owner provides the necessary work instructions without special time constraints, and receptionists must also fulfill unscheduled instructions. Although the receptionists did not have any special work to do, and although they took long breaks or studied during many of the waiting hours, such time is considered to be a waiting time for work, not a recess period completely free from direction and supervision.[29]

4) Postal vehicle drivers

---

[27] Government Guide: Bubmoo 811-28682, issued on May 15, 1980.
[28] Supreme Court ruling on Dec. 13, 2017: 2016da243078.
[29] Seoul Central District Court ruling on June 23, 2017: 2017no922.

시간에 배차가 될지 불확실하여 사업장 내에서 어느 정도 자유롭게 대기는 하고 있으나 사용자로부터 언제 운행 요구가 있을지 모르는 상태에서 대기 중 일 경우에는 그 대기중의 시간은 휴게시간 이라고는 볼 수 없다. 그러나 업무의 성질상 일정 시간의 휴게시간을 미리 일률적으로 정할 수는 없으나 근무 전일 혹은 근무 당일에 출근과 동시에 당일의 배차시간이 명백히 정해져서 배차시간(차량운행시간)과 대기시간의 구분이 명백하고, 근로자가 사전에 대기시간을 알고 있으며, 그 대기시간 중에는 사용자의 지휘·감독을 벗어나 자유로이 이용할 수 있다면 이는 휴게시간이다.[27]

2) 아파트 야간 경비원

한 아파트의 경비원들은 아침 7시부터 다음날까지 24시간을 근무하고, 그 다음날은 쉬는 격일제 근무를 해왔다. 24시간 중 휴게시간은 총 6시간 - 점심 1시간, 저녁 1시간, 야간휴게시간(자정 12시부터 새벽 4시까지) 4시간- 으로 구성됐다. 입주민들은 경비원들에게 야간휴게시간에 가수면 상태라도 급한 일이 발생하면 즉각 반응할 것을 서면으로 지시했다. 경비원들이 야간휴게시간에 근무복을 입고 가수면상태로 휴식을 취하면서 급한 일이 발생하면 즉각 반응할 수 있는 상태로 일했다면, 이러한 야간휴게시간은 근로시간으로 본다.[28]

3) 고시원 총무

고시원 총무들에게는 휴게시간으로 사용할 수 있는 구체적 시간이 미리 정해져 있지 않았다. 방문자나 새로운 세입자가 찾아오는 것은 정해진 시간이 있는 것이 아니므로 고시원을 벗어나지 않고 항상 자리를 지키고 있어야 했다. 고시원 주인은 특별한 시간의 제약이 없이 그때그때 필요한 업무지시를 하였고, 총무는 이에 따른 돌발적인 업무지시를 이행하였다. 비록 고시원 총무들이 특별한 업무가 없어 휴식을 취하거나 공부를 하는 등으로 시간을 보냈다고 하더라도, 그 시간은 고시원 주인의 지휘명령으로부터 완전히 벗어나 자유로운 이용이 보장되는 휴게시간이 아니므로 근로를 위한 대기시간에 해당한다.[29]

4) 우편운송 차량기사

---

[27] 법무 811-28682, 선고일자 : 1980-05-15
[28] 대법원 2017.12.13 선고 2016다243078 판결.
[29] 서울중앙지법 2017. 6. 23 선고 2017노922 판결.

Drivers working in the postal logistics service have often taken breaks (such as eating or sleeping) at work, while working every other day. However, these breaks were taken during gaps in time while waiting to provide labor between the time of going to work and leaving work at a specific time. In other words, such periods were not provided freely away from the employer's direction and supervision.[30]

5) Nursing assistants

The labor contract of nursing assistants who worked a three-shift schedule specified a four-hour rest period during the night shift and the availability of a night-time sleeping room. However, in reality they often could not sleep there due to emergency calls from patients at the nursing hospital where they worked. Such periods should be regarded as waiting hours for work.[31]

3. Recess Periods and Related Working Hour Cases

(1) Recess periods in hotel restaurants

In many restaurants, there are times when it is not busy, such as between breakfast and lunch and between lunch and dinner, so the business closes for two to three hours per day. Workers who are preparing for their work are recognized as working, but other workers are allowed to use this time freely to go out or rest.

In response to this, the Ministry of Employment and Labor presented this opinion: Article 54 of the Labor Standards Act only specifies the minimum standard of a recess period, but there is no regulation on the longest time. Therefore long recess periods (2-3 hours) exceeding statutory recess periods are acceptable, but unlimited long intervals during working hours are against the original intent of the recess system. In order to view such long breaks as a recess period under the Labor Standards Act, there must be objective reasons that can be generally recognized as necessary and socially valid in view of the nature of the work or the working conditions of the workplace. Such recess periods shall be decided in advance through collective agreement, employment rules, labor contract, etc., so that employers cannot change or extend them arbitrarily, and workers shall

---

[30] Supreme Court ruling on May 27, 1993: 92da24509.
[31] Supreme Court ruling on Sept. 8, 2016: 2014do8873.

우편물 운송차량의 운전직에 종사하는 직원들은 격일제 근무형태로 근무하는 도중에 수시로 수면이나 식사 등의 휴식을 취하여 왔다. 그러나 이는 어디까지나 일정한 시각에 출근하여 퇴근할 때까지 항상 사업장 내에서 운전업무 등의 노무제공을 위하여 대기하는 상태에서 그 공백시간에 틈틈이 이루어진 것이지 결코 일정한 수면시간이나 휴식시간이 보장되어 있지 않으므로 사업주의 지휘, 감독으로부터 벗어나 자유로운 휴게시간으로 이용한 것이 아니다.[30]

5) 요양보호사

3교대로 근무하는 요양보호사의 근로계약서에는 야간 근무시간 중 4시간의 휴게시간이 명시되어 있다. 요양보호사들이 잠을 잘 수 있는 야간수면실도 운영했지만 실제로는 요양 대상자가 비상벨을 누르는 경우가 많아 잠을 제대로 이루지 못하고 늘 대기상태에 있었다. 이에 대해 법원은 요양보호사의 당해 야간근무 중 휴게시간은 근로시간으로 보았다.[31]

3. 휴게시간과 관련한 근로시간제도 사례

(1) 호텔 식당의 휴게시간

호텔의 일부 식당에서는 조식과 중식 사이, 중식과 석식 사이 등 고객이 오지 않는 시간대가 있어 일시 사업장의 문을 닫고 영업을 중지하는 시간이 보통 하루에 2~3시간 정도이다. 이 시간 동안 다음 영업의 준비를 위하여 근무하는 사원은 근무로 인정하나 그 외 사원들에게는 외출·휴게 등을 자유로이 이용할 수 있도록 하고 있다.

이에 대해 고용노동부의 의견은 근로기준법 제54조에서는 휴게시간의 최저기준만을 규정하고 있을 뿐 최장 시간에 대한 규제규정이 없다. 법정시간 이상 상당히 긴 시간(2~4시간)을 휴게시간으로 부여하는 것은 무방하나 휴게제도의 본래 취지에 어긋난 무제한 인정은 부당하다. 이러한 장시간의 휴식시간을 근로기준법상 휴게시간으로 보기 위해서는 작업의 성질 또는 사업장의 근로조건 등에 비추어 사회통념상 필요하고 타당성이 있는 객관적인

---

[30] 대법원 1993.5.27 선고 92다24509 판결.
[31] 대법원 2016.9.8 선고 2014도8873 판결.

be guaranteed to use them, free from the need to provide of labor.[32]

(2) Long recess periods at hotels

A break time system refers to a working hour system that allows workers to rest for a time period longer than the time stipulated in law by using time when the work load is significantly less or non-existent (for hotel businesses, a 14:00 ~ 17:00 break is usually used). It is difficult to say if it is illegal for an employer to enforce a break time system for workers because the Labor Standards Act specifies only the minimum standard for a recess period with no maximum regulated limits.[33]

(3) Long recess periods for Korean construction personnel working in the Middle East

In the Middle East, it is objectively recognized that workers cannot work outside on construction sites where the temperature rises rapidly during the day. Instead, they work from 06:00 to 10:00, taking a recess from 10:00 to 16:00, and then work again from 16:00 to 20:00, according to collective agreements, employment rules or labor contracts. During the recess period, workers are completely free from work-related activities. In such cases, even though the recess period is long, such long intervals between working hours can be recognized as recess periods.[34]

4. Conclusion

Whether a break or waiting time set out in a labor contract falls within 'working hours' or 'recess period' cannot be judged exclusively according to the particular kind of business or type of work. It should be judged based upon considerations such as (i) the terms of the employment contract, the rules of employment, or collective agreement applicable to the workplace, (ii) the work provided by the employee and the specific type of work at the workplace, (iii) whether the employer has control and supervision of employees during recess hours, (iv) whether there is a freely-available resting place, and (v) other circumstances such

---

[32] Government Guide: Gungi 01254-1344, Aug. 11, 1992.
[33] Government Guide: Inspection 01254-6504, Nov. 28, 1990.
[34] Government Guide: Bubmoo 811-28682, issued on May 15, 1980.

사유가 있어야 한다. 이러한 휴게시간은 단체협약, 취업규칙, 근로계약 등에 의해 미리 정해져 있어 사용자가 임의 변경하거나 연장할 수 없어야 하고 근로자는 근로 제공처로부터 완전히 이탈하여 자유로이 이용할 수 있도록 보장되어 있어야 한다.[32]

(2) 호텔의 휴게시간

"브레이크타임제"란 근무시간 중 작업량이 현저히 적거나 없는 시간을 이용하여 법이 정한 휴식시간 이상의 장시간을 휴식하게 하는 제도를 말한다(호텔업의 경우 보통 14:00~17:00 브레이크타임 적용). 휴게시간의 최저기준만을 명시할 뿐 기타 상한적 규제가 명시된 바 없으므로 사용자가 근로자에게 브레이크타임제를 실시하는 것은 가능하다.[33]

(3) 중동 건설근로자의 장시간

중동지방에서는 낮에는 기온이 상승하여 야외에서 작업하는 건설공사현장 근로자들이 작업 할 수 없는 것이 사회통념상 객관적으로 인정될 수 있다. 또한 단체협약, 취업규칙 또는 근로계약 등에 매일의 작업시간이 06:00~10:00까지의 작업, 10:00~16:00까지 휴게시간, 16:00~20:00까지 작업시간으로 정하여 작업한 경우, 동 휴게시간 중에는 근로자가 근로행위로부터 완전히 이탈하여 자유로이 활용할 수 있다면 휴게시간이 장시간이라 할지라도 이를 휴게시간으로 인정한다.[34]

4. 시사점

근로계약에서 정한 휴식시간이나 대기시간이 근로시간에 속하는지 휴게시간에 속하는지는 특정 업종이나 업무의 종류에 따라 일률적으로 판단할 것이 아니다. 이는 (ⅰ) 근로계약의 내용이나 해당 사업장에 적용되는 취업규칙과 단체협약의 규정, (ⅱ) 근로자가 제공하는 업무 내용과 해당 사업장의 구체적 업무 방식, (ⅲ) 휴게 중인 근로자에 대한 사용자의 간섭이나 감독 여부, (ⅳ)

---

[32] 근기 01254-1344, 회시일자 : 1992-08-11
[33] 감독 01254-6504, 회시일자 : 1990-11-28
[34] 법무 811-28682, 선고일자 : 1980-05-15

Chapter 1 Working Hours

as whether or not the workers' actual rest can be interrupted or whether there are situations which allow the employer to direct and supervise workers during recess hours.[35]

〈Case Study 1-1〉 Disputes around Working Hours

In early September 2009, five foreign English teachers working at an institute in Incheon visited this labor law firm and we began establishing a case regarding their unpaid overtime allowance. The teachers were supposed to work 30 hours per week, 6 hours per day, to complete their contractual working hours according to their employment contract, but their employer had them working 40 hours a week by keeping them at work for 8 hours a day, which resulted in two hours of overtime every day. The employment contract stipulated, "The employee shall work 30 hours per week, or 120 hours per month. If the employee agrees to work overtime, the employer shall pay a 15,000 won overtime rate per hour." At a meeting between the employer and the teachers on September 1, one female foreign English teacher brought up the issue of working overtime without being paid for overtime, and the employer gave her verbal notice that her employment would be terminated in one month. Uncertain of their rights, the foreign English teachers brought their concerns to this labor law firm as a group, seeking remedy for their situation. Then the English teachers collectively refused to do any more overtime that was not stipulated in the employment contract.[36]

The labor inspector in charge of this petition case investigated both parties. The employer stated that the actual teaching hours were only 6 per day, but the remaining hours were preparation time required for teaching. However, the teachers claimed they had to come to the institute for preparation, and if they were late, they were penalized. Therefore, this mandatory preparation time should be regarded as working hours. In this dispute, the labor inspector confirmed that each day the teachers had to stay in the institute for two hours above the regulated 6 working

---
[35] Supreme Court ruling on June 28, 2018: 2013da28926.
[36] Mr. Jung was the legal attorney representing English teachers for this case at the Gyeonggi Labor Office from September to November 2009.

자유롭게 이용할 수 있는 휴게 장소의 구비 여부, (v) 그 밖에 근로자의 실질적 휴식이 방해 되었다거나 사용자의 지휘·감독을 인정할 만한 사정이 있는 지와 그 정도 등 여러 사정을 종합하여 각각의 사안에 따라 구체적으로 판단한다.[35]

〈실무사례 1-1〉 근로시간 분쟁

2009년 9월 초에 인천에 있는 한 영어학원의 외국인 강사 5명이 노무법인을 찾아와 연장근로에 대해 연장근로수당을 받지 못하였다고 진정사건을 위임하였다. 강사들은 근로계약서에 따라 소정근로시간이 주 30시간으로 하루 6시간을 근무하여야 함에도 불구하고, 사업주는 1일 8시간씩 1주 40시간씩 근무시켜 1일 2시간씩 연장근로가 발생하였다. 근로계약서에는 "주당 30시간 또는 월 단위 총 수업시간 120시간을 근무해야 한다. 만약 근로자가 시간 외 근무에 동의 하였을 때는 사용자는 시간당 15,000원을 지급한다."라고 규정하고 있다. 9월 1일 사업주와의 전체회의에서, 한 여성 외국인 강사가 연장근로에 대한 수당 미지급 문제를 제기하자, 강사의 태도가 불량하다는 이유로 해고예고 통지를 하였다. 이에 불안을 느낀 외국인 강사들은 노무법인을 찾아와 연장근로수당 미지급 사건을 위임하면서, 집단으로 근로계약서에 없는 연장근로를 거부하기 시작하였다.[36]

이 진정사건에 대해 담당 근로감독관은 노사 당사자를 불러 대질 조사를 실사하였다. 사용자는 실제 수업진행시간은 6시간이고, 2시간은 수업 준비 시간이기 때문에 근로시간에 포함하지 되지 않는다고 주장하였다. 그러나 학원 강사들은 회사에 의무적으로 출근해야 하고, 이를 어겼을 때, 징계조치 등 불이익을 받는 부분이 있기 때문에 수업 대기도 근로시간이라 주장하였다. 근로감독관은 근로계약서에 근무시간이 6시간 외에 별도의 규정이 없고, 강사들이 의무적으로 2시간씩 학원에 대기해야 하였기 때문에 이는 근로시간이어야 한다고 판단하였으나, 중간에 저녁 식사 등을 위한 휴게시간을 학원

---

[35] 대법원 2018. 6. 28. 선고 2013다28926 판결
[36] 이 사건은 정봉수 노무사가 2009년 9월부터 11월까지 인천지방 고용노동청에서 원어민 강사 5명을 대리하여 진행한 연장근로수당 미지급 청구사건

hours, but that they had some time for dinner between their working hours. The labor inspector concluded that the employer be ordered to pay 50% of what the teachers claimed as unpaid overtime.

⟨Case Study 1-2⟩ Whether Union Activities by Union Officials is Company Work

I would like to review a union official's union activities to find out whether union activities by a union official are determined to be company work.

1. Criteria to Determine Whether Union Activities Equal Overwork in the Event of Death

(1) Criteria to Determine Overwork as Cause of Death

Death due to overwork is recognized by the Industrial Accident Compensation Insurance Act (IACI Act) as an occupational accident only if it is recognized that the work and disease are related to a significant causality. That is, the IACI Act recognizes that overwork can result in cerebrovascular (brain stroke) or heart disease (Article 34 (3) of the Act). For a death to be recognized as a work-related injury, there must be a considerable causal relationship between work and the incident. To prove this causal relationship, work must have been performed and contributed to the already existing disease if work has been performed, and there is potential for it to be recognized as the cause of the disease-related death . However, for work to be recognized as the main cause of the death when the death occurs while work is not being performed, the surviving family must prove a significant causal relationship between the death and the work. The burden of proof lies with the surviving family: it will not be recognized as a work-related death if they cannot prove the causal relationship.[37]

In order to fall under the IACI Act, which lists work-related injuries, work-related diseases and accidents on commuting (Article 37(1)), there must be a substantial causal relationship between work and accident. When determining that an injury is work-related, the accident needs to (i) occur while the worker is performing work or an act in accordance with his/her employment contract; (ii) occur due to a defect in,

---

[37] Practical Labor Law Research Council, Translation of the Labor Standards Act (III), Parkyoungsa, 2020, p. 607; Lee, Hee-ja, Criteria for Recognizing Work-related Accident concerning Overwork-related Death, Labor Law, monthly magazine, Feb. 2007.

강사들이 임의로 가졌기 때문에 근로자가 청구한 미지급된 연장근로수당 중 50%를 인정하는 선에서 사용자에게 임금지급지시 명령을 내리고 이 연장근로수당 미지급사건은 종결되었다.

〈실무사례 1-2〉 노조간부의 조합활동이 업무인지 여부

노조간부의 조합활동시간이 업무시간에 해당하는지 여부에 따라 산재인정을 받을 수 있어 관련 법령, 지침, 판례 등을 살펴보고자 한다.

1. 과로사의 판단기준과 조합활동

(1) 과로사의 판단기준

과로사는 업무상 과로로 사망하는 질병으로 산업재해보상보험법에서는 업무와 질병이 상당한 인과관계가 있다고 인정되는 경우에 한해 산업재해로 인정하고 있다. 즉, 산재법은 업무상 질병으로 과로로 발생할 수 있는 뇌혈관 질병 또는 심장 질병을 규정하고 있다(제34조 제3항). 과로사 사건에 있어 업무상 재해로 인정받기 위해서는 업무와 재해 간 상당한 인과관계가 있어야 한다. 따라서 인과관계를 입증하기 위해서는 업무수행성과 업무기인성이 동시에 있어야 하고, 업무수행성이 있는 경우에는 업무기인성은 추정될 수 있다. 그러나 업무수행성이 없이 업무기인성을 인정받기 위해서는 재해자가 재해와 업무와 사이에 상당한 인과관계가 있다는 사실을 입증해야 한다. 그 입증책임은 근로자에게 있고 입증을 하지 못하면 산재로 인정받지 못한다.[37]

산재법에서는 업무에 해당되기 위해서는 업무와 재해사이에 상당한 인과관계가 있어야 하며, 그 종류로 업무상 사고, 업무상 질병, 출퇴근 재해에 대해서도 열거하고 있다(제37조 제1항). 업무상 사고의 경우에는 (i) 근로시간 내에 업무수행 중에 일어난 사고, (ⅱ) 사업주의 시설물의 결함으로 발생한 사고,

---

[37] 노동법실무연구회, 「근로기준법 주해」(III), 박영사, 2020, 607면; 이희자, 과로사의 업무상 재해인정기준, 노동법률, 2007년 2월호.

or the careless management of, facilities, etc. provided by the employer while the worker is using these facilities, etc.; (iii) occur while the worker is participating in or preparing an event organized by the employer or an event following the directions of the employer; or (iv) occur during recess hours due to an act that can be seen as under the control of the employer. What should be noted here is that 'an accident that happens while the worker is participating in or preparing an event organized by the employer or an event following the directions of the employer' can also be recognized as a work-related accident. The standard for determining work-related diseases is virtually the same as determining work-related injuries.

(2) Criteria for Determining Whether Union Activities are Work Provided to the Employer

Injuries and diseases caused by union activities are not specified in the IACI Act. However, where union activities of full-time or part-time union officials are recognized as work according to criteria are limited to activities outlined in the collective agreement or activities approved by the employer. In addition, the court considers injury or disease during labor union activities as work-related in accordance with a wider application of the current criteria for work-related injuries.[38]

The court has recognized as work-related accidents involving full-time and part-time union officials that occurred while such officials were engaged in union activities that met the following criteria. First, it involved full-time or part-time union officials using the paid time-off system. Second, the labor union's work was closely related to the company's labor management work, which means that employers allowed union officials to take charge of the work on behalf of their original work. Third, accidents that occur outside of working hours were work-related union activities.

However, the following are union activities by full-time or part-time union officials that are not regarded as work: first, activities unrelated to the work of the company concerned by an umbrella union; second, illegal labor union activities; and third, confrontational labor-management relations over a period of time from the existence of a labor dispute to conclusion of a collective agreement. Fourth, activities outside of working hours that are not specifically related to the employers' labor management work.

1) Union activities approved by the employer shall be those involving company labor management.

The fact that a full-time labor union official has been engaged in labor union activities without having to do the work originally outlined in the labor contract

---

[38] Lim, Jongyul, Labor Law, 17th ed., 2019, p. 497.

(ⅲ) 사업주가 주관하거나 사업주의 지시에 따라 참여한 행사나 행사준비 중에 발생한 사고, (ⅳ) 휴게시간 중 사업주의 지배 관리하에 있다고 볼 수 있는 행위로 발생한 사고를 말한다. 여기서 주목해야 할 점은 사업주가 주관하거나 지시에 따라 발생한 행사 중의 사고나 사업주의 지배관리 하에 있었던 행위에 대해서도 업무로 보았다. 업무상 질병의 경우에도 같은 기준으로 볼 수 있다.

(2) 조합활동이 업무시간에 해당하는지 판단기준

산재법에는 조합활동 중 발생한 사고 및 질병이 '업무상 재해'에 해당되는지에 대하여 구체적으로 명시된 바가 없다. 다만, 판례에서 노조전임자나 조합간부는 단체협약이나 사용자가 승인한 활동에 한해서는 업무상 질병 기준을 적용하여 업무로 인정해준 사례가 다수 있다. 또한 법원은 조합활동을 업무상 재해에 해당하는지 판단과 관련하여 기존의 업무상 사고의 판단기준을 확대하고 있는 경향이다.[38]

판례에서 인정한 노동조합의 전임자 또는 간부의 업무상 재해 인정 기준은 다음과 같다. 첫째, 유급 전임자의 조합활동이나 조합간부가 회사로부터 유급으로 인정받은 활동시간이다. 둘째, 노동조합업무는 회사의 노무관리업무와 밀접한 관련을 가지는 것으로서 사용자가 본래의 업무 대신에 이를 담당하도록 하는 것으로 보고 있다. 셋째, 전임자가 근무시간 외에도 업무와 관련된 조합활동을 하다가 발생한 재해 까지도 인정된다.

한편, 전임자나 조합간부의 조합활동을 근로시간에 해당되지 않는다고 판단한 사례는 다음과 같다. 첫째, 당해 회사의 업무와 무관한 상급단체의 활동이나 불법적인 노동조합 활동. 둘째, 노동쟁의 상태가 된 후부터 단체협약 체결 전까지 회사와 대립적인 노사관계에 있는 기간. 셋째, 전임자나 조합간부가 업무시간 외에 사용자의 노무관리 업무와 구체적인 관련성이 없는 활동이 이에 해당된다.

1) 사용자가 승인한 조합활동인지 여부

노동조합업무 전임자가 근로계약상 본래 담당할 업무를 면하고 노동조합의 업무를 전임하게 된 것이 단체협약 혹은 사용자인 회사의 승낙에 의한 것이다. 이러한 전임자가 담당하는 노동조합업무는 회사의 노무관리업무와

---

[38] 임종률, 「노동법」 제17판, 2019년, 497면

is due to a collective agreement or company consent. Labor union activities allow a full-time union official to engage in company labor management tasks, which can be seen as work provided to the company, instead of his original work. Thus, an illness or accident occurring to a full-time union official in the course of performing or its related labor union activities constitutes a work-related injury or disease.[39]

2) **Paid-time union activities approved by the employer are company labor management duties.**

The same shall be deemed to apply to accidents in the course of union officials, who are not full-time union officials, performing or engaging in ordinary activities approved by the company.[40]

3) **Union activities shall be related to company labor management.**

In the need to form smooth and stable labor-management relations, the full-time union official system allows union officials to take charge of labor union affairs instead of the work originally outlined in the labor contract, while still holding the status of employees. In order for a full-time union worker to be regarded as having a work-related accident under the IACI Act, the labor union activities performed by the full-time union official must be directly and specifically related to company labor management.[41]

4) **Union activities during which accidents or illness are not recognized as work-related**

The following union activities are not considered work: (i) activities related to umbrella unions above or allied to the relevant union and unrelated to the employer's business; ② illegal union activities, and ③ activities that occur during the dispute stage in a conflict with the employer.[42]

2 Cases related to Union Activities and Recognition of Occupational Accidents

(1) Cases where Accidents during Labor Union Activities are Recognized as Work-related

1) **Accidents occurring when a union official was engaged in paid-time union activities.**

---

[39] Supreme Court ruling on Feb. 22, 1994: 92nu14502; Supreme Court ruling on Dec. 8, 1998: 98doo14006; Supreme Court ruling on Mar. 29, 2007: 2005doo11418; Supreme Court ruling on May 29, 2014: 2014doo35232.

[40] Supreme Court ruling on May 29, 2014: 2014doo35232.

[41] Supreme Court ruling on July 14, 2015: 2005doo5246.

[42] Supreme Court ruling on Mar. 29, 2007: 2005doo11418; Supreme Court ruling on May 29, 2014: 2014doo35232.

밀접한 관련을 가지는 것으로서 사용자가 본래의 업무 대신에 이를 담당하도록 하는 것이어서 그 자체를 회사의 업무로 볼 수 있다. 따라서 그 전임자가 노동조합업무를 수행하거나 이에 수반하는 통상적인 활동을 하는 과정에서 그 업무에 기인하여 발생한 재해는 업무상 재해에 해당한다.[39]

2) 사용자가 승인한 조합간부 유급시간 조합활동

노동조합업무 전임자가 아닌 노동조합 간부가 사용자인 회사의 승낙에 의하여 노동조합업무를 수행하거나 이에 수반하는 통상적인 활동을 하는 과정에서 그 업무에 기인하여 발생한 재해의 경우에도 마찬가지로 적용된다고 보아야 한다.[40]

3) 사용자의 노무관리와 관련있는 조합활동

사용자가 원만하고 안정된 노사관계를 형성하기 위한 필요에서 노조간부에게 근로자의 지위는 여전히 보유한 채 근로계약상의 본래 업무 대신 노동조합의 업무를 담당하도록 승낙한 것이 전임자 제도이다. 이러한 전임자 제도의 법적 취지를 고려해 보았을 때 노조전임자가 노동조합의 업무를 수행하던 중 입은 재해를 산재법상 업무상 재해로 볼 수 있으려면, 노조전임자가 수행하던 노동조합의 업무가 사용자의 노무관리업무와 직접적이고 구체적으로 밀접한 관련성이 있어야 한다.[41]

4) 조합활동이 업무로 인정되지 않은 경우

다음의 조합활동의 경우 업무시간으로 판단하지 않았다. ① 그 업무의 성질상 사용자의 사업과는 무관한 상부 또는 연합관계에 있는 노동단체와 관련된 활동이나 ② 불법적인 조합활동 또는 사용자와 대립관계로 되는 쟁의단계에 들어간 이후의 활동 등이다.[42]

2. 조합활동과 업무상 재해 인정 여부와 관련된 사례

(1) 노동조합 활동이 업무상 재해로 인정한 사례
1) 노조간부가 유급으로 인정받은 조합활동을 하다가 발생한 재해

---
[39] 대법원 1994.2.22 선고 92누14502; 대법원 1998.12.8. 선고 98두14006판결; 대법원 2007.3.29. 선고 2005두11418 판결; 대법원 2014.5.29 선고 2014두35232 판결
[40] 대법원 2014.5.29 선고 2014두35232 판결
[41] 대법원 2015.7.14 선고 2005두5246 판결
[42] 대법원 2007.3.29. 선고 2005두11418 판결; 대법원 2014.5.29 선고 2014두35232 판결

Chapter 1 Working Hours

"A delegate of Kumho Tire's labor union participated in a meeting paid for by the company. The delegate applied for industrial accident compensation after losing his footing and breaking his leg while going down the stairs to get the report, which the Supreme Court acknowledged as an occupational accident. The union delegate was paid to attend the meeting, and the company also provided the meeting place. Furthermore, the agenda of the meeting was as closely related to the company's labor management as day-to-day union activities."[43] This is a case where an injury occurring to a non-full-time union official was recognized as work-related as he or she was engaged in union activities during working hours with company approval.

2) **A full-time union official had a heart attack on his way home from a union workshop.**

"Upon conclusion of a collective agreement bargaining, a full-time union official attended a union workshop conducted as part of follow-up actions. This union official had a heart attack on his way home after the workshop. The series of processes in attending the union workshop can be considered company work."[44] The heart attack of a paid full-time union official while returning home after a union workshop was regarded as a work-related accident.

3) **An accident occurred while a full-time union leader was removing a banner used in a union campaign.**

"Prior to collective bargaining, a union official stepped on some plywood while removing a banner used in a union campaign. The plywood fell about 6.5 meters to the floor, during which the official was injured. In order to promote union member solidarity ahead of collective bargaining, the campaign was held between 18:00 and 21:00 after working hours, and was officially permitted by the company in advance and permitted use of the indoor gymnasium facilities on company premises."[45] Although the accident occurred outside working hours, it was recognized as a work-related injury because it happened while handling the incidental tasks for union activities recognized by the company.

4) **A union official had an accident during a workshop hosted by the industrial labor union.**

"The industrial union, like a company labor union, is a single-organization labor union which workers in the same industry directly join and, in principle, have the right to collectively bargain, apply for mediation, and enter into a dispute at an individual company, and so matters in the industrial labor union

---
43) Supreme Court ruling on May 29, 2014: 2014doo35232.
44) Ulsan District Court ruling on Aug. 2, 2006: 2006goohp846.
45) Supreme Court ruling on Dec. 8, 1998: 98doo14006.

"금호타이어 노동조합 대의원이 회사로부터 유급으로 회의에 참석하였다. 그 대의원이 보고자료를 가지러 가기 위해 계단을 내려가다가 발을 헛디뎌서 다리에 골절을 입게 되어 산재신청을 한 사건에서, 대법원은 산재로 인정하였다. 그 사유로 해당 조합간부는 유급으로 회의에 참석하였고, 회의 장소도 회사가 제공하였다. 그 회의 내용도 노동조합의 일상적인 조합활동으로 회사의 노무관리 업무와 밀접한 관련이 있는 회사의 업무로 보았다."[43] 이는 비전임 조합간부가 유급승인을 받아 근무시간 동안 조합활동을 하다가 발생한 사고에 대해 업무상 재해로 인정한 사례이다.

2) 노조 수련회에 참석하였다가 복귀하던 전임자의 급성 심근경색증

"전임자는 단체협약 종료 후 후속조치로 시행된 수련회에 참석하였다. 전임자는 수련회에 참석하였다가 복귀하던 중 급성 심근경색증이 발병한 것으로, 일련의 과정이 전임자로서 활동과 수련회 참가를 회사의 업무로 보았다."[44] 유급 전임자가 조합원 수련회에 참석하고 복귀하던 중에 발생한 급성 심근경색증 사망을 업무상 재해로 보았다.

3) 노조전임자가 결의대회에 사용된 현수막을 철거하던 중 발생한 사고

"단체교섭에 앞서 조합원 결의대회를 위하여 설치한 현수막을 철거하고 내려오다가 나무합판을 밟는 순간 나무합판이 빠지면서 약 6.5m 아래 바닥으로 추락하여 재해를 입었다. 이 사건은 단체교섭을 앞두고 소속 조합원들의 단결력을 과시하기 위해 근무시간 종료 후인 18:00부터 21:00까지 사이에 일부 조합원들이 참가한 가운데 열렸으며, 사전에 회사측에 그 개최사실을 알리고 회사내 실내체육관 시설을 사용하는 것을 허가 받았다."[45] 근로시간 외에 발생한 사그이지만, 회사가 인정한 조합활동의 부수적 업무를 처리하다가 발생한 사고로 업무상 재해로 인정 받았다.

4) 전임자가 산업별 노조가 개최한 수련회 체육행사 도중 발생한 사고

"산업별 노동조합은 기업별 노동조합과 마찬가지로, 동종 산업에 종사하는 근로자들이 직접 가입하고 원칙적으로 소속 단위사업장인 개별 기업에서 단체교섭, 조정신청 및 쟁의권 등을 갖는 단일조직의 노동조합이다.

---

[43] 대법원 2014.5.29 선고 2014두35232 판결
[44] 울산지방법원 2006.8.2 선고 2006구합846 판결
[45] 대법원 1998.12.8. 선고 98두14006 판결.

cannot be treated as umbrella union activities." Labor union work in the industrial union cannot be viewed as activities related to a higher umbrella union or allied labor unions unrelated to the employer's business."[46] In fact, the labor union activities of this industrial union were regarded as activities to improve working conditions at this company because the members had joined the industrial labor union directly.

(2) Cases where Accidents during Labor Union Activities are not Recognized as Work-related

1) **A full-time union official was injured during a union sports competition held after working hours.**

   "A full-time union official was injured during a sports competition, held after working hours, to promote union membership ahead of collective wage bargaining."[47] This is a case where an incident during individual union activities after working hours without the employer's supervision was not recognized as a work-related accident.

2) **An accident involving a full-time union official occurred during the dispute stage of a conflict between labor and management.**

   "By the time of the accident, the company and the labor union had failed to reach a compromise despite several rounds of wage negotiations, and the labor union was at odds with management and in a state of labor dispute after reporting the dispute to the relevant agencies according to the dispute mediation procedures."[48] This accident was not recognized as work-related because it occurred in the middle of conflict between the labor union and the company.

3) **An accident occurred where a full-time union official was injured during a soccer game organized by an umbrella union.**

   "A full-time union official participated in some sports organized by the umbrella labor union as a representative of the union. The company did not give its approval to the union official to participate in the sports in this case, and did not pay any expenses."[49] In this case, incidents during activities of the umbrella union are not recognized as industrial accidents occurring during the activities of an upper level umbrella union, as the activities were not related to the improvement of working conditions for the labor union.

---

46) Supreme Court ruling on Mar. 29, 2007: 2005doo11418.
47) Supreme Court ruling on Mar. 28, 1997: 96noo16170.
48) Supreme Court ruling on Mar. 15, 2004: 2003doo923.
49) Supreme Court ruling on 2005doo5246.

이러한 산업별 노조의 노동조합 업무를 사용자의 사업과 무관한 상부 또는 연합관계에 있는 노동단체와 관련된 활동으로 볼 수는 없다."[46] 당해 조합원들이 산업별 노동조합에 직접 가입하였기 때문에 사실상 산업별 노동조합 활동은 당해 사업장의 근로조건 개선을 위한 활동으로 보았다.

(2) 노동조합 활동을 업무상 재해로 불인정한 사례

1) 전임자가 근무시간 종료 후 개최된 노조 체육대회 경기 도중 부상당한 경우

"노동조합의 전임자인 근로자가 사측과의 임금협상을 앞두고 노동조합 간부들의 단결과시를 위하여 노동조합이 (근무시간 종료 후) 개최한 체육대회에 참가하여 경기 도중 부상을 당한 사례이다"[47] 사용자의 관리 감독을 벗어난 근무시간 이후의 개별적인 조합활동을 업무상 재해로 인정하지 않은 사례다.

2) 노사간의 분쟁 상태에 있는 상태에서 발생한 전임자의 재해

"이 재해를 당할 즈음에 회사와 노동조합은 수차례에 걸친 임금협상에도 불구하고 그 타협점을 찾지 못한 상태에서 관계기관에 쟁의조정 절차를 거쳐 쟁의행위신고를 한 노동쟁의 상태로 노사간에 대립관계에 있었다."[48] 전임자의 사고가 노조와 회사가 분쟁상태에서 발생한 재해이므로 산재로 인정하지 않은 사례이다.

3) 전임자가 상급단체노조의 축구경기 중 부상한 사건

"전임자는 상급단체노조의 체육대회에 당해 노조의 대표자로서 참가하였다. 회사는 원고에게 이 사건 체육대회에 참가하도록 승낙하거나 참가를 강제하거나 경비를 지급하지도 아니하였다."[49] 상급단체의 활동이 당해 노조의 근로조건 개선과 전혀 무관한 상급단체 활동 중 발생한 재해는 산재로 인정하지 않는다는 사례이다.

---

46) 대법원 2007.3.29. 선고 2005두11418 판결.
47) 대법원 1997.3.28. 선고 96누16170 판결.
48) 대법원 2004.03.15. 선고 2003두923 판결.
49) 대법원 2005.07.14 선고 2005두5246 판결.

Chapter 1 Working Hours

〈Case Study 1-3〉 Whether a Study Room Manager's Working Hours can be recognized as Full-time Work

1. Introduction

On July 27, 2022, a Study Room (SR) manager in Seoul filed a lawsuit claiming unpaid wages against the study room's owner, alleging that they did not receive overtime pay and severance pay after they resigned, for their service of 1 year and 2 months. The employee (SR manager) applied for the job after seeing a job advertisement on an online recruitment site that stated, "Looking for a manager for a study room who can work and study at the same time." The terms of employment were from 6 p.m. to 2 a.m. seven nights a week and involved managing the study room, with one day off per month. Specifically, the employee worked as manager of the study room for 2 hours each day and received a monthly salary of 685,000 won as compensation.[50] The duties of the SR manager included handling new member registrations, card payments for monthly fees, visitor guidance and phone inquiries, simple snack preparation and equipment management, facility maintenance and cleaning, and other miscellaneous tasks.

Although the employment contract of the SR manager stated a daily working time of 2 hours, their actual required presence time was 8 hours per day, during which they were free to study but confined to the study room's waiting area. The SR manager was required to perform related tasks whenever requested by users and potential customers. The employee argued that this waiting time be considered actual working hours, totaling 8 per day. Based on this calculation, the employee demanded additional payment of 19,108,000 won for the additional 6 hours per day and claimed a severance pay of 2,706,563 won as they had worked for more than a year.

The main points of contention were: (ⅰ) Whether the study room should recognize only the stated 2 hours of work per day as the SR manager's actual working hours, or if the entire 8-hour period spent studying and waiting should be considered working hours. (ⅱ) Whether evidence exists to consider the 6 hours, excluding the 2 hours of work, as break time, even though the SR manager was obligated to be present for 8 hours.

---

[50] The monthly salary of the employee was 550,000 won. The employer intended to subsidize the individual seat usage fee to the amount of 135,000 won, but the employee chose to receive the seat usage fee in cash and instead used the study room office. Therefore, the employee received a monthly salary of 685,000 won, which included compensation for not using a regular study seat.

〈실무사례 1-3〉 독서실 총무의 근로시간 인정여부

1. 문제의 소재 (사실관계)

2022년 7월 27일 서울의 A독서실 총무가 1년 2개월을 근무하고 퇴직한 뒤, 독서실을 상대로 연장근로수당과 퇴직금을 못 받았다고 법원에 미지급 임금을 청구하는 소송을 제기하였다. 근로자(총무)는 인터넷 채용사이트에서 '공부하면서 일하는 독서실 총무를 구한다'라는 구직광고를 보고 지원하였다. 근로조건은 저녁 6시에 출근하여 새벽 2시까지 독서실을 관리하는 것이고, 월요일부터 일요일까지 1주 7일을 근무하며, 월 1회의 휴무를 한다는 조건이었다. 구체적으로 독서실 총무로서 매일 2시간 근무하고 그에 대한 대가로 월임금은 685,000원을 받는다.[50] 독서실 총무의 일은 신규회원 접수 및 월 사용료 카드결제, 방문객 안내와 문의 전화 답변, 간단한 간식 준비 및 비품 관리, 시설물 관리와 청소업무, 기타 잡무를 수행하였다.

총무의 근로계약서에는 일일 2시간 근무로 기재되어 있지만, 실제 체류시간이 매일 8시간이었고, 이 시간 동안은 자유롭게 공부는 할 수 있지만, 대기장소가 독서실 내로 한정되었다. 총무는 언제든지 고객이나 사용자의 요청이 있는 경우 필요한 업무를 수행하여야 했다. 총무는 이러한 대기시간은 근로시간이므로 하루 8시간을 근로한 것으로 간주하여야 한다고 주장하였다. 그리고 이 기준으로 계산한 추가 6시간에 대한 수당과 주휴수당을 계산한 금액인 19,108,000원 추가적으로 지급해야 하고, 총무가 1년 이상 근무하고 퇴직하였기 때문에 퇴직금 2,706,563원도 지급해야 한다고 청구하였다.

여기서 쟁점은 (ⅰ) 독서실 총무의 실제 근로시간은 독서실에서 인정하는 매일 2시간만을 인정할 것인지, 아니면 실제 공부하며 대기한 8시간 전체에 대해 근로시간으로 보아야 하는지에 있다. 그리고 (ⅱ) 독서실 총무가 구속되는 시간은 8시간임에도 불구하고 근로시간 2시간을 제외한 6시간을 휴게시간으로 볼 수 있는 근거는 어디에 있는지에 있다.

---

[50] 근로자의 월 임금은 550,000원임. 사업주는 개인 좌석 이용료는 135,000원을 보조 하려고 하였으나, 근로자는 개인 좌석 이용료를 돈으로 받고, 그 대신 독서실 사무실을 대신 사용하였다. 따라서 월 임금을 좌석이용료 포함하여 685,000원 수령하였다.

Chapter 1　Working Hours

2. Arguments of the Parties

(1) Employee's Claim :

The SR manager stated that they applied for the position of manager in the study room through an online job advertisement, with the intention of saving money while preparing for the police officer exam. The terms of employment were to study while being on standby 8 hours a day, and receive a monthly salary of 685,000 won. The study room was 230 square meters in size and held 70 seats. The SR manager would study and be on standby in the study room from 6 p.m. to 2 a.m. the next day, spend about 30 minutes cleaning, and then leave. The employer claimed that the SR manager's actual working hours were no more than 2 hours per day, with 30 minutes allocated for cleaning, 30 minutes for new member management, and 60 minutes for other tasks. However, the SR manager argued that tasks such as cleaning, managing residents and visitors, answering phone calls, preparing snacks, organizing equipment, and facility management required more than 2 hours of work per day. They claim that as they were always on standby, the entire 8 hours should be considered working hours. Therefore, the employee demanded unpaid wages, holiday allowances, and a severance pay totaling 26,630,000 won, along with compensation for the delay.

(2) Employer's Argument :

1) The study room hired the SR manager through an internet job advertisement, clearly stating that they were looking for someone to work as a manager while studying. A written employment contract was signed, which stated that the actual work would be 2 hours per day, 7 days a week from Monday to Sunday, with one day off per month. During the interview, the employee stated that they were preparing to become a police officer and applied for the position to reduce study costs and earn pocket money. The employer encouraged and supported the SR manager, hoping that they would succeed in their studies, and provided sufficient study time within the 6 hours of standby each day.

2) The SR manager's tasks as manager of the study room amounted to only about 2 hours per day, and the rest of the time was spent on personal study. The employee had the freedom to engage in personal duties during working hours, and was able to leave for personal matters without affecting their work

2. 당사자의 주장

(1) 근로자(총무)의 주장

　근로자는 경찰공무원을 준비하는 중에, 비용을 아끼기 위해 공부하면서 근무할 수 있는 독서실 총무 자리를 인터넷 구인광고를 보고 지원하였다. 근무조건은 하루 8시간 대기하면서 공부할 수 있고, 월 685,000원을 받는 조건이었다. 독서실 규모는 70평의 공간에 70개의 좌석을 가지고 있었다. 총무는 저녁 6시부터 독서실에서 대기하며, 그 다음날 새벽 2시까지 공부하면서 대기하였고, 약 30분정도 청소를 실시하고 퇴근하였다. 사용자는 총무의 실제 근무시간은 일일 2시간 이내로, 청소업무 30분, 입실자 관리 30분 정도, 그리고 기타 업무 60분으로 처리한다고 설명하였다. 그러나 총무는 청소하기, 입실자 및 퇴실자 관리, 방문객 관리 및 전화 대응, 간식준비와 비품 정리정돈, 시설물 관리 등은 매일 2시간 정도로는 부족하고, 항상 업무대기 상태에서 있어 실제 8시간 전체가 근무시간에 해당이 되므로 하루 8시간을 전제로 계산한 미지급된 임금, 주휴수당, 퇴직금 합계 26,630,000원과 이에 대한 지체손해금을 지급해야 한다고 주장하였다.

(2) 독서실의 주장

1) 독서실은 인터넷 구인광고에 분명히 공부하면서 일하는 독서실 총무를 구직 사이트를 통해서 채용하였다. 채용 시에 근로계약을 작성하고, 실제로 업무는 매일 2시간이고, 월요일부터 일요일까지 1주 7일을 근무하고, 매월 1일의 휴무를 주는 조건이었다. 면접 시에 근로자는 경찰공무원을 준비하고 있으며, 공부하면서 독서실 비용을 아끼고 용돈도 벌기 위해 지원했다고 진술하였다. 이에 사용자는 독서실에서 열심히 공부해서 꼭 합격하기를 바란다고 하며 여러 차례 격려해 주었고, 하루 8시간 대기 중 6시간 중에 공부할 시간을 충분히 마련해 주었다.
2) 독서실 총무업무는 일일 2시간 정도면 충분하고, 나머지는 모두 개인 공부하는데 시간을 사용하였다. 근무시간 중에 자유롭게 개인시간을 가질 수 있었고, 전화를 착신으로 해 놓고 외출하면 업무에 지장이 없기 때문에 근무시간 중에 외출하여 자유롭게 개인업무도 보면서 근무하였다. 실제로

obligations, as long as they left a forwarded phone number. The employer argued that the SR manager's actual work amounted to a maximum of 2 hours per day, with the remaining 6 hours open to personal study or personal tasks without supervision from the employer. Therefore, the employer claims that there were no unpaid wages for the employee, and there was no severance pay as the employee had actually worked very few hours.

3. Relevant Criteria and Precedents

(1) **Relevant Precedent** : A ruling stated, in the context of the Labor Standards Act, that rest time refers to the period during which an employee is completely liberated from the employer's directives and is guaranteed the freedom to use their time as they wish during working hours.[51] The rest time discussed in this precedent refers to a time separated from the employer's management and supervision, indicating a private time with guaranteed freedom of use for the employee.

(2) **Relevant Precedent** : Another ruling stated that the term "working hours" under the Labor Standards Act refers to the time when an employee provides labor under the direction and supervision of the employer as stipulated in the employment contract. Even if an employee is not actively engaged in work during working hours, such as during waiting, rest, or sleep time, if it is effectively under the control and supervision of the employer, it is considered part of the working hours, not as rest time with guaranteed freedom of use.[52]

The SR manager in this study room is obligated to stay for 8 hours, but since the purpose of the stay is 2 hours for official duties and 6 hours for personal study, it can be considered as time in between rest time and waiting time. However, it is deemed difficult to categorize the SR manager's time purely as waiting time for work, as the contract explicitly states that the SR manager may provide labor intermittently while studying as needed.

(3) **Relevant Precedent** : A further ruling stated that, considering that the employer (defendant or Dormitory) did not predefine specific times for the rest time

---

[51] Supreme Court ruling on Apr. 14, 1992, 91da20548.
[52] Supreme Court ruling on Nov. 23, 2006, 2006da41990.

총무의 근무시간은 매일 2시간 이내였고, 나머지 6시간은 사업주의 관리 감독을 받지 않고 모두 개인이 공부하거나 개인 용무를 보는데 사용하였다. 따라서 독서실은 근로자에게 미지급한 임금은 없으며, 퇴직금도 초단시간 근로자이므로 발생하지 않는다.

3. 관련 기준 판례와 적용

(1) **관련판례** : 근로기준법상의 휴게시간이란 근로자가 근로시간의 도중에 사용자의 지휘명령으로 부터 완전히 해방되고 또한 자유로운 이용이 보장된 시간을 의미한다.[51] 이 판례에서 말하는 휴게시간은 사용자의 관리 감독으로부터 벗어난 시간으로, 근로자의 자유로운 이용이 보장된 사적인 시간을 말한다.

(2) **관련판례** : 근로기준법상 근로시간이라 함은 근로자가 사용자의 지휘, 감독 아래 근로계약상의 근로를 제공하는 시간을 말한다. 근로자가 작업시간 도중에 현실로 작업에 종사하지 않은 대기시간이나 휴식, 수면시간 등이라도 하더라도 그것이 휴게시간으로서 근로자에게 자유로운 이용이 보장된 것이 아니고 실질적으로 사용자의 지휘, 감독하에 놓여있는 시간이라면 이는 근로시간에 포함된다.[52]

이번 독서실 총무는 8시간을 의무적으로 독서실에 체류하지만, 그 체류 목적이 공적인 업무 2시간과 개인의 공부를 위한 6시간이므로, 휴게시간과 대기시간 중간에 있는 시간이라고 할 수 있다. 그러나 총무와 독서실이 작성 계약서에서도 독서실 총무는 공부하면서 필요 시에 단속적으로 근로를 제공하는 것으로 순전히 근로를 위한 대기시간으로 보기는 어렵다고 판단이 된다.

(3) **관련판례** : 회사(피고소인 또는 고시원)는 고소인(고시원 총무)들에게 휴게시간으로 사용할 수 있는 구체적 시간을 미리 정하여 주지 않은 점,

---

51) 대법원 1992. 4. 14. 선고 91다20548 판결.
52) 대법원 2006. 11. 23. 선고 2006다41990 판결.

Chapter 1　Working Hours

available to the employee (dormitory manager), and the fact that visitors or new residents could arrive at any time, requiring the dormitory manager to remain in place and be ready to respond without specific time constraints, and taking into account that the employer provided ad-hoc work instructions without specific time constraints, and the employee complied with the employer's spontaneous work instructions, even if the employee spent their time resting or studying, it is reasonable to view that the time falls under waiting time for work rather than rest time completely liberated from the employer's directives."[53]

The wage dispute in the dormitory manager's case revolved around the determination of whether the dormitory manager's waiting time should be considered rest time. In other words, the dormitory declared all the time as waiting time because the dormitory manager did not specify rest time. The key difference with the current study room manager's situation is that the employment contract for the current study room explicitly states 6 hours of rest time for study during rest breaks, and that there is a difference in the information in the hiring notice and the actual use of rest time for studying.

4. Court's Judgment and Implications for Working Hour Disputes

(1) Court's Judgment[54]

1) It is acknowledged that the defendant employee (hereinafter referred to as the SR manager) and the plaintiff (study room) entered into an employment contract on March 10, 2019, agreeing for the SR manager to work 2 hours each day as an overnight SR manager from 18:00 to 02:00, receiving a monthly wage of 685,000 won, and that the SR manager worked until May 9, 2020.

2) The SR manager argues that, as he worked or waited for work from 18:00 to 02:00 daily, the entire 8 hours during this time constitute working hours. Therefore, based on these working hours, the SR manager claims that the employer should have the obligation to pay a total of 19,108,560 won, deducting 685,000 won paid each month, for the period until the resignation date after June 11, 2019, in accordance with the minimum wage set by the Minimum Wage Act.

---

[53] Seoul District Court ruling on June 23, 2017, 2017da922.
[54] Seoul Eastern District Court ruling on Dec. 21, 2023, 200gaso29648.

방문자나 새로운 세입자가 찾아오는 것은 정해진 시간이 있는 것이 아니므로 고시원을 벗어나지 않고 자리를 지키고 있어야 하는 점, 피고인은 특별한 시간의 제약이 없이 그때 그때 필요한 업무지시를 고소인들에게 하였고, 고소인들은 피고인의 돌발적인 업무지시를 이행하였던 점 등을 감안하면, 고소인들이 특별한 업무가 없어 휴식을 취하거나 공부를 하는 등으로 시간을 보냈다고 하더라도, 그 시간은 피고인의 지휘명령으로 부터 완전히 해방되고 자유로운 이용이 보장되는 휴게시간이 아니라 근로를 위한 대기시간에 해당한다고 봄이 타당하다.[53]

위의 고시원 총무의 임금체불 사건은 고시원 총무의 대기시간이 휴게시간인지 아니면 대기시간인지에 대한 판단이다. 즉, 고시원이 고시원 총무의 휴게시간을 명시하지 않아 모두 대기시간으로 판단한 사실이다. 현 독서실 총무와의 차이는 현 독서실 총무의 근로계약서는 휴게시간에 공부를 위한 휴게시간 6시간을 명시하였고, 채용 공고의 내용, 실제 휴게시간을 공부하는 시간으로 보냈다는 사실에서 차이가 있다.

4. 이번 근로시간에 분쟁에 대한 법원의 판단과 시사점

(1) 법원의 판단[54]

1) 피고 근로자 (이하 총무)와 원고 (독서실)와, 총무가 2019. 3. 10. 부터 독서실 야간총무로서 18:00 부터 02:00까지의 시간 중 2시간을 근무하기로 하고 월 685,000원의 임금을 지급 받기로 하는 근로계약을 체결하고 2020.5. 9. 까지 근무한 사실이 인정된다.

2) 독서실은, 근무일 매일 마다 18:00부터 다음날 02:00까지의 8시간을 위 독서실에서 근무하였거나 근무를 위하여 대기하여 이러한 8시간 전부가 근로시간에 해당하므로, 이러한 근로시간을 기준으로 하여 최저임금에 정한 최저시급에 따라 2019. 3. 10. 이후 퇴직일 까지 계산한 임금액 중 매월 685,000원씩 수령액을 공제한 잔액 합계 19,108,560원에 대하여 독서실은 지급 의무가 있다고 주장한다.

---

53) 서울중앙지법원 2017. 6. 23. 선고 2017노922 판결.
54) 서울동부지방법원 2023. 12. 21. 선고 2022가소296948 판결.

However, the agreed working hours of the SR manager were 2 hours, assuming personal study time, and there is no evidence to support the claim that the SR manager worked beyond the agreed-upon hours or that there was a need for additional work beyond the claimed hours. There is also no evidence to suggest that the SR manager needed to wait for work without being able to engage in personal tasks or outings during the study room's operations. Therefore, the SR manager's claim on this matter is deemed unsubstantiated.

3) The SR manager asserts that the study room is obligated to pay severance pay of 2,706,563 won. However, due to the reasons stated in paragraphs 1 and 2, the SR manager falls under the category of a worker who does not qualify as a designated beneficiary of the severance pay system according to Article 4, Paragraph 1, Subparagraph of the Labor Standards Act. This is because the SR manager is in the category of workers with an average weekly working hours of less than 15 over a 4-week period. Therefore, the SR manager's claim on this matter is without merit.

(2) Lessons Learned

1) Waiting time for work is considered part of working hours when calculating working hours (Article 50, Paragraph 3 of the Labor Standards Act). The time when the study room manager is under the supervision of the employer is considered waiting time for work, and this falls within the working hours. However, this study room manager had the flexibility to adjust cleaning or equipment management during the manager's 8-hour stay. Nevertheless, considering that situations such as the entry of study room users or inquiries about study room usage occur irregularly, the SR manager must respond to such occurrences during the designated working hours. Despite this, the study room intentionally stated, from the hiring stage, that it was looking for individuals who could manage the study room while studying. The employment contract also explicitly limited the working hours to 2 within the 8-hour confinement period. Moreover, the actual time the SR manager provided labor amounted to only about 2 hours. Therefore, it can be argued that the study room manager's confined time includes rest time and working hours.

2) In the dispute over the study room manager's working hours, only 2 hours within the 8-hour confinement period were recognized as working hours, while the remaining 6 hours were considered rest time. According to the Labor Standards Act, Article 54, "? If the number of working hours equals 4 hours, the employer must provide a rest time of at least 30 minutes during working

그러나 총무는 18:00부터 02:00까지의 시간 중 본인 공부를 전제로 독서실 업무를 처리하기로 하여 그 업무시간을 2시간으로 약정한 것이고, 위 독서실의 업무처리에 있어서 약정 업무시간을 초과하여 근무하여 근무의 필요가 있었다거나 총무 주장과 같이 실제 근무하였다고 인정할 증거가 없으며, 총무 본인의 공무 등 개인 업무나 외출 등 없이 독서실 업무처리를 위하여 원고가 대기하여야 할 필요가 있었다고 인정할 만한 증거도 없으므로 총무의 이 부분 주장은 이유 없다.
3) 총무는, 독서실이 총무에 대하여 퇴직금 2,706,563원을 지급할 의무가 있다고 주장하나, 위 제1항과 제2항과 같은 이유에서 근로자퇴직급여보장법 제4장 제1항 단서에서 정한 바에 따라 총무는 퇴직급여 제도의 설정대상자에 속하지 않는 '4주간을 평균하여 1주간의 소정근로시간이 15시간 미만인 근로자'에 해당한다고 할 것이므로 총무의 이 부분 주장은 이유 없다.

(2) 독서실 총무 사건에 대한 시사점
1) 업무를 위한 대기시간은 근로시간으로 근로시간의 산정이 대상이 된다 (근기법 제50조 제3항). 독서실 총무가 사용자의 지휘 감독하에 있는 시간은 근무를 위한 대기시간이고 이는 근로시간에 해당이 된다. 그러나 본 독서실 총무의 근로시간은 사용자의 8시간의 체류시간 중에 자신이 결정하여 청소나 비품관리 시간을 조정할 할 수 있다. 다만, 독서실 입실자의 경우나 독서실 사용 상담문의 등의 대해서는 비정기적으로 발생하기 때문에 총무의 근무대상 시간 중에 연락이 오면 이에 대해 대응을 해야 한다. 그럼에도 불구하고, 이 독서실의 총무는 채용 단계부터 공부하면서 독서실 관리를 할 수 있는 자를 모집하였고, 근로계약서 상에서도 8시간 구속시간 중에 근무시간은 2시간으로 한정하였다. 또한 실제로 총무가 근로를 제공한 시간은 2시간 남짓하다. 따라서 독서실 총무의 구속된 시간은 근무시간이 포함된 휴게시간이라고 할 수 있다.
2) 독서실 총무의 근로시간 분쟁에 있어 8시간 구속되는 시간에 대해 2시간만 근로시간으로 인정하고, 나머지 6시간은 휴게시간으로 간주하였다. 휴게시간은 근로기준법 제54조에 ① 사용자는 근로시간이 4시간인 경우

hours. If there are 8 working hours, the rest time must be at least 1 hour. ? Rest time must be provided during working hours, and the worker must be able to use it freely." Rest time must be provided during working hours, and the worker must be able to use this time freely; it is excluded from the calculation of working hours. The specific determination of rest time depends on (1) whether the worker is away from actual work and (2) whether the worker can use the time freely.[55] When applying these legal principles to the case, the study room manager could sufficiently engage in their own studies during the specified rest time. Additionally, considering that they could autonomously determine their actual work hours, it is plausible to consider that, even within the 8-hour confinement period, the actual working time may be considered as 2 hours.

3) To avoid such disputes as this one involving the study room manager, it is necessary to obtain recognition from the Ministry of Employment and Labor for the exclusion of surveillance-type workers from the application of working hours, as per Article 63, Paragraph 3 of the Labor Standards Act. In so doing, the study room manager's working hours could have been adjusted to 2 hours within the 8-hour confinement period, and this arrangement could have been formalized in a revised employment contract, potentially preventing the current dispute.

---

[55] Do, Jae-Hyeong, 'Legal Aspects of Waiting Time,' Ewha Womans University Law Journal, Vol. 16, No. 3 (March 2012), pp. 253.

에는 30분 이상, 8시간인 경우에는 1시간 이상의 휴게시간을 근로시간 도중에 주어야 한다. ② 휴게시간은 근로자가 자유롭게 이용할 수 있다고 규정하고 있다. 휴게시간은 근로시간 도중에 주어야 하고 근로자가 자유롭게 이용할 수 있는 시간이며, 근로시간 계산에서 제외된다. 휴게시간의 구체적인 판단은 (1) 근로자가 현실적인 근로로부터 떠나 있는지 여부, (2) 근로자가 자유롭게 해당 시간을 자유롭게 이용할 수 있는지 여부에 달려 있다.[55] 이러한 휴게시간의 법리를 가지고 판단할 때, 독서실 총무는 해당 휴게시간에 충분히 자신의 공부를 할 수 있었다. 그리고 실제 근로를 스스로 정할 수 있었다는 점에서 비록 8시간 구속시간 중에 실제 근무시간은 2시간으로 간주될 수 있을 것이다.

3) 이러한 독서실 총무의 논쟁을 피하기 위해서는 근로기준법 제63조 제3항의 규정에 따라 감시 단속적 근로자에 대한 근로시간 적용제외를 고용노동부로부터 인정을 받는 것이다. 이렇게 하면 독서실 총무의 근로시간을 조정하여 8시간 구속되는 시간 중에 2시간으로 정하고, 그 내용을 다시 근로계약으로 체결하였다면 이번 독서실 총무의 분쟁사건을 사전에 예방할 수 있었을 것이다.

---

[55] 도재형, 대기시간의 법리, 이화여자대학교 법학논집 제16권 제3호 (2012. 3), 253면.

Chapter 2 Working Hours and Extended Working Hours

Ⅰ. **Legal Standard Working Hours**

Ⅱ. **Contractual Working Hours and Inclusive Wage Systems**

Ⅲ. **Overtime, Nighttime and Holiday Work**

⟨Case Study 2-1⟩ Driver of Director Paid Less than Statutory Allowances

제2장 근로시간과 연장근로수당

I. 법정근로시간
II. 소정근로시간과 포괄임금제
III. 연장근로, 야간근로와 휴일근로

〈실무사례 2-1〉 임원기사의 법정수당 미지급 사건

Chapter 2 Working Hours and Extended Working Hours

Ⅰ. Legal Standard Working Hours

1. Legal Standard Working Hours and Contractual Working Hours

> **The Labor Standards Act:**
> Article 50 (Working Hours) ① Working hours per week shall not exceed 40 hours excluding recess hours.
> ② Working hours per day shall not exceed 8 hours excluding recess hours.
> Article 69 (Work Hours [for minors]) Working hours of a person aged between 15 and 18 shall not exceed 7 hours per day and 35 hours per week. However, the working hours may be extended up to an hour per day, or 5 hours per week, by an agreement between the parties concerned.
>
> **The Occupational Safety and Health Act**
> Article 139 (Restriction on Extension of Working Hours for Harmful or Dangerous Work) With respect to a worker who is engaged in harmful or dangerous work prescribed by Presidential Decree, the employer shall not have him work in excess of 6 hours per day or 34 hours per week.

Working hours stipulated in the Labor Standards Act are regulated in units of one day and one week. The purposes of standard working hours are to rehabilitate the employee from mental and physical fatigue, preserve labor service, and guarantee the employee's right to participate in social and cultural activities.

Contractual working hours are working hours within the legal standard working hours on which the employer and the employees have agreed. It is a concept mainly used to convert daily pay or monthly pay into hourly pay. Accordingly, the hourly ordinary wage is differentiated by the contractual working hours. Contractual working hours determine the hourly ordinary wage, which is calculated by the day, week, or month, then divided by the working hours of the given period.

Ⅰ. 법정근로시간

1. 법정근로시간과 소정근로시간

근로기준법

제50조(근로시간) ① 1주간의 근로시간은 휴게시간을 제외하고 40시간을 초과할 수 없다.

② 1일의 근로시간은 휴게시간을 제외하고 8시간을 초과할 수 없다.

제69조(연소자의 근로시간) 15세 이상 18세 미만인 자의 근로시간은 1일에 7시간, 1주에 35시간을 초과하지 못한다. 다만, 당사자 사이의 합의에 따라 1일에 1시간, 1주에 5시간을 한도로 연장할 수 있다.

산업안전보건법

제139조(유해·위험작업에 대한 근로시간 제한 등) ① 사업주는 유해하거나 위험한 작업으로서 높은 기압에서 하는 작업 등 대통령령으로 정하는 작업에 종사하는 근로자에게는 1일 6시간, 1주 34시간을 초과하여 근로하게 해서는 아니 된다.

　근로기준법은 1일과 1주를 단위로 하여 근로시간을 규제하고 있다. 이는 긴 시간 동안 근로함에 따라 발생하는 정신적·육체적 피로를 회복시켜 근로자로 하여금 노동력을 보전하고 사회적·문화적 활동을 통해 인간다운 생활을 할 수 있도록 하기 위함이다.

　소정근로시간이라 함은 법정근로시간의 범위 안에서 근로자와 사용자 간에 정한 근로시간을 말한다. 소정근로시간은 주로 일급·월급을 시간급으로 환산하기 위해 사용하는 개념으로, 소정근로시간을 얼마로 할 것인가에 따라 시간급 통상임금에 차이가 난다. 소정근로시간은 시간 외 근로에 대한 가산

Chapter 2 Working Hours and Extended Working Hours

Contractual hours also include the wages paid as an additional allowance for overtime work. They are the standard hours of payment for calculating wages.

Legal standard working hours regulated in the Labor Standards Act are as follows:

Type of Employee	Standard working hours	Overtime	Night/holiday work
Employees	8 hours per day; 40 hours per week	Mutual agreement; 12 hours per week	No limit
Female employees within one year after giving birth	8 hours per day; 40 hours per week	Mutual agreement; 2 hours per day; 6 hours per week; 150 hours in one year	Individual agreement; Approval from the Minister of Labor
Pregnant employees	8 hours per day; 40 hours per week	Not allowed	Specified request; Approval from the Minister of Labor
Employees under 18 years of age	7 hours per day; 35 hours per week	Mutual agreement; 1 hour per day; 5 hours per week	Individual agreement; Approval from the Minister of Labor
Employees working under harmful and dangerous conditions	6 hours per day; 34 hours per week	Not allowed	

<Calculating contractual working hours>

(1) In the case of a weekly 5-day work week (8 hours daily) with one day of paid leave and one day of unpaid leave

Week	Month
[8 hrs x 5 days] + 8 hrs = 48 hrs (Duty hours) (Paid leave)	48 hrs × 4.345 weeks ≒ 209 hours

(2) Contractual working hours for employees between the ages of 15 and 18 years (in the case where there is no regulation provided by the company)

임금의 산정에 있어서는 법률상 일·주·월 등에 의한 임금을 그 기간의 소정근로시간으로 나눈 임금을 가지고 계산하도록 하고 있기 때문에 소정근로시간은 임금의 지급대상이 된다.

근로기준법에 규정된 법정근로시간을 요약하면 다음과 같다.

구 분	기준근로시간	연장근로	야간/휴일근로
근로자(원칙)	1일 8시간 1주 40시간	당사자 합의 1주 12시간	제한 없음
산후 1년 미만 여성근로자		당사자 합의 1일 2시간 1주 6시간 1년 150시간	본인 동의 고용노동부장관 인가
임신 중인 근로자		불 가	명시적 청구 고용노동부장관 인가
연소근로자 (15세이상-18세미만)	1일 7시간 1주 35시간	당사자 합의 1일 1시간 1주 5시간	본인 동의 고용노동부장관 인가
유해·위험 작업 근로자	1일 6시간 1주 34시간	연장근로 불가	

<소정근로시간의 계산>

(1) 주 5일(5일 8시간)을 근로하기로 하고 1일은 유급휴일, 1일은 무급휴일로 처리하는 경우

주	월
[8시간×5일] + 8시간 = 48시간 (근로제공의무시간) (유급처리시간)	48시간 × 4.345주 ≒ 209시간

(2) 15세 이상 18세 미만의 월 소정근로시간(노사 간 별도 정함이 없는 경우)

Chapter 2 Working Hours and Extended Working Hours

Week	Month
[7 hrs x 5 days] + 7 hrs = 42 hrs (Duty hours) (Paid leave)	42 hrs × 4.345 weeks ≒ 182 hours

(3) Contractual working hours for employees working under harmful and dangerous conditions (i.e., engaged in submarine or diving work) (in cases of 6 hours for 6 days and 4 hours for one day a week)

Week	Month
[6 hrs x 5 days] + 6 hrs = 36 hrs (Duty hours) (Paid leave)	36 hrs×4.345 weeks≒ 156 hours

II. Contractual Working Hours and Inclusive Wage Systems

1. Introduction

When the Labor Standards Act (LSA) is revised, related rulings also change. A representative example is the change of the Supreme Court ruling in relation to the inclusive wage system as contractual working hours are introduced as mandatory items in employment contracts. Prior to July 1, 2007, the LSA stipulated wages, working hours and other working conditions acceptable for employment contracts, but since that date, it now stipulates wages, contractual working hours, statutory holidays, statutory leave and other working conditions. This means that a previous employment contract that specifies only "working hours" remains unclear in content, but the revised law stipulates that it should include "contractual working hours". Contractual working hours refer to the time set by the employer that the employee is to work, within the allowable total working time (40 hours per week, 8 hours per day) (Article 2, paragraph 8 of the LSA). Therefore, since the revision, the wage in accordance with the contractual working hours has to be specified, which in effect limits the inclusive wage system.[56]

---

[56] Lim, Jongyul, Labor Law, 17th ed., Park Young Sa, 2019, p. 470.

주	월
[7시간 × 5일] + 7시간 = 42시간 (근로제공의무시간) (유급처리시간)	42시간 × 4.345주 ≒ 182시간

(3) 유해·위험작업종사자(잠함·잠수작업근로자)의 월 소정근로시간(노사간 별도 정함이 없고 5일 6시간인 경우)

주	월
[6시간 × 5일] + 6시간 = 36시간 (근로제공의무시간) (유급처리시간)	36시간 × 4.345주 ≒ 156시간

II. 소정근로시간과 포괄임금제

1. 소정근로시간의 이해

근로기준법이 변경되면 관련 판례도 변경된다. 대표적인 것이 근로계약에 소정근로시간이 필수 기재사항으로 도입됨에 따라, 포괄임금제에 관한 대법원 판례의 변경 예이다. 2007년 7월 1일 이전에는 근로기준법상 근로계약 체결 시 임금, 근로시간, 기타의 근로조건을 명시했지만, 그 이후에는 임금, 소정근로시간, 법정휴일, 법정휴가와 기타 근로조건을 명시하였다. 이는 기존의 근로계약은 '근로시간'만을 명시하여 그 내용이 명확하지 않았지만, 개정법은 '소정근로시간'이라 명시하도록 규정하고 있다. 즉, 소정근로시간은 법정근로시간 (1주40시간, 1일 8시간) 내에서 근로자와 사용자가 일하기로 정한 시간을 말한다(근기법 제2조 제8항). 이는 1주 근로시간인 40시간, 1일 8시간 내에서 근로자와 사용자가 근로시간을 정하여야 한다는 것이다. 따라서 개정법 이후에는 소정근로시간에 따른 임금을 명시하도록 되어 있어 사실상 포괄임금제를 제한하고 있다.[56]

Chapter 2 Working Hours and Extended Working Hours

Before revision (prior to July 1, 2007)	After revision: Labor Standards Act [Implemented July 1, 2007]
Article 24 (Stipulation of Working Conditions) The employer shall specify the wages, working hours and other working conditions for workers at the time the employment contract is concluded	Article 24 (Stipulation of Working Conditions) The employer shall notify the employee of the wages, the contractual working hours in accordance with Article 20, holidays in accordance with the provisions of Article 54, annual paid vacation in accordance with the provisions of Article 59, and other working conditions to be determined

In order to understand the content of such changes, it is necessary to examine specifically the meaning of the contractual working hours introduced with revision of the Labor Standards Act in 2007. In this regard, I would like to discuss the judicial precedents introduced due to the revised law, and then look into the types of suitable employment contract where an inclusive wage system is justifiable.

2. Contractual Working Hours

(1) Regulations on contractual working hours

Contractual working hours shall be determined between the worker and employer in the range of working hours pursuant to Article 50 (Work Hours) and Article 69 (Work Hours for Minors) of the Labor Standards Act, or Article 139 (Hazardous and Dangerous Work) of the Occupational Safety and Health Act. This means that the contractual working hours must be set within the statutory working hours. Article 17 of the Labor Standards Act requires wages, contractual working hours and other working conditions to be specified in the process of making an employment contract. Therefore, wages defined in the employment contract are limited to 40 hours a week, and in principle, inclusive wages are a violation of the Labor Standards Act. Article 58 stipulates that if a worker fails to calculate working time by working all or part of the working hours outside the workplace due to business trips or other reasons, he/she shall be deemed to have worked the contractual working hours. Even for part-time workers, "the employer shall obtain

변경 전 (2007.7.1. 이전)	변경 후: 근로기준법 [시행2007.7.1] [법률 제8293호, 2007.1.26, 일부개정]
제24조(근로조건의 명시) 사용자는 근로계약 체결 시 근로자에 대하여 임금, 근로시간, 기타의 근로조건을 명시하여야 한다	제24조(근로조건의 명시) 사용자는 근로계약 체결 시 근로자에 대하여 임금, 제20조의 규정에 따른 소정근로시간, 제54조의 규정에 따른 휴일, 제59조의 규정에 따른 연차유급휴가 그 밖에 대통령령이 정하는 근로조건을 명시하여야 한다

이러한 변화의 내용을 제대로 알기 위해서는 2007년의 근로기준법 변경과 함께 도입된 소정근로시간의 의미는 어떤 것인지에 대해 구체적으로 살펴볼 필요가 있으며, 이와 관련하여 판례의 변경된 내용이 어떤 것이고, 앞으로 변경된 포괄임금제를 타당성 있게 도입하기 위한 근로계약 체결방식에 대해 구체적으로 살펴보고자 한다.

2. 소정근로시간의 내용

(1) 소정근로시간에 관한 법 규정

소정근로시간은 근로기준법 제50조(법정근로시간), 제69조(연소자의 근로시간) 또는 「산업안전보건법」 제139조(유해 위험한 작업)에 따른 근로시간의 범위에서 근로자와 사용자 사이에 정한 근로시간을 말한다. 이는 법정 근로시간 내에서 소정근로시간을 정해야 하는 것을 말한다. 근로기준법 제17조는 근로계약 체결 시 임금과 소정근로시간, 기타의 근로조건을 명시하도록 하고 있다. 따라서 근로계약에서 정하는 임금은 1주 40시간 내에서 정하도록 하고 있으므로, 원칙상 포괄임금은 근로기준법 위반이 된다. 근로기준법 제58조는 근로자가 출장이나 그 밖의 사유로 근로시간의 전부 또는 일부를 사업장 밖에서 근로하여 근로시간을 산정하기 어려운 경우에는 소정근로시간을 근로한 것으로 본다고 규정하고 있다. 단시간 근로의 경우에도 "사용자는 단시간

---
56) 임종률,「노동법」제17판, 박영사, 2019, 470면.

Chapter 2 Working Hours and Extended Working Hours

the consent of the employee concerned if they have a part-time worker work beyond the contractual working hours prescribed in Article 2 of the Labor Standards Act. In this case, such employee cannot work more than 12 hours a week. The employer shall pay the part-time worker an additional 50% or more of the ordinary wage for the overtime exceeding the contractual working hours" (Article 6 of the Act on the Protection Etc. of Fixed-term and Part-time Employees). In the past, overtime pay was introduced only for working hours exceeding legal standard working hours. However, for part-time workers, the overtime pay shall be paid if the working hours exceed contractual working hours (introduced on March 18, 2014). This means that if the part-time worker has 20 contractual working hours per week, an additional wage shall be paid for the hours exceeding those 20 contractual working hours.

(2) Reasons for limiting work hours

Contractual working hours refer to the time within the legal standard working hours that the worker has to work. Here, legal standard working hours generally refer to 40 hours per week and 8 hours per day. The 12-hour limitation on extended work is for hours in excess of statutory working hours (Article 53 of the LSA). Overtime work for part-time workers is also recognized within a limit of 12 hours beyond the weekly contractual working hours of part-time workers. That is, extended hours for part-time workers are judged based on contractual working hours rather than legal standard working hours (Article 6 of the Act on the Protection Etc. of Fixed-term and Part-time Employees). In Article 17 of the LSA, stipulating the contractual working hours in the employment contract is mandatory, and then based upon this, wages and contractual working hours are determined. This limits the maximum working hours and ensures the right of employees to protect their health and pursue happiness.

The inclusive wage system refers to a wage system that does not calculate basic wages in advance for a given working time, but rather stipulates that daily or monthly wages shall include the total amount of statutory working hours plus additional working hours.[57] Since the LSA stipulates that basic wages and contractual working hours shall be defined in the employment contract, the inclusive wage system is in effect in violation of that Act.

---

[57] Lee, Seunggil, "A Study on Judicial Principles and Benefits of the Inclusive Wage System", Labor Law Studies Collection, 29th ed., Korean Comparative Labor Law Study Association, Dec. 2012, p. 575.

근로자에 대하여 근로기준법 제2조의 소정근로시간을 초과하여 근로하게 하는 경우에는 당해 근로자의 동의를 얻어야 한다. 이 경우, 1주에 12시간을 초과하여 근로하게 할 수 없다. 사용자가 단시간 근로자의 소정근로시간을 초과하는 연장근로에 대하여 통상임금의 100분의 50이상을 가산하여 지급하여야 한다" 고 규정하고 있다(기간제법 제6조). 기존에는 법정근로시간을 초과하는 근로시간만 연장근로에 따른 연장근로가산수당을 지급하도록 하였으나, 단시간근로자의 경우에는 법정근로시간에 미치지 못하더라도 소정근로시간을 초과하는 경우 연장근로가산수당을 지급하도록 하고 있다(2014년 3월 18일 도입). 예를 들어, 이는 단시간 근로자의 소정근로시간이 주20시간인 경우 이를 초과했을 때 연장근로에 대한 가산임금을 지급해야 한다는 것이다.

(2) 소정근로시간으로 제한하는 이유

소정근로시간은 법정근로시간 내에서 근로자와 사용자가 일하기로 정한 시간을 말한다. 여기서 법정근로시간이라고 하면 일반적으로 1주 40시간, 1일 8시간을 말한다. 연장근로는 법정근로시간을 초과하여 최대 1주 12시간까지로 제한하고 있다(근기법 제53조). 단시간근로자의 연장근로도 단시간근로자의 1주 소정근로시간에 가산하여 12시간 한도 내에서 인정된다. 즉, 단시간근로자의 연장근로는 법정근로시간이 아닌 소정근로시간을 기준으로 판단한다(기간제법 제6조). 근로기준법 제17조에서는 근로계약서의 소정근로시간을 필수 기재사항으로 하여, 임금과 소정근로시간을 정하도록 하고 있으며, 이는 근로시간을 제한하여 근로자의 건강과 행복추구권을 보장하고 사용자의 권리남용을 방지하기 위한 것이다.

포괄임금제는 소정근로시간에 대한 기본임금을 미리 산정하지 않고, 법정근로시간과 추가 연장근로시간에 대한 제수당을 합한 금액을 월임금액이나 일당임금으로 정해 근로자에게 지급하기로 하는 임금제도를 말한다.[57] 근로기준법상 근로계약 작성시 필수 기재사항인 기본임금과 소정근로시간을 정하도록 명시되어 있는 점을 볼 때, 포괄임금제는 사실상 근로기준법을 위반하는 임금 지급제도라고 할 수 있다.

---

[57] 이승길, "포괄임금제의 법리와 효용성에 관한 연구", 「노동법논총」 제29호, 한국비교노동법학회, 2013.12. 575면.

Chapter 2 Working Hours and Extended Working Hours

3. Changes in Court Rulings Regarding the Inclusive Wage System

(1) Court rulings - details of changes

Related rulings can be divided into those before and those after July 2007. Before July 2007, the courts did not specifically determine contractual working hours because employment contracts were not required to stipulate wage, working time or other conditions. In other words, even if the basic wage was not calculated in advance but the inclusive wage equaled the sum of applicable allowances plus the monthly wage in a way that was not disadvantageous to the employee, it was considered valid. As a result, it was possible to accept the inclusive wage system for both jobs where the working hours were difficult to calculate, and jobs where the working hours were not difficult to calculate, but the system was conducive to convenient management.

<Changes in Court Ruling regarding Inclusive Wages>

Before revision (prior to July 1, 2007)	After revision: (July 1, 2007 on)
The Supreme Court concluded that if an employer receives the consent of the employee as a means of encouraging the convenience of calculating working hours and promoting employee willingness, and it is not disadvantageous to the employee in light of collective agreements and rules of employment, the inclusive wage agreement in a collective wage system is valid".[58]	In 2010, the Supreme Court distinguished between cases where it was difficult to calculate working time and cases where it was not. ① In cases where it is deemed difficult to calculate working hours such as surveillance work, even if a so-called inclusive wage contract is concluded, it is valid if it is not disadvantageous to the employee and is recognized as justified in light of various circumstances. ② If there is little difficulty in calculating working hours, the principle of wage payment according to working hours in the Labor Standards Act shall apply unless there are special circumstances in which it is impossible to apply the provisions of the Labor Standards Act.[59]

[58] Supreme Court ruling on Oct. 25, 1993, 83do1050; Supreme Court ruling on Apr. 25, 1997, 95da4056; Supreme Court ruling on Mar. 24, 2019, 96da24699; Supreme Court ruling on May 28, 1999, 99da2881;

- 35 -

3. 포괄임금제에 대한 판례 변경

(1) 판례의 변경내용

기존의 판례는 2007년 7월 이전의 것으로 근로계약을 체결할 경우 임금, 근로시간 등 기타의 조건을 명시하여야 한다는 내용에 따라 소정근로시간에 대한 부분을 구체적으로 판단하지 않았다. 즉, 기본임금을 미리 산정하지 않은 채 제 수당을 합한 금액을 월 급여액으로 지급하는 포괄임금이 근로자에게 불이익이 없다면 유효한 것으로 인정하였다. 이에 따라 근로시간 산정이 어려운 특수한 형태의 근로뿐만 아니라, 근로시간 계산이 가능하지만 편의를 위해 고정연장근로수당을 신설하여 포괄임금제로 하는 경우도 허용하였다.

<근로기준법의 개정안으로 인해 포괄임금의 판례 변화>

대법원 판례: 변경전 (2007.7.1. 이전)	변경후: 근로기준법 [시행2007.7.1]
대법원은 "근로시간, 근무형태와 업무의 성질 등을 참작하여 계산의 편의와 직원의 근무 의욕을 고취하는 뜻으로 근로자의 승낙을 받고, 그것이 단체협약이나 취업규칙에 비추어 근로자에게 불이익이 없으며 여러 사정에 비추어 정당하다고 인정되면 포괄 임금제의 임금약정은 유효하다"고 판시하여 왔다.[58]	2010년 대법원은 근로시간 산정이 어려운 경우와 그렇지 않은 경우로 구분하였다. ①"감시 단속적 근로 등과 같이 근로시간의 산정이 어려운 것으로 인정되는 경우에는 이른바 포괄임금에 의한 임금지급계약을 체결하더라도 그것이 달리 근로자에게 불이익이 없고 여러 사정에 비추어 정당하다고 인정될 때에는 유효하다." 그러나 ②"근로시간의 산정이 어려운 경우가 아니라면 달리 근로기준법상의 근로시간에 관한 규정을 그대로 적용할 수 없다고 볼 만한 특별한 사정이 없는 한, 근로기준법상의 근로시간에 따른 임금지급의 원칙이 적용된다"고 한다.[59]

In 2010, however, the Supreme Court ruled that the difficulty of calculating working hours would determine whether an inclusive wage system was justified and that such a system was not acceptable if the working hours could be calculated.[60] This case is considered to have set a related precedent because the employment contract specifies contractual working hours in accordance with Article 17 of the LSA. In other words, the basic wage shall be determined on the basis of the contractual working hours when concluding an employment contract, and in principle, the inclusive wage system cannot be introduced when working time can be calculated. Thus, the inclusive wage system is acceptable for workers with supervisory and intermittent duties that make it difficult to calculate working time, but not easily for workers whose working time can be calculated. Amendment of the Labor Standards Act resulted in the following changes in rulings on inclusive wages.

(2) Trends in rulings on the current inclusive wage system

Since July 2007, consistent judicial precedents have been set, denying the existing inclusive wage system. A Supreme Court case in 2014 provides a clear explanation:[61] "In cases where the inclusive wage system can be deemed justifiable, it is necessary to consider the type and nature of the work (such as whether it involves surveillance and intermittent work), and the difficulty of calculating the working hours when considering the working time. The amount of allowance included in the statutory allowance is set as a monthly benefit or daily wage, or the basic wage calculated in advance, but if the statutory allowance is not classified and a fixed amount is set as the statutory benefit allowance, it is valid when a wage contract under the inclusive wage system is concluded. However, it shall not be disadvantageous to the workers. Therefore, it is justified in light of the various circumstances mentioned above."

In addition, the rulings also reject the inclusive wage system if calculation of the working hours is not difficult, unless there is a special situation where the working hours regulation in the Labor Standards Act cannot be applied. In this case, if a

---

Supreme Court ruling on June 11, 1999, 98da26385.
[59] Supreme Court ruling on May 13, 2010, 2008da6052 (Cases regarding Navy Welfare Corporation)
[60] Lim, Dongchae, Cho, Younggil, Kim, Junkeun, "A Study on the Court Ruling of the Navy Welfare Corporation regarding the Effect of the Inclusive Wage System", Kangwon Law Study 25th ed., Feb. 2019, Gangwon University Comparative Law Study Center, p. 453.
[61] Supreme Court Decision 2016.66, Decision 12114, 2011.

그러나 2010년 대법원은 포괄임금제의 유효성을 판단하는 요건으로 '근로시간의 산정이 어려운지의 여부'를 제시하고 근로시간의 산정이 가능한 경우에는 포괄임금제가 허용되지 않는다는 취지의 판결을 내렸다.[60] 이 판례는 근로계약의 내용에 따라 소정근로시간을 필수기재 사항으로 명시하고 있기 때문에 나온 판례라고 본다. 즉, 근로계약 체결 시 기본임금은 소정근로시간을 기준으로 정하여야 하고, 근로시간 산정이 가능한 경우에는 원칙적으로 포괄임금제를 도입할 수 없다. 따라서 포괄임금제는 근로시간 계산이 어려운 감시단속적 근로자 등에 대하여는 적용되지만, 근로시간 산정이 가능한 근로자에 대해서는 포괄임금제로 인정받기가 쉽지 않다(근기법 제17조).

(2) 현행 포괄임금제에 대한 판례의 경향

2007년 7월 이후, 포괄임금제에 대한 일관성 있는 판례가 제시되면서 기존의 포괄임금제를 부정하고 있다. 2014년 대법원 판례는 이와 관련하여 명확한 설명을 하고 있다.[61] 포괄임금제를 인정할 수 있는 경우로, "감시 단속적 근로 등과 같이 근로시간, 근로형태와 업무의 성질을 고려할 때 근로시간의 산정이 어려운 것으로 판단되는 경우에는 사용자와 근로자 사이에 기본임금을 미리 산정하지 아니한 채 법정수당까지 포함된 금액을 월급여액이나 일당임금으로 정할 수 있다. 기본임금을 미리 산정하면서도 법정 제 수당을 구분하지 아니한 채 일정액을 법정 제 수당으로 정하여 이를 근로시간에 상관없이 지급하기로 약정하는 내용이 이른바 포괄임금제에 의한 임금지급계약으로 체결할 수 있다. 이 포괄임금제는 그것이 달리 근로자에게 불이익이 없고 여러 사정에 비추어 정당하다고 인정될 때에는 유효하다."고 판시하고 있다.

또한 판례는 포괄임금제를 부정하는 경우로, "그러나 위와 같이 근로시간의 산정이 어려운 경우가 아니라면 근로기준법상의 근로시간에 관한 규정을 그대로 적용할 수 없다. 특별한 사정이 없는 한 근로기준법상의 근로시간에 따른 임금지급의 원칙이 적용되어야 한다. 이러한 경우에 앞서 본 포괄임금제

---

[58] 대법원 1993.10.25. 선고 83도1050, 대법원 1997.4.25. 선고 95다4056 판결, 대법원 1998.3.24. 선고 96다24699, 대법원 1999.5.28. 선고 99다2881 판결, 대법원 1999 6.11 선고 98다26385 판결 등 다수.
[59] 대법원 2010.5.13. 선고 2008다6052 (해군복지근무지원단 사건).
[60] 임동채, 조영길, 김준근, "포괄임금제 효력에 관한 '해군복지근무지원단 판결'의 타당성 고찰", 「강원법학」제56호, 2019.2. 강원대학교 비교법학연구소, 453면.
[61] 대법원 2014.6.26. 선고 2011도12114 판결

Chapter 2 Working Hours and Extended Working Hours

contract is concluded in advance under the inclusive wage system, the inclusive wage contract shall be judged legal or not after reviewing if the statutory allowance included in the inclusive wage is correct. If the wages paid under the inclusive wage system fall short of the statutory allowance calculated according to the standards established by the LSA, and if it will be disadvantageous to the employee(s), it shall be null and void. In such a case, the company shall compensate the employee(s) equal to the amount to be paid in legal standard allowances.

(3) When it is difficult to calculate working hours

If calculation of working hours is difficult, the inclusive wage system can be introduced. The following types of work to which this system is applicable are presented in the Labor Standards Act.

1) **Supervisory/intermittent work:**

The working hours, rest and holiday regulations in the Labor Standards Act shall not apply to workers engaged in supervisory/intermittent work once the employer has received approval from the Minister of Employment and Labor (Article 63 (3)).

2) **Work outside the workplace:**

If a worker is unable to calculate working time due to working all or part of the working time outside the workplace (or other reasons), he/she shall be deemed to have worked the contractual working hours (Article 58 (1)).

3) **Discretionary work:**

The discretionary work in Article 58 (3) of the Labor Standards Act refers to tasks where it is difficult to calculate working time because of the characteristics or performance rather than the amount of work. Written consent is required from the employee representative in order to qualify the work as within the contractual working hours. Specific tasks include designing and analyzing research and development and information processing systems, organizing articles for newspapers and broadcasts, designing and designing-related job, and producing and supervising broadcasting and film production (Article 58, Clause 3).

4. Case Studies on Introducing an Inclusive Wage System

방식의 임금 지급계약을 체결한 때에는 그것이 근로기준법이 정한 근로계약에 관한 규제를 위반하는지를 따져 포괄임금에 포함된 법정수당이 근로기준법에서 정한 기준에 따라 산정된 법정 수당에 미달한다면 그에 해당하는 포괄임금제에 의한 임금 지급계약 부분은 근로자에게 불이익하여 무효이다. 사용자는 근로기준법의 강행성과 보충성 원칙에 의하여 근로자에게 그 미달하는 법정수당을 지급할 의무가 있다."고 판시하고 있다.

(3) 근로시간 산정이 어려운 경우

근로시간의 산정이 어려운 경우에 대해서는 포괄임금제를 도입할 수 있으며, 이러한 업무는 근로기준법상 제시된 다음과 같은 업무라고 볼 수 있다.

1) 감시 단속적 근로

감시 단속적 근로자로서 사용자가 고용노동부장관의 적용제외 인가를 받은 경우 근로기준법의 근로시간, 휴게, 휴일 규정을 적용하지 아니한다. 이는 고용노동부장관의 승인을 전제로 근로시간의 적용이 제외된다(근기법 제63조 제3항).

2) 사업장 밖 근로

근로자가 출장 및 기타 사유로 근로시간의 전부 또는 일부를 사업장 밖에서 근로하여 근로시간을 산정하기 어려운 경우, 소정근로시간을 근로한 것으로 본다(제58조 제1항).

3) 재량근로

근로기준법 제58조 제3항의 재량근로업무는 전문적 업무로 근로의 양보다는 질이나 성과가 중시되어 근로시간 산정이 어려운 업무를 말한다. 해당업무를 소정근로시간으로 인정받기 위해서는 근로자대표와의 서면합의가 필요하다. 구체적 업무로는 연구개발이나 정보처리시스템의 설계나 분석업무, 신문이나 방송 등 기사의 취재 편성 업무, 디자인이나 고안업무, 방송이나 영화 제작의 프로듀서나 감독 업무 등이 있다(제58조 제3항).

4. 포괄임금제 도입에 대한 실무사례

Chapter 2 Working Hours and Extended Working Hours

(1) Inclusive wage agreement for workers in a restaurant business

1) **Inclusive wage system:** Workers work for 6 days from Monday to Saturday, and work 8 hours a day over the hours from 11 am to 10 pm (resting between 2 pm and 5 pm), and earn a monthly salary of 3 million won, including pay for overtime.

    If the employment contract is written as above, 3 million won will be the basic wage, with an extra wage of 753,588 won per month: 150 percent for an additional 8 hours per week (35 hours per month) paid additionally.

2) **Suggestions for correction:** There are 40 contractual working hours per week and 8 hours per day. The monthly base rate for this is 2,401,560 won, with overtime of 598,437 won for 8 additional working hours per week. Therefore, the monthly total amount is 3 million won. This amount should be divided into two parts: 80 percent as basic pay and 20 percent for overtime pay. To be recognized as a justifiable inclusive wage contract, the monthly wage for the contractual working hours shall be clarified, and the additional working hours and wages stipulated and paid.

(2) Inclusive salary for white-collar workers

1) **Issue:** For some specific white-collar workers, the monthly wage is set at 76% basic wage and 24% fixed overtime allowance. Under this standard, the inclusive wage-based employment contract includes 40 hours of work per week plus an additional 10 hours per week. The company pays inclusive wages every month to the workers regardless of whether they worked overtime or not. Therefore, it is not necessary for the company to pay an additional overtime allowance for up to 10 hours of extended work. Is this inclusive wage system for these white-collar workers possible under current law?

2) **Judging whether the inclusive wage system violates current law:** There have been two judicial precedents for determining whether an inclusive wage system is possible for white-collar workers. The first involved a white-collar worker employed by a foreign life insurance company. In this case, the court deemed it difficult to calculate working hours, unlike production workers, because the business culture common to this company centered on performance tasks due to the nature of the company's insurance sales work. In such cases, the inclusive

(1) **식당 업무의 포괄임금 계약서**
 1) **포괄임금제** : 1주 6일 근무, 1일 근로시간 8시간으로 정하고 오전 11시부터 오후 10시까지 (휴게시간 14:00-17:00 3시간 포함), 급여는 300만 원으로 연장근로 수당을 포함한다.

   위와 같이 포괄임금제 근로계약서를 작성한 경우에는 300만 원이 기본급이 되므로 매월 추가로 1주 8시간(한 달 35시간)에 대한 150%인 연장가산임금 753,588원을 지급해야 한다.

 2) **개선방향** : 소정근로시간은 1주 40시간, 1일 8시간을 근무한다. 이에 대한 월 기본급은 2,401,560원이다. 1주에 1일을 추가로 근무하므로 연장근로수당 598,437원을 추가 지급한다. 따라서 월 수령액은 300만 원으로 한다. 월 임금에 기본급 80%, 고정연장수당 20%를 설정함으로써 1주 8시간, 한 달 35시간에 대한 고정연장수당을 포함한다. 포괄임금으로 인정받기 위해서는 소정근로시간에 대한 월 지급 임금을 명확히 하여야 하고, 추가로 발생하는 연장근로에 대한 근무시간과 임금을 추가 계산하여 지급하면 합법적인 포괄임금 계약서로 인정된다.

(2) **사무직 근로자의 포괄임금**
 1) **예상문제** : 사무직 근로자의 경우, 월 임금 76%를 기본임금으로 24%를 고정 연장수당으로 설정하였다. 이 기준을 가지고 1주 40시간 근무에 추가로 1주10시간의 연장근로를 포함하고 있다는 포괄임금제 근로계약서를 작성하였다. 회사는 근로자에게 연장근로 유무와 상관없이 일정액의 월 임금을 지급하였고, 이 때문에 연장근로 10시간 까지는 고정연장수당을 지급하지 않아도 된다. 이러한 사무직 근로자의 포괄임금제는 현행법상 가능한가?

 2) **포괄임금제의 위반 여부 판단** : 위의 사무직 근로자에 대한 포괄임금제가 가능한지 여부에 대해 판례는 2가지의 기준을 가지고 있다. 첫 번째는 외국계 생명보험회사의 사무직 근로자로 월 20시간의 연장근로에 대한 고정연장수당을 정하여 급여 지급이 이루어졌다. 이 경우 법원은 회사업무 특성상 과업 중심의 업무 문화가 일상화되어 생산직 근로자와 달리 근로시간 산정이 어렵다고 판단하였다. 이와 같은 경우에는 포괄임금제를

wage system was recognized.[62] The second involved white-collar workers who concluded an inclusive wage contract by signing a collective agreement offering a fixed overtime allowance of 10 hours per week for 40 hours of work per week. Workers did not receive any extended allowance for up to 10 hours a week even if overtime was performed that week. The Supreme Court concluded that such a wage system cannot be regarded as monthly remuneration based on an hourly wage or as a legitimate inclusive wage system in light of the fact that workers can calculate their hours easily.[63]

Judging from the principle in rulings on the inclusive wage system and the above two examples, the criteria for determining the justification for an inclusive wage system is whether the working hours of workers can be calculated or not.

5. Conclusion

The purpose for making it mandatory to list the contractual working hours in the employment contract is to ensure that workers are able to pursue happiness and maintain human dignity while providing work within statutory working hours. Since the inclusive wage system promotes long hours of work, it shall be applied only to those industries where there is significant difficulty in calculating hours worked. Long working hours have been the widespread norm for white-collar workers through the inclusive wage system, which is based on a fixed overtime allowance. This can be said to be a violation of the principle that wages must be calculated according to the contractual working hours. Therefore, there should be restrictions on fixed overtime allowances that may result in long hours of work for office workers.

III. Overtime, Nighttime and Holiday Work

---

[62] Seoul Central District Court ruling on Feb. 13, 2018.
[63] Supreme Court ruling on Dec. 10, 2009, 2008da57852.

인정하고 있다.[62] 두 번째는 사무직 근로자의 경우로 1주 40시간 근무에 대해 주당 10시간의 고정연장근로수당을 정한 단체협약을 체결하여 포괄임금제를 실시하였다. 근로자가 1주에 연장근로가 이루어지더라도 주 10시간 까지는 연장근로수당을 지급하지 않았다. 이에 대해 대법원은 임금체계를 월별 보수액을 기준으로한 시간급 금액이 산정되었다고 볼 수 없고, 근로시간 산정이 가능한 근로자에 대한 포괄임금제 제한 법리에 비추어 볼 때, 정당한 포괄임금제로 볼 수 없다고 판단하였다.[63]

본 사안들을 판단해 볼 때, 사무직 근로자의 임금체계에서 고정연장수당을 통한 포괄임금제에 대한 판단 기준은 해당 직종에 대한 근로자의 업무가 **근로시간 산정이 가능한 업종인지 여부에 따라 포괄임금제의 정당성 여부를** 판단할 수 있을 것이다.

5. 시사점

근로계약서에 필수사항으로 소정근로시간을 기재하도록 한 취지는, 근로자가 법정근로시간 내에서 근로를 제공함으로써 인간의 존엄성을 지키면서 행복 추구가 가능한 근로조건을 보장하기 위한 것이다. 포괄임금제는 근로자의 장시간 근로를 조장하고 있기 때문에 근로시간 산정이 어려운 업종에 한해 제한적으로 적용되어야 할 것이다. 특히 사무직 근로자의 경우, 장시간 근로가 고정연장수당인 포괄임금제를 통해서 만연해 왔다. 이는 임금을 소정근로시간에 맞추어 정하여야 하는 임금산정 원칙을 위반하였다고 할 수 있으므로 사무직의 고정연장수당을 통한 장시간 근로는 제한되어야 할 것이다.

Ⅲ. 연장근로, 야간근로와 휴일근로

---

[62] 서울중앙지법 2018.2.13. 선고 2017가단5061696 판결.
[63] 대법원 2009.12.10. 선고 2008다57852 판결.

Chapter 2 Working Hours and Extended Working Hours

The Labor Standards Act:

Article 50 (Work Hours)

① Working hours per week shall not exceed forty hours excluding recess hours.

② Working hours per day shall not exceed eight hours excluding recess hours.

Article 53 (Restrictions on Extended Work)

① If the parties concerned reach agreement, the working hours stipulated in Article 50 may be extended up to twelve hours per week.

② If the parties concerned reach agreement, the working hours stipulated in Article 51 may be extended up to twelve hours per week, and the working hours under Article 52 may be extended up to twelve hours per week averaged during an adjustment period pursuant to subparagraph 2 of Article 52.

Article 56 (Extended, Night or Holiday Work)

① Employers shall pay an additional 50 percent or more of the ordinary wages for extended work (work during the hours as extended pursuant to the provisions of Articles 53 and 59, and the proviso of Article 59).

② Notwithstanding paragraph (1), with regards to holiday work employers shall pay additionally according to the following subparagraphs:

1. Holiday work of 8 hours or less: 50 percent of the ordinary wage
2. Holiday work beyond 8 hours: one hundred percent of the ordinary wage

③ Employers shall pay an additional 50 percent of the ordinary wage for night work (work between 10 P.M. and 6 A.M.)

1. Overtime

(1) Overtime limits

Overtime refers to working hours that exceed the standard working hours specified in the Labor Standards Act. Adult employees may extend their working hours up to 12 hours per week through mutual agreement by the parties concerned,

> 근로기준법
>
> 제50조【근로시간】
>
> ① 1주간의 근로시간은 휴게시간을 제외하고 40시간을 초과할 수 없다.
> ② 1일의 근로시간은 휴게시간을 제외하고 8시간을 초과할 수 없다.
>
> 제53조【연장 근로의 제한】
>
> ① 당사자 간에 합의하면 1주간에 12시간을 한도로 제50조의 근로시간을 연장할 수 있다.
> ② 당사자 간에 합의하면 1주간에 12시간을 한도로 제51조의 근로시간을 연장할 수 있고, 제52조제2호의 정산기간을 평균하여 1주간에 12시간을 초과하지 아니하는 범위에서 제52조의 근로시간을 연장할 수 있다.
>
> 제56조【연장·야간 및 휴일 근로】
>
> ① 사용자는 연장근로(제53조·제59조 및 제69조 단서에 따라 연장된 시간의 근로를 말한다)에 대하여는 통상임금의 100분의 50 이상을 가산하여 근로자에게 지급하여야 한다.
> ② 제1항에도 불구하고 사용자는 휴일근로에 대하여는 다음 각 호의 기준에 따른 금액 이상을 가산하여 근로자에게 지급하여야 한다.
>   1. 8시간 이내의 휴일근로: 통상임금의 100분의 50
>   2. 8시간을 초과한 휴일근로: 통상임금의 100분의 100
> ③ 사용자는 야간근로(오후 10시부터 다음 날 오전 6시 사이의 근로를 말한다)에 대하여는 통상임금의 100분의 50 이상을 가산하여 근로자에게 지급하여야 한다.

1. 연장근로

(1) 연장근로의 제한

연장근로(시간 외 근로)란 근로기준법에서 정한 기준근로시간을 초과하는

Chapter 2 Working Hours and Extended Working Hours

with no limit on daily working hours.

The Labor Standards Act stipulates that the weekly working hours should not exceed 40 hours, and the daily working hours should not exceed 8 hours. However, it allows for overtime work up to 12 hours per week through mutual agreement. Nevertheless, even with mutual agreement, exceeding 12 hours of overtime work is prohibited, and violations may result in criminal penalties, including imprisonment for up to two years or fines of up to 20 million won (Articles 50, 53, and 110 of the LSA).

Regarding the exceeding of the weekly 12-hour extended working hour limit, it is not determined by the cumulative value of extended working hours exceeding 8 hours per day on a weekly basis. Instead, it is assessed whether the time exceeding 12 hours, which is the extended working hour limit, has been surpassed by the time exceeding 40 hours within a week, resulting in exceeding 52 hours per week.[64] However, if the extended working hours exceed 8 hours per day or exceed 40 hours per week, additional allowances must be paid (Article 56 of the LSA).

There has been confusion as to what constitutes "one week". Things used to be based on 5 or 6 days, with the weekly holiday excluded. Therefore, there were 40 working hours plus up to 12 hours overtime, and then 8 hours of holiday work or 16 hours over 2 holidays could be added, which could total 68 hours a week. However, on March 20, 2018, Article 2 of the Labor Standards Act was amended to include the definition that "one week refers to seven days including holidays." Due to this, the maximum working hours per week is now 52 hours including holidays.[65] Employers shall be punished for violations with imprisonment of not more than 2 years or a fine of not more than KRW 20 million (Article 110 of the LSA, Penal Provisions).

Labor Standards Act: Article 2 (Definitions) (1) Terms used in this Act are defined as follows. (revised on March 20, 2018)
7. The term "one week" refers to seven consecutive days including holidays.

---

[64] Supreme Court ruling on December 7, 2023, 2020do15393.
[65] Enforced in phases by size of business
① With regard to businesses that employ 300 people or more: Jul. 1, 2018
② With regard to businesses that employ 50 to fewer than 300 people: Jan. 1, 2020
③ With regard to businesses that employ 5 to fewer than 50 people: Jul. 1, 2021

근로를 말한다. 성인 근로자의 경우, 주 12시간 한도에서 당사자 간의 합의에 의해 연장근로를 할 수 있으나, 1일 연장근로의 한도는 없다.

근로기준법은 1주간의 근로시간이 주 40시간을 초과할 수 없고, 1일의 근로시간은 8시간을 초과할 수 없다고 규정하고 있다. 다만, 당사자 간에 합의하면 1주간 12시간을 한도로 근로시간을 연장할 수 있다고 규정하고 있다. 그러나 당사자가 합의하더라도 원칙적으로 1주간 12시간을 초과하는 연장근로를 하게 할 수 없고, 이를 위반한 경우 형사처벌 된다(2년 이하의 징역 또는 2천만 원 이하의 벌금)의 대상이 된다 (근기법 제50조, 제53조, 제110조).

주 12시간 연장근로한도 초과 여부에 대해 1일 8시간을 초과하는 연장근로시간을 1주 단위로 합산한 값이 12시간을 초과하는지 여부가 아니라, 1주간의 근로시간 중 40시간을 초과하는 시간이 12시간을 초과하여 주 52시간 초과하였는지 이다.[64] 그러나 연장근로수당은 1일 8시간을 초과하는 경우, 1주 40시간을 초과하는 경우 가산수당을 지급하여야 한다(근기법 제56조).

기존에 1주라는 개념에 혼란이 있어왔다. 보통 1주는 휴일을 제외하고 5일이나 6일을 기준으로 하였기 때문에 근로시간이 주 40시간과 최대 12시간까지의 연장근로에 휴일근로 1일 8시간 또는 2일 16시간을 포함하여 총 60시간에서 68시간까지 근무가 가능하였다. 그러나 2018년 3월 20일 근기법 제2조 정의 규정에서 "7항,"1주"란 휴일을 포함한 7일을 말한다"고 명시하고 있다. 이로 인하여 1주의 최대 근무시간은 휴일을 포함하여 52시간이 된다.[65] 이를 위반하는 경우에는 2년 이하의 징역 또는 2천만 원 이하의 벌금에 처한다(근기법 제110조 벌칙).

> 법 제2조(정의) ① 이 법에서 사용하는 용어의 뜻은 다음과 같다.
> 7. "1주"란 휴일을 포함한 7일을 말한다. <개정 2018.3.20.>

---

[64] 대법원 2023.12.7. 선고 2020도15393 판결.
[65] 근로시간 단축 시행시기는 상시근로자 수에 따라 다음과 같이 단계별로 정한다.
  - 근로자 300인 이상 및 국가, 지자체, 공공기관 : '18.7.1.
  * 특례업종에서 제외된 21개 업종은 '19.7.1.
  - 근로자 50~300인 미만 : '20.1.1
  - 근로자 5~50인 미만 : '21.7.1.

Before revision	After revision
Max working hours per week: 68 * 68 hrs = 40 hrs + 12 hrs + 16 hrs (if there are 2 holiday days)	Max working hours per week: 52 * 52 hrs = 40 hrs + 12 hrs

An employer shall not permit a pregnant employee to work overtime. However, an employer can allow a returning female worker within one year after childbirth to work overtime up to two hours per day, six hours per week, and 150 hours per year. A minor's overtime shall not exceed one hour per day and 6 hours per week (Articles 74, 75, and 69).

The term "minor" refers to a worker who is between 15 and 17 years of age. Working hours for minors cannot exceed 7 hours per day and 35 hours per week. However, if agreed between the parties, they may be extended 1 hour per day and 5 hours per week. That is, a minor can work up to 8 hours a day and 40 hours a week. Employers shall be punished for violations with imprisonment of not more than 2 years or a fine of not more than KRW 20 million (Article 110 of the LSA, Penal Provisions).

(2) Overtime and additional allowances

Employers shall pay an additional 50% of ordinary wages for overtime, night, and holiday work. The additional pay shall be made for the employee's overtime after calculating it into his/her ordinary wages. In cases where contractual working hours (e.g., four hours per day) in the Collective Agreement or Rules of Employment are less than the legal standard working hours, an additional allowance needs to be paid for extended working hours exceeding the contractual working hours regardless of whether they exceed the legal standard working hours. In this case, if the part-time employee worked for 8 hours, the employer shall pay the basic pay for four hours and the overtime allowance for six hours: for four hours extended work and an additional two hours for overtime, which will be 10 hours' wage in total (Article 6 of the Act on the Protection Etc. of Fixed-term and Part-time Employees).

2. Night Work

Night working hours range from 10 p.m. to 6 a.m. the following day. Regardless of working hours within the contractual working hours, compensation for night work shall be paid separately as an additional allowance. In cases where overtime,

개정 전	개정 후
1주 최대 근로 가능시간 : 68시간 * 68시간 = 40시간 + 12시간 + 16시간 (휴일이 2일 경우)	1주 최대 근로 가능시간 : 52시간 * 52시간 = 40시간 + 12시간

임신 중인 여성 근로자에 대하여는 연장근로를 시키지 못한다. 다만, 출산 후 1년이 경과되지 아니한 여성 근로자의 경우 1일 2시간, 1주 6시간, 1년 150시간 한도에서 연장근로를 할 수 있다. 연소자의 연장근로는 1일 1시간, 1주 5시간을 초과할 수 없다(근기법 제74조, 제75조, 제69조)

연소자라고 하면 15세 이상 18세 미만인 근로자를 말한다. 연소자의 근로시간도 1일 7시간, 1주 35시간을 초과할 수 없다. 다만, 당사자 간에 합의한 경우 1일 1시간, 1주 5시간 한도로 근로시간을 연장할 수 있다. 즉, 이는 1일 최대 8시간, 1주 40시간이 된다. 이를 위반하는 경우에는 2년 이하의 징역 또는 2천만 원 이하의 벌금에 처한다(근기법 제110조 벌칙).

(2) 연장근로와 가산임금

사용자는 연장·야간·휴일근로에 대하여는 통상임금의 50% 이상을 가산하여 지급해야 한다. 가산임금은 근로자가 연장근로에 대하여 통상임금에 가산하여 지급한다. 단체협약·취업규칙 등에서 법정근로시간에 미달하는 근로시간을 정하고 있는 경우에는 그 소정근로시간(예 : 1일 4시간 근무)을 초과하고 법정근로시간을 초과하지 않는 경우라도 가산임금을 지급해야 한다. 이 경우 하루에 8시간을 일한 경우, 4시간에 대한 임금과 4시간 연장에 근로에 대한 6시간 포함하여 총 10시간의 임금을 주어야 한다(기간제법 제6조 [단시간 근로자의 초과근로 제한]).

2. 야간근로

야간근로란 오후 10시부터 익일 아침 6시까지 사이의 근로를 말한다. 소정근로시간 이내의 근로일지라도 야간근로일 경우에는 가산임금을 지급해야 한다. 연장·야간·휴일근로가 중복된 경우 각각 가산하여 지급한다. 제63조의 적용제외

off-day work, and night work overlap, an additional allowance shall be paid for each one respectively. For employees falling under Article 63 of the Labor Standards Act (exceptions may apply), an additional allowance will not be paid for overtime or off-day work, but shall be paid for night work.

3. Holiday Work

150% of the ordinary wage shall be paid for up to eight hours of holiday work, and 200% shall be paid for hours of holiday work over eight hours. When overtime work and holiday work overlap, in the past it was very confusing to calculate. However, it is meaningful that this amendment clarifies what to do with such overlap. Employers shall be punished for violations with imprisonment of not more than 3 years or a fine of not more than KRW 30 million (Article 109 of the LSA, Penal Provisions).

4. Statute of limitations (extinctive prescription)

> Labor Standards Act, Article 49 (Prescription of Wages) A claim for wages under this Act shall be extinguished by prescription, unless exercised within three years.

(1) Concept

'Extinctive prescription' refers to expiration of a right that has not been exercised. The principle is that the law does not protect those who 'sleep' on it. This means that if people have a right they can exercise but do not for a certain period of time, they will not be able to exercise it, so that the state of legal tranquility already established will be maintained. Most extinctive prescriptions in labor law start at three years. A concept similar to the extinctive prescription under the LSA is 'exclusive period.' After expiration of an exclusive period, no further legal appeal can be made. Since it aims at the rapid establishment of legal relations, exclusive period differs from extinctive prescription.[66]

---

[66] Supreme Court ruling on Sept. 20, 1996 96da25371.

근로자(근로시간·휴게·휴일규정 적용 제외)에 대해서는 연장근로·휴일근로에 대한 가산임금의 지급문제는 발생하지 않으나, 야간근로에 대해서는 가산임금을 지급해야 한다.

3. 휴일근로

1일 8시간 이내의 휴일근로에 대해서는 통상임금의 50%를 가산하여 지급하고, 1일 8시간을 초과하는 휴일근로에 대해서는 통상임금의 100%를 가산하여 지급한다. 이는 연장근로에 해당되어 50% 가산수당을 지급해야 함에도 불구하고 연장근로와 휴일근로가 중복되는 경우 휴일근로 가산수당 할증률 적용하여 연장근로와 휴일근로 가산률(가산율) 중복지급 논란을 법률로 명확히 정리하였다. 이를 위반한 자는 3년 이하의 징역 또는 3천만 원 이하의 벌금에 처한다 (근기법 제109조).

4. 소멸시효제도

> 근로기준법, 제49조(임금의 시효) 이 법에 따른 임금채권은 3년간 행사하지 아니하면 시효로 소멸한다.

(1) 소멸시효의 개념

소멸시효는 권리행사를 할 수 있음에도 해당기간 동안 그 권리를 행사하지 않아 시효가 경과하여 더 이상 권리행사를 할 수 없는 상태를 말한다. 법은 권리 위에 잠자는 자를 보호하지 않는다는 원칙이 적용된다. 이는 행사할 수 있는 권리는 있지만 일정 기간 동안 권리행사를 하지 않는 경우 이를 포기하게 함으로써 이미 형성된 법적 평온 상태를 유지하게 한다는 것이다. 노동법상 대부분의 소멸시효는 3년을 기준으로 한다. 소멸시효와 유사한 개념이 제척기간이다. 제척기간이 지나면 더 이상 법적 이의를 제기할 수 없다. 제척기간은 법률관계의 신속한 확정을 목적으로 하기 때문에 소멸시효와 그 기간에 있어 차이가 있다.[66]

Chapter 2 Working Hours and Extended Working Hours

(2) Details of extinctive prescription
1) Wage bonds under the Labor Standards Act

Wage bonds will expire unless the claims for deferred wages are exercised within three years (Article 49 of the LSA). Wage bonds can be categorized as monthly salary, retirement allowance, unused annual allowance and so on. Monthly wages (base salary, overtime allowance, holiday work allowance, etc.) are paid on the salary payment date and rights can be exercised from the time when they fail to be paid, so salary calculation will begin from the regular payment date. Bonuses shall be calculated when the right to receive the bonus is incurred, while severance pay shall be calculated from the date of retirement due to the obligation to pay the employee on that day.

Annual paid leave is calculated from the date of conversion to a wage claim after using one year for granted annual leave.[67] In other words, if annual paid leave is managed on a yearly basis, if an employee enters 2018, his annual paid leave from January 1, 2019 to December 31, 2019 will be granted on the first day of 2020 if he performs his work 80 percent of the time or more during the period. During 2020, annual leave shall be used. The starting point for a claim for unused annual leave shall be 2021, and this right shall exist for three years (Article 36, Article 60 of the LSA).

(3) Extinctive prescription for wage bonds and for prosecution

Extinctive prescription refers to expiration of the period during which an employee who has the right to receive compensation may exercise a claim against the employer in the event of a delay in the payment of wages or severance pay. The extinctive prescription for prosecution refers to expiration of the period when prosecution can occur for violating labor law, such as delaying the payment of wages, and begins either on the date the violation occurred or the date a continuing violation ends.

The period before the extinctive prescription kicks in for prosecution of violation of labor-related Acts in terms of delayed payment of wages was extended from 3 years to 5 years in 2007 (Article 249, Paragraph 1, Item 5 of the Criminal Procedure Act). The period before the extinctive prescription for prosecution kicks in shall be deemed to have started 14 days from the date the wages should have been paid or the date the violations terminate (Article 252 of the Criminal Procedure Act). According to Article 49 of the LSA, the extinctive prescription for a wage bond kicks in after three years. However, since the extinctive prescription for prosecution is now 5 years, prosecution for delayed payment of wages will

---

[67] Supreme Court ruling on Sept. 14, 1992 92da17754.

(2) 근로기준법상 임금채권

임금채권은 3년간 행사하지 않으면 시효로 소멸한다(근기법 제49조). 임금채권은 월 급여, 퇴직금, 미사용 연차수당 등으로 분류할 수 있으며 각 유형별 소멸시효 기산점이 다르다. 매월 지급되는 월 임금(기본급, 연장근로수당, 휴일근로수당 등)은 임금 지급일에 지급의무가 발생하고 이때부터 권리를 행사할 수 있으므로 기산점은 정기지급일부터 진행된다. 상여금은 상여금에 관한 권리가 발생한 때 지급의무가 발생하며, 퇴직금은 근로자가 퇴직한 날 지급의무가 발생하므로 퇴직일로부터 기산한다.

연차유급휴가는 휴가 사용기간인 1년 완료 후 임금청구권으로 전환되는 시점부터 기산된다.[67] 즉, 연도별 관리로 판단할 경우 2018년 입사자의 경우, 2019년 1월 1일 부터 2019년 12월 31일까지 80퍼센트 이상 출근한 경우에 한해 15일의 연차휴가가 발생한다. 다음 년도인 2020년 1년 동안 연차휴가를 사용하여야 한다. 2021년 1월 1일부터 미사용 연차휴가에 대한 임금청구권의 기산점이 되며, 이는 3년간 청구가 가능하다(근기법 제36조, 제60조).

(3) 임금채권 소멸시효와 공소시효

소멸시효는 돈을 받을 권리가 있는 근로자가 사용자를 상대로 임금이나 퇴직금의 체불이 있는 경우에 청구권을 행사할 수 있는 기간을 말한다. 이에 대해 공소시효는 임금체불 등 노동법 위반 사용자를 법 위반행위가 있는 날 또는 법 위반행위가 계속되는 경우 종료일로부터 형벌권을 행사할 수 있는 기간을 말한다.

임금체불로 인한 노동관계법령 위반 범죄의 공소시효 기간은 2007년에 기존 3년에서 5년으로 연장되었다(형사소송법 제249조 제1항 제5호). 공소시효 기산점은 "범죄행위가 종료된 때부터(형소법 제252조) 임금지급일 또는 퇴직일로부터 14일이 경과한 때"까지를 말한다. 이에 반해 임금채권의 소멸시효는 3년이다(근기법 제49조). 임금채권의 소멸시효 3년이 완성되었다 하더라도 공소시효가 아직 남아 있기 때문에 임금체불사업주에 대한 형사처벌이 가능하다.[68] 따라서 공소시효를 근거로 하여 근로자는 체불된 임금에 대해 5년간

---
66) 대법원 1996.9.20. 선고 96다25371 판결
67) 대법원 1992.9.14. 선고 92다17754 판결.
68) 고용노동부 근로기준정책과, 「체불사건 업무처리 요령」, 2016. 31-32면.

continue to be possible.[68] Thus, an employee may file a claim for unpaid wages for a period of five years.

5. The Compensatory Leave System and the Vacation Savings Account System for Working Hours

> Labor Standards Act, Article 57 (Compensatory Leave System) An employer may, in lieu of paying additional wages, grant the leave to worker to compensate for the extended, night and holiday work, etc. prescribed in Articles 51-3, 52 (2) 2 and 56, pursuant to a written agreement with the workers' representative.

(1) The compensatory leave system under current law

The compensatory leave system is introduced only upon written agreement with the workers' representative, and involves vacation being granted in lieu of the wages that normally must be paid for overtime work, night work, and holiday work. The specifics of implementation must also be agreed upon in writing with the employee representative, and can be decided freely by labor and management within the scope of the existing Labor Standards Act.[69] The details of the written agreement with the workers' representative should include ① the scope of eligible workers, ② the scope of compensatory working hours, ③ the settlement period, and ④ how compensatory leave is to be used.

(1) Scope of eligible workers: The system can apply uniformly to all workers or only to specific workers.
(2) Scope of compensatory working hours: Overtime, holiday, and night work shall be subject to the system. What needs to be decided is whether or not any additional wage will be paid for the working hours subject to the compensatory leave system.
(3) Settlement period: This is where the length of time for which compensatory leave can be banked, which shall be no more than three years, in consideration of the extinctive prescription for wages.
(4) How compensatory leave is to be used: Does accumulated compensatory leave

---

68) MOEL Guide, Guide on Handling Unpaid Wages, 2016, pp. 31-32.
69) Kim, Ki-seon, Introduction of the Vacation Savings Account System for Working Hours, Monthly Labor Review, June 2018, p. 24.

청구가 가능하다.

5. 보상휴가제와 근로시간 저축휴가제도

> 근로기준법, 제57조(보상 휴가제) 사용자는 근로자대표와의 서면 합의에 따라 제51조의3, 제52조제2항제2호 및 제56조에 따른 연장근로·야간근로 및 휴일근로 등에 대하여 임금을 지급하는 것을 갈음하여 휴가를 줄 수 있다.

(1) 보상휴가제

보상휴가제는 근로자대표와의 서면 합의에 따라 가산임금을 지급해야 하는 연장근로, 야간근로, 그리고 휴일근로에 대하여 임금을 지급하는 것을 갈음하여 휴가를 지급하는 제도이다. 보상휴가에 대한 구체적인 시행방법을 근로자대표와의 서면합의로 정하도록 하고 있고, 세부적인 시행방법에 대해 기술한 내용이 없으므로 기존의 근로기준법을 적용하는 범위내에서 노사 간에 자유롭게 정할 수 있도록 하고 있다.[69] 보상휴가제의 실시에 관하여 근로자대표와의 서면합의의 내용은 ① 대상근로자의 범위, ② 대상근로시간의 범위, ③ 정산기간, ④ 보상휴가의 사용방법 등을 포함하여야 할 것이다.

(1) 대상근로자의 범위: 전체 근로자에게 일률적으로 적용할 것인지, 희망하는 근로자에 한하여 적용할 것인지에 대한 대상근로자의 범위를 설정할 수 있다.

(2) 대상근로시간의 범위: 보상의 대상이 되는 근로시간은 연장근로, 휴일근로, 야간근로이다. 소정근로시간 외에 추가로 지급되는 가산임금 전체를 할 것인지 여부를 결정한다.

(3) 정산기간: 적립 가능한 보상기간에 대해 단기로 할 것인지, 장기로 할 것인지에 대해 결정한다. 이 경우 최대 임금소멸시효를 감안하여 3년 이내로 한다.

(4) 보상휴가의 사용방법: 축적된 보상휴가에 대해 개별적으로 사용할 것인지,

---

[69] 김기선, 근로시간저축휴가제의 도입방향, 월간 노동리뷰, 2018년 6월호, 24면.

have to be used at once or is it divisible? In addition, measures necessary for the company to guarantee long-term leave need to be described, as do details on monetary compensation for the compensatory leave not used during the settlement period.

(2) Vacation savings account for working hours

In order for a workplace to change the compensatory leave system to a vacation savings account system for working hours, the accumulated vacation savings must be used within the framework of current law on the premise of a labor-management agreement. The most problematic areas are deciding how long additional wages can be saved and the company's long-term vacation guarantee policy. Current law requires a settlement period be decided for vacation and monetary compensation for unused vacation. The Ministry of Employment and Labor (MOEL) considers the saving and use of overtime, holiday work and night work hours positively, and considers it legal for an employer to allow employees to use all the compensatory leave gained for working overtime, nights and holidays during a one-year period, the following year. If it is not used the following year, a written agreement must already be in place with the workers' representative that employees are to be financially compensated for the unused portion on the first regular wage payment date of the year following the year during which the leave was to be used.[70] Otherwise, the employer must ensure that the compensatory leave accumulated in lieu of overtime, holiday and night work performed by an employee in a specific year can be properly used up to three years after it is gained. In consideration of the extinctive prescription for wage claims, employees must be compensated for leave that has not been used within 3 years, even if leave has not been used due to reasons attributable to the employee.[71] Even if labor and management agree that the employer is not obligated to pay wages for any compensatory leave not used by the employee for causes not attributable to the employer within the settlement period for compensatory leave, such agreement has no effect.[72]

---

[70] Ministry of Employment and Labor Guidelines on Sept. 23, 2019: Retirement Welfare Dept.-4046.
[71] Ministry of Employment and Labor Guidelines on Feb. 20, 2020: Wage & Working Hours Dept.-376.
[72] Ministry of Employment and Labor Guidelines on Dec. 10, 2004: Labor Standards Dept.-6641.

아니면 집단적으로 사용할 것인지에 대해 결정한다. 그리고 장기간의 휴가사용이 가능하도록 회사에서 필요한 조치 등에 대해 기술하여 장기간의 휴가보장이 될 수 있도록 한다. 또한 보상휴가의 정산기간에 대해 사용하지 못한 보상휴가에 대한 금전보상 내용을 포함한다.

(2) 근로시간의 저축휴가제도

보상휴가제를 근로시간 저축휴가제도로 변경하기 위해서는 노사합의를 전제로 하여 현행법의 테두리 내에서 활용되어야 한다. 가장 문제가 되는 것은 가산임금을 언제까지 저축할 수 있는지 여부와 회사의 장기휴가 보장 정책이라 할 수 있다. 보상휴가제를 저축휴가제로의 변경 시 현행법상 고려해야 하는 것이 휴가사용의 정산기간과 미사용한 휴가에 대한 금전보상이다. 고용노동부는 연장근로, 휴일근로 및 야간근로를 저축하여 사용하는 것에 대해 긍정적으로 판단하고 있다. 고용노동부는 사용자가 근로자대표와 서면합의에 의하여 1년간 연장근로, 야간근로 및 휴일근로시간을 계산하여 다음 연도에 1년간 휴가를 사용하게 하고, 미사용한 휴가에 대하여 그 다음 연도 첫 번째 달의 임금정기지급일에 금전으로 보상하더라도 위법하지 않다고 판단하였다.[70] 따라서 사용자는 특정 해에 발생한 근로자의 연장근로, 휴일근로 및 야간근로에 대한 대가로 저축된 보상휴가를 그 후 3년간 적절하게 사용할 수 있도록 보장해야 한다. 임금채권의 소멸시효를 고려하여 3년간 사용하지 못한 휴가는 반드시 임금보상을 하여야 할 것이다. 근로자의 귀책사유로 휴가를 사용하지 않는 경우에도 남아 있는 보상휴가에 대해 금전보상을 하여야 한다.[71] 이는 노사가 '보상휴가 사용기간 내에 사용자의 귀책사유 없이 근로자가 사용하지 않은 보상휴가에 대해 사용자는 임금 지급의무가 없다'고 합의하더라도 그러한 합의의 효력이 없 다.[72] 이러한 취지를 볼 때, 매년 1년 간 발생한 보상휴가는 그 후 3년간 사용하고, 소멸시효를 고려하여 3년간 미사용 휴가에 대해 임금보상을 하는 방식으로 이용할 수 있다.

---

[70] 행정해석 2019.9.23. 퇴직연금복지과-4046.
[71] 행정해석 2020.2.20. 임금근로시간과-376.
[72] 행정해석 2004.12.10. 근로기준과-6641.

Chapter 2 Working Hours and Extended Working Hours

〈Case Study 2-1〉 Driver of Director Paid Less than Statutory Allowances

> The exclusive driver of a director (hereinafter referred to as "the Employee") of Company A (hereinafter referred to as "the Company") resigned after serving approximately 6 years, and filed a petition to the Ministry of Employment & Labor for severance pay owed him, as well as statutory allowances for overtime, night, and holiday work, which were significantly different than what he received from the Company.[73]
>
> The Employee was hired by the Company on September 29, 2005 as a temporary employee and driver of the director's car. His employment contract was renewed every year for four years, after which the Company made him a dispatched employee of another company due to the limitations on continued employment of fixed-term employees, and had him continue doing the same duties. The Employee resigned on August 13, 2011, after working two additional years. The reason the Employee filed the petition is because the Company just paid a fixed allowance for overtime exceeding the fixed overtime and holiday work. These fixed allowances were much lower than the allowances calculated by the Labor Standards Act, and the same situation existed for his severance pay.
>
> The legal issues in this labor case were 1) overtime and holiday work allowances for an intermittent worker and 2) method used in calculation of overtime, night, and holiday work.

1. Details of the Petition

(1) The Company's fixed allowance and statutory requirement

As the director's exclusive driver, the Employee's working hours were according to the director's work schedule. While employed, the Employee constantly worked overtime hours exceeding the contractual working hours of 8 hours per day and 40 hours per week, as stipulated in the employment contract. Working hours were stipulated as between 9 am and 6 pm, with a one hour recess during that time. Wages included basic pay and a certain allowance which was set to cover a fixed

---

[73] Mr. Park Kyuhee of KangNam Labor Law Firm handled this petition case from Nov. 2011 to Feb. 2012.

〈실무사례 2-1〉 임원기사의 법정수당 미지급 사건

> A회사 (이하 "회사"라 함)의 임원전속기사로 6년여를 일하고 회사를 퇴사한 기사(이하 "진정인"이라 함)는 연장·야간·휴일 근로에 대한 수당 뿐 아니라 퇴직금도 적게 지급되었다고 고용노동부에 진정을 제기하였다.[73]
>
> 진정인은 2005년 9월 29일 A회사의 임원차량을(임원 차량을) 운전하는 계약직 사원으로 입사하여, 1년 단위로 계약을 갱신하면서 4년동안 근무하였고, 2009년 9월 29일 기간제 근로자 사용기간 제한 때문에 파견회사로 소속을 옮겨서 동일한 보직으로 동일한 업무를 수행하였다. 추가로 2년여를 더 근무한 후 2011년 8월 13일에 퇴사하였다. 법정수당과 관련하여 다툼이 된 것은 고정연장시간을 초과하는 연장, 휴일 근로에 대해 정해진 정액수당만을 지급하였는데, 이 정액수당이 근로기준법에 근거해 계산된 수당보다 터무니없이 낮았다는 점이다. 이에 진정인은 지난 3년간의 법정수당 차액, 이로 인한 퇴직금 차액에 대해 임금체불이라고 주장을 하였다.
>
> 이 진정사건의 법적 쟁점은 1) 단속적 근로자에 대한 연장·휴일 근로수당과 2) 연장·야간·휴일의 근로 계산방법이다.

1. 진정내용

(1) 회사의 정액지급과 법정수당

진정인은 계약기간 동안 임원차량기사로 임원의 업무 스케줄에 따라 차량을 운행해야 하므로 근로계약서상에 명시된 1일 8시간, 주 40시간을 수시로 초과하여 연장근로를 하였다. 근무시간은 오전 9시부터 오후 6시까지로 되어 있으며, 휴게시간 1시간을 근무시간 중에 부여하였다. 임금은 기본급과 매일 2시간의 연장근로 (저녁 8시까지)에 대하여 고정연장근로 수당으로 설정하여

---

[73] 진정사건: 강남노무법인 박규희 노무사 처리 (2011. 11 ~ 2012. 2)

Chapter 2 Working Hours and Extended Working Hours

overtime of two hours every day. For overtime, night, and holiday work, a fixed allowance was paid of a minimum ₩5,000 (for daily overtime exceeding 2 hours) and a maximum ₩80,000 (for holiday work exceeding 8 hours).

The calculation of statutory allowance according to the Labor Standards Act is not to pay a fixed allowance stipulated in the employment contract, but to multiply the number of overtime and holiday working hours by ordinary hourly wages, and then add 50% as the statutory allowance.

The Employee's employment contract: Article 2 (wages)

① Wage details

Basic pay	₩2,086,000
Fixed OT allowance	₩783,000
Total	₩2,869,000 / month

② Overtime allowance for hours before 8 pm is replaced with the fixed OT allowance in ① above.

③ ₩5,000 for overtime beyond 8 pm, but before 10 pm;
₩10,000 for overtime beyond 10 pm, but before 12 am;
₩20,000 for overtime past 12 am.

④ ₩40,000 for holiday work of 4 hours or more; ₩80,000 for holiday work of 8 hours or more. (However, no pay will be given for fewer than 4 hours.)

< **Calculation of unpaid overtime and holiday work** >[74]

1) **Regular work day:** Arrived at 6 am on Wednesday, Nov 19, 2008. Started driving and finished at 2 am the following day for a total of 11 hours overtime and 4 hours night work.

   Payment from the Company: ₩20,000 fixed overtime allowance.

   Statutory allowance: 150% of 9 hours excluding 2 hours already included in the fixed OT allowance, plus 50% of 4 hours for night work. That is, 13.5

---

[74] Working details were recorded in "car operation details" and calculated by the Company.

일정액을 지급 하였다. 연장·야간·휴일근로에 대한 금전적 보상을 최저 5,000원 (평일 2시간 이상연장)에서 최대 80,000원까지(휴일 8시간 이상 근무) 정액으로 지급하여 왔다.

근로기준법에 의한 법정수당계산은 근로계약서에 명시된 정액방식이 아닌 근로자의 시간급 통상임금에 연장·휴일 근로시간을 곱한 후, 법정가산임금 50%를 추가하여 지급하여야 하나 회사는 진정인의 추가 근로에 대해 그렇게 계산하지 않았다.

진정인의 근로계약서: 제2조(임금)
① 임금내역

기본급	2,086,000원
고정OT수당	783,000원
계	2,869,000원/월

② 평일 20시 미만 근무와 관련된 시간외 수당은 제1항의 고정OT수당으로 대체한다.
③ 평일 20시 이상 22시 미만 근로 시 ₩5,000; 22시 이상 24시 미만 근로 시 ₩10,000; 24시 이상 근로 시 ₩20,000
④ 휴일 근무시 4시간 이상 근로 시 ₩40,000; 8시간 이상 근로 시 ₩80,000 (단, 4시간 미만 근로 시는 별도 추가 금액 지급 없음)

〈미지급 임금계산〉[74]

1) **평일의 경우** : 2008년 11월 19(수) 새벽 6시부터 운행을 시작하여 익일 새벽 2시까지 근로를 제공하여 연장근로 11시간, 야간근로 4시간이 발생
   회사지급 : 추가 연장수당 정액 2만 원 지급
   법정수당[75] : 기존 연장 2시간 고정연장수당 포함된 2시간 제외한 9시간에

---

[74] 진정인 근무내역이 다행히 모두 차량운행일지에 기록되어 있어 기록을 근거로 하여 계산하였음.
[75] 시간당 통상임금 산식: 월 통상임금액 2,086,000원 / 월 소정근로시간 209시간 = 9,980원

hours for overtime and 2 hours for night work equal 15.5 hours. Ordinary hourly wages of ₩9,980 x 15.5 hours = ₩154,690. As ₩20,000 was already paid, ₩134,690 is the amount due.

2) **Saturday work**[75]: Arrived at 7:30 am on Saturday, May 30, 2009, and finished working 12:20 am that night for a total of 16 hours overtime and 2.5 hours night work.

Payment from the Company: Regarded as holiday work exceeding 8 hours, so ₩80,000 was paid as a fixed allowance.

Statutory allowance: 150% of 16 hours, plus 50% of 2.5 hours for night work. That is, 24 regular hours for the overtime and 1.25 (1¼) hours for night work equals 25.25 hours. Ordinary hourly wages of ₩9,980 x 25.25 hours = ₩251,995. As ₩80,000 was already paid, ₩171,995 is due.

3) **Sunday work:** Arrived at 5:30 am on Sunday, September 20, 2009, and finished working at 10:30 pm for a total of 16 hours holiday work, 8 hours for overtime and 30 minutes for night work.

Payment from the Company: ₩80,000 in fixed holiday allowance.

Statutory allowance: 150% of 16 hours for holiday work, 50% of 8 hours for overtime, and 50% of 8 hours for night work. That is, 24 regular hours for holiday work, 4 hours for overtime, and 0.25 hours for night work for a total of 28.25 hours. Ordinary hourly wages of ₩9,980 x 28.25 hours = ₩281,935. As ₩80,000 was already paid, ₩201,995 is the amount due.

(2) Calculation of average wages to calculate severance pay

The Employee's employment contract stipulates, "30 days' average wages as severance pay are payable to employees who serve one year or more, upon contract expiry." In calculating average wages, the Company included only the basic pay and fixed OT allowance into the total amount of wages received for the three months prior to the date of resignation, excluding other allowances. In addition, the Company also paid his severance pay every year when his employment contract was renewed. The average wages calculated under the Labor Standards Act shall include not only basic pay and fixed OT allowance, but also meal and statutory allowances like overtime, night work, and holiday work. The Employee requested that the excluded allowances be calculated as part of his severance pay.

---

[75] Calculation of ordinary hourly wages: Monthly ordinary wage (₩ 2,086,000) / Monthly contractual working hours (209) = ₩9,980.

대한 150% 지급과 야간수당 4시간에 대한 50% 가산금을 합한 금액. 즉 연장 13.5시간과 야간근로 2시간 분을 더한 총 15.5시간임. 시간당 통상임금 9,980원에 15.5 시간을 곱한 154,690원을 지급해야함. 따라서 기 지급된 2만 원을 제외한 134,690원이 적게 지급되었음.

2) **토요일의 경우** : 2009년 5월 30일(토) 아침 7시30분부터 24시30분까지 근로를 제공하여 연장근로 16시간, 야간근로 2시간 30분이 발생
회사지급 : 휴일근로로 간주, 8시간을 초과하였으므로 8만 원 지급
법정수당 : 연장근로 16시간에 대한 150%의 가산임금과 야간수당 2시간 30분에 50% 가산금을 합한 금액. 즉, 연장근로 24시간과 야간근로 1.15시간을 더한 총 25.15시간임. 시간당 통상임금 9,980원에 25.15시간을 곱한 250,990원이 지급되어야 함. 따라서 기 지급된 8만 원을 제외한 170,190원이 적게 지급되었음.

3) **일요일의 경우** : 2009년 9월 20일(일) 새벽 5시 30분부터 22시 30분까지 근로를 제공하여 휴일근로 16시간, 연장근로 3시간, 야간근로 30분이 발생
회사지급 : 휴일근로 8시간을 초과하였으므로 8만 원을 지급
법정수당 : 휴일근로 16시간에 150% 지급, 연장근로 8시간에 50%, 야간수당 30분에 50%의 가산임금을 각각 지급함. 즉, 휴일근로수당 24시간, 연장근로수당 4시간, 야간수당 0.15시간 분을 더한 총 28.15시간에 시간당 통상임금 9,980원을 곱한 280,430원. 따라서 기 지급된 8만 원을 제외한 200,430원이 적게 지급되었음.

(2) 퇴직금 산정을 위한 평균임금 산정

근로계약서에 "퇴직금은 만 1년 이상 근로 시에 한해 30일분의 평균임금을 계약기간 만료 시 정산하여 지급한다."라고 명시되어 있다. 회사는 진정인의 평균임금에 대한 계산에 있어 퇴직일 이전 3개월간 지급받은 임금총액에 기본급과 고정OT 수당만 산입하고 기타수당은 제외하여 평균임금을 산정하였다. 또한 회사는 진정인에게 매년 재계약 형태로 퇴직금을 매년 지급하였다. 그러나 근로기준법에 의한 평균임금 계산은 임금총액에 기본급과 고정 OT수당뿐만 아니라 식대와 연장·야간·휴일근로수당을 포함하여 산정하여야 한다. 이에 진정인은 제외된 수당을 포함한 퇴직금 차액을 청구하였다.

Chapter 2 Working Hours and Extended Working Hours

(3) Details of unpaid wages

1) Unpaid statutory allowances: ₩93,961,874

	Employment	Actual Payment	Statutory Allowance	Difference
Company A (Employment: Sep 2005 ~ Sep 2009)	Application[76]: Dec 2008 ~Sep 2009	₩15,064,200	₩27,547,762	₩12,483,562
Dispatch Co B	Sep 2009 ~Aug 2011	₩18,900,000	₩100,378,312	₩81,478,312

2) Unpaid severance pay: ₩10,946,582

	Employment	Daily Average Wages	Severance Pay	Difference
Company A (Employment: Sep 2005 ~ Sep 2009)	Application[77]: Aug 2008 ~Sep 2009	₩80,928 (actual:₩186,374)	Paid: ₩2,382,837 (actual: ₩5,591,234)	₩3,208,397
Dispatched to Company B	Sep. 2009 ~Aug. 2011	₩102,933 (actual: ₩257,078)	Paid: ₩5,841,880 (actual: ₩13,580,065)	₩7,738,185

3) Total amount claimed: ₩104,908,456

2. Major Issues

(1) Overtime and holiday work allowances for an intermittent worker

Generally, drivers of directors have long working hours, with the majority of these hours spent waiting, so it is not really fair to consider a driver's working hours as equal to a regular employee's working hours. Due to this, companies who

---

[76] Due to the three year statute of limitations, the Employee only claimed what was due for the applicable period.

[77] As the employment contract was renewed each year, severance pay was paid yearly, so severance pay for the previous three years has been claimed.

(3) 체불임금 내역

1) 연장, 야간, 휴일근로수당 미지급액: ₩93,961,874

	사용기간	회사지급	실제 법정수당	차액
A 회사 (2005.9 ~2009.9)	적용된 근무기간[76]: 2008.12 ~2009.09	15,064,200	27,547,762	₩12,483,562
B 파견회사	2009.09 ~2011.08	18,900,000	100,378,312	₩81,478,312

2) 퇴직금 미지급액: 10,946,582원

	사용기간	일일 평균임금	퇴직금 지급	차액
A 회사 (2005.9 ~2009.9)	적용된 근무기간[77]: 2008.09 ~2009.09	기존: 80,928 (실제: 186,374)	기지급: 2,382,837 (실제: 5,591,234)	₩3,208,397
B 파견회사	2009.09 ~2011.08	기존: 102,933 (실제: 257,078)	기지급: 5,841,880 (실제: 13,580,065)	₩7,738,185

3) 총 청구액 (법정수당 및 퇴직금 차액분): 104,908,456원

2. 주요 법적 쟁점

(1) 단속적 근로자에 대한 연장·휴일근로수당

임원차량 운전기사의 경우 근무시간이 길고, 그 반 이상이 대기시간이므로 일반적인 근로자의 근로시간으로 판단할 수 없는 경우가 많다. 이 경우,

---

[76] 임금채권의 소멸시효가 3년이라 A회사의 근무기간 1년에 대해서만 청구하였음.
[77] 근로계약이 1년 단위로 갱신되어 퇴직금 지급함. 퇴직금 차액은 최초 3년에 대해 청구함.

Chapter 2 Working Hours and Extended Working Hours

receive permission can be exempt from paying additional overtime and holiday work allowances. However, the Company in this case did not receive an exemption from the Minister of Employment and Labor, so statutory allowances cannot be excluded, and the driver's allowances shall be recalculated according to the Labor Standards Act.

Even though the characteristics of the work make it surveillance or intermittent work, if the employer has not obtained approval from the Minister of Employment and Labor, provisions in the Labor Standards Act concerning working hours, recess, and holiday shall apply.[78]

(2) Method of calculation for overtime, night, and holiday work

The Company paid fixed allowances for the driver's overtime, night and holiday work. However, until obtaining approval for exemption "for a surveillance or intermittent worker", the Company shall pay additional statutory allowances for overtime, night and holiday work exceeding the legal standard working hours just like it would for ordinary workers. In cases where the Company pays fixed allowances for overtime, night and holiday work, if the fixed allowances exceed the statutory allowances, it is allowed. However, if the fixed amount is lower than statutory allowances, the Company shall pay the additional amount.

(3) Employer responsible for payment of overtime for dispatched employees

Article 34 of the Act on the Protection, etc. of Dispatched Workers (Special Cases relating to Application of Labor Standards Act) regulates that the sending employer is regarded as the employer responsible for matters concerning employment and wages, and that the using employer is regarded as the employer for matters concerning working hours. Accordingly, the sending employer directly determined and paid such wages as monthly salary, meal allowances and the fixed overtime allowance stipulated in the Employee's employment contract, but the using employer paid the Employee additional variable overtime allowances exceeding the fixed overtime allowance, as decided by the Company's regulations (according to its car operation records). Therefore, the using employer shall be responsible for statutory allowances for additional work performed as requested by the Company.

---

[78] Administrative Guideline, Kungi 68207-1215, Oct. 2, 2003

단속적 근로자로 고용노동부의 승인을 받은 경우에 한해서 근로기준법상 연장근로와 휴일근로의 법정 수당을 지급하지 않을 수 있다. 따라서 진정인의 경우, 고용노동부의 승인을 받지 않았기 때문에 추가 근로에 대해 근로기준법에 의한 계산을 적용 제외시킬 수 없고, 행정해석처럼 현행 근로기준법 기준으로 추가 근로분이 재 계산되어야 한다.

 근로의 성격이 감시·단속적이라 하더라도 적용제외 승인을 얻지 못한 경우라면 근로기준법에 의한 근로시간, 휴게와 휴일에 관한 규정이 적용되어야 한다.[78]

(2) 연장·야간·휴일근로 계산방법

 A회사는 진정인의 연장·야간·휴일근로에 대하여 일정액의 수당을 지급하여 왔다. 그러나, 근로기준법에 명시된 '감시·단속적 근로자 적용제외 선청서'를 고용노동부에서 제출하여 승인을 받기 전까지는 일반 근로자와 동일하게 법정근로시간을 초과하는 연장·야간·휴일 근로에 대해 추가된 가산임금을 지급해야 한다. 연장·야간·휴일 근로에 대해 정액의 수당을 지급하는 경우에는 그 지급하는 금액이 근로기준법 상 법정기준인 가산임금을 초과하는 경우에 그 효력을 가지며, 초과하지 못하는 경우에는 그 차액을 지급해야 한다.

(3) 파견근로자의 법정가산임금에 대한 지급 주체

 "파견근로자 보호 등에 관한 법률" 제34조 [근로기준법의 적용에 관한 특례]에 있어 고용 관계와 임금 부분에 대해서는 파견사업주를 사용자로 보고, 근로시간에 대해서는 사용사업주를 사용자로 본다. 본 사안에서 있어서는, 파견사업주와의 근로계약서상 임금 지급항목인 월급여, 식대, 고정연장수당에 대해서는 파견사업주가 정하여 지급하였고, 고정연장 수당을 초과하는 부분에 대해서는 A회사의 차량운행일지에 따라 A회사의 정액지급 규정에 근거하여 추가 지급하였다. 따라서 A회사의 추가 업무요청 수행에 따라 발생한 법정수당에 대하여는 사용사업주가 책임을 지고 지급해야 함이 타당하다.

---

[78] 행정해석, 근기 68207-1215, 2003.10.2.

(4) Statute of limitations regarding unpaid wages

According to Article 49 of the Labor Standards Act (Prescription of Wages), as the statute of limitation to exercise a claim for wages is three years, the Employee can claim his unpaid statutory allowances and severance pay for the past three years, and not the past six.

(5) Method of calculating average wages for severance pay

Severance pay is calculated based on average wages, and on the total amounts paid in meal, overtime, night, and holiday work allowances, but the Company intentionally excluded these. As long as the meal allowance is paid periodically and uniformly, this cannot be pure welfare or a bonus expressing favor, but shall be regarded as money characteristic of wages paid as remuneration for labor service.[79]

As the total wages calculated for average wages are any money and valuable goods an employer pays to a worker for his/her work, what the worker receives continuously and regularly, and what the employer has to pay according to the collective agreement and rules of employment, regardless of how such payments are termed, the holiday work allowance shall be included [in calculation of severance pay.[80]

As the overtime allowance is not money paid under friendly and favorable conditions, but rather, is remuneration that the employer has to pay for an employee's work, regardless of its label, the overtime allowance shall be included into average wages when calculating severance pay.[81]

3. Conclusion

This petition case for unpaid allowances is a case of wages that were unpaid due to the HR manager's ignorance of labor law and lack of work-related preparation. The Company concluded this case by paying the difference between what they had already paid in fixed amounts and the statutory allowances occurring due to actual work. Through this case, the Company learned to recognize the fact that wages remained unpaid from a neglect to follow the procedural rules and calculation methods under labor law, even though the Company paid enough in

---

[79] Supreme Court, 2001do1186, May 15, 2001.
[80] Supreme Court 91da5587, Apr. 14, 1992.
[81] Seoul District Court 2005na175, May 26, 2005.

(4) 임금채권의 소멸시효

근로기준법 제49조(임금의 시효)에 따라 3년간 임금채권을 청구할 수 있기 때문에 법정수당과 퇴직금에 대해 3년 이내의 금품에 대해서만 청구할 수 있다. 그래서 본 진정인은 총 6년의 기간 중 임금채권의 효력이 유효한 3년의 기간에 대해서만 청구할 수 있었다.

(5) 퇴직금 산정을 위한 평균임금 계산방법

퇴직금 계산을 위한 평균임금에 있어, 식대, 연장·야간·휴일근로 수당을 포함하여야 함에도 불구하고 이를 누락시켰다.

식대가 정기적 일률적으로 지급되는 한 그것을 근로제공과 무관한 단순한 복리 후생적이거나 은혜적인 급부라 할 수 없으므로 근로 대가로서의 임금의 성질을 지닌 것으로 보아야 할 것이다.[79]

평균임금의 산정기초인 임금총액에는 사용자가 근로의 대상으로 근로자에게 지급하는 일체의 금품으로서 근로자에게 계속적·정기적으로 지급되고 단체협약, 취업규칙 등에 의하여 사용자에게 그 지급의무가 있는 것이면 그 명칭이 어떠하든 모두 포함된다고 할 것이므로, 휴일근로수당이 이에 포함됨은 당연하다.[80]

연장근로수당은 임의적·은혜적으로 지급된 급여라 할 수 없고 그 명칭을 불구하고 근로의 대상으로써 사용자에게 지급의무가 발생하는 임금이라고 할 것이므로, 퇴직금산정의 기초인 평균임금에 연장근로수당도 포함된다.[81]

3. 시사점

진정인의 법정수당 미지급 진정사건은 회사의 인사담당자가 근로기준법에 대한 이해 부족과 업무상 준비사항을 갖추지 못해서 발생한 임금체불사건이라 할 수 있다. 이 진정사건은 회사에서 기 지급한 고정수당을 제하고 실제 발생한 법정수당의 차액을 지급하면서 해결되었다. 여기서 얻을 수 있었던 교훈은 회사가 급여를 지급함에도 불구하고, 노동법에 정해진 절차규정이나

---

[79] 대법 2001도1186, 2001.05.15
[80] 대법 91다 5587, 1992.04.14
[81] 서울중앙지법2005나175, 2005.05.26

regular wages.

This case happened because the Company was used to paying fixed allowances for overtime, night and holiday work over a long period of time, due to the convenience of calculation. 1) If the Company had adjusted its wages by reducing the basic pay and increasing fixed allowances, or 2) if the Company had previously submitted to the Labor Office "an application for exemption for surveillance and intermittent workers" and received the necessary approval while keeping the current wage system, there would have been no problem related to unpaid wages. Accordingly, companies are required to understand the wage rules in the Labor Standards Act first, before establishing their wage systems.

계산방식을 지키지 않으면 임금체불이 된다는 것이다.

이 사례는 회사가 오랫동안 계산의 편리를 위해 일정액의 연장·야간·휴일수당을 고정적으로 지급해오던 관행으로 인해 발생하였다. 만약, 회사가 1) 임금조정을 통해 기본급을 낮추고, 고정된 즉액수당을 인상하여 지급하였더라면, 또는 2) 현 급여지급 시스템을 유지하면서도 "감시·단속적 근로자 적용제외신청서"를 미리 제출하여 승인을 받아두었다면 임금체불이 발생하지 않을 수 있었던 사건이었다. 따라서 회사는 임금설정시 근로기준법상 임금관련 규정을 충분히 사전에 숙지한 후 적용이 필요하다고 할 수 있다.

Chapter 3 Exceptions from Application of Working Hours

I. Surveillance · Intermittent Employees
II. Managerial and Supervisory Positions
III. Workplaces Ordinarily Employing Fewer than Five People
IV. Part-time Workers
V. Working Conditions for Minors

〈Case Study 3-1〉 Whether a Managing Director is Considered to Hold a Managerial and Supervisory Position

제3장 근로시간 적용의 제외와 특례

Ⅰ. 감시 단속적 근로자
Ⅱ. 관리 감독자
Ⅲ. 5인 미만의 사업장
Ⅳ. 단시간 근로자
Ⅴ. 연소근로자

〈실무사례 3-1〉 외국기업의 상무 관리감독자 여부 판단

Chapter 3 Exceptions from Application of Working Hours

I. Surveillance · Intermittent Employees

1. Introduction

If an employer has received permission from the Minister of Employment and Labor, some rules of the Labor Standards Act concerning working hours, recess, and holidays will not apply to surveillance or intermittent employees, and the employer will not be obligated to pay overtime allowances and holiday work allowances.[82] This means, when paying fixed monthly wages to surveillance or intermittent employees, the employer does not have to pay additional overtime allowance or holiday work allowance for overtime or holiday work. The employer can even pay lower than minimum wage. Here, "surveillance or intermittent employees" mean those employees whose jobs require a relatively lower intensity of labor and less physical fatigue and mental tension than others. Although some jobs share similar characteristics to surveillance or intermittent work, identical rules to normal employees concerning working hours shall continue to apply to those jobs, if the employer hasn't applied for approval to have them recognized as exceptions by the Minister of Employment and Labor, or if the employer's application for exception was rejected. In relation to this matter, I would like to look into the necessity for exceptions to the Labor Standards Act for certain jobs, requirements for approval, and cases that have been approved or have not been approved.

2. Times When Approval for 'Exceptions to Application' is Necessary

While reviewing labor cases that deal with surveillance or intermittent work, I have found it very important, and sometimes essential, for employers to receive approval to make exceptions to the Labor Standards Act for surveillance or intermittent employees.

(1) Exclusive driver (chauffeur) for a company executive:
In the morning, a chauffeur employed by Company "A" picks up the executive assigned to him, drives him to the office, and then finishes the day by taking him home in the evening. In cases where the director provides special receptions for corporate clients, the driver has to leave the workplace in the middle of night. In some cases, he may have to drive the executive to golf courses or other places on weekends or holidays. In situations like this, the time involved in picking up the executive before work, time spent waiting in the evening, and time spent waiting during dinners or golf meetings for clients shall be calculated as working hours and paid in overtime allowance for the extra working hours. If the inclusive wage

---

[82] Supreme Court ruling on November 22, 1996, 96da30751.

Ⅰ. 감시 단속적 근로자

1. 개념

감시 단속적 근로자에 대하여 노동부장관의 승인을 받은 경우에는 근로기준법 상 근로시간, 휴게 및 휴일에 관한 규정이 적용되지 않게 되어, 원칙적으로 사용자는 근로자에게 시간외근로수당 및 휴일근로수당을 지급할 의무가 없다.[82] 즉, 감시 단속적 근로자에 대해서는 월 일정액의 임금을 지급하고 연장, 휴일근로에 대해 별도의 연장근로수당, 휴일근로수당 등을 지급하지 않아도 된다. 여기서 감시 단속적인 근로는 다른 일반근로자와 비교하여 노동강도가 낮고 신체적 피로나 정신적 긴장이 적은 업무를 말한다. 비록 업무의 특징이 감시 단속적 근로라고 추정되더라도 노동부의 승인을 받지 않았거나 적용제외 신청이 거부된 경우에는 일반근로자와 동일한 근로시간에 관한 규정이 적용된다. 이와 관련하여 적용제외 승인의 필요성, 승인요건 및 승인/불승인 사례를 살펴보고자 한다.

2. 적용제외 승인의 필요성

감시 단속적 근로와 관련하여 본인이 직접 수임하여 처리하였던 사례를 몇 가지 살펴보면, 감시 단속적 근로자에 대한 '적용제외 승인'을 받는 것이 얼마나 중요한가를 알 수 있다.

(1) 전속 운전기사

A 회사에 고용된 전속 운전기사는 담당 임원을 픽업하여 출근시키고, 또한 저녁에는 퇴근 시켜 주면 하루의 일과가 끝난다. 그런데 임원은 사업상 접대를 할 경우에는 심야에 퇴근해야 하고, 또한 주말이나 휴일에도 골프 모임 등에 동행하여 운전을 해야만 했다. 이러한 경우, 출근시간 전에 픽업하는 시간, 저녁 퇴근시 대기시간, 손님 접대나 골프접대에서의 대기시간 모두 근로시간으로 간주하여 모두 연장근로수당을 지급해야 한다. 포괄임금으로 적용하는

---
[82] 대법원 1996.11.22. 선고 96다30571 판결.

Chapter 3 Exceptions from Application of Working Hours

system is applied, the maximum working hours per week (including overtime) are 52 hours, so working hours exceeding 52 hours per week shall be paid an additional overtime allowance. Since inclusive wages only include the legally allowed extended working hours (12 hours per week), the company would have to pay extra overtime wages for hours worked above 52, to cover the extended working hours and holiday work. In order to deal with this situation more appropriately, the employer should submit an application to the Minister of Employment and Labor for exception to be made to the statutory rules regulating working hours, recess and holiday work for surveillance and intermittent employees. Once approval is received, the employer does not have to calculate working hours for surveillance and intermittent employees concerning extended working hours or holiday work.[83]

(2) Employees responsible for maintenance of air-conditioning, heating equipment and electricity:

Company "B" is a manufacturer that runs three shifts in its plant. Employees responsible for maintaining air-conditioning, heating equipment and electricity work 12 hour days in two shifts. Their annual wages at entry level were about ₩30 million or less, but the actual wages they received amounted to not less than ₩50 million after accumulation of overtime and weekly holiday work allowances, etc. Despite having long working hours, the intensity of work is lower than for other employees, and the number of hours they actually have to perform some service is less than half of their total shift hours. In order to maintain an acceptable wage level under such long working hours, the company has to receive permission from the Ministry of Employment and Labor for exception to be made to the statutory rules regulating working hours, recess and holiday work for such employees If permission is given, the company is free of legal obligations to pay extra allowances for employees on duty beyond the weekly maximum extended working hours, or holiday work.

3. Requirements for 'Exclusions from Application' to be Approved

(1) Provision of 'exceptions to application' (Labor Standards Act)

> Article 63 (Exclusion from Application) The provisions of this Chapter, and Chapter V, as to working hours, recess, and holidays shall not be applicable to workers who are engaged in any work described in the following subparagraphs:

---

[83] MOEL Guidelines, Kungi 68207-1215, Oct. 2, 2003

경우에도 일주일에 최대 52시간에 대한 임금까지는 일정액으로 지급할 수 있으나 주 52시간을 초과하는 근로시간에 대해서는 모두 연장근로수당을 지급해야만 한다. 이유는 포괄임금으로 지급하는 것은 법정 연장근로시간 (주 12시간) 까지만 포함한 범위이므로 회사는 추가 연장근로, 휴일근로에 대하여 그 초과분의 임금을 지급할 의무가 발생한다. 이와 같은 문제를 해결하기 위해서는 '감시 단속적 근로'에 대한 근로시간, 휴게, 휴일에 대한 근로기준법 적용제외 신청을 하여 노동부로부터 승인을 받아야 한다. 승인된 이후부터는 근로시간, 휴일 근로 등에 대한 시간계산과 가산임금의 적용이 제외된다.[83]

(2) 냉난방, 전기 등의 관리 직원

회사 B는 제조업체로 3교대제로 공장을 가동시키고 있었다. 공장의 냉난방 및 전기를 담당하는 직원들의 경우에는 1일 12시간씩 2교대로 투입되었다. 이들의 입사 시 연봉은 약 3000만 원 이었지만, 실제 수령하는 금액은 연장근로수당, 휴일근로수당 등이 가산되어 5000만 원 이상에 달하였다. 장시간 근무라 하지만, 실질적으로 업무의 강도나 실제 근무시간은 총 근로시간의 절반에도 미치지 못했다. 이에 대해 적법한 근로시간 관리와 적합한 임금 수준을 유지하기 위해서 회사가 당장 취하여야 할 조치는 해당 직원들 업무에 대해 '감시 단속적 근로'에 대한 '적용제외 승인'을 노동부로부터 받는 일이었다. 그렇게 되면, 가산임금이나 연장근로의 법리로부터 자유로워 진다.

3. 적용예외 승인

(1) 적용예외에 대한 법 규정 (근로기준법)

> 제63조 (적용의 제외) 이 장과 제5장에서 정한 근로시간, 휴게와 휴일에 관한 규정은 다음 각 호의 어느 하나에 해당하는 근로자에 대하여는 적용하지 아니한다.

---

83) 노동부 행정해석, 근기 68207-1215,2003.10.2.

Chapter 3 Exceptions from Application of Working Hours

1. cultivation of arable land, reclamation work, seeding and planting, gathering or picking-up or other agricultural and forestry work;
2. livestock breeding, catching of marine animals and plants, cultivation of marine products or other cattle-breeding, sericulture and fishery business;
3. surveillance or intermittent work, for which the employer has obtained the approval of the Minister of Employment and Labor;
4. any other work prescribed by Presidential Decree. ("Work provided for by Presidential Decree" in subparagraph 4 of Article 63 of the Act means managerial and supervisory work and work of handling secret affairs irrespective of types of work.)

(2) Approval procedures (Enforcement Decree of the LSA)

Article 10 (Application of exceptions to working hours, etc. under the LSA)
① When an employer wants to receive permission to exclude employees from application of the Labor Standards Act regarding working hours, etc. for those engaged in surveillance or intermittent work in accordance with Article 63 (paragraph 3) of the LSA, he shall submit an application for exemption from the statutory rules for surveillance or intermittent employees with the designated form, Attachment #7, to the head of the Regional Labor Office.
② A surveillance employee, stipulated in Paragraph 1, is an employee who provides surveillance as his main function and has relatively less mental and physical fatigue.
③ An intermittent employee, stipulated in Paragraph 1, is an employee who works intermittently and has more recess hours than actual working hours or has long waiting hours.
④ If the head of the Regional Labor Office approves the application according to Paragraph 1, a certificate permitting exemption for surveillance or intermittent employees, Attachment #8, shall be issued.

(3) Criteria for approval (Working Regulations of Labor Inspectors)

1. 토지의 경작·개간, 식물의 재식(栽植)·재배·채취 사업, 그 밖의 농림사업
2. 동물의 사육, 수산 동식물의 채포(採捕)·양식 사업, 그 밖의 축산, 양잠, 수산 사업
3. 감시 또는 단속적으로 근로에 종사하는 자로서 사용자가 노동부장관의 승인을 받은 자
4. 대통령령으로 정하는 업무에 종사하는 근로자 (법 제63조 제4호에서 "대통령령으로 정한 업무"란 사업의 종류에 관계없이 관리·감독 업무 또는 기밀을 취급하는 업무를 말한다.)

(2) 승인절차에 대한 규정 (근로기준법 시행규칙)

제10조 (근로시간 등의 적용제외 승인 신청 등)
① 사용자는 법 제63조 제3호에 따라 감시 또는 단속적으로 근로에 종사하는 자에 대한 근로시간 등의 적용 제외 승인을 받으려면 별지 제7호 서식의 감시적 또는 단속적 근로종사자에 대한 적용 제외 승인 신청서를 관할 지방노동관서의 장에게 제출하여야 한다.
② 제1항에 따른 승인 대상이 되는 감시적 근로에 종사하는 자는 감시업무를 주 업무로 하며 상태적(狀態的)으로 정신적·육체적 피로가 적은 업무에 종사하는 자로 한다.
③ 제1항에 따른 승인 대상이 되는 단속적으로 근로에 종사하는 자는 근로가 간헐적·단속적으로 이루어져 휴게시간이나 대기시간이 많은 업무에 종사하는 자로 한다.
④ 관할 지방노동관서의 장은 제1항에 따른 신청에 대하여 승인을 할 경우에는 별지 제8호 서식의 감시적 또는 단속적 근로종사자에 대한 적용 제외 승인서를 내주어야 한다.

(3) 승인여부 판단기준 (근로감독관 업무지침)

Article 68 (Approval of exceptions for those working in surveillance and intermittent workers)

① Approval of exceptions for "those working in surveillance", according to Article 63 (paragraph 3) of the Labor Standards Act and Article 10 (paragraph 2) of the Enforcement Decree of the LSA, shall be issued when the following criteria are satisfied:
  1. the employee holds a position requiring less mental and physical fatigue, such as a guard, security guard, watchman of products, or keeper of measurement machines, or in exceptional cases, other jobs requiring continuous watch and mental tension;
  2. the employee works on a surveillance job as an occupation, but often engages in other temporary jobs; or in exceptional cases, if the employee has to implement other jobs repeatedly or is engaged in other plural duty;
  3. the employee works fewer than 12 hours per day under the employer's supervision, or works a 24-hour shift every other day, and either
    a) 8 or more consecutive hours are provided for sleep or recreation, OR
    b) there is an agreement between the employer and apartment building security guards and the employer provides the guards with an off-period of 24 hours the following day.

② Approval of exceptions for "those working in intermittent work", according to Article 63 (paragraph 3) of the Labor Standards Act and Article 10 (paragraph 2) of the Enforcement Decree of the LSA shall be issued when the following criteria are satisfied:
  1. the employee is free during ordinary hours, but his/her job entails a lot of waiting to prevent such things as machinery breakdowns or accidents, or for machine maintenance;
  2. the employee's actual working hours are fewer than the waiting hours within an 8-hour period, provided that, if the employee works a 24-hour shift every other day, the employee must be granted a 24-hour off-day on the day following the shift;
  3. the employee with waiting hours shall be provided with rest facilities

제68조(감시.단속적 근로에 종사하는 자에 대한 적용제외 승인)
① 「근로기준법」 제63조제3호 및 같은 법 시행규칙 제10조제2항에 따른 "감시적 근로에 종사하는 자"의 적용제외 승인은 다음 각 호의 기준을 모두 갖춘 때에 한한다.
　1. 수위·경비원·물품감시원 또는 계수기감시원 등과 같이 심신의 피로가 적은 노무에 종사하는 경우. 다만, 감시적 업무이기는 하나 잠시도 감시를 소홀히 할 수 없는 고도의 정신적 긴장이 요구되는 경우는 제외한다.
　2. 감시적인 업무가 본래의 업무이나 불규칙적으로 단시간 동안 타 업무를 수행하는 경우. 다만, 감시적 업무라도 타 업무를 반복하여 수행하거나 겸직하는 경우는 제외한다.
　3. 사업주의 지배하에 있는 1일 근로시간이 12시간 이내인 경우 또는 다음 각 목의 어느 하나에 해당하는 격일제(24시간 교대) 근무의 경우
　　가. 수면시간 또는 근로자가 자유로이 이용할 수 있는 휴게시간이 8시간 이상 확보되어 있는 경우
　　나. 가목의 요건이 확보되지 아니하더라도 공동주택 경비원에 있어서는 당사자 간의 합의가 있고 다음 날 24시간의 휴무가 보장되어 있는 경우
② 「근로기준법」 제61조 제3호 및 같은 법 시행규칙 제10조 제3항에 따른 "단속적 근로에 종사하는 자"의 적용제외 승인은 다음 각 호의 기준을 모두 갖춘 때에 한한다.
　1. 평소의 업무는 한가하지만 기계고장 수리 등 돌발적인 사고발생에 대비하여 대기하는 시간이 많은 업무인 경우
　2. 실 근로시간이 대기시간의 반 정도 이하인 업무로 8시간 이내인 경우. 다만, 격일제(24시간 교대) 근무인 경우에는 당사자간의 합의가 있고 다음 날 24시간의 휴무가 보장되어야 한다
　3. 대기시간에 근로자가 자유로이 이용할 수 있는 수면 또는 휴게

Chapter 3 Exceptions from Application of Working Hours

> free of charge.
> ③ Working hours for employees who fit under Paragraph 1 and Paragraph 2 shall be calculated as averages per certain period (one week or one month).

4. Cases Approved and Rejected

(1) Approved cases

1) Those working on weekends or at night to maintain a building and its facilities are considered intermittent employees.[84]

2) Security guards at apartment buildings and those working in an electrical or boiler room are considered to be engaged in surveillance or intermittent work and LSA rules concerning working hours, recess and holidays shall not be applicable.[85]

3) A guard supervisor who is in charge of general management of security resources is considered to be engaged in surveillance work.[86]

4) A private policeman whose job requires a relatively lower intensity of labor than others in his/her field, is considered to be engaged in surveillance work.[87]

(2) Rejected cases

1) A watchman at a railroad crossing (flagman) is not a surveillance or intermittent employee.

A certain watchman at a railroad crossing controls the trains passing 42 to 50 times per day, and also helps prevent accidents with pedestrians or passing cars. In reviewing the frequency of this watchman's checks and the constant attention needed to prevent accidents, this job cannot easily be classified as surveillance or intermittent work.[88]

2) Janitors at court are not intermittent employees.

---

[84] MOEL Guideline: Sept. 5, 1987, Gungi 01254-14337.
[85] MOEL Guideline: Feb. 5, 1990, Gungi 01254-1626.
[86] MOEL Guideline: July 27, 1993, Supreme Court 92da46462.
[87] Apr. 25, 1997, Supreme Court 95da4056.
[88] MOEL Guideline: Nov. 14, 2001, Gungi 68207-3901.

시설이 확보되어 있는 경우
③ 제1항 및 제2항의 근로시간은 일정기간(주 또는 월 등)의 평균적 개념으로 산정한다.

4. 승인 및 불승인 사례

(1) 승인사례
1) 건물시설관리를 위해 휴일 및 야간에 대기하는 자는 단속적 근로에 종사하는 자에 해당된다.[84]
2) 아파트 경비원과 아파트 관리소 내의 전기실, 기관실 직원은 감시·단속적 근로자로 근로시간, 휴게, 휴일에 관한 적용이 제외된다.[85]
3) 경비계장은 경비원들을 관리·감독하여 경비업무 전반을 총괄하는 것이므로 감시적 근로에 종사하는 경비직 직원어 해당된다.[86]
4) 청원경찰은 업무의 성격상 통상의 근로보다 노동의 밀도나 강도가 낮은 감시적 근로에 해당한다.[87]

(2) 불승인 사례
1) 철도 건널목 관리원은 감시·단속적 근로자에 해당되지 않는다.
    철도 건널목 관리원의 업무가 1일 42~50회의 열차통행에 대한 업무 뿐 아니라 건널목 통행자 및 차량의 건널목 통행 시 발생될 수 있는 각종 사고예방에 관한 업무를 하고 있는 경우라면 업무의 빈도, 안전사고 방지를 위한 주의 정도 등을 감안할 때 감시·단속적 근로로는 보기 어렵다고 사료된다.[88]
2) 법원 청소직 근로자는 단속적 근로자에 해당되지 않는다.
    법원 청소직 근로자는 매일 아침 일찍 업무를 시작, 일정한 시간표에

---

[84] 행정해석: 1987.09.05, 근기 01254-14337
[85] 행정해석 1990.02.05, 근기 01254-1626
[86] 대법원 1993.7.27 선고 92다46462 판결
[87] 대법원 1997.4.25 선고 95다4056 판결
[88] 행정해석: 2001.11.14, 근기 68207-3901

Janitors at court start work early in the morning, and continue according to a certain work schedule, excluding designated recess hours. Some individuals have to work even during recess hours. They are not classified as intermittent employees, because they do not provide work intermittently.[89]

II. Managerial and Supervisory Positions

1. Concept

Managerial and supervisory positions refer to employees who have managerial or supervisory authority over other employees or deal with classified information and whose start/finish time at work is not strictly regulated because he/she is given discretion in his/her work. Article 63 (Exclusions from Application) of the LSA regulates that the provisions regarding working hours, recess and holiday shall not apply to managerial and supervisory positions.

Article 63 (Exclusions from Application) The provisions of this Chapter and Chapter V as to working hours, recess, and holidays shall not apply to workers engaged in any of tasks described in the following subparagraphs:

1. 2. 3. (Omitted)

4. any other work prescribed by Presidential Decree. [Implementation Decree (Article 34) - Work prescribed by Presidential Decree means managerial and supervisory work and work of handling confidential information, irrespective of the type of business.]

---

2. Ministry of Employment and Labor Guidelines

---

[89] July 12, 2003, Seoul District Court 2002 Guhap 19050.

따라 정해진 휴식시간을 제외하고는 계속 업무를 수행하고 있고, 개인에 따라서는 휴식시간에도 업무를 계속해야 하는 경우가 있으므로 반드시 간헐적으로 근로를 제공하고 있다고 볼 수 없어 단속적 근로자에 해당하지 않는다.[89]

Ⅱ. 관리 감독자

1. 관리 감독자의 개념

노무관리상 지휘, 감독 권한이 있으며 업무에 있어 재량권이 인정되어 출·퇴근시간이 엄격하게 제한되지 않는 감독이나 관리의 지위에 있는 자 또는 기밀취급자를 말한다. 현행 근로기준법 제63조(적용제외)에는 관리감독자에 대해서는 근로시간, 휴게와 휴일에 관한 규정을 적용하지 않는다고 규정하고 있다.

제63조【적용의 제외】제4장과 제5장에서 정한 근로시간, 휴게와 휴일에 관한 규정은 다음 각 호의 어느 하나에 해당하는 근로자에 대하여는 적용하지 아니한다.
1. 2. 3. (생략)
4. 대통령령으로 정하는 업무에 종사하는 근로자 (사업의 종류에 관계없이 관리 감독 업무 또는 기밀을 취급하는 업무를 말한다: 시행령 제34조)

---

2. 행정해석

---

[89] 서울행판 2003.6.12, 2002구합19050

Chapter 3 Exceptions from Application of Working Hours

"The provisions of Chapter 4 and Chapter 5 of the LSA as to working hours, recess, and holidays shall not apply to persons engaged in management and supervision" (Article 63 (4ho) of the LSA and Article 34 of its Enforcement Decree). Here, "persons engaged in management and supervision" refers to those in managerial positions in the decision-making process of working conditions. This position shall be determined collectively in consideration of whether the person participates in deciding labor management or has authority for supervision and control in labor management regardless of his/her formal designation, whether the person's working hours are strictly regulated (such as time to arrive at and leave the workplace), whether the person receives a special allowance due to the position, etc.

Administrative guidelines explain, for those in the position of 'section manager' who are authorized to plan and implement general duties and detailed job assignments for their subordinates, and control their business trips, overtime, and vacations, even though the section manager did not receive a special allowance in accordance with that position, if the section manager has not been strictly regulated in time of arrival at and leaving the workplace, the section manager shall be considered as a person who is in line with the employer in determining working conditions and other forms of labor management.[90]

3. Judicial Ruling

The Supreme Court has ruled that working hours, recess and holidays stipulated by the Labor Standards Act do not apply to persons in managerial and supervisory positions in terms of deciding subordinates' working conditions, and do not have their times of arrival at and leaving the workplace strictly regulated, and have flexibility in their own working hours. Persons in these positions cannot receive additional allowances for overtime exceeding contractual working hours or holiday work according to the Labor Standards Act.[91]

---

[90] MOEL Guidelines Kunjung-41, on Mar. 3, 2011.
[91] Supreme Court ruling on Feb. 28, 1989, 88DaKa2974.

"관리.감독업무에 종사하는 근로자(제63조 제4호 및 시행령 제34조)"는 근로기준법 제4장 및 제5장에서 정한 근로시간, 휴게와 휴일에 관한 규정을 적용하지 않는다. 여기서 "관리.감독업무에 종사하는 자"라 함은 근로조건의 결정 기타 노무관리에 있어서 경영자와 일체적인 지위에 있는 자를 말하는 것으로 사업장 내 형식적인 직책에도 불구하고 노무관리방침의 결정에 참여하거나 노무 관리상의 지휘.감독 권한을 가지고 있는지의 여부, 출.퇴근 등에 있어서 엄격한 제한을 받는지 여부, 그 지위에 따른 특별수당을 받는 여부 등을 종합적으로 검토하여 판단하여야 할 것이다.

행정해석은 회사의 위임전결규정 등의 자료에 의하여 실장이 일반 업무에 대한 방침 및 소관업무에 관한 세부계획 수립 및 집행 등에 대한 결정권과 소속 직원에 대한 출장, 연장근로 지시, 휴가 승인 등 노무관리상의 지휘.감독 권한을 가지고 있는 것으로 보이는 경우 비록 그 지위에 따른 특별수당을 지급받지 않는다고 하더라도 일반 직원과 달리 출.퇴근 등에 있어서 엄격한 제한을 받지 않는 경우라면 전반적으로 근로조건의 결정 기타 노무관리에 있어 경영자와 일체적인 지위에 있는 자로 볼 수 있다고 해석하고 있다.[90]

3. 판례

판례는 부하직원의 근로조건 결정 및 기타 노무관리에 있어 경영자의 지위에 있으면서 기업 경영상의 필요에 의하여 출·퇴근에 관하여도 엄격한 제한을 받지 아니하고 자기의 근무시간에 관한 융통성을 가지고 있어 회사의 감독, 관리의 지위에 있던 자는 근로기준법에서 정한 근로시간, 휴게와 휴일에 관한 규정이 적용되지 아니한다. 이러한 위치에 있는 자는 평일의 규정 내 잔업시간은 물론, 일요일 근무에 대해서도 근로기준법 소정의 시간 외 또는 휴일근무라 하여 같은 근로기준법에서 정한 가산금을 지급받을 수는 없다고 판시하고 있다.[91]

---

[90] 행정해석: 2011.03.03. 근정과-41.
[91] 대법원 1989.02.28. 선고 88다카2974 판결.

Chapter 3   Exceptions from Application of Working Hours

III. Workplaces Ordinarily Employing Fewer than Five People

1. Introduction

Some workers are not protected by Korean labor law, or have limits to the protection offered. Representative examples include 1) workers at workplaces ordinarily employing fewer than five people, and 2) domestic workers. Article 11 of the Labor Standards Act (LSA) stipulates that "The Labor Standards Act shall apply to all businesses or workplaces in which five or more workers are ordinarily employed. This Act, however, shall not apply to any business or workplace which employs only relatives living together, or to workers hired for domestic work."

In relation to such limitations on application of the Labor Standards Act, some problems have recently emerged. The first is that while labor rights are not completely applicable to people employed by workplaces ordinarily employing fewer than five people, they are now finding themselves eligible for severance pay, which in the past was not the case. This new situation has been at the heart of more labor disputes for those workers looking out for their own labor rights. Accordingly, it is necessary for workplaces ordinarily hiring fewer than five people to be aware of which articles of the LSA are applicable to their workers.

The second problem is that while it is evident that domestic workers exclusively working for a particular house are completely excluded from application of the LSA, this gets confusing when someone works for a company but is paid to be a housekeeper, butler, driver, etc. at the company president's house. In particular, there are disputes related to workers getting injured at work, or whether the workers should receive severance pay or not.

2. Employees at Workplaces Ordinarily Employing Fewer than Five People

(1) Background

In December 2012, employees at workplaces employing fewer than five people became eligible for severance pay. This has brought a lot of attention to those workers in inferior situations. Major articles of the LSA that are not applicable to such workers include, among others, 1) restrictions on dismissal, 2) suspension allowances, 3) restrictions on extended work, 4) extended work, night work and holiday work, and 5) annual paid leave. Due to their exclusion from these

Ⅲ. 5인 미만의 사업장

1. 관련 규정의 이해

근로자이지만 노동법의 적용을 받지 못하거나 노동법의 보호를 제한적으로 받는 근로자들이 있다. 그 대표적 사례가 5인 미만 사업장의 근로자와 가사사용인이다. "근로기준법은 상시 5명 이상의 근로자를 사용하는 모든 사업 또는 사업장에 적용된다. 다만, 동거하는 친족만을 사용하는 사업 또는 사업장과 가사(家事)사용인에 대하여는 적용하지 아니한다(근로기준법 제11조)"라고 명시하고 있다.

근로기준법의 적용제한과 관련하여 다음과 같은 문제가 대두되고 있다. 첫째, 5인 미만 사업장에 근무하는 근로자에게는 근로기본권이 제대로 보장되지 않았으나 최근에 적용되지 않았던 퇴직금 조항이 적용되면서 5인 미만 사업장 근로자들이 자신들의 권리를 찾는 분쟁이 자주 발생하고 있다는 점이다. 따라서 이들 5인 미만의 근로자에 대한 근로기준법 적용 조항들에 대해서도 살펴볼 필요가 있다고 하겠다.

둘째, 가사사용인이 특정 가정에 전속되어 가사일에 종사하는 경우에는 근로기준법이 적용되지 않는 것이 분명하다. 하지만, 가사사용인이 회사에 소속되어 회사로부터 급여를 받으면서 회사 사장의 집에서 가정부, 집사, 운전기사 등으로 일하는 있는 경우 근로기준법의 적용을 받을 수 있는지가 쟁점이 된다. 특히, 업무수행 중 업무상 상해를 입은 경우 산업재해 처리 여부, 퇴직금의 지급 여부 등에 대해 분쟁이 발생하고 있다.

2. 상시 5인 미만 사업 또는 사업장에 근무하는 근로자

(1) 법규정

2010년 12월부터 5인 미만 사업장의 근로자들도 퇴직금 규정을 적용받게 됨에 따라 이들 취약 근로자들에 대해 사회적 곤심을 쏠리고 있다. 적용되지 않는 주요 규정으로는 1) 해고의 제한 2) 휴업수당 3) 법정근로시간의 제한 4) 연장/야간/휴일 근로에 대한 가산임금 5) 연차유급휴가 등이 있다. 이러한

Chapter 3 Exceptions from Application of Working Hours

protections, such employees often work in inferior working environments. In the following pages, I would like to look at and explain conditions which require and do not require LSA application.

(2) Major articles applicable to workplaces ordinarily employing fewer than five people

Topics related to major articles applicable to workplaces ordinarily employing fewer than five people include, among others, 1) written statement of the employment contract, 2) weekly holidays, 3) recesses, 4) accident compensation, 5) payment of money and valuables, 6) payment of wages, 7) restrictions on dismissal timing, 8) advance notice of dismissal, and 9) maternity leave.

Even though the restrictions on dismissal are not applicable, advance notice of dismissal is required, which means that an employer shall give at least thirty days' advance notice to a worker the employer intends to dismiss. If notice is not given thirty days before the dismissal, ordinary wages of at least thirty days shall be paid to the worker. Most articles regarding wages to be paid for labor service are also applicable. That is, minimum wage applies, payment of wages shall be observed, and penalty provisions for delayed payment of wages are applicable. Of particular note, severance pay became mandatory on December 1, 2010 for the first time: for the two years until December 1, 2012, the employer had to pay 50% of full severance pay to resigning employees, and pay 100% for the period beginning January 2013. Regardless of the length of service, severance pay only began accruing from December 1, 2010. Also, according to Industrial Accident Compensation Insurance requirements, accident compensation for occupational injury, including medical treatment, suspension compensation, handicap compensation, etc. are applicable in the same way as for regular employees.

<Laws Applicable to Workplaces Ordinarily Employing Fewer than Five People>

Division		Applicable articles
Labor Standards Act	Chapter 1. General Provisions	Article 1~Article 13
	Chapter 2. Labor Contracts	Article 15, Article 17, Article 19-(1), Article 20 ~ 22, Article 23-(2), Article 26, Article 35 ~ 42
	Chapter 3. Wages	Article 43 ~ 45, Article 47 ~ 49

핵심 조항이 적용되지 않으므로 근로기본권의 보호를 받지 못하는 취약한 근로환경에서 근무하는 근로자들이라고 할 수 있다. 이하에서는 근로기준법에 적용되는 내용과 적용되지 않는 부분을 구분하여 구체적으로 살펴보고자 한다.

(2) 5인 미만 사업장에 적용되는 주요 규정

5인 미만 사업장 적용되는 주요 규정으로는 1) 근로계약의 서면작성, 2) 주 휴일, 3) 휴게, 4) 재해보상, 5) 임금청산, 6) 임금지급, 7) 해고시기 제한, 8) 해고예고, 9) 출산휴가 등 관련 조항이 적용된다.

해고의 제한규정이 적용되지 않지만, 근로자를 해고하고자 할 경우에는 적어도 30일 전에 해고예고를 하여야 하고 이를 하지 못한 경우 1개월의 해고예고수당을 지급해야 한다. 근로의 대가인 임금에 대해서는 대부분 최저임금이 적용되고, 임금 지급시기를 준수해야 하며, 임금체불에 대한 벌칙 조항이 적용된다. 특히 퇴직금의 경우, 2010년 12월 1일부터 적용되어 최초 2년이 되는 2012년 12월 1일 까지는 법정 퇴직금의 50%, 그 이후부터는 100%를 지급해야만 한다. 근로연수가 많은 경우라도 이 퇴직금규정 시행시기부터 계산하여 지급해야 한다. 그 뿐 아니라, 업무상 재해를 당한 경우에는 일반근로자와 동일하게 산업재해보상보험법에 따른 요양보상, 휴업보상, 장해보상 등 보상규정 일체를 적용 받는다.

<상시 5인 미만의 근로자를 사용하는 사업 또는 사업장에 적용하는 법 규정>

구분		적용 법 규정
근로기준법	제1장 총칙	제1조부터 제13조까지의 규정
	제2장 근로계약	제15조, 제17조, 제18조, 제19 조 제1항, 제20조부터 제22조까지의 규정, 제23조 제2항, 제26조, 제35조부터 제42조까지의 규정
	제3장 임금	제43조부터 제45조까지의 규정, 제47조부터 제49조까지의 규정
	제4장 근로시간과 휴식	제54조, 제55조, 제63조

Chapter 3 Exceptions from Application of Working Hours

	Chapter 4. Working Hours and Recess	Article 54, Article 55, Article 63
	Chapter 5. Women and Minors	Article 64, Article 65-(1) & (3) (restricted to pregnant women and minors), Article 66~Article 69, Article 70-(2)&(3), Article 71, Article 72, Article 74
	Chapter 6. Safety & Health	Article 76
	Chapter 8. Accident Compensation	Article 78 ~ 92
	Chapter 11. Labor Inspectors, etc.	Article 101 ~ 106
	Chapter 12. Penalty Provisions	Article 107 ~ 116 (restricted to cases where an employer violates articles applying to businesses and workplaces ordinarily employing fewer than 5 people)
Minimum Wage Act		All employees
Equal Employment Act		All employees
Industrial Accident Compensation Insurance Act		All employees: Companies in certain sectors (including companies in agriculture, forestry and fisheries with 4 employees or fewer) are excluded
.Employment Insurance Act		All employees: Companies in certain sectors (including companies in agriculture, forestry and fisheries with 4 employees or fewer) are excluded

(3) Major articles not applicable to workplaces ordinarily employing fewer than five people

As the following LSA provisions do not apply to workers at workplaces ordinarily employing fewer than five people, working conditions for such employees are quite inferior.

1) Restrictions on dismissal, etc.

① An employer can arbitrarily dismiss or discipline workers without justifiable reason;

	제5장 여성과 소년	제64조, 제65조 제1항·제3항(임산부와 18세 미만인 자로 한정한다), 제66조부터 제69조까지의 규정, 제70조 제2항·제3항, 제71조, 제72조, 제74조
	제6장 안전과 보건	제76조
	제8장 재해보상	제78조부터 제92조까지의 규정
	제11장 근로감독관	제101조부터 제106조까지의 규정
	제12장 벌칙	제107조부터 제116조까지의 규정 (제1장부터 제6장까지, 제8장, 제11장의 규정 중 상시 4명 이하 근로자를 사용하는 사업 또는 사업장에 적용되는 규정을 위반한 경우로 한정한다)
최저임금법		전 사업장
남녀고용평등과 일·가정 양립 지원에 관한 법률		전 사업장
산업재해보상보험법		전 사업장(단, 5인 미만 농, 임, 어민 등 일부 업종은 제외)
고용보험법		전 사업장(단, 5인 미만 농, 임, 어민 등 일부 업종은 제외)
노동조합 및 노동관계 조정법		전 사업장

(3) 5인 미만 사업장에 적용되지 않는 주요 규정

5인 미만의 사업장에 근로하는 근로자에게는 아래의 규정이 적용되지 않기 때문에 근로기본권의 보호를 받지 못하고 열악한 근로환경에 처해 있다고 할 수 있다.

1) 해고 등의 제한
   ① 정당한 이유가 없어도 근로자들을 마음대로 해고하거나 징계할 수 있다.

Chapter 3 Exceptions from Application of Working Hours

② Even though a worker is unfairly dismissed, the worker cannot apply to the Labor Relations Commission for remedy;
③ An employer does not have to notify workers in writing of reasons for dismissal;
④ As the restrictions on dismissal for managerial reasons do not apply to such workers, an employer can dismiss workers at any time if business conditions deteriorate;
⑤ The two-year limitation on the use of temporary workers such as dispatch employees or short-term contract workers does not apply, and the employer can dismiss such workers at any time.

2) Allowances during suspension of business

When an employer suspends business operations, the workers are not entitled to receive suspension allowances. Even though business operations are suspended for reasons attributable to the employer, the employer does not have to pay allowances to workers during such suspensions.

3) Restrictions on working hours

Workplaces ordinarily employing fewer than five people do not have to follow the 40 hours per week limitation or keep to a 5 day workweek. There are no restrictions on extending the work day beyond 8 hours, or even beyond 12 hours, nor does the employer have to pay additional allowances (50%) for overtime, night shift (10:00 pm to 6:00 am) or holiday work.

4) Annual paid leave

When a worker at a workplace employing at least five people has worked continuously for one year, 15 days of annual paid leave are granted, but workers at workplaces ordinarily employing fewer than five people are not guaranteed any paid, non-statutory holidays. A worker at such workplaces must get permission to take a day off, and the employer can deduct one day's salary.

3. Domestic Workers Employed by a Company

(1) Background

"Domestic worker" refers to a person paid to engage in work that runs a particular

② 근로자가 부당한 해고를 당했어도 노동위원회에 의한 구제를 받을 수 없다.
③ 사용자의 일방적인 해고에 대한 서면통지 의무가 없으며,
④ 경영상 해고제한 규정에도 적용되지 않으므로 회사 사정이 좋지 않을 때에는 언제든지 해고할 수 있다.
⑤ 파견근로나 단시간 근로자를 사용할 경우에 자유롭게 언제든지 해고할 수 있기 때문에 2년의 사용기간제한 규정 적용 없이 계속 사용할 수 있다.

2) 휴업수당

회사가 휴업해도 휴업수당을 받을 수 없다. 따라서 회사가 필요시 임의적 휴업을 하더라도 특별히 휴업수당을 지급하지 않기 때문에 사용자의 귀책사유로 휴업을 하여도 근로자들은 그 휴업기간 동안 임금이 지급되지 않는다.

3) 근로시간의 제한

5인 미만의 사업장은 주40시간 근로나 주5일제도 해당이 없고 하루 8시간을 초과하여도 무제한으로 연장근로를 시킬 수 있다. 연장근로도 주12시간 한도에 대한 제한이 없고, 연장근로나 야간근로(22시~06)에 근무를 하거나 휴일에 근무를 해도 50%의 할증임금을 받지 못한다.

4) 연차유급휴가

일반 근로자는 1년 근무에 15일의 연차휴가를 유급으로 사용할 수 있으나, 5인 미만 사업장 근로자들은 유급휴가가 발생하지 않는다. 따라서 휴가를 사용하고자 할 경우에는 사용자의 승인을 얻어 무급으로 휴가를 사용할 수 있다.

3. 사업장 소속의 가사사용인의 근로기준법 적용여부

(1) 가사사용인의 이해

가사사용인이란 가정의 가사업무에 종사하는 가정부, 파출부, 유모, 집사 등의 근로자를 말한다. 가사사용인은 주로 개인의 사생활과 관련된 가사에 종사하므로 국가가 그들의 근로시간이나 임금에 관하여 감독하기 어렵기

Chapter 3 Exceptions from Application of Working Hours

home as a housekeeper, a cleaner, a nanny, a butler, etc. As "domestic work" exclusively involves housekeeping related to an individual's private life, it is not preferable for the nation to intervene in and audit working hours or wages, which is why domestic workers are excluded from the Labor Standards Act. Therefore, even though a domestic worker for a company president is employed by the company, the LSA is not applicable. However, in cases where a worker is employed by a company and is covered by company regulations, but was assigned to work as a gardener, guard, butler, driver, etc. at the company president's house, the situation is different. I would like to review some cases that deal with this issue.

(2) Domestic worker not covered by the Labor Standards Act

This labor case involved an application for remedy for unfair dismissal, but was dropped as the domestic worker was not covered by the Labor Standards Act. The ruling stated: "Even though this worker claimed he applied for a position posted by the company, his workplace was the summer house owned privately by the company president, and he was employed by the president and her husband. Caretaking of the summer house was not related to the company's main business of construction. In addition, the worker has not done anything to contribute to the profit gaining activities of the company. In light of these facts, this worker, privately employed by the employer, is considered a domestic worker to which Article 11 of the LSA applies. It is therefore not necessary to review the facts of the dismissal or its justification."[92]

(3) Domestic worker covered by the Labor Standards Act

In looking into the background to the worker beginning to work at the CEO's house, it was found that he had been employed by the company to work in the Management Department, and then was immediately assigned to work at the CEO's house. Since that time, the company had managed the worker's general matters regulated by labor law such as wages, service regulations, and payment of severance pay. The company had also handled the worker's social security insurance and other income deductions. Even though the type of work was at the discretion of the CEO, the worker still belonged to the company organization. This

---

[92] Gyunggi Labor Relations Commission: 2012 buhae 1130.

때문에 근로기준법의 적용에서 제외되어 있다. 따라서 회사에서 고용한 자라 하더라도 회사 사장의 가정에서 가사노동에 종사하는 경우에는 근로기준법이 적용되지 않는다. 그러나, 회사에 채용되어 회사 규정의 적용을 받고 사장 집에 파견되어 정원 관리, 경비원, 집사, 운전기사 등의 업무를 담당 할 경우 근로기준법 적용여부에 대해 논란이 있을 수 있다. 이 문제와 관련하여, 유사한 사례를 가지고 판단해보고자 한다.

(2) 근로기준법이 적용되지 않는 가사사용인으로 각하 판정한 사례

근로자가 해고되어 부당해고 구제신청을 했던 경우로 "이 사건 근로자들은 사용자의 채용공고를 보고 채용되었다고 주장하나 근무장소가 사용자인 대표이사가 개인적으로 소유한 별장이었다는 점, 별장에서 대표이사와 그의 남편에 의한 면접을 통하여 채용되었다는 점, 별장관리업무는 건설업을 주로 행하고 있는 이 사건 사용자의 사업내용과 직접적인 연관이 없고 사용자에게 수익을 창출하는 업무를 하였다고 보기 어려운 점 등을 비추어 볼 때 사용자가 채용한 근로자가 아닌 대표이사가 개인적으로 채용한 근로자로 근로기준법 제11조의 가사사용인에 해당하여 해고처분의 존재 및 정당성 여부에 대하여는 별도로 논할 필요 없다"라고 하여 근로기준법의 적용을 배제하고 있다.[92]

(3) 근로기준법이 적용된다고 본 사례

근로자가 대표이사의 자택에서 근무하게 된 경위를 살펴보면, 회사에서 채용하여 회사의 관리부로 소속을 두게 하고 대표이사의 자택에서 근무하도록 명령을 내린 것으로 확인되고, 이후 임금지급관계, 복무규정, 퇴직금 지급 등 노동관계법에 따라 발생하는 제반 사항에 대하여 회사에서 일괄적으로 관리해온 것이 확인되며, 제세공과금의 납부와 사회보장제도 등 대외적인 권리·의무관계에 있어서도 회사에 귀속되어 행하여진 점을 종합할 때 근로자는 대표이사가 사적인 용도로 사용하였다 하나, 법인인 회사 소속 근로자로 보는 것이 타당하며, 독립적인 지위에서 개인 가정에 고용되어 개인 가사서비스, 운전기사, 정원 관리원 등의 활동을 행하는 가사사용인과는 달리 보아야 할

---

[92] 경기지노위, 2012부해1130 (주)건교산업 부당해고구제 신청사건

worker is clearly different from a worker hired independently by an individual as a private housekeeper, driver, or gardener. Accordingly, the decision by the Employee Welfare Corporation to reject the family's application for the survivors' pension because of the worker's supposed status as a domestic worker was inaccurate.[93]

(4) Judgment

A review of these two cases reveals two things: 1) In cases where a worker is employed by a company and is exclusively engaged in housekeeping duties, the worker shall be regarded entirely as a housekeeper excluded from coverage by the Labor Standards Act; 2) However, in cases where a worker was employed by the company and assigned to the company president's house as a guard, exclusive driver, gardener, etc., that worker is likely considered to be covered by the LSA. In light of this, it is necessary to consider the worker's job characteristics, job scope, and work relations with the company in deciding whether the LSA applies or not.

4. Conclusion

Employees of workplaces ordinarily employing fewer than five people are at times excluded from or have restrictions on their coverage by the Labor Standards Act. Such restrictions or exclusion from basic labor rights normally granted to other workers have resulted in poorer working conditions for them in terms of dismissal, disciplinary action, restrictions on working hours, etc. To protect their minimum labor rights, protections in three more areas shall be given: restrictions on working hours, allowances for suspension of business due to the reasons attributable to the employer, and additional allowances for extended work, night time work, and holiday work. As for domestic workers, although they are workers (since they work for payment), because they work exclusively for a particular house as housekeeper, butler, gardener, etc., they are not considered as workers covered by the LSA. However, in cases where a domestic worker is assigned to a particular director's house, if the company manages his/her payment etc., and supervises his/her work, the person can be regarded as a worker under the LSA. This requires an understanding by employers of the concrete details of the work performed by the domestic worker, regardless of his/her title of "domestic worker".

---

[93] Industrial Accident Compensation Insurance Review Committee 2004-910, Sept. 14, 2004.

것이다. 따라서, 원처분기관에서 근로자가 사업주의 자택에서 근무하였다는 이유로 가사사용인으로 잘못 판단하여 유족급여 및 장의비청구서를 반려 처분한 것은 부당하다.[93]

(4) 시사점

사례를 살펴보면, 회사에서 채용되어 사장 집에서 가사를 맡고 있는 가정부로 업무를 수행하는 경우에는 순수 가사사용인으로 근로기준법에 적용되지 않으나, 사장 집에 파견되어 경비업무, 전속기사, 조경업무 등을 할 경우에는 근로기준법에 적용되는 경향이 있다. 따라서 그 가사사용인의 업무의 성격, 업무의 범위, 회사업무와의 관계 등을 구체적으로 파악하여 근로기준법 적용 여부를 판단하여야 할 것이다.

4. 종합의견

근로기준법 적용이 제외되거나 제한되는 대상은 5인 미만의 사업장에 근무하는 근로자와 가사사용인이다. 5인 미만의 사업장 근로자는 근로자로 마땅히 보장받아야 할 해고 등 제한 규정, 근로시간 제한 규정 등의 적용에서 배제됨으로써 노동기본권을 제한받고 있다. 영세 사업장에 근무하는 근로자들도 최소한의 노동기본권 보장을 위해서는 근로시간의 제한, 사업주의 귀책사유에 대한 휴업수당 및 연장·야간·휴일 근로에 대한 가산임금 규정이 확대적용 되어야 할 것이다. 또한 가사사용인도 임금을 목적으로 근로를 제공하는 자이므로 근로자의 영역에 속하지만, 특정 개인의 가정집에서 가정부, 집사, 정원사 등으로 근로를 제공한다는 점과 개인 가정에 전속되어 업무를 수행하므로 근로기준법상의 근로자라 할 수 없다. 그러나 사업장에서 특정 임원의 개인 집에서 파견근무를 하고 회사 자체적으로 인사관리를 하는 경우에는 일반 근로자로 볼 수도 있다. 따라서 가사사용인이라는 명칭에 구애됨이 없이 구체적인 업무내용을 가지고 근로자인지 여부를 최종 판단하여야 할 것이다.

---

93) 산심위2004-910, 2004.09.14

Chapter 3   Exceptions from Application of Working Hours

IV. Part-time Workers

The term "part-time worker" in Article 2 of the Labor Standards Act (LSA) means an employee whose contractual working hours per week are shorter than those of a full-time worker engaged in the same kind of job in the same workplace. For example, since a full-time worker works 40 hours per week, a worker who has worked 8 hours for 4 days in a week (32 hours per week) is considered a part-time worker.

Working conditions for part-time workers shall be determined on the basis of the relative ratio of their working hours in comparison to those of full-time workers engaged in the same kind of job in the same workplace (Article 18 of the LSA). That is, even part-time workers are subject to all the provisions of the Labor Standards Act, but for statutory holidays and leaves, the principle of proportional working hours of ordinary workers is applied.[94]

1. Working hours

(ⅰ) The contractual working hours of part-time workers are strictly protected. The employer must obtain the consent of the part-time worker if having the part-time worker work beyond the contractual working hours, and in instances such as this the APF also stipulates that the part-time worker shall not work more than 12 additional hours per week over the contractual working time. The employer shall pay part-time workers at least 50/100 of the ordinary wage for overtime exceeding the contractual working hours within the legal working hours (8 hours per day, 40 hours per week). Under the Labor Standards Act, an additional wage of 50% or more of ordinary wage is paid only for overtime exceeding legal working hours, but for part-time workers, payment of additional wages is prescribed even if the contractual working hours are exceeded within the legal working hours (Article 6 of the APF).

(ⅱ) Part-time workers are also paid an additional 50% for holiday work as specified in the rules of employment, and 100% for holiday work exceeding 8 hours (Article 56 of the LSA). (iii) If a part-time worker performs night work between 10 pm and 6 am on the following day, the employer shall pay wages with an additional allowance equivalent to 50/100 of ordinary wage (Article 56

---

[94] For details, related information is in the Labor Standards Act and Article 9 of the Enforcement Decree to the LSA attached, Table 2, the APF, the Minimum Wage Act, etc.

Ⅳ. 단시간 근로자

"단시간근로자"란 1주 동안의 소정근로시간이 그 사업장에서 같은 종류의 업무에 종사하는 통상 근로자의 1주 동안의 소정근로시간에 비하여 짧은 근로자를 말한다(근로기준법 이하 '근기법' 제2조). 즉, 통상근로자의 1주 소정근로시간이 40시간이라면, 1일 8시간씩 1주 4일 근무한 경우에도 1주 근로시간이 32시간이 되기 때문에 단시간근로자에 속한다.

단시간근로자의 근로조건은 그 사업장의 같은 종류의 업무에 종사하는 통상 근로자의 근로시간을 기준으로 산정한 비율에 따라 결정되어야 한다(근기법 제18조). 즉, 단시간근로자도 근로기준법상 제 규정을 모두 적용받지만, 법정 휴일이나 휴가에 있어서는 통상근로자의 근로시간 비례원칙이 적용된다.[94]

1. 근로시간

(ⅰ) 단시간근로자의 소정근로시간은 엄격하게 보호되고 있다. 사용자는 단시간근로자에 대하여 소정근로시간을 초과하여 근로하게 하는 경우에는 당해 근로자의 동의를 얻어야 하며, 이 경우에도 1주 소정근로시간에 12시간을 초과하여 근로하게 할 수 없다고 명시하고 있고 소정근로시간을 초과하여 연장근로를 하는 경우에는 법정근로시간(1일 8시간, 1주 40시간) 이내에도 불구하고 그 초과근로에 대한 통상임금의 100분의 50 이상을 가산하여 지급하여야 한다. 근로기준법의 경우 법정근로시간을 초과하는 연장근로에 대해서만 통상임금의 100분의 50 이상의 가산임금을 지급하지만, 단시간근로자의 경우에는 소정근로시간을 초과할 경우에도 가산임금의 지급을 규정하고 있다(기단법 제6조).

(ⅱ) 단시간근로자도 취업규칙에 명시된 휴일근로에 대해 100분의 50을 가산해서 지급하고, 8시간을 초과하는 휴일근로에 대해서는 100분의 100을 가산한다(근기법 제56조). (ⅲ) 단시간근로자가 오후 10시부터 다음 날 오전 6시 사이 야간근로를 하는 경우에는 100분의 50을 가산한 임금을

---

[94] 그 자세한 내용은 근기법 및 근기법 시행령 제9조, [별표 2]), 기단법, 최저임금법 등에 따라 정리함.

of the LSA).

2. Holidays and annual paid leave

Holidays and annual paid leave for part-time workers are applied equally in accordance with the principle of proportional working hours for full-time workers.

(i) **Holidays:** An average of one paid holiday per week worked shall be guaranteed, for which the contractual working hours of one day must be paid. When calculating wages according to hourly wage, the employer shall pay an additional weekly holiday allowance. However, in the case of a part-time worker who has been employed for weekend or holiday work, the weekly holiday should be given as a paid holiday on a non-weekend day.

① Calculating 6 hours per day from Monday to Friday, 5 days' work per week for full-time workers and payment of KRW 10,000 per hour: [(30 hours x 4 weeks)/(5 days x 4 weeks) = 6 hours], results in [6 hours x KRW 10,000 = KRW 60,000].

② However, if full-time workers are working for 6 days a week: [(30 hours x 4 weeks)/(6 days x 4 weeks) = 5 hours], the result is [5 hours x KRW 10,000 = KRW 50,000].

(ii) **Annual paid leave:** The employer shall grant part-time workers a number of days of annual paid leave equal to that of full-time workers. Annual paid leave is calculated in hours, with less than one hour counting as one hour. Also, in case of monthly paid leave for those working less than one year, the contractual working hours of one day per each month should be given as monthly paid leave. The criteria for granting annual paid leave for part-time workers are as follows:

$$\text{Number of annual leave days for full-time workers} \times \frac{\text{Number of hours worked for part-time workers}}{\text{Number of hours worked for full-time workers}} \times 8 \text{ hours}$$

지급해야 한다(동법 제56조).

2. 휴일과 연차유급휴가

 단시간근로자의 휴일과 연차유급휴가는 통상근로자의 근로시간 비례원칙에 따라 동일하게 적용된다.

(ⅰ) **휴일** : 1주에 평균 1회 이상의 유급휴일을 보장하여야 한다. 1일의 소정근로시간을 유급으로 주어야 한다. 시간급으로 임금을 계산할 경우에는 유급 주휴수당을 추가적으로 계산하여 지급해야 한다. 다만, 주말 근무나 휴일을 대체하기 위해 채용된 단시간 근로자의 경우에는 주말이 아닌 날에 주휴일을 유급으로 주어야 한다.
① 월요일부터 금요일까지 매일 6시간, 통상근로자는 주5일 근무하고, 시간급 1만 원인 경우: [(30시간 × 4주) / (5일 × 4주) = 6시간]이 되므로 [6시간 × 1만 원 = 6만 원]이 된다.
② 그러나 통상근로자가 주6일을 근무하는 경우: [(30시간 × 4주) / (6일 × 4주) = 5시간]이 된다. [5시간 × 1만 원 = 5만 원]이 된다.

(ⅱ) **연차유급휴가** : 사용자는 단시간근로자에게 연차유급휴가 횟수를 통상근로자와 같이 동등하게 부여하여야 한다. 이 경우 연차유급휴가는 시간 단위로 계산하고, 1시간 미만은 1시간으로 본다. 또한 근속년수 1년 미만자의 월차유급휴가의 경우에도 매월 1일의 소정근로시간을 월차유급휴가로 주어야 한다. 단시간근로자의 연차휴가부여의 기준은 다음과 같다.

$$\text{통상근로자의 연차휴가일수} \times \frac{\text{단시간근로자의 소정근로시간}}{\text{통상 근로자의 소정근로시간}} \times 8\text{시간}$$

Chapter 3 Exceptions from Application of Working Hours

If a part-time worker works 20 hours a week, this works out to [15 days x (20 hours/40 hours) x 8 hours = 60 hours]. In other words, each four hours is guaranteed as an annual paid leave day.

(iii) **Maternity Leave:** The employer shall give 90 days of pre-and post-natal maternity leave for pregnant part-time female workers, with the first 60 days of maternity leave being paid. ① The maternity leave allowance is the amount calculated as the hourly wage of a part-time worker multiplied by the contractual working hours of one day and multiplied by 60 days. ② The remaining 30 days can be paid as maternity leave benefits as stipulated by the Employment Insurance Act (Article 74 of the LSA). Assuming that a part-time worker is paid KRW 10,000 per hour, and the contractual working hours is 5 hours per day. ① The maternity leave allowance is KRW 10,000 x 5 hours x 60 days = KRW 3,000,000. ② The maternity leave benefit is KRW 10,000 x 5 hours x 30 days = KRW 1,500,000.

3. Exceptions to application for part-time workers

With respect to workers whose contractual working hours are an average of less than 15 hours per week over a four-week period (or the employment period, if they have been employed for less than four weeks), ① weekly holiday allowance (Article 55), ② annual paid leave (Article 60), ③ monthly paid leave (Article 60), and ④ severance pay (Article 34) shall not apply. In addition, employment insurance, national pension and national health insurance are excluded, while industrial accident compensation insurance is not.

If the employer sets the contractual working hours of one week to 14 hours, and concludes the employment contract by adding 2 hours of fixed overtime every day (for 5 days), the Ministry of Employment and Labor has decided that the total working hours, including fixed extended working hours, are defined as working hours actually performed, as long as there is no reason to believe otherwise. In such case, part-time workers are eligible for severance pay. However, it is possible to exclude from fixed working hours if it is not fixed overtime but extended work due to an agreement with the company at that time.[95]

---

[95] MOEL Guidelines: Working Standards-5085, Dec. 1, 2009.

단시간근로자가 주20시간 근무하는 경우, "15일 × (20시간/40시간) × 8시간 = 60시간"이다. 즉, 1일 연차유급휴가로 4시간이 보장되어야 한다.

(iii) **산전후휴가** : 사용자는 임신중인 단시간 여성근로자에 대하여 출산 전과 출산 후를 통합하여 90일의 출산전후휴가를 부여하여야 한다. 이 경우 출산전후휴가 중 최초 60일은 유급으로 한다. 단시간근로자의 시간급에 1일의 소정근로시간을 곱하고 이에 60일을 곱한 금액을 ① 산전후휴가 유급수당을 지급해야 한다. 나머지 30일분은 고용보험법에서 정한 바에 따라 ② 산전후휴가급여를 지급받을 수 있다. (근기법 제74조). A의 시간급이 10,000원이고, 1일 소정근로시간이 5시간인 경우 ① 산전후휴가 유급수당은 10,000원 × 5시간 × 60일 = 3,000,000원이고, ② 산전후휴가급여는 10,000원 × 5시간 × 30일 = 1,500,000원으로 계산된다.

3. 단시간근로자의 적용제외

4주 동안(4주 미만으로 근로하는 경우에는 그 기간)을 평균하여 1주 동안의 소정근로시간이 15시간 미만인 근로자에 대하여는 ① 주휴일(제55조), ② 연차유급휴가(제60조), ③ 월차유급휴가(제60조), ④ 퇴직금(제34조), ⑤ 4대 보험 중 산재보험을 제외한 고용보험, 국민연금, 국민건강보험이 적용되지 않는다.

사용자가 1주 소정근로시간을 14시간으로 정하고 추가로 매일 2시간씩 (5일) 고정연장근로를 하는 것으로 근로계약을 체결한 경우, 노동부는 '필요에 따라 연장근로를 실시하기로 정했다고 보기는 어려운 점 등으로 보아 달리 볼 사정이 없는 한(고정연장근로를 포함한 시간이) 당사자 간 근로하기로 미리 정한 근로시간'이라며 해당근로자는 퇴직금 지급 대상이라고 판단했다. 다만, 고정된 연장근로가 아니라 그때그때 일시적 필요에 따라 당사 합의로 연장근로가 이루어졌다면 소정근로시간에서 제외할 수는 있을 것이다.[95]

---

[95] 근로기준과-5085, 2009.12.1.

Chapter 3 Exceptions from Application of Working Hours

V. Working Conditions for Minors

1. Scope of Working Minors

In principle, no person under the age of 15 shall be employed as a worker. However, those 13 to 15 years of age with an employment permit issued by the Minister of Employment and Labor may be so employed, as long as the employment does not interfere with their compulsory education (Article 64 of the LSA and Article 35 of its Enforcement Decree). The employer shall keep in the workplace a certificate proving the family relationships and written consent from their parent or guardian for each working minor under 18 (Article 66).

2. Special Protection of Working Hours and Rest

The working hours of persons aged 15 to 18 shall not exceed 7 hours per day and 35 hours per week. However, this may be extended by up to 1 hour per day and 5 hours per week if there is agreement between the parties. Since 1 week refers to 7 days including holidays, the longest working hours for working minors shall be 40 hours a week. Therefore, flexible working hours and selective working hours are not applicable to working minors (MWA, Articles 51 and 52).

An employer shall allow a recess period of 30 minutes or more for every 4 working hours and at least 1 hour for every 8 working hours during the work day. During these rest hours, rest should be freely available to working minors (Article 54).

If working minors continue to work for 15 hours or more per week, they are given paid weekly holidays (Article 55). If they have completed their contractual working hours for one week, they are entitled to a weekly leave allowance of one or more days (Article 55). The weekly leave allowance for working minors is determined according to the ratio calculated by the working hours of ordinary workers engaged in the same type of work at the workplace, just as the working conditions for part-time workers (Article 18).[96]

When working minors have worked for more than the contractual working hours, employers must pay overtime allowance amounting to 50% or more of the normal

---

[96] For 4 hours a day, 5 days a week, and an hourly wage of 10,000 won, the weekly vacation allowance is calculated according to the proportional principle of short-time workers. (20 hours / 40 hours per week) x 8 hours = 4 hours; 4 hours x 10,000 won = 40,000 won.

V. 연소근로자

1. 연소근로자의 범위

사용자는 15세 미만인 사람은 근로자로 사용하지 못한다. 다만, 예외적으로 고용노동부장관이 의무교육에 지장이 없다고 판단하여 취직인허증을 발급하는 경우에 한해 13세이상 15세미만자도 근로자로 사용할 수 있다(근기법 제64조, 시행령 제35조). 사용자는 18세 미만인 사람에 대하여는 그 연령을 증명하는 가족관계기록사항에 관한 증명서와 친권자(부모) 또는 후견인(친권자 부재)의 동의서를 사업장에 갖추어 두어야 한다(제66조).

2. 근로시간과 휴식의 특별보호

15세 이상 18세 미만인 사람의 근로시간은 1일에 7시간, 1주에 35시간을 초과하지 못한다. 다만, 당사자 사이의 합의에 따라 1일에 1시간, 1주에 5시간을 한도로 연장할 수 있다. 1주란 휴일을 포함한 7일을 말하기 때문에 연소근로자가 근로할 수 있는 최장시간은 주40시간이 된다. 따라서 연소근로자에 대해서는 탄력적 근로시간제와 선택적 근로시간제가 적용되지 않는다(제51조, 제52조).

사용자는 연소근로자의 근로시간이 4시간인 경우에는 30분 이상, 8시간인 경우에는 1시간 이상의 휴게시간을 근로시간 중에 주어야 한다. 이 경우 휴게시간은 연소근로자가 자유롭게 이용할 수 있어야 한다(제54조).

연소근로자가 1주 15시간 이상 계속 근무한 경우에는 유급 주휴일을 부여받는다(제55조). 연소근로자가 1주간 소정근로일수를 개근한 경우에는 1일 이상의 주휴수당을 주어야 한다(제55조). 연소자의 주휴수당은 단시간 근로자의 근로조건과 같이 그 사업장의 같은 종류의 업무에 종사하는 통상 근로자의 근로시간을 기준으로 산정한 비율에 따라 결정된다(제18조).[96]

연소근로자가 소정근로시간을 초과하여 근무한 경우에는 통상임금의 100

---

[96] 1일 4시간, 1주일에 5일, 시간급 10,000원 인 경우, 주휴수당은 단시간근로자의 비례원칙에 따라 계산된다. (주 20시간 / 40시간) × 8시간 = 4시간; 4시간 × 10,000원 = 40,000원이 된다.

Chapter 3 Exceptions from Application of Working Hours

wage, in addition to the normal wage (Article 6 of the Fixed-Term Employment Act).

Employers are not allowed to have those under the age of 18 work from 10 pm to 6 am or on holidays, unless the employer obtains the consent of those under the age of 18 and approval from the Minister of Employment and Labor (Article 70). According to the approval standards of the MOEL,[97] if nighttime operations are inevitable for fast food restaurants where many minors work part-time, in consideration of the safety of working children, their health, and protecting their ability to learn during the day, the limit is 12 midnight, unless approval from the MOEL is gained for special reasons. Here, the term special reasons refers to cases where the necessity for night work is accepted and will have no detrimental effect on the health of working minors.

Employers shall give 15 days of annual leave when working minors have attended the workplace for at least 80% of the contracted work hours during one year. Employers shall also provide one day of paid leave for each month to working minors who have continued to work for less than one year or those who have attended the workplace for less than 80 percent of the contracted work hours during one year (Article 60).

〈Case Study 3-1〉 Whether a Managing Director is Considered to Hold a Managerial and Supervisory Position

1. Introduction

In the Seoul office of a foreign company (hereinafter referred to as "the Company") that employed about 300 people and is engaged in the apparel business, a labor case occurred due to escalating disputes between directors in April 2015. With two departments of the Company combining into one, the executive managing director told the managing director that it would be not desirable to have two directors in one department, and told the managing director that she would need to resign. The managing director (hereinafter referred to as "the Employee") told the Company that she would sue it for violating the Labor Standards Act (LSA) and would also report additional claims of other employees unless the Company paid her a severance bonus of two years' annual wages. The Company responded that it did not order the Employee to resign, rejected her demand for a severance bonus, and explained that the Company had not violated the LSA. Just after that, the

---

[97] MOEL Guidelines on approval for minors to engage in night work (Equality Policy Division-July 26, 2004).

분의 50 이상을 가산한 연장근로수당을 지급하여야 한다(기간제법 제6조).

사용자는 18세 미만자를 오후 10시부터 오전 6시 까지의 시간과 휴일에 근로시키지 못한다. 다만, 사용자가 18세 미만자의 동의와 고용노동부장관의 인가를 받으면 야간시간과 휴일에 근로를 할 수 있다(제70조). 고용노동부의 인가기준에 따르면,[97] 연소자가 다수 아르바이트를 하고 있는 패스트푸드점에 대하여 업종의 특성상 야간 가동(영업)이 불가피 하다고 볼 수 있지만, 연소 근로자의 건강보호 및 학습보장, 귀가 등 안전을 고려하여 특별한 사유가 없는 한 오후 12시까지 제한적으로 인가한다. 여기서 특별한 사유라 함은 사업주의 야간근로 필요성과 연소근로자의 건강 등에 무리가 없는 경우를 말한다.

사용자는 연소근로자가 1년간 80%퍼센트 이상 출근한 경우에 15일을 연차 휴가를 주어야 한다. 사용자는 계속하여 근로한 기간이 1년 미만인 연소근로자 또는 1년간 80퍼센트 미만 출근한 연소근로자에게는 1개월 개근 시 1일의 유급휴가를 주어야 한다(제60조).

〈실무사례 3-1〉 외국기업의 상무가 관리감독자인지 여부 판단

1. 사실관계

서울에 사무소를 두고 300여 명을 고용하여 의류 사업을 하고 있는 한 외국기업에서, 2015년 4월에 임원 간의 갈등이 노동사건으로 확대된 사건이 발생하였다. 부서가 통폐합되면서 한 부서에 전무와 상무가 같이 근무하게 되었는데, 전무가 상무에게 하나의 부서에 임원 둘이 같이 근무하는 것은 바람직하지 않으니 퇴사할 것을 권유하였다. 이에 상무(이하, "이 사건의 근로자"라 함)는 회사가 근로기준법을 위반하였다고 주장하면서, 2년 치 퇴직위로금을 주지 않을 경우 회사를 고용노동부에 고소하고, 다른 직원들에 대한 위반 사항도 고발할 것이라고 압박하였다. 이에 대해 회사는 이 사건의

---
[97] 고용노동부의 연소근로자 야간근로 인가업무 처리지침(평등정책과-2004.7.26)

Chapter 3 Exceptions from Application of Working Hours

Employee began a lawsuit against the Company and visited the Gangnam Labor Office to claim the Company had violated the Labor Standards Act, and had not paid an additional allowance for her overtime.

The main item in these accusations is that, as the Employee's job title of managing director placed her in the "directors" group, the question is whether or not this high position is included in 'persons to be excluded from the application of working hours, recess and holidays' stipulated by the LSA. Herein, I would like to look substantially into these two main points of dispute to confirm whether or not the Company had violated the LSA.

2. Overtime Allowance for Personnel in Managerial and Supervisory Positions

(1) Current Situation

The Employee claimed that she had never received any additional allowance for overtime or holiday work during her service period, and that she was entitled to such allowances for the past three years. The Employee requested the information of her office PC's "on-and-off" data to verify her working time as she had not recorded it in the related documents.

The Company responded that the Employee is not entitled to overtime work allowance or holiday work allowance due to her high position as managing director, putting her in a managerial and supervisory position according to Article 63 of the LSA.

(2) Related Law, Guidelines and Judicial Rulings
1) The LSA

Article 63 (Exclusion from Application) of the LSA regulates that the provisions regarding working hours, recess and holiday shall not apply to personnel in managerial and supervisory positions.[98]

2) Related guidelines

---

[98] Article 63 (Exclusions from Application) The provisions of this Chapter and Chapter V as to working hours, recess, and holidays shall not apply to workers engaged in any of tasks described in the following subparagraphs:
1. cultivation of arable land, reclamation work, seeding and planting, gathering or picking-up or other agricultural and forestry work;
2. livestock breeding, catch of marine animals and plants, cultivation of marine products or other cattle-breeding, sericulture and fishery business;
3. surveillance or intermittent work, for which the employer has obtained the approval of the Minister of Employment and Labor;
4. any other work prescribed by Presidential Decree. [Implementation Decree (Article 34) - "Work provided for by Presidential Decree" means managerial and supervisory work and work of handling confidential information, irrespective of the type of business.]

근로자에게 퇴직을 권유하지 않았으며, 근로기준법을 위반한 사실도 없다고 하면서 퇴직위로금의 지급을 거부하였다. 그러자 이 사건의 근로자는 회사가 연장근로에 대한 가산임금을 지급하지 않는 등 근로기준법을 위반하였다고 '강남고용지청'에 회사를 고소하였다.

이 고소내용에 대한 주요 쟁점사항을 살펴보면, 이 사건의 근로자 직급은 임원에 속하는 '상무'로 근로기준법상 '근로시간 휴게, 휴일의 적용제외자'로 인정받을 수 있는지의 여부이다. 위 사항과 관련하여 회사가 근로기준법을 위반했는지 구체적으로 살펴보고자 한다.

2. 관리감독자에 대한 연장근로수당

(1) 현 상황

이 사건의 근로자는 근무기간 중 연장근로와 휴일근로를 많이 하였음에도 불구하고 한 번도 가산임금을 받아본 적이 없다고 주장하면서, 과거 3년간의 연장근로수당과 휴일근로수당을 청구하였다. 근로자는 관련된 자료를 기록하고 있지 않았기 때문에 '본인 업무용 컴퓨터 사용기록(on-off 자료)'을 요청하였다.

이에 대해 회사는 이 사건의 근로자는 직급상 상무로 회사의 임원에 해당되므로 근로기준법 제63조의 규정에 따른 '관리감독자'로 연장근로, 휴일근로에 대해 적용대상자가 아니라고 판단하여 수당 등을 지급하지 않았다.

(2) 관리감독자에 대한 연장근로수당의 법 규정, 행정해석의 판례
1) 근로기준법 규정

현행 근로기준법 제63조(적용제외)에는 관리감독자에 대해서는 근로시간, 휴게와 휴일에 관한 규정을 적용하지 않는다고 규정하고 있다.[98]

2) 행정해석

---

[98] 제63조【적용의 제외】제4장과 제5장에서 정한 근로시간, 휴게와 휴일에 관한 규정은 다음 각 호의 어느 하나에 해당하는 근로자에 대하여는 적용하지 아니한다.
  1. 토지의 경작·개간, 식물의 재식·재배·채취 사업, 그 밖의 농림 사업
  2. 동물의 사육, 수산 동식물의 채포·양식 사업, 그 밖의 축산, 양잠, 수산 사업
  3. 감시 또는 단속적으로 근로에 종사하는 자로서 사용자가 고용노동부장관의 승인을 받은 자
  4. 대통령령으로 정하는 업무에 종사하는 근로자 (사업의 종류에 관계없이 관리·감독 업무 또는 기밀을 취급하는 업무를 말한다: 시행령 제34조)

Chapter 3 Exceptions from Application of Working Hours

'The provisions of this Chapter and Chapter V as to working hours, recess, and holidays shall not apply to persons engaged in management and supervision' (Article 63 (4ho) of the LSA and Article 34 of its Enforcement Decree). Here, 'persons engaged in management and supervision' refers to those in managerial positions in the decision-making process of working conditions. This position shall be determined collectively in consideration of whether the person participates in deciding labor management or has authority for supervision and control in labor management regardless of his/her formal designation, whether the person's working hours are strictly regulated (such as time to arrive at and leave the workplace), whether the person receives a special allowance due to the position, etc.

Administrative guidelines explain that, for those in the position of 'section manager' who are authorized to plan and implement general duties and detailed job assignments for their subordinates, and manage their business trips, overtime, and vacations, even though a section manager does not receive a special allowance in accordance with that position, if the section manager's time of arrival at and departing from the workplace has not been strictly regulated, the section manager shall be considered as a person who is in line with the employer in determining working conditions and other forms of labor management.[99]

3) Judicial ruling

The Supreme Court ruled that working hours, recess and holidays stipulated by the LSA do not apply to persons in managerial and supervisory positions in terms of deciding subordinates' working conditions, does not have their times of arrival at and departure from the workplace strictly regulated, and is managing his/her own working hours flexibly. Persons in this position cannot receive additional allowances for overtime exceeding contractual working hours or holiday work according to the Labor Standards Act.[100]

(3) The Employer's countermeasures

Even though the 'managing director' for the foreign company in this case had a

---

[99] MOEL Guideline: Guideline Kunjung-41, Mar. 3, 2011.
[100] Supreme Court ruling on Feb. 28, 1989, 88daka2974.

'관리·감독업무에 종사하는 근로자(제63조 제4호 및 시행령 제34조)'는 근로기준법 제4장 및 제5장에서 정한 근로시간, 휴게와 휴일에 관한 규정을 적용하지 않는다. 여기서 '관리·감독업무에 종사하는 자'라 함은 근로조건의 결정 기타 노무관리에 있어서 경영자와 일체적인 지위에 있는 자를 말한다. 사업장 내 형식적인 직책에도 불구하고 노무관리방침의 결정에 참여하거나 노무 관리상 지휘·감독 권한을 가지고 있는지의 여부, 출·퇴근 등에 있어서 엄격한 제한을 받는지 여부, 그 지위에 따른 특별수당을 받고 있는지 여부 등을 종합적으로 검토하여 판단하여야 할 것이다.

행정해석은 회사의 위임전결규정 등의 자료에 의하여 '실장'이 일반업무에 대한 방침 및 소관업무에 관한 세부계획 수립 및 집행 등에 대한 결정권과 소속 직원에 대한 출장, 연장근로 지시, 휴가 승인 등 노무관리 상의 지휘·감독 권한을 가지고 있는 것으로 보여지는 경우 비록 그 지위에 따른 특별수당을 지급 받지 않는다 하더라도 일반 직원과 달리 출·퇴근 등에 있어서 엄격한 제한을 받지 않는 경우라면 전반적으로 근로조건의 결정 기타 노무관리에 있어서 경영자와 일체적인 지위에 있는 자로 볼 수 있다고 해석하고 있다.[99]

3) 판례

판례는 부하직원의 근로조건의 결정, 기타 노무관리에 있어 경영자의 지위에 있으면서 기업 경영상의 필요에 의하여 출·퇴근에 관하여도 엄격한 제한을 받지 아니하고 자기의 근무시간에 관한 융통성을 가지고 있어 회사의 감독, 관리의 지위에 있던 자는 근로기준법에서 정한 근로시간, 휴게와 휴일에 관한 규정이 적용되지 아니한다. 이러한 위치에 있는 자는 평일의 법 내 잔업시간은 물론 일요일 근무에 대해서도 근로기준법 소정의 시간 외 또는 휴일근무라 하여 같은 근로기준법에서 정한 가산금을 지급 받을 수는 없다고 판시하고 있다.[100]

(3) 회사의 대응 및 처리결과

본 사건에서 외국기업의 '상무'와 같이 상당한 직급을 가지고 있음에도

---

[99] 행정해석: 2011.03.03. 근정과-41
[100] 대법원 1989.02.28. 선고 88다카2974 판결

considerably high position, it is not clear whether this high-ranking person was working just as a manager, and not a department head which would place her in a managerial and supervisory position.

The Employee in this case was not a department head due to the combination of two departments, but had received the high salary of a director, twice the incentives of other employees, and her time of arrival at and leaving the workplace was not strictly controlled as was done with other employees. In consideration of these facts, the Gangnam Labor Office in charge of this case concluded that the Employee in this case held a managerial and supervisory position and could be excluded from the provisions on working hours, recess and holiday provisions in Article 63 of the Labor Standards Act. In the end, as the Employee recognized that she could not receive a severance bonus from the Company, she withdrew the lawsuit and instead of resigning, took childcare leave.

3. Conclusion

The labor case herein is a very common one that can occur easily for companies. On the second point of whether the managing director of a foreign company shall be entitled to an additional allowance for overtime work shall be determined collectively in consideration not only of the official designation of the employee as being in a high position but also the manager's authority, observance of commuting time, and any special allowances assigned to the position.[101] Through this evaluation, companies should prepare measures to avoid having to later deal with matters regarding overtime and holiday work for such a position.

This labor case began with the Employee's demand to receive a severance bonus from the Company through a claim that the Company had violated labor law. When a company has violated labor law and has to settle with certain employees to end labor disputes, other employees will rush to claim compensation from the company as well. In particular, for many foreign companies with registered representative directors working as directors in their home countries, those representative directors have to come to Korea to attend investigation procedures in the Labor Office, which will cause considerable embarrassment for their local Korean branches. On this point, companies need to thoroughly observe labor law to avoid labor disputes with potentially dissatisfied employees and reduce in advance the risk of related damages.

---

[101] Ha, Kaprae,The Labor Standards Act (27th ed.) Joongang Economy, 2015, p. 315.

불구하고, 단지 관리자이지 부서장이 아닌 경우에 관리 감독자인지 여부에 대해 판단을 하기 어려운 경우가 많다.

이 사건의 근로자인 경우에는 부서의 통폐합으로 인해 부서장은 아니지만, 고위의 직급에 임원급의 임금, 일반 근로자의 2배 이상의 인센티브를 받고 있으며, 출퇴근 시간에 대해서도 일반근로자와 달리 엄격히 통제 받지 않았다. 이러한 사정을 고려하여 이 사건을 담당한 강남노동지청은 이 사건의 근로자를 근로기준법 제63조에 따른 근로시간, 휴일, 휴게에 대해 예외를 인정받을 수 있는 관리·감독자로 인정하였다. 결국, 이 사건의 근로자는 퇴직위로금을 받지 못하자 퇴직하는 대신 고소사건을 취하하고 육아휴직을 청구하여 휴직하게 되면서 이 사건은 종결되었다.

3. 시사점

위에서 다루었던 사례는 기업에서 일상적으로 일어날 수 있는 사건이다. 또한, 외국기업 상무의 연장근로에 대한 가산임금 지급여부에 대한 판단은 직급의 고하(高下)만을 가지고 판단할 것이 아니라 관리자로서의 권한, 출퇴근 시간준수 의무, 특별수당 지급여부 등을 복합적으로 고려하여 판단하여야 할 것이다.[101] 이를 잘 살펴 연장근로나 휴일근로에 대해 차후 문제가 발생하지 않도록 하여야 할 것이다.

이 노동사건의 발단은 회사의 노동법 위반사항을 빌미로 근로자가 회사를 압박하여 퇴직위로금을 받기 위해서였다. 회사가 노무관리를 잘못하였을 때나, 근로자의 퇴직위로금 요구를 일부 수용하여 합의하는 경우 다른 직원들도 얼마든지 동일한 노동사건을 제기할 수 있다는 점에서 시사점이 크다고 할 수 있다. 특히, 외국인 회사의 경우 등기된 대표이사가 본사의 중역을 맡고 있는 경우 대표이사가 고소사건 조사에 직접 출석하여 조사를 받아야 하기 때문에 상당한 곤욕을 치르는 경우가 많다. 이러한 점에서 회사는 노동법을 준수하는 철저한 노무관리를 통해 잠재적 불만이 있는 근로자에게 합법적으로 대응하여 부당한 손해를 보는 일이 없도록 해야 하겠다.

---

[101] 하갑래,『근로기준법(제27판)』, 중앙경제, 2015, 315면.

Chapter 4 Flexible Working Hours

I. **Requirement Before Introducing Flexible Working Hours**

II. **Flexible Working Hour System**
   〈Table 4-1〉 Rules of Employment on Flexible Working Hours for 2-Week Units
   〈Table 4-2〉 Labor-Management Agreement on Flexible Working Hours for 3-Month Units

III. **Selective Working Hour System**
   〈Table 4-3〉 Selective Working Time Policy
   〈Table 4-4〉 Labor-Management Agreement on Selective Working Hour System

IV. **Deemed Working Hour System**
   〈Table 4-5〉 Labor-Management Agreement on Deemed Working Hours for Outside Work

V. **Discretionary Work System**
   〈Table 4-6〉 Rules of Employment for Discretionary Working Hour System
   〈Table 4-7〉 Labor-Management Agreement on Discretionary Working Hour System〉

VI. **Compensatory Leave System**
   〈Table 4-8〉 Labor-Management Agreement regarding the Compensatory Leave System

VII. **Work-from-Home Systems**
   〈Table 4-9〉 Working from Home in the Rules of Employment
   〈Table 4-10〉 Regulation Example: Work-from-Home Service Regulations
   〈Table 4-11〉 Example Working from Home Policy
   〈Table 4-12〉 Working from Home Checklist
   〈Table 4-13〉 Agreement to Protect Security while Working from Home

VIII. **Work-from-Home Systems**
   〈Table 4-14〉 Selective Working Time Policy
   〈Table 4-15〉 Labor-Management Agreement on Selective Working Hour System

제4장 유연 근로시간제도

Ⅰ. 도입요건: 근로자대표 선정
Ⅱ. 탄력적 근로시간제
  〈표 4-1〉 2주 이내 탄력적 근로시간제 취업규칙
  〈표 4-2〉 3개월 이내 탄력적 근로시간제 노사합의서
Ⅲ. 선택적 근로시간제
  〈표 4-3〉 선택적 근로시간제 규정 - 시차 출근
  〈표 4-4〉 선택적 근로시간제 노사합의서
Ⅳ. 간주 근로시간제
  〈표 4-5〉 사업장 밖 간주근로시간제 노사합의서
Ⅴ. 재량 근로시간제
  〈표 4-6〉 재량근로시간제 취업규칙
  〈표 4-7〉 재량근로시간제 노사합의서
Ⅵ. 보상휴가제
  〈표 4-8〉 보상휴가제 노사합의서
Ⅶ. 재택근로제
  〈표 4-9〉 취업규칙 규정
  〈표 4-10〉 취업규칙 중 재택근무제 복무규정
  〈표 4-11〉 재택근무 규정
  〈표 4-12〉 재택근무 체크리스트
  〈표 4-13〉 재택근무 보안서약서
Ⅷ. 연차유급휴가를 이용한 저축휴가제도
  〈표 4-14〉 근로시간 저축휴가제 노사합의서
  〈표 4-15〉 취업규칙을 통한 도입 내용

Chapter 4 Flexible Working Hours

> Productivity refers to the amount produced or achieved in a limited time. The term "52-hour week" originated from the introduction of 'one week' in Article 2 of the Labor Standards Act, which states that "one week is seven days, including a holiday."[102]
>
> For this reason, 40 hours constitute a statutory work week, while the weekly working hours become a maximum 52 hours when maximum overtime (up to 12 hours a week) is allowed. To see greater results while reducing working hours, a flexible working time system that focuses on the characteristics of the work is urgently needed. When I was engaged in wage consultations for a French company responsible for operation of Subway Line 9 in 2006, what the manager told me remains vivid. "Koreans are working 44 hours per week, but are less productive than those who work 32 hours per week." When I thought about it at the time, I figured this was because Koreans are constantly working extended hours and on holidays due to labor market rigidity. Most Korean companies still work from 9 am to 6 pm, Monday through Friday. To be more efficient during these traditional working hours, various flexible working hours urgently need to be introduced into the Labor Standards Act.

The Labor Standards Act includes (i) flexible working hours, (ii) selective working hours, (iii) deemed working hours, and (iv) discretionary working hours, (v) paid time-off leave, etc. Ways to adopt and use these flexible working hours are described in more detail below.[103]

I. Requirement before Introducing Flexible Working Hours: Selection of Employee Representatives[104]

1. Reasons to Select an Employee Representative

---

[102] The Labor Standards Act for the related article was revised around the concept of one week (Mar. 30, 2018).

[103] Ministry of Employment and Labor (MOEL), "Flexible Working Hour System Guides", Sept. 2019; MOEL, "Q&As on a Flexible Working Hour System", Dec. 2017.

[104] This article is based upon the Administrative Guide: Kungi 68207-735 (June 5, 1997) including related administrative guidance and judicial rulings.

제4장 유연적 근로시간제

> 생산성은 제한된 시간에 더 많은 성과를 내는데 달려 있다. 최근 주 52시간제라는 용어가 생기게 된 것은 근로기준법 제2조에서 "1주라 함은 휴일을 포함한 7일로 한다"고 명시하면서 부터다.[102] 1주의 법정근로시간인 40시간에 연장근로 한도인 12시간을 더하면 52시간이 된다. 근로시간이 줄어들면서도 더 많은 성과를 내기 위해서는 업무의 특성에 맞추어 집중하는 유연근로시간제가 절실히 필요하다. 필자가 2006년도 지하철 9호선 관리를 맡게 된 프랑스회사를 임금컨설팅 하던 중 관리자가 한 말이 아직도 귀에 생생하다. "한국인들은 주당 44시간 근무하면서 주당 32시간 근무하는 자신들보다 생산성이 떨어진다"고 하였다. 이는 우리나라는 경직된 근무시간으로 인해 연장, 휴일근로 등이 보편화 되었기 때문이라고 생각한다. 아직도 우리나라 대부분의 기업은 근무시간이 월요일부터 금요일까지, 오전 9시부터 오후 6시까지 일한다. 이러한 전통적인 근무시간에 업무의 효율을 극대화하기 위해서는 근로기준법에서 허용하고 있는 다양한 유연근로시간제의 도입이 절실히 요구된다.

근로기준법에는 이와 관련하여 (ⅰ) 탄력적 근로시간제, (ⅱ) 선택적 근로시간제, (ⅲ) 간주근로시간제, (Ⅳ) 재량근로시간제, (Ⅴ) 보상휴가제 등이 있다. 이러한 유연 근로시간제에 대해 보다 구체적으로 살펴보고자 한다.[103]

Ⅰ. 도입요건: 근로자대표의 선정[104]

1. 근로자대표 선정이유

---

[102] 근로기준법 개정(2018.3.20)으로 1주의 개념 도입
[103] 고용노동부, "유연근로시간제 가이드", 2019.9; 고용노동부, "유연근무제 Q&A", 2017.12.
[104] 근기 68207-735 (97.6.5) 행정해석기준으로 유사행정해석 및 판례 추가하여 정리

Chapter 4 Flexible Working Hours

While individual working conditions are determined by employment contracts, the determination of collective working conditions shall follow the principles in the Labor Standards Act regarding equal decision-making between labor and management. According to Article 4 of that Act, "Working conditions shall be determined through free and voluntary agreement between workers and employers, on the basis of equality." Based on this principle, changes in collective working conditions require written agreement of the employee representative.[105] An employee representative refers to a labor union organized by the majority of employees in cases where such a labor union exists, or an individual representing the majority of employees if there is no labor union representing the majority of employees.

Specifically, the role of an employee representative under the Labor Standards Act can be divided into three categories. First, when employers seek to change statutory working hours according to the Labor Standards Act and implement flexible, optional or discretionary working hours, compensatory leave, or alternative paid leave, they are required to obtain written agreement of the employee representative. Unilaterally changing the statutory working hours (40 hours per week, 8 hours per day) by the employer can lead to criminal punishment. However, if written agreement is obtained from the employee representative, there will be no criminal punishment.[106]

Second, for management layoffs, employers are required to engage in prior consultations with the employee representative. Management layoffs refer to cases where the company undergoes restructuring due to unavoidable business difficulties, without fault on the part of the employees. When implementing management layoffs, employers must notify the employee representative 50 days in advance, make efforts to avoid layoffs, and engage in sincere consultations regarding the employees to be laid off. The consultation process with the employee representative is a critical requirement for justifying the legitimacy of management layoffs (Article 24 of the Labor Standards Act).

Third, when making adverse changes to working conditions stipulated in the rules of employment, the consent of a majority of employees is necessary. In the case we are discussing herein, the consent of the employee representative representing the majority of employees is necessary. Changes to working conditions that do not receive consent of the employee representative shall be legally ineffective (Article 94 of the LSA).

2. Purpose to change statutory working hours

---

[105] Kim, Mi-young & Park, Eun-jeong, "Workplace Autonomy, Labor-Management Council, and Employee Representatives," Labor Law Forum, Vol. 34 (2021), p. 122.

[106] Lee, Seung-wook, "A Study on Measures for Improving the Employee Representative System in Labor Relations Law," MOEL, p. 25.

개별적 근로조건은 근로계약에 따라 정해지지만, 집단적 근로조건의 결정은 근로기준법의 근로조건 노사대등결정의 원칙에 따라 결정된다. 이에 대해 근로기준법 제4조는 근로조건은 근로자와 사용자가 동등한 지위에서 자유로운 의사에 의하여 결정되어야 한다는 원칙을 명시하고 있다. 이 원칙에 따라 집단적 근로조건의 변경은 근로자대표와의 서면합의를 필요로 한다.[105] 여기서 근로자대표라고 하면 근로자의 과반수로 조직된 노동조합이 있는 경우에는 그러한 노동조합, 근로자의 과반수를 대표하는 노동조합이 없는 경우에는 대상 근로자의 과반수를 대표하는 자를 말한다.

구체적으로, 근로기준법상 근로자대표의 역할은 세 가지로 구분이 된다. 첫째는 사용자가 근로기준법상 법정근로시간을 변경하여 운영하는 경우에 근로자대표와의 서면합의를 요구하고 있다. 관련된 근로시간의 변경은 탄력적 근로시간제, 선택적 근로시간제, 재량근로시간제, 보상휴가제, 유급휴가의 대체 등이다. 사업주가 일방적으로 법정근로시간(1주 40시간, 1일 8시간)을 집단적으로 변경하는 경우 형사처벌의 대상이 되지만, 근로자대표와의 서면합의를 하게 되면 형사처벌이 면책 된다.[106]

둘째로 경영상 해고에 있어서 근로자대표와의 사전협의를 요구하고 있다. 경영상 해고는 근로자의 귀책사유 없이 회사의 경영상 어려움으로 구조조정이 불가피 한 경우를 말한다. 사용자가 경영상 해고를 할 경우에는 50일 전에 근로자대표에게 통보하고 해고회피노력과 해고대상자에 대해 성실히 협의 해야 한다. 이러한 사용자의 근로자대표와의 협의절차는 경영상 해고의 정당성 입증에 있어 필수 요건에 해당된다(근기법 제24조).

셋째로 취업규칙에 있는 근로조건을 불이익하게 변경할 때에는 근로자 과반수의 동의를 받아야 한다고 규정하고 있다. 여기서 근로자의 과반수를 대표하는 근로자대표의 동의가 필요하다. 근로자대표의 동의를 받지 못한 사용자의 근로조건 불이익 변경은 정당한 규정으로써의 효력을 상실한다(근기법 제94조).

2. 근로시간제도 도입을 위한 근로자 대표 선정

---

[105] 김미영, 박은정, 사업장 자치, 노사협의회와 근로자대표, 노동법도럼 제34호(2021), 122면.
[106] 이승욱, 노동관계법상 근로자대표제도의 개선방안연구, 고용노동부, 25면.

Chapter 4 Flexible Working Hours

The Labor Standards Act requires written agreement from or consultation with the employee representative for matters such as changes in working hours, etc. "This employee representative refers to the labor union, where there is an organized labor union representing more than half the employees at a business or workplace; or shall refer to a person who represents more than half the employees, where there is no such organized labor union" (Article 24 (3) of the LSA). However, this article does not explain the entire scope of "employee" covered by employee representation, the selected unit or method used in selecting the employee representative, manner of representation, effect of the written agreement, etc. Here, I would like to bring attention to clear administrative guidance and judicial rulings concerning these matters to better understand related laws and operations.

Items Requiring Written Agreement from or Consultation with Employee Representative

LSA	Written Agreement or Consent Required
Article 51/51-2	Three-month (or six-month) flexible working hour system
Article 52	Selective working hour system
Article 57	System of using leave as compensation
Article 58 (2)	Hours deemed working hours for "those ordinarily required to carry out duty
"Article 58 (3)	Discretionary working hours
Article 59	Exceptions in applying working and recess hours for such particulars as transportation
Article 62	Substitution of paid leave

3. Scope of "Employee" and Unit Selected for Employee Representation

(1) Scope of "Employee"

The following criterion is used to evaluate whether or not there is an organized labor union representing more than half the employees. The scope of employees participating in voting for the employee representative is calculated as follows:

근로기준법은 사용자가 근로시간제도의 변경 등에 있어 일정한 사항에 대하여 근로자 대표와 서면합의 또는 협의를 하도록 하고 있다. 이 경우 근로자 대표는 "당해 사업 또는 사업장에 근로자의 과반수로 조직된 노동조합이 있는 경우에는 그 노동조합, 근로자의 과반수로 조직된 노동조합이 없는 경우에는 근로자의 과반수를 대표하는 자"를 의미한다. (근기법 제24조 제3항). 그러나 동 규정만으로 근로자 대표를 선출하는 근로자의 범위, 근로자 대표의 선정단위 및 선정방법, 근로자 대표의 대표권 행사방법, 서면합의서의 효력 등이 명확하지 않다. 따라서 이에 관련한 문제에 대한 명확한 행정해석 기준과 판례 내용을 제시하여 법 해석과 운영을 이해하고자 한다.

<근로자대표와의 서면합의/동의 및 협의내용>

근로기준법	서면합의 또는 동의
제51/51조의2	3개월 이내 (6개월 이내) 단위르 탄력적 근로시간제
제52조	선택적 근로시간제의 도입과 관련된 사항
제57조	선택적 보상휴가제
제58조 제2항	사업장 밖 간주근로시간제에 있어 '업무수행에 통상 필요한 시간 간주
제58조 제3항	재량근로에 있어 근로시간으로 간주하는 시간
제59조	운수업 등 특수업종에 있어 연장근로 및 휴게시간의 특례
제62조	연차휴가 유급휴가의 대체

3. 근로자의 범위 및 근로자 대표의 선정단위

(1) 근로자의 범위

노동조합이 근로자의 과반수를 조직하고 있는지의 여부를 판단하는 기준이 되거나 근로자 대표를 선출함에 있어 투표에 참여하는 근로자의 범위는 다음과 같이 산정한다.

Chapter 4 Flexible Working Hours

> The scope of employees covered by employee representation
> = Employees under LSA Guidelines − Employers under LSA Guidelines
>   (Article 2 of the LSA (1))   (Article 2 of the LSA (2))

The term "employer" under the LSA means 1) a business owner, or 2) a person responsible for management of a business or 3) a person who works on behalf of a business owner with respect to matters relating to employees. Here, 'a person who works on behalf of a business owner with respect to matters relating to employees' is an employee who has the dual position of employee and employer, and so shall be excluded from employees covered by employee representation. Although he/she is considered an employee to whom agreements apply, he/she acts specifically in the interest of the employer in the course of making written agreements.

(2) Unit Selected for Employee Representation

The employee representative shall be selected from a unit of a business or workplace. Accordingly, in cases where one business is composed of several workplaces, if the company wants to introduce new working hour systems to the business unit, the employee representative shall be selected from that business unit, or if the company wants to introduce items to some designated workplace, the employee representative shall be selected from employees at those workplaces.

(3) Ministry of Employment and Labor (MOEL) Guidelines and Precedents Related to Selection of an Employee Representative
 1) MOEL Guidelines

Under the Labor Standards Act, employee representative refers to an entity/individual representing the majority of employees within a specific business or workplace unit. Therefore, in principle, the employee representative shall be elected for the entire business. However, if certain provisions apply to specific occupations or job categories, solely basing selection of the employee representative on the entire workforce of the business might fail to adequately represent the interests of the affected employees. In regards to the "majority of employees in the business or workplace" mentioned in Article 94 of the Labor Standards Act concerning changes to rules of employment, the Supreme Court has stated that "if the adverse changes to the rules of employment only affect a

> 근로자대표를 선출하는 = 근로기준법상의 근로자 - 근로기준법상의 사용자
> 근로자의 범위   (법 제2호 제1호)   (법 제2호 제2호)

근로기준법상 사용자는 1) 사업주, 2) 사업경영담당자, 3) 그 밖에 근로자에 관한 사항에 대하여 사업주를 위하여 행위하는 자를 말한다. 여기서 '그 밖에 근로자에 관한 사항에 대하여 사업주를 위하여 행위하는 자'는 근로자와 사용자의 이중적 지위를 갖는 자로 근로자 산정에서 제외된다. 이유는 설사 이들이 근로자로 향후 합의 내용의 적용을 받더라도 노사서면 합의과정에서는 사용자를 위하여 대리하는 자로 볼 수 있기 때문이다.

(2) 근로자 대표의 선정단위

근로자 대표는 당해 사업 또는 사업장 단위로 선정되어야 한다. 따라서 하나의 사업이 수 개의 사업장으로 구성되어 있는 경우, 근로시간제도를 사업단위로 도입하고자 하면 근로자 대표는 사업단위로 선정하고, 일부 사업장에만 도입하고자 하면 일부 사업장단위로 선정해야 한다.

(3) 근로자대표 선정대상 관련 행정해석과 판례

1) 행정해석

근로기준법 상 근로자대표는 해당 사업 또는 사업장 단위로 소속 근로자의 과반수를 대표하는 자를 의미하므로 근로자대표는 원칙적으로 전체 사업(장) 단위로 선출하여야 한다. 다만, 특정 직군이나 직종에 한정하여 적용되는 사항의 경우에도 일률적으로 사업(장) 전체 근로자를 기준으로만 근로자대표를 선정해야 한다고 하면, 오히려 적용대상 근로자의 이해관계가 적절히 대변되지 못할 가능성을 배제할 수 없다. 한편, 취업규칙 변경에 관한 근로기준법 제94조에서의 사업 또는 사업장의 근로자 과반수에 대해서 대법원은 '일부 근로자 집단에 적용되는 취업규칙 불이익 변경과 관련하여 다른 근로자 집단에게 적용되지 않거나 적용이 예상되지 않는다면 해당 근로자 집단만이 취업규칙 변경의 동의 주체가 된다'고 판시를 하고 있다.[107] 따라서 사업장의 특정 직종(시설직 등)만을 대상으로 탄력적

specific group of employees and do not apply or are not expected to apply to other employee groups, then only the affected employee group becomes the subject of consent for the changes to the rules of employment."[107] Therefore, when introducing flexible working hour systems limited to specific occupations or job categories (such as facility workers), it would be permissible to select an employee representative who represents the majority of employees within that specific occupation or job category. The employee representative in such cases should be elected or determined through democratic methods such as voting or polling, involving the participation of a majority of employees in that occupation or job category.[108]

2) Related Precedents

① When multiple employee groups are part of a single system of working conditions and even if only one employee group directly suffers from the adverse changes to the rules of employment, if application of the changed rules is expected to affect other employee groups, both the directly affected employee group and the employee groups that can anticipate future application of the changed rules become the subjects of consent. However, if the working conditions are differentiated, and the changed rules only apply to specific employee groups, resulting in direct disadvantages for those specific employee groups, without anticipation that the changed rules will apply to other employee groups, only the disadvantaged employee group(s) become the subject of consent.[109]

② In a case where a hospital laid off employees ranked 4th grade or higher, the Supreme Court stated that "when a hospital seeks to downsize primarily employees of 4th grade or higher, it is also necessary to engage in consultations with the employee representative who can represent the interests of the employees in that rank. In this case, the employee representative claiming to have engaged in consultations regarding the layoffs consists mostly of employees ranked 5th grade or lower, temporary employees, and non-administrative staff, and since the majority of union members in the labor union, composed mainly of employees ranked 5th grade or lower, are not the target of layoffs and have little connection to the layoffs, it is unreasonable to consider the selection of the employee representative as fair."[110]

③ The Seoul Administrative Court determined that "if an employer intends to

---

[107] Supreme Court ruling on May 28, 2009, 2009doo2238.
[108] MOEL Guidelines, Labor Standards section-1356, May 7, 2021.
[109] Supreme Court ruling on May 28, 2009, 2009doo2238.
[110] Supreme Court ruling on Sept. 29, 2005, 2005doo4403.

근로시간제를 도입하는 등 특정 직종이나 직군에 한정하여 적용되는 사항일 경우에는 해당 직종이나 직군 근로자의 과반수를 대표하는 자를 근로자대표로 선정할 수 있을 것이다. 이 경우 근로자대표 또한 해당 직종이나 직군 근로자 과반수가 참여한 투표거수 등의 민주적인 방식에 의하여 선출 또는 결정되어야 한다.[108]

2) 관련 판례

① 여러 근로자 집단이 하나의 근로조건 체계 내에 있어, 비록 취업규칙의 불이익 변경 시점에는 어느 근로자 집단만이 직접적인 불이익을 받더라도, 다른 근로자 집단에도 변경된 취업규칙의 적용이 예상되는 경우에는 일부 근로자 집단은 물론 장래 변경된 취업규칙 규정의 적용이 예상되는 근로자 집단을 포함한 근로자 집단이 동의 주체가 된다. 그렇지 않고 근로조건이 이원화되어 있어 일부 근로자 집단에만 변경된 취업규칙이 적용되어, 직접적으로 불이익을 받게 되는 해당 근로자 집단 이외에는 변경된 취업규칙의 적용이 예상되는 근로자 집단이 없는 경우에는 불이익을 받는 근로자집단만이 동의 주체가 된다.[109]

② 한 병원이 4급 이상의 근로자들을 정리해고한 사건에서, 대법원은 "근로자 중 주로 4급 이상의 직원을 감원하기로 하는 경우 4급 이상 직원들의 이해관계를 대변할 수 있는 근로자대표와의 협의도 필요하다. ○○○병원이 정리해고와 관련하여 협의하였다고 하는 근로자대표는 신○○를 제외하고는 모두 5급 이하의 직원, 고용원, 기능직 직원들로 구성되어 있고, 근로자의 과반수를 넘지 않고 주로 5급 이하의 근로자로 구성된 노동조합 조합원은 대부분 정리해고대상자가 아니어서 이 사건 정리해고와 거의 이해관계를 갖고 있지 아니하고, 근로자대표의 선출도 공정하게 이루어졌다고 보기 어렵다고 판시했다.[110]

③ 서울행정법원은 "사용자가 근로자들 중의 일부 직급을 대상으로 정리해고를 실시하려면 특별한 사정이 없는 한, 그 대상이 되는 근로자들을

---

107) 대법원 2009.5.28. 선고 2009두2238 판결
108) 행정해석 근로기준정책과-1356,2021.05.07.
109) 대법원 2009.5.28. 선고 2009두2238 판결
110) 대법원 2005.9.29. 선고 2005두4403 판결

Chapter 4　Flexible Working Hours

carry out layoffs targeting only certain ranks of employees, unless there are exceptional circumstances otherwise, they shall engage in consultations with a representative who can represent the affected employees. It is not permissible to engage in consultations with a labor union that lacks representativeness. If interpreted differently, it would result in entrusting the fate of certain employee groups to individuals who cannot adequately reflect the opinions and interests of those certain employee groups."[111]

4. Choosing the Employee Representative

(1) Principles of Employee Representative Selection

If there is a labor union representing the majority of employees, that union becomes the employee representative. If there is no labor union representing the majority of employees, an individual shall be chosen who represents the majority of employees. Therefore, in cases where a majority labor union does not exist, a separate election shall be held to select an employee representative who represents the majority of the employees. Labor laws do not provide any specific regulations regarding the election of such an employee representative. Therefore, a fair procedure is necessary to adequately reflect the intentions of the employees in the respective business or workplace. Such a procedure shall involve a democratic election method that obtains the support of the majority of employees and does not allow for employer appointment or nomination.[112]

1) Selection of an employee representative shall follow a collective decision-making method, such as an election (including a meeting-based approach). The election of an employee representative shall be determined through an appropriate method (including anonymous voting) that allows individual employees to freely express their opinions in a meeting where employees gather in the same location. The elected individual, chosen by the majority of employees based on the results of such a process, shall be appointed as the employee representative.[113]

2) Selecting an employee representative through individual circulation and signing cannot be considered a valid election method.[114] However, in exceptional cases where employees are dispersed across multiple workplaces or when it is not feasible to hold elections or meetings at the same location, a method where employees freely nominate employee representatives by workplace or

---

[111] Seoul Administrative Court ruling on Aug. 22, 2000, 99goo27292.
[112] Do, Jae-hyung, Labor Representatives and the Written Agreement System under the Labor Standards Act, Labor Law Studies, Vol. 37, 2011, p. 102.
[113] Supreme Court ruling on July 26, 1977, 773da355.
[114] Supreme Court ruling on June 24, 1994, 92da28556.

대표할 수 있는 자와 정리해고에 관한 협의를 진행하여야 할 것이고, 대표성을 지니지 못한 노동조합과 협의를 진행할 수는 없다 할 것이다. 만약 이와 달리 해석한다면, 일부 계층의 근로자들로 하여금 자신들의 의사와 이익을 제대로 반영할 수 없는 자에게 운명을 맡기는 것을 감수하도록 하는 결과가 될 것이라고 판단했다.[111]

4. 근로자대표 선정방법

(1) 근로자대표 선정원칙

근로자대표라고 하면, 근로자의 과반수를 대표하는 노동조합이 있는 경우에는 그 노동조합이 근로자대표가 되고, 근로자의 과반수를 대표하는 노동조합이 없는 경우에는 근로자의 과반수를 대표하는 자를 말한다. 따라서 과반수 노동조합이 존재하지 않는 경우에는 과반수 근로자대표를 따로 선출하여야 한다. 노동관계법령에서는 과반수 근로자대표의 선출과 관련하여 아무런 규정을 두고 있지 않다. 따라서 당해 사업 또는 사업장 소속 근로자의 의사를 공정하게 반영할 수 있는 절차가 필요하다. 이러한 절차는 민주적인 선출 방법으로 근로자의 과반수 지지를 얻어 선출되어져야 하며, 사용자의 지명이나 임명은 허용되지 않는다.[112]

1) 근로자대표의 선출은 선거와 같은 집단적 의사결정 방식(회의방식 포함)을 원칙으로 한다. 근로자대표의 선출은 근로자가 같은 장소에 집합한 회의에서 근로자 개개인의 의견표명을 자유롭게 할 수 있는 적절한 방법(무기명 투표 등)으로 의결한 결과 근로자의 과반수가 선출한 자를 근로자대표로 정해야 한다.[113]

2) 개별적 회람 및 서명을 통하여 근로자대표를 선출하는 것은 유효한 선출로 볼 수 없지만,[114] 근로자가 여러 사업장에 분산되어 있는 등 동일한 장소에서 선거나 회의가 불가능한 경우에는 예외적으로 사업장 및 부서별로 근로자가 자유롭게 근로자대표를 지명하고 이를 취합하는 방식은 허용된다.[115]

---

111) 서울행정법원 2000.8.22. 선고 99구27292 판결
112) 도재형, 근로기준법상 근로자대표 및 서면 합의제도, 노동법학, 제37호, 2011, 102면.
113) 대법원 1977.7.26. 선고 773다355판결
114) 대법원 1994.6.24. 선고 92다28556 판결
115) 대법원 2005.5.12. 선고 2003다52456 판결

department and consolidate those nominations is permitted.[115]
3) In cases where a majority labor union does not exist, designating labor-management council workers as employee representatives without a separate election procedure is not recognized. This is because the labor-management council serves a different legal purpose, with limited decision-making authority, while the flexible working hour system performs functions related to determining employment conditions.[116]

(2) Where there is an organized labor union representing more than half the employees

Whether the labor union represents more than half the employees shall be estimated in the unit of the business where the employer wants to select an employee representative; and shall be estimated in a unit of the workplace for that unit of the workplace. If the labor union represents more than half the employees, it is taken for granted that the labor union becomes the union representative (e.g. the chairman of the union branch) who has been authorized to represent the labor union.

(3) Where there is no organized labor union representing more than half the employees

Where there is no organized labor union representing more than half the employees, an employee representative shall be selected. In this case, there are no particular restrictions to the method of selection, but in situations where the employees are informed that an employee representative will be authorized to represent them in introduction of a working hour system, it is acceptable to receive employee opinions. Accordingly, direct voting is not always necessary; it is also possible to choose multiple representatives. In cases where a Labor-Management Council has been established by the Act on the Promotion of Workers' Participation and Cooperation (the Labor-Management Council Act) in a business or workplace to introduce a new working hour system, the employee members can be regarded as employee representatives.

The employee representative for the purpose of consulting with the employer shall be selected by independent and voluntary decision-making by the employees after they are informed of the reason for choosing employee representation. It is also acceptable to choose the employee representative through employees' general meeting or individual signatures on circulating representative lists. If an employer asks the employees to choose an employee representative, the employees autonomously determine procedures and methods of selection without intervention

---

[115] Supreme Court ruling on May 12, 2005, 2003da52456.
[116] Supreme Court ruling on June 24, 1994, 92da28556.

3) 과반수 노동조합이 존재하지 않는 경우, 별도의 선출절차 없이 노사협의회 근로자위원을 근로자대표로 하는 것은 인정되지 않는다. 근로시간 유연화 제도가 근로조건 결정 기능을 수행하는데 반해, 노사협의회는 의결사항이 제한되는 등 그 법적 취지가 다르기 때문이다.[116]

(2) 근로자 과반수로 조직된 노동조합이 있는 경우

노동조합이 근로자의 과반수를 조직하고 있는지의 여부는 사업단위로 도입하는 경우는 사업단위에서, 사업장단위로 도입하는 경우는 사업장단위에서 판단해야 한다. 노동조합이 근로자 과반수를 조직하고 있으면 근로자 대표는 당연히 노동조합의 대표자 또는 노동조합으로부터 대표권을 위임받은 자(예, 노동조합지부장)가 된다.

(3) 노동조합이 근로자 과반수를 조직하지 못하고 있는 경우

노동조합이 근로자의 과반수를 조직하지 못하고 있는 경우에는 근로자의 과반수를 대표하는 자를 선정하여야 한다. 이 경우 선정방법에는 특별한 제한이 없으며, 근로시간제도에 대한 대표권을 행사한다는 것을 근로자에게 주지시킨 상태에서 근로자의 의사를 모으는 적당한 방법이면 된다. 따라서 반드시 직접 투표에 의하지 않아도 되며, 1인의 대표는 물론 복수의 근로자 대표를 선정하는 것도 가능하다. 근로시간제도를 도입하고자 하는 사업 또는 사업장단위에 '근로자참여 및 협력증진에 관한 법률'(이하 '근참법')에 의한 노사협의회가 설치되어 있으며 그 근로자위원을 근로자 대표로 볼 수 있다.

경영상의 이유에 의한 해고 문제에 대하여 "사용자와 협의를 할 근로자의 대표자를 선출한다는 것을 근로자들에게 주지시킨 상태에서 근로자들의 자유로운 의사결정이 보장되는 적당한 방법이면 될 것으로 사료되는 바, 근로자들의 집회를 통한 선출이나 회람을 통한 서명 등의 방법도 무방할 것이다. 사용자가 근로자 대표의 선출을 요청하고 그에 따라 근로자들이 사용자의 개입이 배제된 상태에서 자율적으로 근로자대표 선출을 위한 절차나 방법을 결정하고 근로자대표를 선출하였다면 그 과정에서 일부 근로자들이 참여하지 못하였다 하더라도 선출된 자가 근로자의 과반수에 대한 대표성을

---

116) 대법원 1994.6.24 선고 92다28556 판결

Chapter 4 Flexible Working Hours

by the employer, and select someone (even though some employees could not participate) that represents more than half of the employees, the person shall be regarded as the employee representative.[117]

(4) Invalid employee representatives

Agreement from or consultation with an employee who does not justifiably represent the employees is not legally valid.

1) In cases where a company does not receive written agreement from the employee representative in introducing a three month or less flexible working hour schedule, but instead receives individual written agreements from more than half the employees, this is a violation of related labor laws.[118]

2) Article 3 of the rules for implementation of the Labor-Management Council Act stipulates that the employee representative shall be selected by direct and secret vote, but this does not include the method of voting. Vote counting is frequently computerized according to laws related to elections, but electronic voting has not yet been stipulated and related technical matters were not yet officially verified, and so it is difficult to accept its official use in reality.[119]

4. Method of Representation by the Employee Representative

(1) In cases where a written agreement is made as a supplement to the collective agreement

In cases where the employer makes a supplementary agreement to the collective agreement with the union chairman or the person commissioned to be the employee representative, the agreement can affect the collective agreement.

(2) In cases where a written agreement is made with an employee representative of the Labor-Management Council

Since a written agreement cannot change the existing collective agreement, if such agreement is incompatible with the current collective agreement, separate procedures to revise the collective agreement shall be taken so as to apply to the employees under the collective agreement. Employees to whom the collective agreement does not apply can be included in the written agreement. This written agreement can be applicable without revising the existing rules of employment.

---

117) MOEL Guides 68207-1472, Nov. 13, 2003.
118) MOEL Guides 1167, Apr. 29, 2008.
119) MOEL Guides 68107-335, Nov. 12, 1998.

가지고 있다면 근로자대표가 아닌 자로 보기는 어렵다."[117]

(4) 근로자대표로서 인정받지 못한 사례

근로자대표로서 대표성이 없는 자와의 승인 또는 협의는 법적인 효력을 가질 수 없다.

1) 3개월 이내 단위 탄력적 근로시간제를 도입하면서 근로자 대표와의 서면합의가 아닌 대상 근로자 과반수의 개별적 서면 동의를 받는 경우에는 법적 요건을 갖추지 못한 것이다.[118]

2) 근참법 시행령 제3조 제1항은 근로자위원을 직접·비밀·무기명투표에 의하여 선출하도록 명시하고 있으나 투표방법에 관한 사항은 명시된 바가 없다. 현행 선거관련법상 전산조직을 이용한 개표는 명문화되어 실시 중이나 전자투표에 관하여는 명시된 바가 없으며 기술적인 문제가 검증되지 않아 아직까지는 현실적으로 활용하기에 곤란하다.[119]

4. 근로자 대표의 대표권 행사방법

(1) 노동조합이 대표권을 행사하는 경우

노동조합의 대표자 또는 노동조합으로부터 대표권을 위임받은 자가 대표권을 행사한다. 단체협약의 보충협약으로 체결하거나, 단체협약과는 별개의 서면합의서로 작성할 수 있다.

(2) 노사협의회 근로자 위원이 대표권을 행사하는 경우

서면합의의 방식은 노사협의회의 근로자위원들이 정한 대표권 행사방법에 따르면 되고, 1) 1인의 대표자를 선출하거나, 2) 당해 사업에 한하여 1인의 근로자위원에게 대표권을 위임하거나 3) 별도의 의사결정방법을 설정하거나 (예를 들어 과반수의 찬성, 2/3 이상의 찬성 등) 4) 근로자위원 전원이 서면합의에 참여하는 등의 모든 방법이 가능하다. 사용자가 일방적으로 일부 근로자위원과만 서면합의 하는 경우에는 법적 효력이 발생하지 않는다.

---

117) 행정해석: 근기 68207-1472, 2003.11.13
118) 행정해석: 근로조건지도과-1167, 2008.04.29
119) 행정해석: 노사 68107-335, 1998.11.12

Chapter 4 Flexible Working Hours

However, revising the existing rules of employment is highly recommended in order to maintain consistency in working conditions.

The purpose of a labor-management council is to promote the common interests of labor and management through participation and cooperation, but it does not involve making decisions regarding employment conditions (Article 1 of the Act on the Promotion of Employees' Participation and Cooperation). Therefore, a labor-management council representative cannot be considered as delegated with the authority of a workplace employee representative, such as the power to change substitute holidays. Consequently, the consent of the majority of employees cannot be equated with consent for changes in employment conditions by a labor-management council representative.[120]

If the exercise of employee representative authority is explicitly specified and communicated in a manner that is easily recognized by the employees, such as through prior notice and public disclosure of the fact that the elected labor-management council worker will exercise employee representative authority, then that labor-management council worker can be considered an employee representative.[121]

(3) In cases where a written agreement is made with a new employee representative

The effectiveness is considered to be the same as a written agreement with the employee representative of the Labor-Management Council.

II. Flexible Working Hour System

1. Purpose

'Flexible working hours' means shortening the working hours of other working days or other weeks instead of extending working hours on particular working days or particular weeks, so that the average working hours of a certain period shall be within the statutory standard working hours (40 hours per week). For an example,

---

[120] Kim, Kisun, "Regulatory Status and Legislative Issues of the Employee Representative System in Labor Relations Law" National Assembly Legislative Research Institute, 2016, p. 64; Supreme Court ruling on June 24, 1994, 92Da28556.
[121] MOEL Guidelines, Labor Standards section-1356, May 7, 2021.

노사협의회의 목적은 근로자와 사용자 쌍방이 참여와 협력을 통하여 노사 공동의 이익을 증진하는데 있지, 근로조건의 결정을 하는데 있지 않다(근참법 제1조). 그래서 노사협의회의 근로자대표는 근로자위원 선정시에 대체휴일 변경과 같이 사업장 단위의 근로자대표의 권한을 위임 받았다고 할 수 없으므로, 노사협의회의 근로자대표는 근로조건의 불이익 변경에 대해 근로자 과반수 동의와 동일시 할 수 없다.[120]

노사협의회 근로자위원 선출 당시에 근로자대표 권한행사 사실이 주지된 경우에는 해당 근로자위원을 근로자대표로 볼 수 있다. 이 경우 근로자대표 권한 행사 사실은 선출되는 근로자위원이 근로자대표 권한을 행사하게 된다는 사실과 권한 범위 등을 구체적으로 명시하고 이를 공고게시하는 등 사회통념상 근로자들이 쉽게 인지할 수 있는 방식으로 주지하여야 한다.[121]

(3) 새롭게 근로자 대표를 선정하는 경우

1인의 근로자 대표가 선정된 경우는 선정된 대표가 대표권을 행사하면 된다. 복수의 근로자 대표가 선정되는 경우는 노사협의회 근로자 위원이 대표권을 행사하는 방법에 준하여 대표권을 행사한다.

Ⅱ. 탄력적 근로시간제

1. 의의

'탄력적 근로시간제'란 어떤 근로일이나, 어떤 주의 주당 근로시간을 연장시키는 대신 다른 근로일, 다른 주의 근로시간을 단축시킴으로써, 일정 기간의 평균 근로시간을 법정기준근로시간(1주 40시간) 내로 맞추는 제도를 말한다. 예를 들어, 2주 단위 탄력적 근로시간제에서 첫째 주에 45시간(9시간×5일), 둘째 주에 35시간(7시간×5일) 근무 시, 주당 평균 근로시간이 40시간이므로,

---
[120] 김기선, 노동관계법상 근로자대표제의 규율현황 및 입법과제 국회입법조사처, 2016. 10. 64면. 대법원 1994.6.24. 선고 92다28556 판결
[121] 행정해석 근로기준정책과-1356,2021.05.07.

if you work 45 hours (9 hours x 5 days) in the first week and 35 hours (7 hours x 5 days) in the second week, they will equal 40 hours per week on average, meaning an overtime allowance will not have to be paid for the 5 extended working hours in the first week.

From the perspective of workers, it is easy to utilize leisure time by reducing working hours, decreasing the number of commuting days, and increasing holidays, while they face changes in biorhythm that cause greater fatigue while their real wages decrease due to reduced overtime allowance. From the perspective of employers, it is possible to reduce labor costs by increasing the efficiency of working hours and reducing the demand for overtime by arranging working hours to proactively respond to market conditions and management, avoiding a fixed statutory time system that is too strict.

The flexible working hour system is designed to increase efficiency in a workforce by adjusting the length of working time according to seasonal, monthly, or daily fluctuations in workload.

Under it, the employee works additional hours the legal standard working hours for a specific period such as two weeks, one month or three months on the condition that the average working hours for a certain period of a day or week shall not exceed the standard working hours. In this case, the employer is not violating the working hour rules of the LSA, nor is he/she obliged to pay an additional allowance for the extended hours. This system is designed to benefit the employer by allowing him/her to adjust working hours according to seasonal changes in production volume.

2. Introducing a Flexible Working Hour System

Article 51 (Flexible Working Hour System)
① An employer may have a worker work in accordance with the rules of employment (or in accordance with rules or regulations equivalent thereto) for a specific week in excess of working hours prescribed in Article 50 (1), or for a specific day in excess of working hours prescribed in Article 50 (2), on condition that average working hours per week in a certain unit period of not more than two weeks do not exceed the working hours under Article 50 (1), and provided that working hours

첫째 주에 법정근로시간을 초과한 5시간 분에 대한 가산수당이 발생하지 않는다.

근로자의 입장에서는 실 근로시간 단축, 출퇴근일수의 감소 및 휴일의 증가로 여가활용이 쉬워지는 장점이 있는 반면, 근로시간 변경에 따른 생체리듬 변화, 피로증대, 연장근로수당의 지급축소에 따른 실질 임금이 감소되는 단점이 있다. 사용자의 입장에서는 고정적 법정 기준시간제도가 가지는 엄격성을 탈피하여 시장 상황, 경영 등에 탄력적으로 대응하도록 근로시간을 배치하여 근로시간의 효율성을 높이고 연장근로수요를 줄임으로써 인건비 절감이 가능하다는 장점이 있다.

탄력적 근로시간제는 계절별·월별·요일별 업무량의 변화가 있는 경우에 근로시간을 탄력적으로 배치함으로써 효율적인 인력관리를 하려는 데 그 목적이 있다.

탄력적 근로시간제란 2주간, 1개월간, 3개월간 등과 같이 일정한 기간을 평균하여 1일간 또는 1주일간 근로시간이 법정기준 근로시간을 초과하지 않으면 특정일 또는 특정 주에 기준근로시간을 초과하더라도 근로시간 위반이 아님은 물론 초과한 시간에 대해 연장근로에 대한 가산수당을 지급하지 않아도 되는 장점이 있는 제도이다. 일이 많을 때는 근로를 길게 하고 일이 적을 때는 근로시간을 짧게 하는 등 근로시간 운용에 탄력성을 부여하기 위한 제도이다.

2. 도입방법

근로기준법: 제51조【탄력적 근로시간제】
① 사용자는 취업규칙(취업규칙에 준하는 것을 포함한다)에서 정하는 바에 따라 2주 이내의 일정한 단위기간을 평균하여 1주 간의 근로시간이 제50조 제 1항의 근로시간을 초과하지 아니하는 범위에서 특정한 주에 제50조 제 1항의 근로시간을, 특정한 날에 제5조 제 2항의 근로시간을 초과하여 근로하게 할 수 있다. 다만, 특정한 주의 근로시간은 48시간을 초과할 수 없다.

Chapter 4   Flexible Working Hours

in any particular week shall not exceed forty-eight hours.

② Where an employer reaches an agreement in writing with a workers' representative on the following enumerated items, the employer is allowed to have a worker work for a specific week in excess of the working hours under Article 50 (1), or for a specific day in excess of the working hours under Article 50 (2), on the condition that average working hours per week in a certain unit period of not more than three months do not exceed the working hours under Article 50 (1). However, working hours for a specific week, and for a specific day shall not exceed fifty-two hours and twelve hours respectively:

1. scope of workers subject to this paragraph:
2. unit period (a unit period not exceeding three months):
3. working days in a unit period and working hours for each working day: and 4. other matters prescribed by Presidential Decree.

③ The provisions of paragraphs (1) and (2) shall not apply to workers aged between fifteen and eighteen, and pregnant female workers.

④ If an employer needs to have a worker work in accordance with the provisions of paragraphs (1) and (2), the employer shall prepare measures to ensure that the existing wage level is not lowered.

Enforcement Decree

Article 28 (Agreed-upon Matters regarding Flexible Work Hours System)

① "Other matters prescribed by Presidential Decree" in Article 51 (2) 4 of the Act mean the valid period of a written agreement.

② If necessary for deciding on whether or not to devise measures to ensure the existing wage level as prescribed in Article 51 (4) of the Act, the Minister of Employment and Labor may order the employer to present the contents of such measures, or may check them directly.

An employer may adopt "flexitime" on a 2-week basis by modifying the rules of employment and on a 3-month basis by reaching agreement with the employee representative. In a flexitime scheme on a 2-week basis, the hours of work in a

② 사용자는 근로자대표와의 서면 합의에 따라 다음 각 호의 사항을 정하면 3개월 이내의 단위기간을 평균하여 1주 간의 근로시간이 제5조 제1항의 근로시간을 초과하지 아니하는 범위에서 특정한 주에 제50조 제1항의 근로시간을, 특정한 날에 제50조 제2항의 근로시간을 초과하여 근로하게 할 수 있다. 다만, 특정한 주의 근로시간은 52시간을, 특정한 날의 근로시간은 12시간을 초과할 수 없다.
   1. 대상 근로자의 범위
   2. 단위기간(3개월 이내의 일정한 기간으로 정하여야 한다)
   3. 단위기간의 근로일과 그 근로일별 근로시간
   4. 그 밖에 대통령령으로 정하는 사항
③ 제1항과 제2항은 15세 이상 18세 미만의 근로자와 임신 중인 여성 근로자에 대하여는 적용하지 아니한다.
④ 사용자는 제1항 및 제2항에 따라 근로자를 근로시킬 경우에는 기존의 임금 수준이 낮아지지 아니하도록 임금보전방안(賃金補塡方案)을 강구하여야 한다.

시행령

제28조【탄력적 근로시간제에 관한 합의사항 등】
① 법 제51조 제 각 호의 2항제4호에서 "그 밖에 대통령령으로 정하는 사항"이란 서면 합의의 유효기간을 말한다.
② 고용노동부장관은 법 제5조 제4항에 따른 임금보전방안을 강구하게 하기 위하여 필요한 경우에는 사용자에게 그 보전방안의 내용을 제출하도록 명하거나 직접 확인할 수 있다.

취업규칙 변경을 통하여 2주 이내 단위의 탄력적 근로시간 제도를, 근로자대표와의 합의를 통하여 3개월 이내 단위의 탄력적 근로시간 제도를 도입하여 운영할 수 있다. 취업규칙(2주 단위) 또는 근로자대표와의 서면합의(3개월 단위)에 의하여 탄력적 근로시간제를 도입하는 경우, 일정한 기간(2주 또는 3개월)을 평균하여 1주간의 근로시간이 40시간을 초과하지 않는 범위 내에서 1일 8시간, 1주 40시간을 초과하여 근로 시킬 수 있다. 다만, 2주 단위의

Chapter 4 Flexible Working Hours

particular week may not exceed 48; in a flexitime scheme on a 3-month basis, the hours of work in a particular week and on a particular day may not exceed, respectively, 52 and 12 (Article 51 of the LSA).

(1) Introduction of flexible working hours up to two weeks

Flexible working time up to two weeks can be prepared through the establishment and revision of employment rules. In order to introduce this system through the employment rules, the opinion of the labor union representing the majority of workers or an employee representative representing the majority of workers shall be heard, and consent obtained if introduction of the system will disadvantage the workers.

(2) Introduction of flexible working hours up to 3 months

This system requires a labor-management agreement. The employer shall receive a written agreement from the labor union which comprises a majority of the workers, or the employee representative representing the majority of workers. The contents of the written agreement shall include (i) the scope of the affected workforce, (ii) the unit period, (iii) the working day in the unit period, and the working hours for each working day, and (iv) the validity period of the written agreement.

1) The scope of the covered workers does not necessarily have to include all workers, and can apply only to some workers engaged in certain business sectors, industries and occupations. However, it cannot apply to young workers (between 15 and 18 years old) and pregnant women workers.

2) Since the unit period is up to 3 months, it can be implemented in various unit periods such as 3 months, 2 months, 1 month, or 3 weeks.

3) The working days and working hours for each working day shall be specified. Workers shall be notified of the work schedule before the start of the unit period by specifying the work day by work type and working hours by work day in the work schedule. Working hours in a particular week may not exceed 52, and working hours on a particular day shall not exceed 12. If more than that, an overtime allowance shall be paid.

4) There is no special limitation on the validity of a written agreement. If an expiration date is set, an automatic renewal clause or an auto-expansion clause may be provided if the expiration date has passed.

탄력적 근로시간제의 경우 특정주의 근로시간이 48시간을 초과할 수 없고, 3월 단위의 탄력적 근로시간제의 경우 특정주의 근로시간은 52시간을, 특정일의 근로시간은 12시간을 초과할 수 없다.

(1) 2주 이내 탄력적 근로시간제 도입

2주 이내 탄력적 근로시간제는 취업규칙의 작성 및 변경을 통하여 도입할 수 있다. 취업규칙을 통해 제도를 도입하고자 할 때에는 근로자 과반수를 대표하는 노동조합 또는 근로자 과반수의 의견을 들어야 하며, 동 제도 도입으로 근로자에게 불이익하게 작용하는 경우에도 그 동의를 얻어야 한다.

(2) 3개월 이내 탄력적 근로시간제 도입

3개월 이내 탄력적 근로시간제의 경우는 노사 서면합의로 도입하여야 하는데, 서면합의하여야 할 대상은 근로자의 과반수로 조직된 노동조합이 있는 경우에는 그 노동조합, 그렇지 않은 경우에는 근로자 과반수를 대표하는 자가 이에 해당한다. 서면합의 내용에 포함해야 할 사항은 (ⅰ) 대상근로자의 범위, (ⅱ) 단위기간, (ⅲ) 단위기간에 있어서의 근로일 및 그 근로일별 근로시간, (ⅳ) 서면합의의 유효기간이다.

1) 대상근로자의 범위는 반드시 전체 근로자를 대상으로 하여야 하는 것은 아니어서 일정 사업부문, 업종, 직종 등에 따라서 그에 종사하는 일부 근로자에 한하여만 적용할 수 있다. 다만, 연소근로자(15세 이상 18세 미만) 및 임신 중인 여성근로자에게는 적용할 수 없다.
2) 단위기간은 3개월 이내의 기간이므로 3개월 단위, 2개월 단위, 1개월 단위, 3주 단위 등 다양한 단위기간으로 실시 가능하다.
3) 근로일 및 근로 일별 근로시간을 명시해야 한다. 근무일정표에 근무형태별 근무일과 근무일별 근로시간을 명시한 근무일정을 단위기간 개시 전까지 근로자에게 고지하면 된다. 특정 주의 근무시간이 52시간을, 특정일의 근로시간이 12시간을 초과할 수 없으며, 초과할 경우 연장근로에 해당한다.
4) 서면합의 유효기간에 대해서는 특별한 제한이 없다. 또한 유효기간을 설정하는 경우 유효기간이 경과할 경우를 대비하여 자동갱신 조항을 두거나 자동연장조항을 둘 수 있다.

Chapter 4 Flexible Working Hours

	Two week flexible working hour system	Three month flexible working hour system (or less)
Concept	Two-week flexible working hours can be efficiently used anytime without employees' additional consent.	This system is extended to flexible working hours longer than two weeks, which is effective when used in seasonal business, construction, exporting companies, etc.
Eligibility	① Specified in the rules of employment ② Equal to or less than 48 hours per week ③ Specific weeks and days fixed	① An employer shall obtain a written agreement from the employee representative on the following items: - Scope of the employees affected; - Unit period; - Working days in the unit period and working hours for each working day; and - Effective period of the written agreement ② To a maximum of 3 months ③ Working hours do not exceed 52 per week, 12 per day
Effect	① Exclusion of additional allowances - No obligation for an additional allowance is given for extended working hours exceeding legal standard hours for a specific week or a specific day. ② Measures to maintain current wages - An employer shall take measures to ensure that the existing wage level is not lowered (Paragraph ④ of Article 51, LSA). - The above rules are instructions without penalty, which is subject to administrative rules of the Labor Office	
Except-ions	① Minor (Ages 15 to 18) ② Pregnant employees	

구분	2주 단위 탄력적 근로시간제	3월이내 단위 탄력적 근로시간제
의의	2주 단위 탄력적 근로시간제는 취업규칙에서 정하는 바에 의해 실시되므로, 근로자들의 별도의 동의 없이 유용하게 활용할 수 있다.	이 제도는 2주단위 탄력적 근로시간제 보다 탄력성의 범위를 넓힌 것으로서 주로 계절적 사업, 건설업, 수출산업 등에서 유용하게 활용할 수 있다.
실시 요건	① 취업규칙에서 규정해야 함. ② 1주 48시간 이내일 것 ③ 특정주, 특정일을 명확히 지정할 것	① 근로자대표와 아래 사항을 서면 합의 - 대상근로자의 범위 - 단위기간 - 근로일 및 근로일별 근로시간 - 서면합의 유효기간 ② 3월 이내 ③ 1주52시간, 1일 12시간을 초과하지 못함
실시 효과	① 가산임금 적용제외 - 특정주 또는 특정일에 법정기준근로시간을 초과하여 근로 하더라도 연장근로가 아니므로 가산임금을 지급할 의무가 없음 ② 임금보전방안 강구 - 사용자는 탄력적 근로시간제를 도입할 경우 기존의 임금수준이 저하되지 않도록 임금보전방안을 강구해야 함(근로기준법 제51조 제4항) - 위의 조항은 벌칙규정이 없는 훈시규정	
적용 제외	① 연소자(15세 이상 18세 미만자) ② 임신 중인 여성 근로자	

Chapter 4 Flexible Working Hours

(3) Flexible Work Hours System Exceeding Three Months

Labor Standards Act: Article 51-2 (Flexible Work Hours System Exceeding Three Months) (1) When an employer has determined matters falling under the following subparagraphs by a written agreement with the representative of employees, the employer may extend work hours in excess of those as referred to in Article 50 (1) in a particular week, or may extend work hours in excess of those as referred to in Article 50 (2) in a particular day, to the extent that average work hours per week during a certain unit period of more than three months and not more than six months that do not exceed the work hours referred to in Article 50 (1): Provided, That work hours in any particular week or in any particular day shall not exceed 52 hours or 12 hours respectively:
1. The scope of employees to whom the agreement is applicable.
2. Unit period (It shall be determined as a fixed period within six months and exceeding three months);
3. Work hours by week during the unit period;
4. Other matters prescribed by Presidential Decree.
② If an employer orders a worker to work pursuant to paragraph (1), the employer shall give the worker an 11-hour or more of an uninterrupted recess starting from the end of a working day until the beginning of the next working day: Provided, That if it is inevitable to be prescribed by Presidential Decree, such as a natural disaster, it shall be followed if there is a written agreement with the representative of employees.
③ An employer shall notify an employee of the work hours of each working day of the relevant week by not later than two weeks before the beginning of the working days of each week referred to in paragraph (1) 3.
④ When there arises an unavoidable cause, such as a natural disaster, mechanical malfunction, and rapid increase in the quantity of work, which was unexpected at the time of a written agreement with the representative of employees referred to in paragraph (1), the employer may change the matters referred to in paragraph (1) 3 after consulting with the representative of employees within the unit period of paragraph (1) 2. In such cases, the relevant employee shall be notified of the changed work hours of each working day before the changed working day commences.

(3) 3개월 초과하는 탄력적 근로시간제

근로기준법: 제51조의2(3개월을 초과하는 탄력적 근로시간제) ① 사용자는 근로자대표와의 서면 합의에 따라 다음 각 호의 사항을 정하면 3개월을 초과하고 6개월 이내의 단위기간을 평균하여 1주간의 근로시간이 제50조제1항의 근로시간을 초과하지 아니하는 범위에서 특정한 주에 제50조제1항의 근로시간을, 특정한 날에 제50조제2항의 근로시간을 초과하여 근로하게 할 수 있다. 다만, 특정한 주의 근로시간은 52시간을, 특정한 날의 근로시간은 12시간을 초과할 수 없다.
1. 대상 근로자의 범위
2. 단위기간(3개월을 초과하고 6개월 이내의 일정한 기간으로 정하여야 한다)
3. 단위기간의 주별 근로시간
4. 그 밖에 대통령령으로 정하는 사항

② 사용자는 제1항에 따라 근로자를 근로시킬 경우에는 근로일 종료 후 다음 근로일 개시 전까지 근로자에게 연속하여 11시간 이상의 휴식 시간을 주어야 한다. 다만, 천재지변 등 대통령령으로 정하는 불가피한 경우에는 근로자대표와의 서면 합의가 있으면 이에 따른다.

③ 사용자는 제1항제3호에 따른 각 주의 근로일이 시작되기 2주 전까지 근로자에게 해당 주의 근로일별 근로시간을 통보하여야 한다.

④ 사용자는 제1항에 따른 근로자대표와의 서면 합의 당시에는 예측하지 못한 천재지변, 기계 고장, 업무량 급증 등 불가피한 사유가 발생한 때에는 제1항제2호에 따른 단위기간 내에서 평균하여 1주간의 근로시간이 유지되는 범위에서 근로자대표와의 협의를 거쳐 제1항제3호의 사항을 변경할 수 있다. 이 경우 해당 근로자에게 변경된 근로일이 개시되기 전에 변경된 근로일별 근로시간을 통보하여야 한다.

⑤ 사용자는 제1항에 따라 근로자를 근로시킬 경우에는 기존의 임금

⑤ Every employer shall, if the employer employs an employee falling under paragraph (1), adjust or establish wage items so that the existing wage level does not decrease, or prepare wage conservation measures such as payment of additional wages and report them to the Minister of Employment and Labor: Provided, That the foregoing shall not apply where a plan for wage conservation has been prepared by a written agreement with the representative of employees.

⑥ The provisions of paragraphs (1) through (5) shall not apply to employees aged 15 years or older and under 18 years or to female employees who are pregnant.

<LMC: Presidential Decree>

Article 28-2 (Matters Agreed upon Flexible Work Hours System Exceeding Three Months) (1) "Other matters prescribed by Presidential Decree" in Article 51-2 (1) 4 of the Act means the effective term of a written agreement.

(2) "if it is inevitable to be prescribed by a presidential decree, such as a natural disaster" in the proviso of Article 51-2 (2) of the Act means the following:
1. Where emergency measures are required to prevent disasters or corresponding accidents prescribed in the Framework Act on the Management of Disasters and Safety, which occurred or are likely to occur, in order to prevent such disasters or accidents;
2. Where an emergency measure is required to protect human life or to ensure safety;
3. Where it is deemed difficult to give a break time under the main clause of Article 51-2 (2) of the Act due to reasons falling under subparagraphs 1 and 2 of the Act.

3. Cases of Use

(1) At a brick factory[122]

"We are using sand, special cement, and water to make differentiated bricks in the factory. In January each year, temperatures drop below 20 degrees below zero, and when the water completely freezes at 20 degrees below zero, it is almost impossible to produce bricks. So, workers come to work normally and perform

---

[122] Kim, Boksoo, "Practical Use of the Flexible Working Hour System," Labor Law, June 2018.

수준이 낮아지지 아니하도록 임금항목을 조정 또는 신설하거나 가산임금 지급 등의 임금보전방안(賃金補塡方案)을 마련하여 고용노동부장관에게 신고하여야 한다. 다만, 근로자대표와의 서면합의로 임금보전방안을 마련한 경우에는 그러하지 아니하다.
⑥ 제1항부터 제5항까지의 규정은 15세 이상 18세 미만의 근로자와 임신 중인 여성 근로자에 대해서는 적용하지 아니한다.

시행령

제28조의2(3개월을 초과하는 탄력적 근로시간제에 관한 합의사항 등)
① 법 제51조의2제1항제4호에서 "그 밖에 대통령령으로 정하는 사항"이란 서면 합의의 유효기간을 말한다.
② 법 제51조의2제2항 단서에서 "천재지변 등 대통령령으로 정하는 불가피한 경우"란 다음 각 호의 어느 하나에 해당하는 경우를 말한다.
 1. 「재난 및 안전관리 기본법」에 따른 재난 또는 이에 준하는 사고가 발생하여 이를 수습하거나 재난 등의 발생이 예상되어 이를 예방하기 위해 긴급한 조치가 필요한 경우
 2. 사람의 생명을 보호하거나 안전을 확브하기 위해 긴급한 조치가 필요한 경우
 3. 그 밖에 제1호 및 제2호에 준하는 사유로 법 제51조의2제2항 본문에 따른 휴식 시간을 주는 것이 어렵다고 인정되는 경우

3. 활용방법

(1) 벽돌공장 도입사례[122]

"우리 공장은 모래, 시멘트 특수원료, 물을 배합해서 차별화된 벽돌을 만들고 있다. 그런데 매년 1월이 되면 기온이 영하 20도 밑으로 내려가고 영하 20도에서는 물이 완전히 얼어 버리기 때문에 벽돌 생산을 할 수가 없다. 그렇지만, 직원들은 정상적으로 출근해서 청소 등 잡무를 수행한다. 그런데

---

[122] 김복수, "탄력적 근로시간제도의 실무적 활용", <노동법률>, 2018년 6월호,

Chapter 4 Flexible Working Hours

chores such as cleaning rather than producing bricks. But in March, the situation is completely different. As construction starts in earnest, there is no choice but to work overtime due to the large volume of brick orders." In this company, a flexible working hour system can solve the problem. Workers work 30 hours per week in January, 40 hours per week in February, and 50 hours per week in March. In this case, the average working hours per week are 40, and so the company is not obligated to pay overtime allowance in March, even though their weekly work exceeds 40 hours.

(2) Luxury brand stores

December is the peak season, and so customers shop a lot and store workers work overtime. On the other hand, January is off-season and customers don't go to luxury brand stores, leaving workers with not much to do. In these stores, the introduction of flexible working hours can reduce labor costs and increase work efficiency. In December, during the peak season, workers work 52 hours a week, but in January, the off-season, workers can work 28 hours a week.

<Table 4-1> Rules of Employment on Flexible Working Hours for 2-Week Units

Article ○○ (Flexible Working Hour System)
① The Company shall provide the following for workers in production for ○ months from ○ (month) to ○ (month). A flexible working hour system is implemented every two weeks as prescribed in each subparagraph.
   1. Working hours per week: 48 hours in the first week, 32 hours in the second week
   2. Working hours per day in the first week: ○○ hours from ○ (day) to ○ (day) (from ○○:○○ to ○○:○○)
   3. Working hours per day in the second week: ○○ hours from ○ (day) to ○ (day) (from ○○:○○ to ○○:○○)
② The Company shall consider that 8 hours were worked even if the worker worked ○○ hours in the first week in accordance with paragraph 1. No additional allowance will be paid for overtime.
③ Employees aged between 15 and 18 and pregnant workers shall not be placed into a flexible working hour system.
④ The period of validity for this system is one year from the time the system is applied

3월이 되면 상황이 완전히 달라진다. 건설공사가 본격적으로 시작되기 때문에 벽돌 주문이 밀려들어 연장근로를 할 수 밖에 없다." 이러한 회사의 경우 탄력적 근로시간제도를 통해서 문제를 해결할 수 있다. 1월은 주당 30시간, 2월은 주당 40시간, 3월은 주당 50시간 근로한다. 이 경우 주 평균이 40시간이 되기 때문에 회사는 주당 40시간을 초과하는 3월에도 연장수당을 지급해야 할 의무가 없다.

(2) 명품매장의 도입사례

연말인 12월은 성수기라 고객들이 쇼핑을 많이 하기 때문에 일손이 많아 직원들은 연장근로를 한다. 이에 반해 1월에는 비수기라 고객들이 매장을 많이 찾지 않기 때문에 매장은 한가한 편이다. 이러한 매장의 경우, 탄력적 근로시간제를 도입하여 인건비를 줄이고 업무의 효율을 가져올 수 있다. 성수기인 12월에는 매 주 52시간을 근무하고, 비수기인 1월은 매 주 28시간을 근무하게 한다면 매장의 생산성을 향상시킬 수 있다.

<표4-1> 2주 이내 탄력적 근로시간제 취업규칙

제○○조(탄력적 근로시간제)
① 회사는 ○월부터 ○월까지 ○개월 동안 생산직 사원에 대하여 다음 각 호에 정하는 바에 따라 2주 단위의 탄력적 근로시간제를 시행한다.
  1. 주당 근무시간 : 첫째 주 ○○시간, 둘째 주 ○○시간
  2. 첫째 주의 1일 근무시간 : ○요일부터 ○요일까지 ○○시간(○○:○○부터 ○○:○○까지)
  3. 둘째 주의 1일 근무시간 : ○요일부터 ○요일까지 ○○시간(○○:○○부터 ○○:○○까지)
② 회사는 제1항에 따라 사원이 첫째 주에 ○○시간을 근무한 경우 8시간을 초과한 시간에 대하여는 가산수당을 지급하지 아니한다.
③ 15세 이상 18세 미만의 사원과 임신 중인 여성사원은 탄력적 근로시간제를 적용하지 아니한다.
④ 본 제도의 유효기간은 제도 적용 시점부터 1년으로 한다.

Chapter 4 Flexible Working Hours

<Table 4-2> Labor-Management Agreement on Flexible Working Hours for 3-Month Units

The Company and worker representative agree to the following regarding flexible working hours for up to 3 months at a time.

Article 1 (Purpose) This Agreement is designed to stipulate the rules necessary to implement flexible working hours in 3-month units in accordance with Article 51 (2) of the Labor Standards Act.

Article 2 (Scope of Application) This Agreement applies to all production workers.

Article 3 (Unit Period) The unit period of this Agreement is from the beginning of each quarter to the end of each quarter.

Article 4 (Working Hours) Flexible Working Hours in 3-month units are described in the following table for each day of work, start time, finish time and recess hour.

	Daily working hours	Start time	Finish time	Recess hour
○ month	First day ~last day: 7 hours (Mon~Fri)	09:00	17:00	12:00~13:00
○ month	First day ~last day: 8 hours (Mon~Fri)	09:00	18:00	12:00~13:00
○ month	First day ~last day: 9 hours (Mon~Fri)	09:00	19:00	12:00~13:00

Article 5 (Holidays) The Company shall be closed two days a week (Saturdays and Sundays) during the unit period, but only Sundays shall be paid holidays.

Article 6 (Exclusions) This Agreement does not apply to minority-age (15 to 18 years old) or pregnant workers.

Article 7 (Additional Wages for Overtime) In the event the set working hours of a particular day are exceeded, overtime pay shall consist of the ordinary wage +50% for each hour worked above the set working hours.

Article 8 (Overtime, Night, Holiday Work) Overtime, nighttime, and holiday work will be compensated in accordance with overtime allowance as specified in Article 56 of the Labor Standards Act and Article ○○ of the Rules of Employment.

<표4-2> 3개월 이내 탄력적 근로시간제 노사합의서

주식회사 ○○ 대표이사와 근로자대표는 3월 단위 탄력적 근로시간제에 관하여 다음과 같이 합의한다.

제1조 (목적) 이 합의서는 근로기준법 제51조 제2항에 따라 3월 단위 탄력적 근로시간제를 실시하는데 필요한 사항을 정하는 것을 목적으로 한다.

제2조 (적용대상자) 이 합의서의 내용은 전체 생산직 근로자에 적용한다.

제3조 (단위기간) 이 합의서의 단위기간은 대 분기 초일부터 매 분기 말일까지로 한다.

제4조 (근로시간) 3월 단위 탄력적 근로시간제 단위기간에 있어 1일의 근로 시간, 시업시간, 종업시간 및 휴게시간은 다음과 같다.

구분	1일 근로시간	시업시간	종업시간	휴게시간
○월	1일~말일 7시간(월~금)	09:00	17:00	12:00~13:00
○월	1일~말일 8시간(월~금)	09:00	18:00	12:00~13:00
○월	1일~말일 9시간(월~금)	09:00	19:00	12:00~13:00

제5조(휴일) 단위기간 중 주 2일(토.일요일)은 휴무하되, 휴일은 일요일로 한다.

제6조(적용제외) 연소근로자(15세 이상 18세 미만)와 임신 중인 여성 근로자에게는 본 합의를 적용하지 아니한다.

제7조(연장근로 가산임금) 근로일별 근로하기로 정한 시간을 초과한 경우 통상임금의 50%를 가산임금으로 지급한다.

제8조(연장.야간.휴일근로) 연장.야간.휴일근로에 대해서는 근로기준법 제56조 및 취업규칙 제○○조에 따라 가산하여 지급한다.

Chapter 4 Flexible Working Hours

> Article 9 (Effective Period) The period of validity for this Agreement shall be one year from _____ (date).
>
> Signed on _____ (date).
>
> Company Representative _____   Worker Representative _____

III. Selective Working Hour System

1. Purpose

The selective working hour system is a system that, by setting only the total working hours of the settlement period within one month, allows workers to select their own working time for days and for weeks within the standard working time range, and to freely determine the commute time of each day and each week. In other words, the system sets only the total working hours within one month and leaves the start and end times of working hours up to the workers. A selective working hour system therefore gives workers the choice of specific commute time, which enables them to increase work efficiency and improve their quality of life.

The selective working hour system introduced in Korea allows employees to decide for themselves the time of their arrival and departure from the office, or choose the daily working hours within the range of total working hours described by a specific period unit within one month. This system is useful in helping professionals or business managers improve work efficiency and providing housewives with work opportunities. Under this system, employees have convenience in commuting and the right to a more relaxing social life, while the employer benefits from higher productivity and a reduction in inefficient working hours.

2. Types of Selective Working Hour Systems

> 제9조(유효기간) 이 합의서의 유효기간은 ○○○○년 ○월 ○일부터 1년간으로 한다.
>
> 20○○. . .
>
> 주식회사 ○○ 대표이사_____(인)   근로자대표_____ (인)

Ⅲ. 선택적 근로시간제

1. 의의

   선택적 근로시간제란 1개월 이내의 정산기간의 총 근로시간만을 정하고 각 일, 각 주의 출퇴근 시각을 자유롭게 결정하여 기준근로시간 범위에서, 근로자가 근로시간을 임의로 선택할 수 있는 제도로 1개월 이내의 총 근로시간만 정하고 근로시간의 시작 및 종료시각을 근로자의 결정에 맡기는 제도이다. 따라서 선택적 근로시간제는 구체적으로 출퇴근 시각에 대한 근로자의 선택권을 인정함으로써 근로자가 일과 생활의 조화를 이루어 업무의 효율성을 높이고 삶의 질을 향상시킬 수 있다.

   우리나라에서 도입하고 있는 선택적 근로시간제는 1개월 이내의 일정기간 단위로 정하여진 총 근로시간 범위 내에서 출·퇴근시간 및 1일의 근로시간을 근로자가 자율적으로 결정할 수 있는 제도로 전문직·사무관리직 등의 업무 능률향상과 주부의 취업을 용이하게 할 수 있다는 장점이 있다. 이 제도를 도입할 경우 근로자에게는 출·퇴근 편의나 여유 있는 사회생활의 기회가 주어지고, 경영자에게는 생산성 증대나 낭비 작업시간의 감소 등의 효과가 있어 사회 전체의 생산성이 증가될 것이다.

2. 선택적 근로시간제의 종류

Chapter 4　Flexible Working Hours

1) Fully selective working hour system

Under a fully selective working hour system, the employee decides on the commuting hours during the period of flexible working hours and the employer does not interfere with the allocation of employee working hours. That is, there is no mandatory range of working hours other than the selective working hours.

2) Partly selective working hour system

Under a partly selective working hour system, the employee is entrusted with the decision to begin and finish tasks, while receiving hourly supervision and concrete job directions from the employer during specified hours. However, during a different range of working hours, the employee decides when to begin and finish work and arranges the amount of working hours.

The mandatory range of working hours is called the "core time," while the selective range is called the "flexible time." Usually, the core time and flexible time are settled automatically through a written agreement between employer and employee. The employer makes the most of the core time, during which he/she can give necessary orders and manage meetings, directions, etc.

3. Introducing a Selective Working Hour System

(1) Introduction through the rules of employment

Employers shall stipulate that the start and end times of work are left to the worker's decision for a group of workers subject to selective working hours through the establishment or revision of employment rules.

(2) Written agreement with the employee representative

To introduce the selective working hour system, a written agreement with the labor union or worker representative representing the majority of the workers is required. The written agreement shall include (i) scope of workers subject to this system, (ii) adjustment period (within one month), and the total working hours within an adjustment period, (iii) starting and finishing time of working hours, if a mandatory work period is in force (core time), (iv) starting and finishing time of working hours which are allowed to be selected by workers (selective time), and (iv) standard working hours to form the basis for granting paid leave.

1) 완전 선택적 근로시간제

정산기간 중에 출·퇴근이 근로자의 결정에 맡겨 있고 근로자의 근로시간배열에 사용자가 관여하지 않는 선택적 근로시간제로 의무 근로시간대는 없고 선택적 근로시간대만 있는 경우를 말한다.

2) 부분 선택적 근로시간제

정산기간 중의 출·퇴근을 근로자의 결정에 맡긴 상태에서 일정한 시간대를 정하여 그 시간에는 근로자가 사용자로부터 시간적 구속과 구체적 업무지시를 받고 나머지 시간에 대해서는 출·퇴근 및 근로시간 배열이 근로자의 결정에 맡겨지는 근로시간제를 말한다.

근로자가 의무적으로 출근해야 하는 시간대를 의무적 근로시간대(Core Time), 재량에 맡겨진 시간대를 선택적 근로시간대(Flexible time)라고 부른다. 선택적 근로시간대와 의무적 근로시간대를 구분하여 설정하는 것은 노·사가 서면합의를 통해 자율적으로 결정할 사항이며, 회의, 지시사항 등 필요한 지휘명령을 위하여 의무 근로시간대를 설정한다.

3. 도입방법

(1) 취업규칙을 통해 도입

사용자는 취업규칙의 작성 또는 변경을 통해 선택적 근로시간제의 대상이 되는 근로자 집단에 대해 업무의 시작 및 종료시각을 근로자의 결정에 맡긴다는 내용을 기재하여야 한다.

(2) 근로자대표와의 서면합의

선택적 근로시간제를 도입하려면 근로자의 과반수를 대표하는 노동조합 또는 근로자대표와 서면합의를 해야 한다. 서면합의 내용에 포함되어야 할 사항은 (ⅰ) 대상근로자의 범위, (ⅱ) 정산기간(1개월 이내) 및 그 기간에 있어 총 근로시간, (ⅲ) 반드시 근로하여야 할 시간대를 정한 경우에는 그 시작 및 종료시각(core time), (ⅳ) 근로자가 그의 결정에 따라 근로할 수 있는 시간대를 정하는 경우에는 그 시작 및 종료시각(selective time), (ⅴ) 유급휴가 부여 등의 기준이 되는 표준근로시간이다.

Chapter 4 Flexible Working Hours

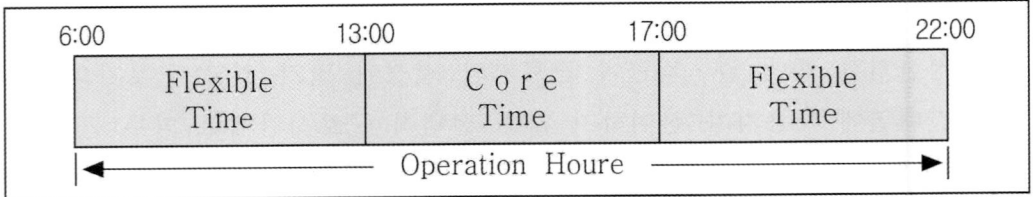

1) The scope of the covered workers: In general, it is easy to apply the system to managers, supervisors who do not have strict restrictions on commuting, etc., and professional, research, and office workers who place more emphasis on quality than the amount of work. However, this system can be introduced at any workplace.

The Labor Standards Act:
Article 52 (Selective Working Hour System)
   Where an employer has reached a written agreement on each of the following subparagraphs with the workers' representative regarding a worker who is entrusted with the decision as to when to begin and finish work in accordance with the rules of employment (including those equivalent to rules of employment), the employer may have workers work in excess of the working hours per week set by paragraph (1) of Article 50, or the working hours per day set by paragraph (2) of Article 50 on the condition that average working hours per week computed on the basis of adjustment period of not more than one month do not exceed the working hours prescribed in paragraph (1) of Article 50:
1. scope of workers subject to this paragraph (excluding workers between the age of 15 and 18);
2. adjustment period (a finite period not more than one month);
3. total working hours within an adjustment period;
4. starting and finishing time of working hours, if a mandatory work period is in force;
5. starting and finishing time of working hours which are allowed to be selected by workers; and
6. other matters as determined by Presidential Decree.

Enforcement Decree to the Labor Standards Act
Article 29 (Agreed-upon Matters regarding Selective Work Hours System)

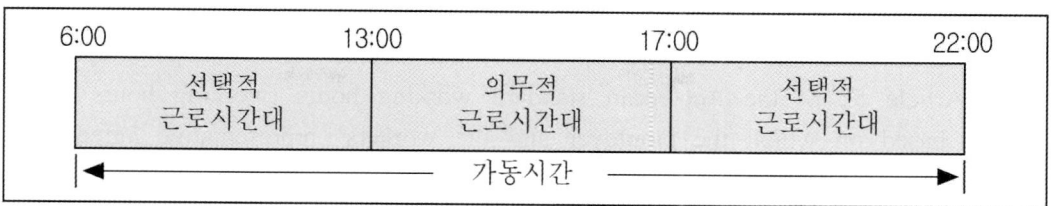

1) 대상근로자의 범위: 일반적으로 출퇴근 등에 엄격 제한을 받지 않는 관리, 감독업무 종사자, 근로의 양보다는 질이 중시되는 전문직, 연구직, 사무직 종사자 등에 제도 적용이 용이하나, 사업장 여건이 허락되는 경우 대부분 사업장에서도 도입이 가능하다.

근로기준법

제52조【선택적 근로시간제】

　사용자는 취업규칙(취업규칙에 준하는 것을 포함한다)에 따라 업무의 시작 및 종료 시각을 근로자의 결정에 맡기기로 한 근로자에 대하여 근로자대표와의 서면 합의에 따라 다음 각 호의 사항을 정하면 1개월 이내의 정산기간을 평균하여 1주간의 근로시간이 제50조 제1항의 근로시간을 초과하지 아니하는 범위에서 1주 간에 제50조 제1항의 근로시간을, 1일에 제5조 제2항의 근로시간을 초과하여 근로하게 할 수 있다.

1. 대상 근로자의 범위(15세 이상 18세 미만의 근로자는 제외한다)
2. 정산기간(1개월 이내의 일정한 기간으로 정하여야 한다)
3. 정산기간의 총 근로시간
4. 반드시 근로하여야 할 시간대를 정하는 경우에는 그 시작 및 종료 시각
5. 근로자가 그의 결정에 따라 근로할 수 있는 시간대를 정하는 경우에는 그 시작 및 종료 시각
6. 그 밖에 대통령령으로 정하는 사항

근로기준법 시행령

제29조【선택적 근로시간제에 관한 합의사항】

Chapter 4 Flexible Working Hours

> "Other matters as prescribed by Presidential Decree" under subparagraph 6 of Article 52 of the Act mean standard working hours (working hours per day based on which the employer and the workers' representative agree to calculate paid leave, etc.).

2) Settlement period and total working hours: The period for which the worker chooses to provide the work by themselves can be set to up to one month, such as two weeks or four weeks. The total working hours are usually calculated as the total sum of the contractual working hours within the settlement period (such as 40 hours x 30 days / 7 days = 171.4 hours) prior to introduction of the system. If the total working hours are set, even if the working hours exceed the legal working hours per day or per week within the total working hours of the settlement period, they will not be considered extended working hours subject to overtime allowance.
3) Core working hours and selective working hours: Core working hours is the time when the worker must work, while selective working hours is the time when the worker can decide on their own whether to provide work.
4) Standard working hours: Standard working hours refers to the one day's working hours set by labor and management, which becomes the basis for calculation of paid leave, etc. in the selective working hour system. When using paid leave, it is considered that the standard working hours of 1 day are used.

4. Using the Selective Working Hour System

If the above conditions are satisfied, the employer may extend weekly working hours to more than 40 and daily working hours beyond 8 to the extent that the average working hours per week during the period of flexible working hours within the given month do not exceed 40. In this case, additional allowance for extended work is not provided.

(1) General selective working hour system

Selective working hours are divided into mandatory working hours and selective working hours. The standard working hours, based on the calculation of paid leave, are from 09:00 to 18:00. For example, workers are given discretionary hours at 07:00-11:00 for coming to the office and 15:00-20:00 for leaving the office. The

> 법 제52 조 제6호에서 "그 밖에 대통령령으로 정하는 사항"이란 표준근로시간(유급휴가 등의 계산 기준으로 사용자와 근로자대표가 합의하여 정한 1일의 근로시간)을 말한다.

2) 정산기간, 총 근로시간: 근로자가 스스로 선택하여 근로를 제공할 정산기간을 1개월 이내에서 2주, 4주 등으로 설정할 수 있다. 총근로시간은 일반적으로 제도 도입 전을 기준으로 정산기간 상당의 소정근로시간 합계로 계산한다(예: 40시간 × 30일 / 7일 = 171.4시간). 총 근로시간을 정하게 되면 정산기간의 총 근로시간 범위 내에서 일, 주 단위 법정근로시간을 초과하여 근무하더라도 연장근로가 되지 않는다.
3) 의무 근로시간대 및 선택적 근로시간대: 의무 근로시간대는 근로자가 반드시 근로하여야 할 시간대이며, 선택 근로시간대는 근로자가 스스로의 결정에 의하여 근로제공 여부를 결정할 수 있는 시간대를 말한다.
4) 표준근로시간: 표준근로시간은 선택적 근토시간제에서 노사가 유급휴가 등의 계산기준으로 정한 1일의 근로시간을 말한다. 유급휴가 사용 시 1일의 표준근로시간을 사용한 것으로 간주한다.

4. 활용방법

상기 실시요건을 충족하는 경우 1월 이내의 총 근로시간을 평균하여 1주의 평균 근로시간이 40시간을 초과하지 아니하는 범위 안에서 근로기준법 제50조에 규정된 1주 40시간, 1일 8시간의 기준근로시간을 초과하여 연장근로할 수 있다. 이 경우에 연장근로수당이 발생하지 않는다.

(1) 의무 선택적 근로시간제

일반적 근로시간제로 의무 근로시간대와 선택 근로시간대로 나누어 운용한다. 유급휴가 등의 계산을 기준으로 삼는 표준근로시간대는 오전 9시에서 저녁 6시이다. 예를 들어, 근로자에게 재량이 주어지는 출근시간대는 오전 7시에서 오전 11시, 퇴근시간대는 오후 3시에서 저녁 8시이다. 그리고 모든 근로자가

Chapter 4 Flexible Working Hours

mandatory (core) working hours for all workers are 11:00-15:00.

(2) Jobs where it is difficult to check working hours and with significant waiting time (00 company, which specializes in renewable energy)

Employees were dissatisfied because they did not get paid overtime due to difficulty in verifying their work hours. Also, as for after-sales service, irregular overtime occurred frequently and there were many hours spent waiting. The company introduced a selective working hour system on a monthly basis for sales and after-service teams through written agreements with labor representatives after consultations between labor and management. As a result, it was possible to adjust working hours according to the work volume while reducing unnecessary waiting time and overtime, improving flexibility and efficiency in work.[123]

(3) Jobs related to types of irregular work

Company 00, which is a refrigeration facility installation and management company, works according to project schedules requested by clients and their companies due to the nature of work. There has been a lot of overtime due to irregular work schedules (including nighttime and holiday work). The company introduced a selective working hour system, which allowed each worker to manage their arrival time to work and their departure time from work according to the circumstances of their client companies. This has minimized unnecessary overtime. As a result, workers were able to adjust their working hours according to their clients' schedules, which made it possible to reduce overtime that had been due to irregular schedules.[124]

<Table 4-3> Selective Working Time Policy

1. Purpose   Selective working is the term applied to any working arrangement that

---

[123] MOEL, "Flexible Working Hour System Guides", Sept. 2019, p. 52.
[124] Ibid., pp. 53-54.

의무적으로 근무해야 하는 의무 근로시간대는 오전 11시에서 오후 3시까지이다.

(2) 근무시간 확인이 어렵고 대기시간이 많은 업종의 경우
(예 : 신재생 에너지 전문업체인 00기업)

영업직의 경우 근무시간을 확인하기 어렵다는 이유로 연장근로수당을 지급하지 않아 직원들의 불만이 많았다. 특히, A/S 업무는 업무 특성상 불규칙적인 연장근로가 자주 발생하였고 대기상태가 많았다. 이 회사는 노사 간 협의 과정을 거쳐 근로자대표와의 서면합의로 영업직과 A/S 팀을 대상으로 1개월 단위로 선택적 근로시간제를 도입하였다. 그 결과 업무량에 따른 근로시간 조정이 가능하여, 유연하고 효율적인 업무 수행으로 불필요한 대기시간 및 연장근로를 감소시켰다.[123]

(3) 불규칙적인 근로가 이루어지는 업종

냉동기기 설치와 관리 업체인 00기업은 업무 특성상 고객사 및 거래처가 원하는 프로젝트 일정에 따라 근로가 이루어져 불규칙적인 연장, 야간, 휴일 근무가 발생하는 등 장시간 근로가 많이 발생했다. 이 기업은 선택적 근로시간제를 도입하여 각 근로자가 담당하고 있는 고객사의 사정에 맞게 출, 퇴근시간을 운영할 수 있도록 하여 일률적인 출, 퇴근시간에 따른 불필요한 연장근로 발생을 최소화하였다. 그 결과, 고객사의 스케줄에 따라 근로자 스스로 근로시간을 조정할 수 있게 되어 불규칙한 근로시간에 따른 연장근로를 감소시켰다.[124]

<표4-3> 선택적 근로시간제 규정

1. 목적 　선택적 근로라는 용어는 근로자가 전통적인 근로 시간으로부터 보다 선택적인 스케줄로 이동해 갈 수 있도록 하는 근로 계약에 적용되는

---
[123] 고용노동부, "유연근로시간제 가이드", 2019.9, 52면.
[124] 고용노동부, "유연근로시간제 가이드", 2019.9, 53-54면.

Chapter 4 Flexible Working Hours

allows an employee to transfer from traditional hours to a more flexible schedule. This is only approved where the new hours, first and foremost, better suit the business requirements, and secondly, the employee's individual circumstances.

It has been recognized that more selective working patterns and practices may enable employees with primary childcare duties or other caring responsibilities to combine their personal domestic arrangements with employment needs and enable the Company to retain expertise which may otherwise be lost.

2. Eligibility

All employees, regardless of length of service, are eligible to apply for such working arrangements. However, eligibility is always discretionary, subject to the operational needs of the business and the satisfactory performance of the individual up to that time.

3. Working time range

| AM 7 | 8 | 9 | 10 | 11 | 12 | 1 | 2 | 3 | 4 | 5 | 6 | 7 PM |

Lunch Time

| Flexible | Core Time | Flexible |

Standard Time (9:00 ~ 18:00)

4. Principles & Guidelines
- Team members have to provide their working time quarterly to their team leader with the prior approval of the team leader/supervisor. HR will list up the working time plan for individuals and revise it quarterly.
- Unavoidable working time changes can be accepted with prior approval of the team leader/supervisor and notification given to HR of the revised working time.

용어이다. 이것이 승인되기 위해서는 첫째, 새로운 근로 시간이 사업의 요구사항에 잘 맞아야 하며 둘째, 근로자의 개인적인 상황과도 잘 맞아야 한다.

보다 선택적인 근로 형태와 관행은 근로자로 하여금 자녀 양육뿐만 아니라 그들의 개인적인 가정생활과 직업적인 요구를 결합하기 위한 기타 책임들을 더 잘 수행할 수 있도록 해주며, 또한 회사는 잃을지도 모르는 숙련자들을 보유할 수 있도록 하는데 기여한다.

2. 적용 대상

근무년수에 상관없이 모든 직원들은 탄력적 근로시간을 신청할 수 있다. 그러나 그러한 자격은 사업 운영상의 요구와 개인의 현재까지의 만족스러운 업무 성과에 따라 항상 임의적으로 결정된다.

3. 근로 시간대

4. 원칙 및 지침
- 팀원들은 부서장으로부터 사전 승인을 득한 후 부서장에게 분기마다 본인의 근로 시간을 제출해야 한다. 인사부는 분기마다 개인의 근로 시간 계획을 취합하여 재검토할 것이다.
- 어쩔 수 없는 근로 시간 변경은 부서장이나 상사의 사전 승인이 있으면 허용될 수 있으며, 수정된 근로 시간은 인사부에 반드시 통보한다.
- 모든 근로자는 핵심 시간 (오전 10시 ~ 오후 5시)은 반드시 지켜야 한다.

Chapter 4 Flexible Working Hours

- The core time (10:00 AM ~ 17:00 PM) has to be kept by all employees.
- Starting and closing times must be observed by all employees, in keeping with the mutual agreement between labor and management.
- Exemptions can be arranged for business trips or work performed off Company premises.
- This selective working time system will begin Jan. 01, 2020. The quarterly plan for each team shall be submitted to HR by each team leader.

This policy will be effective from January 1, 2020, and reviewed annually to maintain competitiveness in terms of the Korean market situation.

<Table 4-4> Labor-Management Agreement on Selective Working Hour System

The Company and worker representative agree to the following regarding selective working hours.

Article 1 (Purpose) This Agreement aims to determine what is necessary for a selective working hour system in accordance with Article 52 of the Labor Standards Act and Article ○ of the Rules of Employment.

Article 2 (Scope of Application) Selective working hours shall apply to employees at the managerial level or higher.

Article 3 (Settlement Period) The settlement period for working hours shall be from the beginning of the month to the end of the month.

Article 4 (Total Working Hours) Calculated as '8 hours per day × contractual working days in the month (excluding holidays and holidays).'

Article 5 (Standard Working Hours) The standard working hours for one day shall be 8 hours.

Article 6 (Mandatory Work Period) The mandatory work period shall be from 10 am to 4 pm, excluding the one hour between noon and 1 pm for lunch break.

Article 7 (Selective Time Period) The selective time period shall be from 8 to 10 am for start time and from 4 to 7 pm for finish time.

Article 8 (Additional Allowance) In the event business operations are unavoidable during holidays or at night, or exceeding the working

- 근무의 시작과 종료 시각의 준수는 상호 합의와 모든 직원들의 자주적인 이해에 따라 지켜져야 한다.
- 출장이나 외근의 경우는 면제될 수 있다.
- 탄력적 근로 시간제는 2021년 1월 1일부터 시작될 것이며, 부서장은 각 팀의 분기별 계획을 인사부에 제출해야 한다.

    이 정책은 2020년 1월 1일부터 유효하며, 국내 다른 경쟁업체들이나 국내 시장 상황에 비추어 경쟁성을 유지할 수 있도록 매년 재 검토 된다.

<표4-4> 선택적 근로시간제 노사합의서

주식회사 ○○ 대표이사 와 근로자대표는 선택적 근로시간제에 관하여 다음과 같이 합의한다.

제1조(목적) 이 합의서는 근로기준법 제52조와 취업규칙 제○조에 의해 선택적 근로시간제에 필요한 사항을 정하는 것을 목적으로 한다.

제2조(적용범위) 선택적 근로시간제는 과장급 이상의 기획 및 관리·감독 업무에 종사하는 자를 대상으로 한다.

제3조(정산기간) 근로시간의 정산기간은 매월 초일부터 말일까지로 한다.

제4조(총 근로시간) '1일 8시간 × 해당 월의 소정근로일수(휴일·휴무일은 제외)'로 계산한다.

제5조(표준근로시간) 1일의 표준근로시간은 8시간으로 한다.

제6조(의무시간대) 의무시간대는 오전 10시부터 오후 4시까지로 한다. 다만, 정오부터 오후 1시까지는 휴게시간으로 한다.

제7조(선택시간대) 선택시간대는 시작시간대 오전 8시부터 10시, 종료시간대 오후 4시부터 7시로 한다.

제8조(가산수당) 업무상 부득이한 경우에 사용자의 지시 또는 승인을 받고 휴일 또는 야간시간대에 근무하거나, 제4조의 근무시간을 초과하여 근무한 시간에 대해 가산수당을 지급한다.

Chapter 4 Flexible Working Hours

> hours specified in Article 4, an additional allowance shall be paid, under the direction or approval of the employer.
> Article 9 (Wage Deduction) Workers shall have their wages deducted in accordance with the number of hours they did not work during the mandatory work period.
> Article 10 (Effective Period) The period of validity for this Agreement shall be one year from the date this Agreement is signed.
> Signed on _____(date).
>
> Company Representative _____
> Worker Representative _____

IV. Deemed Working Hours System

1. Purpose

The deemed working hours system is a system for recognizing working hours when it is difficult for a worker to calculate all or part of his or her working time outside the workplace due to business or other reasons. In this case, in principle, the prescribed contractual working hours are considered to be worked. However, in cases where work in excess of the predetermined working hours is normally required for the performance of the work, the required time is generally regarded as working time. If labor and management have determined in advance the generally necessary working hours in writing, such working hours are regarded as performed. The deemed working hour system outside the workplace is sometimes referred to as an authorized labor system, and was established to make calculation of working hours more reasonable in consideration of the increasing number of working hours outside the workplace due to development of the service industry and automation. Areas where difficulties exist in calculating working hours include sales, AS service, business trips, taxi driving, reporters' work, and working from home.

> 제9조(임금공제) 의무 출근 시간대에 근무하지 않은 경우, 근무하지 않은 시간만큼 임금을 공제하며 의무출근시각을 지나 출근하거나 의무퇴근시각 전에 퇴근한 경우에는 지각, 조퇴로 처리한다.
> 제10조(유효기간) 이 합의서의 유효기간은 ○○○○년 ○월 ○일부터 1년간으로 한다.
>
> 20○○. . .
>
> 주식회사 ○○ 대표이사_____(인)
> 근로자대표_____ (인)

Ⅳ. 간주 근로시간제

1. 의의

간주 근로시간제란 근로자가 출장 또는 그 밖의 사유로 근로시간의 전부 또는 일부를 사업장 밖에서 근로하여 근로시간을 실제로 측정하기 어려운 경우에 근로시간을 인정하는 제도이다. 이 경우에 원칙적으로 소정근로시간을 근로한 것으로 보나, 당해 업무의 수행을 위해 통상적으로 소정근로시간을 초과한 근로가 필요한 경우에는 통상 필요한 시간을 근로시간으로 인정하며, 통상 필요한 시간을 노사가 따로 서면 합의한 경우에는 그 시간을 근로시간으로 인정한다. 사업장 밖 간주 근로시간제는 인정근로제로 표현하기도 하는데 서비스산업의 발달과 자동화의 진전 등으로 사업장 밖에서 근로하는 사례가 증가하고 있는 현실을 반영하여 근로시간을 보다 합리적으로 정하기 위하여 제정된 것이다. 근로시간의 산정이 어려운 업무로 영업, A/S 업무, 출장업무, 택시운전업무, 기사 취재업무, 재택근무 등을 들 수 있다.

Chapter 4 Flexible Working Hours

2. Introducing a Deemed Working Hours System

> Labor Standards Act, Article 58: Special Cases for Calculation of Work Hours
> ① When it proves difficult to calculate the work hours of an employee because he/she performs his duty in whole or in part outside the workplace owing to a business trips or other reasons, the hours shall be calculated as contractual working hours, provided that, in cases where it is ordinarily necessary for an employee to work in excess of contractual working hours to carry out said duty, it shall be deemed that the employee has worked for the hours ordinarily required to carry out that duty.
> ② Notwithstanding the proviso of paragraph ①, in cases where there exists a written agreement between the employer and the employee representative of the workplace concerned, the hours determined in the agreement shall be regarded as those ordinarily required to carry out the relevant duty

(1) Provision of work outside the workplace

Work outside the workplace shall be judged by comprehensive consideration of the place of work and the type of work performed. Working outside the workplace is a situation in which a worker deviates from the management of working hours at his or her own place of work. The form of work performance refers to the conduct of work without specific direction and supervision from the employer's working time management organization.

(2) Difficulty in calculating working hours

It is difficult to calculate working hours, because the work start and finish time outside the workplace are discretionary for the workers concerned, and because the workers concerned work the length of working hours according to their working conditions. Therefore, if it is possible to calculate working hours when the specific direction and supervision of the employer directly affects the workers working outside, the deemed working hour system shall not apply to those workers.

(3) Introducing the system

If (1) and (2) above are met, the agreed-upon working hours shall be considered

2. 도입방법

> 제58조【근로시간계산의 특례】
> ① 근로자가 출장이나 그 밖의 사유로 근로시간의 전부 또는 일부를 사업장 밖에서 근로하여 근로시간을 산정하기 어려운 경우에는 소정근로시간을 근로한 것으로 본다. 다만, 그 업무를 수행하기 위하여 통상적으로 소정근로시간을 초과하여 근로할 필요가 있는 경우에는 그 업무의 수행에 통상 필요한 시간을 근로한 것으로 본다.
> ② 제1항 단서에도 불구하고 그 업무에 관하여 근로자대표와의 서면합의를 한 경우에는 그 합의에서 정하는 시간을 그 업무의 수행에 통상 필요한 시간으로 본다

(1) 사업장 밖의 근로제공 일 것

사업장 밖 근로는 근로 장소와 근로수행 형태를 종합적으로 고려하여 판단해야 한다. 근로장소는 소속 사업장에서의 장소 이탈을 전제로 하여 근로자가 자신의 본래 소속 사업장의 근로시간 관리로부터 벗어나 있는 상황을 말한다. 근로수행형태는 사용자의 근로시간 관리조직으로 부터의 구체적인 지휘, 감독을 받지 않고 근로를 수행하는 것을 말한다.

(2) 근로시간을 산정하기 어려울 것

근로시간 산정이 어려운 경우는 사업장 밖 근로의 시업시각과 종업시각이 해당 근로자의 자유에 맡겨져 있고, 근로자의 조건이나 업무상태에 따라 근로시간의 장단이 결정되는 경우를 말한다. 따라서 사업장 밖 근로라 하더라도 사용자의 구체적인 지휘, 감독이 미치는 경우에는 근로시간의 산정이 가능하므로 그 적용대상에서 제외된다.

(3) 도입방법

Chapter 4 Flexible Working Hours

as working hours, regardless of actual working hours, as one of three: (i) predetermined working hours, (ii) time normally required for the performance of work, or (iii) agreed working hours between labor and management.

3. Using the Deemed Working Hours System

(1) Overseas business trips

When traveling overseas for business or returning home, flight time, immigration procedures, and travel time are likely to exceed actual working hours. In such cases, it is desirable to establish a written agreement with the worker representative. Generally, the company guarantees paid or alternative leave for the time required for the work through overseas business regulations. In this regard, the courts and the Ministry of Employment and Labor consider working time spent abroad as working hours.[125]

(2) If the working hours are difficult to calculate because the employee performs duty outside the workplace, disputes are likely to arise between employee and employer about calculation of wages. As a solution, the deemed working hour system has been introduced to recognize those outside working hours as fixed working hours.

<Table 4-5> Labor-Management Agreement on Deemed
Working Hours for Outside Work

The Company and worker representative agree to the following, regarding the calculation of working hours according to Article ○○ of the Rules of Employment for workers having to work outside the workplace.

Article 1 (Scope of Application) This Agreement applies to those engaged in outside work in departments such as sales or customer relations.

Article 2 (Recognized Working Hours) In cases where the workers specified in Article 1 are engaged in work outside the workplace for all or part of the normal working hours and there is significant difficulty in calculating their working hours, they shall be regarded as having worked 8 hours a day,

---

[125] Suwon District Court ruling on Nov. 25, 2016: 2015 gadan 505758; MOEL Guidelines on June 14, 2001: 68207-1909.

위의 (1)과 (2)을 충족한 경우, 근로자가 실제 근로한 시간과 관계없이 (ⅰ) 소정근로시간, (ⅱ) 업무수행에 통상적으로 필요한 시간, (ⅲ) 노사가 서면으로 합의한 시간 중 어느 하나를 근로시간으로 본다.

3. 활용방법

(1) 해외출장

장거리 해외출장을 위해 이동하거나 귀국 시 비행시간, 출입국 수속시간, 이동시간 등은 실제 시간이 소정근로시간을 초과할 가능성이 높다. 이러한 경우 근로자대표와 서면 합의를 통해 정하는 것이 바람직하다. 일반적으로 회사는 해외출장규정을 통해서 그 업무에 필요한 시간만큼 유급이나 대체 휴무를 보장한다. 이와 관련하여 법원과 고용노동부는 해외출장 중 소비한 시간은 근로시간으로 판단하고 있다.[125]

(2) 사업장 외에서의 근무로 근로시간 산정이 어려운 경우 근로시간과 임금의 계산 등을 둘러싸고 노·사간 분쟁의 소지가 있으므로, 간주근로시간제를 도입하여 일정시간을 근로한 것으로 인정할 수 있는 근거를 마련한 것이다.

<표4-5> 사업장 밖 간주근로시간제 노사합의서

주식회사 ○○ 대표이사 와 근로자대표 000는 취업규칙 제○○조에 따라, 근로자에 대하여 사업장 밖 근로를 시키는 경우의 근로시간 산정에 관하여 다음과 같이 합의한다.
제1조(대상의 범위) 이 합의서는 영업부 및 판매부에 해당하는 것으로 주로 사업장 밖의 업무에 종사하는 자에게 적용한다.
제2조(인정근로시간) 제1조에 정한 직원이 통상근로시간의 전부 또는 일부를 사업장 밖의 업무에 종사하고, 근로시간을 산정하기 어려운

---

[125] 수원지방법원 2016.11.25.선고 2015가단505758 판결; 근기 68207-1909, 2001.6.14.

excluding rest hours.

Article 3 (Recess Hour) The rest time specified in Article ○○ of the Rules of Employment shall apply to workers specified in Article 1. However, if the type of business engaged in is not conducive to taking a break during the designated recess time, a predetermined rest period shall be given at a different time.

Article 4 (Holiday Work) In cases where the worker specified in Article 1 has to work on holidays stipulated in Article ○○ of the Rules of Employment in accordance with special instructions to do so, the Company shall pay that worker an additional holiday work allowance based on Article ○○ of the Rules of Employment.

Article 5 (Night work) In cases where the worker specified in Article 1 has to work at night (22:00 ~ 06:00) in accordance with special instructions to do so, the Company shall pay a nighttime work allowance based on Article ○○ of the Rules of Employment.

Article 6 (Overtime) In cases where the worker specified in Article 2 has to work hours in excess of the contractual working hours, the Company shall pay the overtime allowance specified in Article ○○ of the Rules of Employment.

Article 7 (Effective Period) The period of validity for this Agreement shall be one year from the date this agreement is signed.

Signed on _____(date).

Company Representative_____

Workers Representative _____

V. Discretionary Work System

1. Concept

The discretionary work system is a system that requires the delegation of work method to worker discretion in light of the nature of the work.

Workers have a lot of discretion in the way they work according to technological advances, information-orientation of work, increasing economic share

> 경우에는 휴게시간을 제외하고 1일 8시간을 근로한 것으로 본다.
> 제3조(휴게시간) 제1조에 정한 직원에 대해 취업규칙 제○○조에 정한 휴게시간을 적용한다. 다만, 업무에 따라서는 정해진 휴게시간에 휴게할 수 없는 경우에는 별도의 시간대에 소정의 휴게시간을 부여하는 것으로 한다.
> 제4조(휴일근로) 제1조에 정한 직원이 특별한 지시에 따라 취업규칙 제○○조에 정한 휴일에 근무한 경우에는 회사는 취업규칙 제○○조에 기초하여 휴일근로 가산수당을 지급한다.
> 제5조(야간근로) 제1조에 정한 직원이 특별한 지시에 따라 야간시간(22:00~06:00)에 근무한 경우에는 취업규칙 제○○조에 기초하여 야간근로 가산수당을 지급한다.
> 제6조(연장근로) 제2조에 따라 근무로 인정된 시간 중 소정근로시간을 넘는 시간에 대해서는 취업규칙 제○○조에서 정한 연장근로 가산수당을 지급한다.
> 제7조(유효기간) 이 합의서의 유효기간은 ○○○○년 ○월 ○일부터 1년간으로 한다.
>
> 20○○. . .
>
> 주식회사 ○○ 대표이사_____(인) 근로자대표_____ (인)

V. 재량근로시간제

1. 의의

재량근로시간제란 업무의 성질에 비추어 업두수행방법을 근로자의 재량에 위임할 필요가 있는 업무로 사용자가 근로자대표와 서면합의로 정한 근로시간을 소정근로시간으로 인정하는 제도이다.

Chapter 4 Flexible Working Hours

of the services industry, increasing share of knowledge labor, etc., and so their remuneration depends on the quality of work rather than the amount of working hours.

Professional work that requires creativity, such as research and development, information processing system analysis, design, news article composition, and editorial work, is not appropriately regulated by the amount of working hours like general workers. But it is desirable for both labor and management to leave their working hours to the discretion of such professional workers rather than to directly control them.

2. Introducing a Discretionary Work System

Labor Standards Act: Article 58 (Special Cases for Calculation of Work Hours)
③ For tasks designated by Presidential Decree as those tasks which need, in light of their characteristics, worker discretion with regard to the ways to perform them, the worker shall be deemed to have worked such working hours as determined by a written agreement between the employer and the workers' representative. Such written agreement shall contain each of the items described in the following subparagraphs:
1. provisions as to work to be provided;
2. provisions in which the employer will not give directions to the worker regarding how to perform the work, and how to allocate working hours; and
3. provisions in which computation of working hours shall be determined by the written agreement concerned.

Enforcement Decree

Article 31 (Jobs Eligible for Discretionary Work System)

"Work prescribed by Presidential Decree" in the former part of Article 58 (3) of the Act means work falling under any of the following subparagraphs:
1. Research and development of new products or technologies, and research in the areas of the humanities or social or natural sciences;
2. Design or analysis for data processing systems;
3. Gathering, compiling and editing of news for a newspaper, broadcasting or publication business;
4. Design or creation of clothing, interior decoration, industrial goods, advertisement, etc.;

산업전반에서 기술혁신, 정보화, 서비스업 비중 증가, 지식노동 증가 등에 따라 일하는 방식에 있어서 근로자의 재량 여지가 많고, 그 보수도 근로시간의 양보다 근로의 질(성과)에 따라 결정되는 것이 적합한 전문적 업무가 증가하고 있다.

연구개발 업무, 정보처리시스템 분석, 설계업무, 기사의 취재, 편집업무 등 창의성 발휘가 필요한 전문적 업무에 대해서는 일반근로자와 같이 근로시간의 양으로 동일하게 규제하는 것이 부적절하므로 사용자의 구체적 지시에 따라 업무를 수행케 하는 것보다 근로자의 재량에 맡기는 것이 노사 쌍방을 위하여 바람직하다.

2. 도입방법

> 근로기준법: 제58조【근로시간 계산의 특례】
> ③ 업무의 성질에 비추어 업무 수행 방법을 근로자의 재량에 위임할 필요가 있는 업무로서 대통령령으로 정하는 업무는 사용자가 근로자대표와 서면 합의로 정한 시간을 근로한 것으로 본다. 이 경우 그 서면 합의에는 다음 각 호의 사항을 명시하여야 한다.
>   1. 대상 업무
>   2. 사용자가 업무의 수행 수단 및 시간 배분 등에 관하여 근로자에게 구체적인 지시를 하지 아니한다는 내용
>   3. 근로시간의 산정은 그 서면 합의로 정하는 바에 따른다는 내용
>
> 시행령
> 제31조【재량근로의 대상업무】
>   법 제58조 제3항 전단에서 "대통령령으로 정하는 업무"란 다음 각 호의 어느 하나에 해당하는 업무를 말한다. <개정 2010.7.12.>
> 1. 신상품 또는 신기술의 연구개발이나 인문사회과학 또는 자연과학 분야의 연구 업무
> 2. 정보처리시스템의 설계 또는 분석 업무

Chapter 4 Flexible Working Hours

> 5. Work as a producer or director in the business of producing broadcasting programs, motion pictures, etc.; and
> 6. Other jobs as determined by the Minister of Employment and Labor.

(1) Work considered discretionary

Work that may be targeted as discretionary is limited to the work prescribed in Article 31 of the Enforcement Decree to the Labor Standards Act. In view of the nature of the work, it must be given to worker discretion. Workers shall not be given specific instructions on how to perform the work, but this shall be left to their full discretion, while the employer can direct the basic content of the work. However, the employer shall not give specific instructions regarding the distribution of working hours to workers.

(i) Research and development of new products or technologies, and research in the areas of the humanities or social or natural sciences;

(ii) Design or analysis for data processing systems;

(iii) Gathering, compiling and editing of news for a newspaper, broadcasting or publication business;

(iv) Design or creation of clothing, interior decoration, industrial goods, advertisement, etc.;

(v) Work as a producer or director in the business of producing broadcasting programs, motion pictures, etc.; and

(vi) Consultation, advice, appraisal or agency with the delegation or commission of others in the affairs of accounting, legal cases, tax payment, legal affairs, labor management, patents, appraisal, etc.

(2) There must be written agreement on statutory matters

To introduce a discretionary work system, the employer must specify the tasks concerned, and other necessary items through a written agreement with the employee representative. The statutory matters that must be included in the written agreement include: (i) provisions as to tasks to be provided; (ii) provisions in which the employer would not give directions to the worker regarding method of performance, and how to allocate working hours; and (iii) provisions in which the computation of working hours shall be determined by the written agreement concerned.

> 3. 신문, 방송 또는 출판 사업에서의 기사의 취재, 편성 또는 편집 업무
> 4. 의복·실내장식·공업제품·광고 등의 디자인 또는 고안 업무
> 5. 방송 프로그램·영화 등의 제작 사업에서의 프로듀서나 감독 업무
> 6. 그 밖에 고용노동부장관이 정하는 업무

(1) 재량근로의 업무에 해당할 것

재량근로의 대상으로 할 수 있는 업무는 근로기준법 시행령 제31조에서 규정한 업무에 한정된다. 업무의 성질에 비추어 업무수행방법은 근로자의 재량에 위임할 필요가 있는 업무여야 한다. 수행 수단에 관한 구체적인 지시를 받지 않아야 하지만 업무수행을 완전히 근로자 재량에 맡겨야 한다는 것은 아니므로 업무의 기본적 내용을 지시할 수 있다. 그러나 사용자는 근로자의 근로시간 배분에 관하여 구체적인 지시를 하지 않아야 한다.

(ⅰ) 신상품 또는 신기술의 연구개발이나 인문사회과학 또는 자연과학분야의 연구 업무
(ⅱ) 정보처리시스템의 설계 또는 분석 업무
(ⅲ) 신문, 방송 또는 출판 사업에서의 기사의 취재, 편성 또는 편집 업무
(ⅳ) 의복, 실내장식, 공업제품, 광고 등의 디자인 또는 고안 업무
(ⅴ) 방송 프로그램, 영화 등의 제작 사업에서의 프로듀서나 감독 업무
(ⅵ) 회계, 법률사건, 납세, 법무, 노무관리, 특허, 감정평가 등의 사무에 있어 타인의 위임, 위촉을 받아 상담, 조언, 감정 또는 대행을 하는 업무

(2) 법정 사항에 대한 서면합의가 있어야 함.

재량근로제를 도입하기 위해서는 사용자가 근로자대표와 서면합의를 통하여 대상업무를 등을 구체적으로 명시하여야 한다. 서면합의에 반드시 포함시켜야 할 법정사항은 (ⅰ) 대상업무, (ⅱ) 사용자가 업구의 수행 수단 및 시간 배분 등에 관하여 근로자에게 구체적인 지시를 하지 아니한다는 내용, (ⅲ) 근로시간의 산정은 그 서면 합의로 정하는 바에 따른다는 내용이다.

Chapter 4 Flexible Working Hours

3. Using a Discretionary Working Hour System

In order for the company to adopt and use discretionary work hours in certain occupations, departments, and duties within the organization, (i) it must apply only to the six discretionary work tasks mentioned above, (ii) discretionary rights in work performance shall be allocated and (iii) a written agreement with the worker representative shall pre-exist the discretionary work hours.

<Table 4-6> Rules of Employment for a Discretionary Working Hour System

Article ○ (Application of Discretionary Working Hour System)
① The discretionary working hour system applies to those workers selected under mutual agreement between the employer and the worker representative.
② Workers to whom the discretionary working hour system applies, pursuant to paragraph (1), are considered to have worked the fixed working hours decided through mutual agreement between the employer and the worker representative, regardless of the working hours prescribed in Article ○.
③ If the deemed working hours determined by the agreement in subparagraph ② above exceed the working hours specified in Article ○, an additional allowance shall be paid for those overtime hours.
④ Working hours shall be allocated at the discretion of the relevant discretionary worker.
⑤ Holidays and vacation for discretionary workers shall be as prescribed in Article ○.
⑥ Before discretionary workers intend to work on holidays or at night, they shall obtain permission from their superior.
⑦ In cases where discretionary workers work holidays or at night after obtaining permission as prescribed in paragraph 6, the Company shall pay additional allowances in accordance with Article ○

<Table 4-7> Labor-Management Agreement
on Discretionary Working Hour System>

The Company and worker representative agree to the following, regarding discretionary working hours according to Article 58 (3) of the Labor

3. 활용방법

　기업이 조직 내 특정 직종이나 부서, 직무 등에 재량 근로시간제를 도입해 활용하기 위해서는 그 적용대상이 (ⅰ) 위에 언급한 6가지의 재량근로대상업무에 해당되어야 하고, (ⅱ) 대상업무 수행에 있어 재량이 인정되어야 하고, (ⅲ) 근로자대표와의 서면합의가 있어야 한다.

<표4-6> 재량근로시간제 취업규칙

제○조(재량근로시간제 적용)
① 재량근로시간제는 노·사 합의로 정하는 대상 근로자에게 적용한다.
② 제1항에 따라 재량근로시간제가 적용되는 근로자(이하 "재량근로자"라 한다)에 대해서는 제○조에서 정하는 근로시간에 관계 없이 노·사 합의에서 정하는 근로시간을 근로한 것으로 본다.
③ 제2항의 노·사 합의에서 정하는 간주근로시간이 제○조에서 정한 근로시간을 초과하는 부분에 대해서는 가산수당을 지급한다.
④ 재량근로자의 근무시간은 재량근로자의 재량에 의해 구체적인 시간 배분을 결정하는 것으로 한다.
⑤ 재량근로자의 휴일, 휴가는 제○조에서 정한 바에 따른다.
⑥ 재량근로자가 휴일 또는 야간에 근로하는 경우에는 미리 소속 부서장의 허가를 얻어야 한다.
⑦ 제6항에 따른 허가를 받고서 휴일 또는 야간에 업무를 행한 경우 회사는 제○조에 따라 가산수당을 지급한다

<표4-7> 재량근로시간제 노사합의서

주식회사 ○○ 대표이사 와 근로자대표 000는 근로기준법 제58조 제3항에 기반하여 재량근로시간제에 관하여 다음과 같이 합의한다.
제1조(적용 대상업무 및 근로자) 본 합의는 각 호에서 제시하는 업무에

Chapter 4 Flexible Working Hours

Standards Act.

Article 1 (Applicable Business and Workers) This Agreement applies to workers engaged in the areas of business presented in the following subparagraphs.
1. Workers engaged in R&D for new products or technologies at the headquarters research center;
2. Workers engaged in design or analysis of the information processing system in the information processing center attached to the head office;

Article 2 (Method of Task Performance)
① In principle, the workers specified in Article 1 shall be able to determine independently the method of work and the time allocated, and the Company shall not give instructions to them. However, they will be assigned basic tasks and required to report at certain stages, such as when selecting a new research project.
② Notwithstanding paragraph 1 of this Article, the Company can give orders not directly related to performance, but to the Company's service principles or in-company facility management instructions.

Article 3 (Calculation of Working Hours) The workers specified in Article 1 shall be regarded as having worked 8 hours a day (weekly working hours) regardless of the actual working hours, as prescribed in Article ○ of the Rules of Employment.

Article 4 (Overtime Allowance) Workers working hours exceeding the deemed working hours under Article 3 are prescribed by Article ○ of the Rules of Employment to receive an overtime allowance.

Article 5 (Holidays and Night Work)
① On the day when the workers specified in Article 1 are to work, the Company shall record the time of arrival and departure via ID card.
② Workers described in Article 1 as performing business on holidays or at night (22:00 ~ 06:00) shall obtain advance permission from the department head.
③ Once this permission in the preceding paragraph is obtained and the holiday or night hours worked, the Company shall pay additional allowances as described in Article ○ of the Rules of Employment.

종사하는 근로자에게 적용한다.

1. 본사 연구소에서 신상품 또는 신기술의 연구개발 업무에 종사하는 근로자
2. 본사 부속 정보처리센터에서 정보처리시스템의 설계 또는 분석의 업무에 종사하는 근로자

제2조(업무의 수행방법)

① 제1조에서 정한 근로자에 대해서는 원칙적으로 그 업무수행의 방법 및 시간 배분의 결정 등을 본인에 위임하고 회사 측은 구체적 지시를 하지 않는다. 다만, 연구과제의 선택 등 종사할 기본적인 업무 내용을 지시하거나 일정 단계에서 보고할 의무를 지울 수 있다.

② 이 조 제1항에도 불구하고, 업무 수행과 직접 관련이 없는 직장 질서 또는 회사 내 시설 관리상 지시는 할 수 있다.

제3조(근로시간의 산정) 제1조에서 정한 근로자는 취업규칙 제○조에서 정하는 근로시간에 관계없이 1일 8시간(간주근로시간) 근로한 것으로 본다.

제4조(연장근로수당) 제3조의 간주근로시간이 취업규칙 제○조에서 정한 소정 근로시간을 초과하는 부분에 대해서는 연장근로로 취급하여 가산수당을 지급 한다.

제5조(휴일 및 야간근로)

① 제1조에서 정한 근로자가 회사에 출근하는 날에는 입·퇴실 시에 ID카드에 의한 시간을 기록해야 한다.

② 제1조에서 정한 근로자가 휴일 또는 야간(22:00~06:00)에 업무를 행하는 경우에는 미리 소속 부서장의 허가를 얻어야 한다.

③ 전항에 따른 허가를 받고서 휴일 또는 야간에 업무를 행한 경우 회사는 취업규칙 제○조의 정한 바에 따라 가산수당을 지급한다.

제6조(휴게, 휴일 및 휴가) 제1조에서 정한 근로자의 휴게, 휴일 및 휴가는 취업규칙에서 정하는 바에 따른다.

제7조(재량근로의 적용 중지) 제1조에서 정한 근로자에 대하여 사용자는

Chapter 4 Flexible Working Hours

Article 6 (Recess, Holidays and Vacation) Rest, holidays and vacations specified in Article 1 shall follow the Rules of Employment.

Article 7 (Suspension of Application for Discretionary Work) The employer shall not, in any of the following cases, apply discretionary work to the workers specified in Article 1:
 1. When it is not appropriate to apply the discretionary working hour system due to changes in work;
 2. When a worker applies for suspension of his/her eligibility for the discretionary work system.

Article 8 (Effective Period) The period of validity for this Agreement shall be one year from the date this Agreement is signed.

Signed on _____(date).

Company Representative _____
Worker Representative _____

VI. Compensatory Leave System

Labor Standards Act: Article 57 (Compensatory Leave System)
   An employer may, in lieu of paying additional wages, grant leave to a worker to compensate for the extended, night and holiday work prescribed in Article 56, pursuant to a written agreement with the workers' representative.

1. Requisites to Utilizing a Compensatory Leave System

There shall be a written agreement between the employer and the employee representative. Without such an agreement, the system shall not be legally in effect. If there is a labor union organized by the majority of employees, the union shall represent all workers. If there is no union, then an employee representative shall represent the workers. The written agreement shall be a document signed by both parties concerned.

> 다음 각 호의 어느 하나에 해당하는 경우 해당 근로자에게 재량근로제를 적용하지 않을 수 있다.
> 1. 업무의 변경 등으로 인해 재량근로시간제를 적용하는 것이 적정하지 않다고 판단된 경우
> 2. 근로자가 재량근로제의 적용 중지를 신청한 경우
>
> 제8조(유효기간) 이 합의서의 유효기간은 ○○○○년 ○월 ○일부터 1년간으로 한다.
>
> 20○○. . .
>
> 주식회사 ○○ 대표이사_____(인)   근로자대표_____ (인)

VI. 보상휴가제

> **근로기준법 제57조【보상 휴가제】**
> 사용자는 근로자대표와의 서면 합의에 따라 제56조에 따른 연장근로·야간근로 및 휴일근로에 대하여 임금을 지급하는 것을 갈음하여 휴가를 줄 수 있다.

1. 보상휴가제 도입 요건

근로자대표와의 서면합의가 있어야 하며, 동 요건을 갖추지 못하면 효력이 없다. 근로자대표는 근로자 과반수로 조직된 노동조합이 있으면 그 노동조합, 근로자 과반수로 조직된 노동조합이 없으면 근로자 과반수를 대표하는 자이며, 서면합의는 노사당사자가 서명한 문서의 형태로 작성되어야 한다.

2. Criteria for using leave as compensation

Wages paid for extended work, night work, and holiday work, and leave rendered as compensation, shall be of equal value. Accordingly, an additional allowance mentioned in Article 56 of the LSA shall be considered. This means that, if two hours were spent in extended work, wages would be valued at 3 hours, including additional allowances. In cases where extended work, holiday work, and night work overlap, wages including each additional allowance shall be compensated with leave.

The parties concerned shall agree upon whether compensatory leave should be rendered as total wages with an additional allowance or only as an additional allowance.

3. Providing Compensatory Leave

Leave, according to the regulations, shall be rendered within contractual working hours. Whether the leave shall be used in a unit of hours or days in regards to accumulation depends on the agreement between the parties concerned.

4. Items to be Considered in a written Agreement

In the Act, where the system of using leave as compensation is regulated in a written agreement, details shall be specified in separate written agreements between the parties concerned. They include: ① whether the rendering of leave will be decided by the employee or the employer, and ② whether the leave will be applied to all employees uniformly or selectively. It also considers ③ whether the employer shall allow workers to ask for allowances, and ④ whether the employer will allow workers to ask for leave, if they are not allowed to ask for allowances.

Accordingly, in cases where all employees agree upon using leave uniformly in the written agreement, the employer shall not have to pay an allowance for each employee, since Article 56 of the Labor Standards Act (Extended, Night or Holiday Work) is not being violated.

2. 보상휴가 부여 기준

 연장·야간·휴일근로에 대한 임금과 이에 갈음하여 부여하는 휴가 사이에는 동등한 가치가 있어야 하므로 근로기준법 제56조에 의한 가산임금까지 감안되어야 한다. 따라서 연장근로를 2시간 한 경우 가산임금을 포함하면 총 3시간분의 임금이 지급되어야 하므로 3시간의 휴가가 발생한다. 연장·휴일·야간근로가 중복된 경우에는 가산임금을 포함하여 산정된 임금에 해당하는 휴가가 발생한다.
 보상휴가제의 적용대상을 연장근로 등에 대한 가산임금을 포함한 전체 임금으로 할지, 가산임금 부분만 할지는 노사 서면합의로 정한 바에 따른다.

3. 휴가 부여 방법

 동 규범에 의한 휴가는 소정근로시간 중에 부여되어야 한다. 휴가를 "시간" 단위로 부여할지 이를 "일" 단위로 부여할지는 노사 서면합의로 정하는 바에 따른다.

4. 노사 서면합의에 포함되어야 할 사항

 법 규정에는 노사 서면합의로 보상휴가제를 도입할 수 있는 근거만 있으므로 세부적인 사항은 노사 서면합의에 의해 노사가 자율적으로 정할 수 있다. 즉, 부여 방식은 ① 근로자의 청구에 의할 것인지 사용자가 일방적으로 지정할 것인지, ② 전 근로자에게 일률적으로 적용할 것인지 희망하는 근로자에 한하여 적용할 것인지 등의 사안과 ③ 임금청구권은 휴가 청구권과 임금청구권의 선택을 인정할 것인지 ④ 임금청구권을 배제하고 휴가 청구권만 인정할 것인지 등이다.
 노사 서면합의에 의해 전 근로자에게 일률적으로 적용하고 휴가사용권만 인정하기로 한 경우에는 개별 근로자가 이에 불구하고 임금을 청구하더라도 사용자는 이에 응할 의무가 없으며, 근로기준법 제56조(야간·연장 및 휴일근로) 위반 등의 문제가 발생하지 않는다.

Chapter 4 Flexible Working Hours

5. Obligation to Pay Allowance for Unused Leave

Using leave as compensation is a system in which an employer provides leave instead of allowances, which means the employer shall have to pay allowances if the leave cannot be granted. Unlike annual paid leave, the employer cannot waive wage payment with measures to promote the use of leave.

The right to ask for an allowance is given from the day following the expiry date of the unused leave. If this rule is violated, it is regarded as a violation of Article 56 of the Labor Standards Act. It is not a violation of the Act if the employer pays the allowance sometime between the expiration date of leave and the regular payment date of wages in the first following month.

<Table 4-8> Labor-Management Agreement regarding the Compensatory Leave System

---

The Company and the worker representative agree to the following, regarding the compensatory leave specified in Article 57 of the Labor Standards Act.

Article 1. The compensatory leave given for overtime, nighttime and holiday work shall be calculated from the first day to the last day of every month, which will be given as paid time-off leave instead of additional payment in the following month in principle. Workers shall be free to decide their paid time-off period. However, if the time specified by the worker creates an unreasonable burden on business operations, the employer can change the timing.

Article 2. If an individual worker explicitly requests it, wages can be paid instead of vacation time given.

Article 3. If the worker does not use any part of the compensatory leave in the following month, monetary compensation must be provided instead.

Article 4. (Effective Period) The period of validity for this Agreement shall be one year from the date this Agreement is signed.

Signed on _____ (date).

Company Representative _____
Worker Representative _____

5. 휴가를 사용하지 않을 경우 임금지급 의무

　보상휴가제는 임금지급에 갈음하여 휴가를 부여하는 제도이므로 어떠한 이유로든 휴가를 부여하지 않은 경우에는 그에 대한 임금이 지급되어야 한다. 연차유급휴가와는 달리 사용자가 휴가사용촉진조치를 통해 임금지급의무를 면제받을 수 없다.

　임금청구권은 휴가를 사용할 수 없게 된 것이 확정된 날의 다음 날부터 행사할 수 있으며, 위반 시에는 근로기준법 제56조 위반이 된다. 다만, 휴가를 사용할 수 없게 된 것이 확정된 날의 다음 날부터 최초로 도래하는 임금 정기지급일에 위 임금을 지급한 경우에는 법 위반으로 보지 않는다.

<표4-8> 보상휴가제 노사합의서

주식회사 ○○ 대표이사 와 근로자대표 는 근로기준법 제57조에 따른 보상휴가에 대하여 다음과 같이 합의한다.

제1조 보상휴가의 기준이 되는 연장 . 야간 . 휴일근로의 기준일은 매월 1일부터 말일까지로 하고 보상휴가는 익월에 실시함을 원칙으로 하되, 그 시기는 근로자의 자유의사에 따른다. 단, 근로자가 지정한 시기가 사업운영에 막대한 지장을 줄 경우 사용자는 그 시기를 변경할 수 있다.

제2조 개별근로자가 명시적으로 청구하는 경우 휴가 대신 임금으로 지급할 수 있다.

제3조 만약 근로자가 익월에 보상휴가를 일부라도 사용치 않을 경우에는 미사용 분에 대해 금전보상을 실시해야 한다.

제4조(유효기간) 이 합의서의 유효기간은 ○○○○년 ○월 ○일부터 1년간으로 한다.

　　　　　　　　　　　　20○○. . .
　　　　　　주식회사 ○○ 대표이사 _____(인)
　　　　　　　　　　　　근로자대표 _____ (인)

Chapter 4　Flexible Working Hours

VII. Work-from-Home Systems

As of March 23, 2020, the number of persons confirmed to have been infected by the coronavirus in Korea was approaching 9,000, with over 100 dead. COVID-19 is spreading worldwide and showing signs of prolongation. In this emergency situation, many companies are putting work-from-home procedures in place to protect workers while continuing business. However, these procedures have been introduced without preparation, lowering work efficiency and causing many negative side-effects.

To maintain efficiency while a work-from-home system is in place, the following three criteria must be met in the introduction process: (i) the jobs must be suitable for working from home; (ii) the employee(s) must have the necessary work environment to work from home; and (iii) there must be continuous management supervision of those working from home. First, a work-from-home system should be introduced only for jobs in suitable fields. Second, an IT work environment must be in place for the employee(s). Only then will it be possible to manage and supervise the work and address the security concerns related to working from home. Third, application of the Labor Standards Act to maintain and manage the working conditions of those working from home must be made clear. From this point of view, I would like to review the concept of working from home and suggest concrete methods to make a work-from-home system sustainable.[126]

1. Jobs Suitable for Working from Home and Required Equipment

(1) The concept of working from home

Working from home provides flexibility when a work space is provided in a home and utilizes information & communication technology and the facilities and equipment necessary for the work. Regular working from home involves most of

---

[126] Reference: MOEL, "Manual on the Introduction and Operation of a Systematic Flexible Working System", Dec. 2017; MOEL, "How Korean Companies Will Put Flexible Work into Action", Nov. 2016; MOEL Guidelines (kungi 68201-4085, Dec. 29, 2000): "Standards for Application of the Labor Standards Act with Those Working from Home"; MOEL, "Flexible Working Hours Guide", Aug. 2019; Lee, Seurggil, "Status of Those Working from Home in Terms of Labor Law", Labor Law, Aug. 2001, vol. 123.

Ⅶ. 재택근무제 도입

> 2020년 3월 23일 현재, 한국에서 코로나바이러스 확진자가 9000명에 육박하고 있고, 사망자도 100명을 넘어서고 있다. 이 전염병은 전 세계적으로 확산되고 있고, 그나마 장기화 조짐을 보이고 있다. 이러한 비상상황에서 많은 기업들은 재택근무제를 도입하여 근로자를 보호하고 사업수행을 계속하려 노력하고 있다. 이 경우 비대면으로 업무를 계속할 수 있다는 장점도 있지만 다른 한편으로는 사전에 충분한 준비 없이 갑작스러운 도입으로 업무 효율이 저하되는 등의 부작용도 있다.
>
> 재택근무를 통해 업무의 효율을 높이기 위해서는 (ⅰ) 재택근무 도입의 필요성을 우선적으로 고민해 보고, (ⅱ) 관련 업무환경을 구비하고, (ⅲ) 마지막으로 재택업무의 효율적인 관리·감독이 이루어져야만 한다. 다시 말해 재택업무는 적합한 업무분야에 도입되어야 하고, 재택업무를 수행하기 위한 IT 업무 환경이 우선적으로 갖추어져 있어야 한다. 또한 재택근무자의 근로조건을 유지하고 관리하기 위한 근로기준법 적용을 명확히 하여야 한다. 그래야만 업무를 안정적으로 모니터링 하고, 업무상 보안 문제 등을 사전에 예방할 수 있을 것이다. 이러한 점에서 재택근무에 대해 살펴보고, 일회성이 아닌 지속적 재택근무가 가능한 방안에 대해서도 구체적으로 살펴보고자 한다.[126]

1. 재택근무제의 적합한 업무과 업무환경 구비요건

(1) 재택근무의 의의

재택근무란 정보통신기술을 활용하여 "자택"에 업무공간을 마련하고, 업무에 필요한 시설과 장비를 구축한 환경에서 근무하는 유연한 근무 형태이다. 재택

---

[126] 참고자료: 고용노동부, "체계적인 유연근무제 도입·운영을 위한 매뉴얼, 2017. 12; 고용노동부, "유연근로제 우리 기업은 어떻게 운영할까요", 2016. 11; 고용노동부 행정해석(근기 68201-4085, 2000.12.29): "재택근로자에 대한 근로기준법 적용기준"; 고용노동부, "유연근로시간제 가이드", 2019.8; 이승길, "재택근로자의 노동법적 지위", 노동법률, 2001년 8월호, vol.123.

the work being done from home, while occasional working from home involves only part of the week spent working from home and the other part at the office. This would include, for example, Mondays and Tuesdays at home working and the rest of a 5-day work week in the office.

(2) Jobs suitable for working from home

   Jobs that allow workers to work independently and involve the performance of individual tasks, jobs that have little or no face-to-face contact with customers, and jobs that do not need to be performed at a specific location are all suitable for a work-from-home system. Such a system is particularly easy to introduce into fields such as program and game development, web design, book publication, distance education, financial and insurance marketing, civil complaint consulting, planning and administrative processing, and computational work.

1) Suitable tasks:
① Work with little or no face-to-face contact with customers;
② Work allowing a high degree of independence and little need for approval or reporting, or organizational management that allows a high degree of independence due to little need for cooperation between organizations;
③ Work easy to quantify in work performance evaluations; and
④ Jobs determined by managers with approval authority after considering business characteristics and working conditions of the department.

2) Unsuitable tasks:
① Jobs where there is significant security risk due to insufficient security measures in the relevant business;
② Jobs involving safety inspections, equipment inspections, and accident handling measures, etc., where the person responsible should be there to do such jobs, or the risk will inevitably and significantly increase if the work were to be done from home;
③ Jobs where the work must always be carried out in a specific place for the purpose of receiving and processing civil complaints;
④ Jobs where other serious obstacles are expected before business (administrative) objectives can be achieved.

(3) Equipment needed when working from home

근무는 대부분의 근무를 재택으로 하는 상시형 재택근무와 일주일 중 일부만을 재택근무를 하는 수시형 재택근무로 구분할 수 있다. 수시형 재택근무는 근무일 중 일부는 재택근무, 일부는 사무실에서 근무하는 형태로 실시할 수 있다. 예를 들면, 주 5일 중 월요일과 화요일에는 재택근무를 하고, 나머지 수요일에서 금요일은 사무실에서 근무하는 방식이다.

(2) 재택근무제에 적합한 업무

재택근무는 독립적이면서도 개별적인 업무수행이 가능하거나, 고객과의 대면 접촉이 거의 없는 직무, 특정한 장소에서 이루어지지 않아도 되는 직무 등에 적합하다. 특히, 프로그램 및 게임개발, 웹 디자인, 도서출판, 원격교육, 금융 및 보험마케팅 등의 업종이나, 민원 상담, 기획 및 행정처리 업무, 전산 업무 등의 분야에 도입이 용이하다.

1) 적용 가능 업무
   ① 고객과의 대면접촉이 거의 없는 업무
   ② 결재·보고가 적은 독립성이 강한 업무, 기관 간 업무협조가 적어 조직 운영의 독립성이 높은 업무
   ③ 업무실적 평가의 계량화가 쉬운 업무
   ④ 승인권자가 업무특성 및 부서 근무여건을 고려하여 정한 업무

2) 근무허가가 불가능한 경우
   ① 해당업무의 보안대책이 미흡하여 재택근무를 수행하는 경우 심각한 보안위험이 예상되는 경우
   ② 안전점검, 장비점검, 사고처리 등 해당업무의 수행을 위하여 반드시 특정의 장소에 항상 위치하여야 하거나 재택근무를 수행하는 경우 현저히 그 위험성이 증가하는 경우
   ③ 민원사무의 접수 및 처리 등을 위하여 특정의 장소에서 항상 업무를 수행하여야 하는 경우
   ④ 그 밖에 사업(행정)목적을 달성하는 것에 심각한 지장이 발생할 수 있는 경우

(3) 재택근무 업무환경의 구비요건

A certain level of working environment and work facilities (seats, PCs, etc.) are needed at home so that the work can be performed in an identical or very similar environment to the regular office.

1) Preparing work space

As contact with family members can disrupt work performance, employers need to ensure that those working from home have an independent space dedicated to work.

2) Construction of an IT infrastructure

The company will need to provide the basic IT devices and networks needed to do business at home. These would include computers and accessories, printers, communication equipment, and personal web cameras for video conferencing. The company will also need to provide the necessary solutions (electronic payment, messenger, file sharing, project management, etc.) when accessing office systems or performing company work.

3) Cost burden

It is common for the employer to bear the communication expenses related to working from home, the cost of information and communication equipment, and work-related consumable items.

4) Security measures

Working from home requires measures to protect information security. Such measures may include (i) providing a solution to security threats that may occur when accessing an office system from home, and to support with related technologies, (ii) introduction of a computer that leaves all work and records on the cloud rather than individual computers, (iii) actions to prevent family members of the employee working from home from accessing any company data, (iv) safe disposal of document waste, and (v) preparation of measures to ensure security of the home office space and computers (such as shutting them down automatically) when the employee is not at the work-from-home location.

2. Introducing a Work-from-Home System

Introduction of a work-from-home system requires (i) a written agreement with the workers' representative, (ii) changes in the labor contract with individual workers, and (iii) changes in the rules of employment. Even when a work-from-home system needs to be revised, the employer must follow the above 3

재택근무자가 사무실에서 업무를 수행할 때와 동일하게 업무를 수행하기 위해서는 재택근무지에 근무환경 및 업무시설(좌석, PC 등)을 구축하는 것이 필요하다.

1) 업무수행 공간 확보

재택근무는 가족이나 친지 등과의 접촉으로 업무수행에 차질을 야기할 수 있으므로 재택근로자로 하여금 업무수행을 위한 독립된 전용공간을 확보하도록 한다.

2) IT 인프라 구축

회사는 자택에서 업무를 수행하는 데 필요한 기본적인 IT 기기 및 네트워크를 제공한다. 컴퓨터 및 부속장비, 복합기, 통신장비, 화상회의를 위한 개인용 웹 카메라 등 업무 속성에 따라 관련 장비를 지원한다. 사무실 시스템에 접속하거나 업무를 수행할 때 필요한 솔루션(전자결재, 메신저, 파일공유, 프로젝트 관리 솔루션 등)도 제공한다.

3) 비용부담

재택근무와 관련된 통신비, 정보통신기기 비용, 소모성 비품 등은 사용자가 부담하는 것으로 하는 것이 일반적이다.

4) 보안대책

재택근무는 일반 가정에서 업무를 수행하기 때문에 정보보안 등을 위한 대책을 마련해야 한다. 예를 들어, (ⅰ) 가정에서 사무실 시스템 접속 시 발생할 수 있는 보안 위협에 대해 해결방안을 마련하고 관련 기술을 개발, (ⅱ) 단말기에 기록을 남기지 않는 클라우드 방식의 컴퓨터 도입, (ⅲ) 재택근무자의 다른 가족 구성원이 정보 보호 관련 데이터 등에 접근하지 못하도록 할 것, (ⅳ) 폐기문서의 안전한 처리, (ⅴ) 재택 사무공간 및 컴퓨터 잠그기 등이 있다.

2. 재택근로제 도입 방법

재택근무제의 도입을 하기 위해서는 (ⅰ) 근로자대표와 서면합의, (ⅱ) 개별 근로자와 근로계약서 작성 (ⅲ) 취업규칙의 변경 절차가 필요하다. 일부 조건을 변경할 경우에도 위의 3가지 절차를 거쳐야 한다. 다만, 특정 근로자에 대한

Chapter 4 Flexible Working Hours

steps again. However, when the work-from-home system will apply only to a particular worker, only that worker's consent is needed.

(1) Written agreement with the workers' representative

The Labor Standards Act (Article 58 (2)) requires a written agreement with the employees' representative when working outside the workplace, such as working from home. The time required for the performance of work is usually determined through a written agreement, but the content of the rest of the written agreement is not otherwise specified. Eventually, if the working hours for a work-from-home system are determined in a written agreement, the details of place of work and those to whom the agreement applies should be included.

(2) Changes to the employment contract

① Since the details of workplace and working hours are legally required to be specified in the employment contract, the working contract must reflect the changed workplace and working hours under the work-from-home system (regular work from home).

② For occasional work from home at a certain frequency and time while the company workplace remains the main workplace, it is necessary to state in the employment contract that work at a certain frequency and time outside the workplace is possible. However, as is the case for remote work, it is common for employment contracts to stipulate that uniform working conditions such as working place, working hours, and holidays are subject to employment rules or collective agreements. In this case, even if it is not specified in the employment contract, it is recognized in the employment rules that the company fulfilled its obligation to notify workers of compulsory working conditions.[127]

(3) Changes to rules of employment

When introducing a work-from-home system, whether there is a need to change the existing rules of employment needs to be confirmed. Any changes shall be reflected in the existing rules of employment.

① If there is no change to the rules of employment: When comparing the working conditions of working from home with those of ordinary workers at

---

[127] MOEL Guidelines: Labor Standards Team-5809, Aug. 7, 2007.

재택근무의 경우, 혹은 간헐적으로 이루어지는 재택근무의 경우에는 해당 근로자의 동의만으로도 제도의 도입이 가능하다.

(1) 근로자대표와 서면합의 내용

근로기준법(제58조 제2항)에서는 재택근무처럼 사업장 밖에서 근무가 이루어질 경우 근로시간을 근로자대표와의 서면합의로 정할 수 있는 규정을 두고 있다. 다만, 업무수행에 기본적으로 필요한 시간을 서면합의를 통해 정할 수 있도록 하고 있을 뿐, 나머지 서면합의에 꼭 포함되어야 하는 내용에 대해서는 달리 규정하고 있지 않으므로 재택근무제 도입 운영에 따른 근로시간을 서면합의에서 정할 경우, 업무수행에 필요한 평균 근로시간 이외의 근무장소, 적용대상자 등에 대한 내용을 기본적으로 포함시킬 수 있을 것이다.

(2) 근로계약서의 작성 및 변경

① 근무장소와 근로시간에 대한 내용은 법적으로 근로계약서에 명시해야 할 사항이기 때문에 제도도입에 따라 변경된 근무장소 내지 근로시간의 내용을 반영하여 근로계약서를 작성 또는 변경해야 한다(재택근무 상시형).
② 사업장을 주된 근무장소로 하면서 일정 빈도 및 시간을 재택근무 방식으로 근무하는 수시형의 경우에는 주 근무장소와 함께 일정 빈도 및 시간을 주된 근무장소 외의 장소에서 근무할 수 있다는 내용을 근로계약서에 함께 명시하여야 한다. 다만, 원격근무와 마찬가지로 근무장소·근로시간·주휴일 등 통상적인 근로조건에 대해서는 취업규칙이나 단체협약 등에 따른다고 규정하는 경우가 일반적이다. 이 경우 근로계약서에 명시되어 있지 않은 사항이라도 취업규칙에 명시되어 있고 이를 해당 근로자에게 주지시키면 명시의무를 이행한 것으로 인정된다.[127]

(3) 취업규칙 변경

재택근무제 도입 시 기존 취업규칙을 변경할 필요가 있는지 검토하고 변경이 필요한 항목이 있다면 선별하여 기존의 취업규칙에 반영한다.
① 취업규칙의 변경이 없는 경우: 재택근무를 하는 근로자와 통상근로자를

---

[127] 노동부 행정해석: 근로기준팀-5809, 2007.8.7.

the workplace, if there are no changes in working conditions besides workplace, individual consent of the worker who wants to work from home is all that is needed. There is no need to change the rules of employment.
② When the rules of employment need to be changed: If the employer requires all workers in the business or workplace to work from home.

<Table 4-9> **Working from Home in the Rules of Employment**

Article 00 (Working from home)
① The company may introduce a work-from-home system for workers desiring to work part or all of their working hours at home.
② Th working hours of workers to work from home are considered to be 8 hours a day. However, working hours may be determined separately according to the work performed. When the working hours are determined by written agreement with the workers' representative, the hours in the agreement shall be considered working hours that have been worked.
③ If those working from home want to work overtime, at night or during holidays, the approval of the head of the department must be obtained in advance. In this case, 50% of the normal wage is added and paid.
④ Requests to come to the company workplace due to reasons such as business meetings, work orders, work performance evaluation, education, events, etc. must be followed.

---

3. Application of the Labor Standards Act

(1) Attendance management

The Labor Standards Act regulations on working hours and rest also apply to workers working from home. However, working from home is a form of labor in which working hours and daily home life cannot easily be separated due to the nature of the workplace. It is difficult to manage and supervise such working hours as the employees are at home. In the end, it is left to the worker whether to

비교하여 근무장소 외의 다른 근로조건에 변경이 없는 경우에는 재택근무를 하고자 하는 근로자의 개별적 동의를 받아 실시하는 것으로 가능하며, 반드시 취업규칙을 변경할 필요는 없다.

② 취업규칙을 변경해야 하는 경우: 사용자가 해당 사업 또는 사업장의 근로자 전체를 대상으로 일괄적으로 재택근무를 시행하는 경우에는 취업규칙을 변경해야 한다.

<표4-9> 취업규칙 규정

제○○조 재택근무

① 회사는 근로시간의 전부 또는 일부를 자택 등에서 근로를 희망하는 근로자에 대하여 재택근무제를 도입할 수 있다.

② 재택근무제를 실시하는 근로자의 근로시간은 1일 8시간 근로한 것으로 본다. 다만 수행업무에 따라 근로시간을 별도로 정할 수 있으며, 근로자대표와 서면합의로 근로시간을 정한 경우에는 이에 따른다.

③ 재택근무자가 연장, 야간, 휴일근로를 하고자 하는 경우에는 사전에 부서장의 승인을 받아야 하며, 이때에는 통상임금의 50%를 가산하여 지급한다.

④ 업무회의, 업무지시, 업무수행평가, 교육, 행사 등의 사유로 인하여 회사의 출근요청이 있는 경우에는 이에 따라야 하며, 월 정기 출근일이 정해져 있는 경우 이를 준수하여야 한다.

---

3. 근로기준법의 적용

(1) 근태관리

재택근무에 종사하는 근로자도 근로기준법상의 근로시간 및 휴식에 관한 규정이 적용된다. 다만, 재택근무는 그 성질상 근로자의 근무시간대와 일상생활 시간대가 혼재되지 않을 수 없는 근로형태이며 "자택"에서 근로가 이루어지기 때문에 사생활의 침해없이 근로자가 소정근로시간 동안 성실히 업무에

fulfill the duty to provide work during the specified working hours. However, online attendance records and information and communication devices can provide some assistance with worker management.

<Table 4-10> Regulation Example: Work-from-Home Service Regulations

Article ○○ (Work-from-Home Service Regulations)
① Workers who have been approved to work from home are expected to manage their time and attendance well, including the time they start and finish their work each day. If necessary, an authorized person can confirm this by telephone or an in-person visit.
② Workers shall not leave the at-home workplace for personal reasons during the performance of work. If they need to work outside their home or at the applicable "smart work" location, this must be approved by the relevant company authority in advance. However, if it is unreasonably difficult to obtain this relevant authority's prior approval, the worker must immediately report to the relevant authority after changing the place of work for a late approval.
③ The worker shall immediately report any emergency while working from home to the approval authority, who shall respond with appropriate instructions.
④ Those working from home must provide an electronic report of their work plan and outcomes to the approval authority at least once a week

(2) Working hours, overtime, night work allowance

When the work-from-home system is introduced, whether or not an overtime allowance, night work allowance, or holiday work allowance occurs depends on the specified working time for the worker or the time normally required to perform the work and the range of working hours established by the labor-management agreement.

In principle, if the teleworkers (which is another term referring to those working from home for an employer) required to perform a specific task in accordance with the employer's instructions work overtime, at night or during a holiday, overtime or nighttime work allowance must be paid. However, it is desirable to prepare a similar procedure for general workers to apply for overtime, night, and holiday work in advance and be approved by the employer before working those hours. For example, a procedure might include reporting in advance plans to work over a

전념하였는가를 관리·감독하는 것은 어렵다. 결국 소정근로시간 동안의 근로제공의무나 직무전념의무의 이행 여부는 근로자에게 맡겨질 수 밖에 없고, 정보통신기기를 통한 온라인 출퇴근기록 등으로 재택근무자의 근로시간을 관리하는 것은 가능하다.

<표4-10> 취업규칙 중 재택근므제 복무규정

제 ○ 조 재택근무제 복무규정

① 재택근로를 승인받은 직원은 출·퇴근시간 등 근태관리에 철저를 기해야 하며, 승인권자는 필요한 경우 전화 또는 방문을 통해 근무상황을 확인할 수 있다.

② 직원은 업무수행 중 개인적인 사정을 이유로 임의로 근무장소를 무단이탈 할 수 없으며, 자택 또는 신청한 스마트워크센터 이외의 장소에서 근무가 필요한 경우에는 사전에 승인권자의 승인을 받아야 한다. 다만, 관리자의 사전승인을 얻는 것이 곤란한 경우에는 근무지 변경 후 즉시 관리자에게 보고하여 사후승인을 받아야 한다.

③ 재택근무 수행 중 긴급상황 발생 시 승인권자에게 이를 즉시 보고하고 적절한 지시를 받아 대처하여야 한다.

④ 재택근무 직원은 업무 계획 및 실적을 온라인으로 주 1회 이상 승인권자에게 서면보고 하여야 한다.

---

(2) 근로시간, 연장근로수당, 야간근로수당

재택근무제 도입 시 반드시 해당 근로자에 대한 소정근로시간 또는 업무수행에 통상 필요한 시간, 그리고 노사합의로 정한 근로시간의 범위에 따라 연장근로수당이나 야간근로수당, 휴일근로수당에 대한 발생 여부가 달라지게 된다.

사용자의 지시에 따라 특정업무를 수행하는데 필요한 시간이 연장·야간·휴일근로를 발생시킬 경우 원칙적으로 그에 대한 연장근로, 야간근로수당을 지급해야 한다. 다만, 전술한 바와 같이 재택근무제도 특성상 명확한 근로시간 산정이 어려우므로 근로자가 연장·야간·휴일근로를 사전에 신청하여

Chapter 4 Flexible Working Hours

holiday to obtain the employer's permission and then report the outcome in detail.

(3) Leave and rest time for teleworkers

If the rules of employment do not provide separate rules for leave and rest for ordinary workers working from home, the employment rules on working hours, leave, and rest for ordinary workers apply. In this regard, it is desirable for the employer to set in advance the matters concerning working hours and non-working hours (for example, non-working hours due to vacation or sick leave).

(4) Job training and compulsory training

It is unavoidable that workers who work remotely or from home are susceptible to some concern that they may lag behind their colleagues in development of their abilities, etc., because working from home does make it difficult to have the educational opportunities normally obtained during on-the-job training (OJT). When a separate in-house education or training system or legally-required program is run, this should be reflected in the employment rules. In particular, as education on safety and health (Article 29 of the Industrial Safety and Health Act), preventing sexual harassment (Article 13 of the Equal Employment Act), and protecting personal information (Article 28 of the Personal Information Protection Act) is normally run for workplace workers, the employer will need to provide equal training opportunities to those working from home.

(5) Safety and health standards

Depending on the nature of their work, if it falls under the safety and health standards in the Occupational Safety and Health Act, those working from home will need to follow those rules. Accidents arising during the work at home will be considered occupational accidents and those injured/ill are eligible to insurance benefits under the Industrial Accident Compensation Insurance Act. However, accidents caused by workers' actions unrelated to work are not recognized thus.[128]

(6) Performance evaluation

When employees are working from home (full time), it is desirable to establish a system so that workers do not worry about performance evaluation and personnel

---

[128] MOEL Guidelines: Medical Care 0509-90, Feb. 14, 1996.

사용자의 허가를 받도록 하는 유사한 절차를 마련하는 것이 바람직하다.

(3) 재택근무자의 휴가와 휴식 시간

취업규칙에서 재택근로에 종사하는 통상 근로자들에 대한 휴가 및 휴식에 관해서 별도의 규정을 두고 있지 않는 경우에는 통상적 근로에 종사하는 근로자들의 근로조건이 그대로 적용된다. 이와 관련하여 사용자는 근로시간과 비 근로시간(예컨대 휴가나 병가 등으로 인하여 근로하지 못하는 시간)에 관한 사항을 사전에 약정에 두는 것이 바람직하다.

(4) 직무교육과 의무교육

원격이나 재택근무를 하는 근로자는 OJT(On the Job Training)에 의한 교육기회를 얻기 어려운 측면이 있으므로 능력개발 등에서 다른 동료근로자들에 비하여 뒤쳐질 수 있다는 불안감을 갖지 않도록 조치를 취하는 것이 바람직하다. 따라서 통상근로자와는 별도의 사내교육이나 연수제도, 법정교육을 위한 프로그램 등을 운영하는 경우에는 이를 취업규칙에 반영하여야 한다. 특히, 법정교육인 산업안전·보건교육(산업안전보건법 제29조), 성희롱 예방교육 (남녀고용평등법 제13조), 개인정보 보호교육(개인정보 보호법 제28조) 등은 사업장 근로자와 차등적 적용되어서는 안되기 때문에 그에 대한 대처방안을 마련하는 것이 좋다.

(5) 안전보건 기준

업무의 특성에 따라 산업안전보건법상 안전보건기준에 해당하는 경우에는 이를 준수하여야 한다. 재택근무 중에 해당업무가 원인이 되어 발생한 재해는 업무상 재해로 산업재해보상보험법상 보험급여의 대상이 된다. 다만, 근로자의 사적 행위를 원인으로 하여 발생한 재해는 업무상 재해로 인정되지 않는다.[128]

(6) 성과평가

재택근무(상시형)의 경우 근로자가 사무실에 출근하지 않기 때문에 성과평가 등을 걱정하는 일이 없도록 별도의 성과평가 및 인사관리 제도를 구축

---

128) 노동부 행정해석(요양 0509-90, 1996.2.14)

management issues because they are not working at the normal workplace. The most difficult thing for companies who have workers providing work from home is ensuring efficiency from those workers. In the course of evaluating work performance, teleworkers are often less productive and feel less managed. It is a good idea for the company to do the following: (i) measure the performance of teleworkers based on visible results; (ii) manage the quality of work from teleworkers, and (iii) implement performance evaluations for teleworkers as necessary, and report summary results and explain to them their ongoing progress.

4. Conclusion

In order to increase work efficiency and promote the morale of workers working from home, it is necessary that a work environment is put in place that is suitable for independent work. In addition, it is important to separate work duties from the private lives of the workers so that they can continue to work from home. Therefore, rather than having them work from home the entire week at the beginning, it is necessary to introduce working from home on an occasional basis to ensure it is possible to do so on a regular basis later.

<Table 4-11> Example: Working from Home Policy

Article 1. Purpose

The Company recognizes that working from home is one way of providing a more flexible approach to working conditions. This "Working from Home" policy has been developed to provide guidelines for employees working from home

Article 2. Definitions and Guidelines
1. In all cases, the employee may only work from home with prior approval from their team leader and management through HR.
2. Team leaders are responsible for the establishment and administration of each working from home case.
3. The guidelines offered are intended to provide a checklist of issues that all team leaders and employees must agree to prior to the commencement of any working from home arrangements. They address management and administrative issues for

하는 것이 바람직하다. 재택근무를 제공하는 회사가 가장 어렵게 느끼는 점은 재택근무의 효율성이다. 따라서 (ⅰ) 회사는 보이는 결과에 의해 재택근무자의 결과물을 측정하고, (ⅱ) 재택근무자의 업무의 질을 관리하며, (ⅲ) 필요시 재택근무자에 대해 수행평가를 시행하고, 요약 결과나 진행과정 등에 대해 보고하도록 하는 것이 좋다.

4. 시사점

재택근로제를 도입하여 업무의 효율을 높이고 근로자의 사기를 진작시키기 위해서는 재택근로에 적합한 업무의 발굴과 업무환경을 구비하여야 한다. 이와 함께 근로자들의 업무와 사생활 영역을 명확히 하여 지속적 재택근무가 가능하도록 관리하는 것이 중요하다. 따라서 1주일 전일을 재택근무 하기 보다는 수시형 재택근무제를 도입하여 어느 정도 재택근무의 가능성을 확인 후에 상시형 재택근무제를 도입하는 것이 바람직할 것이라 하겠다.

<표4-11> 재택근무 규정

제1장 목적
회사는 재택근무를 제공하여 좀 더 나은 탄력적 근무환경을 만들고자 한다. "재택근무"정책은 재택근무를 하는 근로자들을 위한 지침서로서 마련되었다.

제2장 정의 및 지침
1. 모든 경우 근로자는 인사부서를 통하여 그들의 팀장이나 경영진으로 부터 사전 승인을 받아야만 재택근무를 할 수 있다.
2. 팀장들은 각 재택근무 요청에 관한 근무 원칙들을 확립하고 관리할 책임이 있다.
3. 제시된 지침들은 재택근무를 실시하기 전에 팀장과 근로자가 사전에 동의해야 하는 의제의 체크리스트를 제공하며, 부분적으로나 전체적 으로 정기적 재택근무를 하는 근로자들에 대한 관리와 감독 문제들을

Chapter 4 Flexible Working Hours

employees working partly or fully from home on a regular basis.

Article 3. Authorization

In all cases, the employee may only work from home with prior approval from their team leader & management. HR will be responsible for maintaining this policy and for reviewing, ensuring consistency of the terms of employment, employment itself and work practices.

Article 4. Terms of Employment

Working partly or fully from home on a regular basis constitutes a variation to the employment contract which should be documented in the form indicated in the Standard Letters (e.g. allowances).

Article 5. Equipment and Facilities

1. The provision of additional equipment and facilities is at the discretion of the team leader in conjunction with the HR adviser and occupational health and safety. The facilities offered may vary between businesses according to the needs of different jobs. Additional equipment and facilities may also be provided for employees who are working from home on a regular basis and for significant periods. The level of support provided in this respect will depend on each individual situation.

2. Employees working from home should discuss and agree to their requirements for additional equipment with their leader and Company management (additional phone line for computer, desk etc.) prior to beginning to work from home. Should additional equipment be required, where possible spare Company equipment shall be provided. Record must be kept of all equipment/facilities provided to an employee working from home. Team leaders shall ensure that unnecessary expense is avoided.

3. Any arrangements made with respect to equipment/facilities will cease if the employee's worksite changes and the employee no longer works from home, or if the employee leaves the Company. Any Company equipment, furniture or files etc. must also be returned to the Company at such a time.

4. In all cases, occupational health and safety issues must be addressed and rectified.

규정하고 있다.

제3장 권한

모든 경우에 근로자는 그들의 팀장 및 경영진의 사전동의를 통해서만 재택근무를 할 수 있다. 인사부서는 이 정책을 유지하고, 재검토하며, 고용 조건과 고용 및 노동 관례와의 일관성을 유지해야 할 책임이 있다.

제4장 고용 조건

정기적인 부분적 또는 전체적 재택근무는 표준 서식(예, 수당)에 따라 지정된 양식에 고용 계약의 변동사항을 문서화 한다.

제5장 장비 및 시설

1. 추가적인 장비 및 시설의 제공은 직업적 건강 및 안전에 관하여 인사부와 팀장의 재량에 따른다. 제공된 시설들은 다양한 업무상의 요구에 따라 다르다. 추가적인 장비 및 시설은 정기적으로 상당한 기간 동안 재택근무를 하는 근로자에게 제공되어질 수 있으며 지원의 수준은 각 개인의 상황에 따라 다르다.
2. 재택근무를 하고자 하는 근로자는 재택근무를 시작하기 전에 추가적으로 필요한 장비, 예를 들어 컴퓨터를 위한 추가적인 전화선, 책상 등과 같은 것들을 팀장 및 경영진과 미리 상의하고 동의를 받아야 한다. 추가 장비가 요구되면, 가능한 한 회사가 가진 여분의 장비가 먼저 제공되어야 한다. 재택근무를 하는 근로자에게 제공된 모든 장비/시설에 대해서는 기록을 하여야 하며, 팀장은 불필요한 비용의 지출이 생기지 않도록 해야 한다.
3. 근로자의 작업장이 변경되거나, 근로자가 재택근무를 중단하거나, 회사를 퇴사할 때에는 장비/시설과 관련하여 맺은 모든 계약은 중단되며 회사 장비와 가구 및 파일 등도 동시어 회사에 반납되어야 한다.
4. 모든 경우에 직업적 건강 및 안전의 문제는 다루어지고 조정되어야 한다.

Chapter 4 Flexible Working Hours

Article 6. Additional Expenses

Where working from home is required by the Company, and with team leader & management approval, employees may receive compensation from the Company for additional expenses borne by running an office at home, such as telephone expenses.

Article 7. Space

Employees will need to set aside a suitable area in their home to use as an office area. While the Company may assist the employee by helping to provide adequate equipment / furniture to allow the employee to work from home, it is not Company policy to relocate an employee or finance home extensions to accommodate an office.

Article 8. Work Practices

1. Team leaders shall ensure that adequate contact is maintained with the employee working from home, and that communication links (e.g. Company notices and information) reach the employee. Employees shall be urged to attend team meetings and training courses as appropriate.
2. Team leaders and employees shall substitute the reduced day-to-day contact experienced by employees working from home with a more detailed work program and revised job objectives and performance measures. It is particularly important that a work program (including expected deliverables) be developed, clearly outlining the specific tasks that will apply e.g. arrangements for supervision of family dependents, hours worked and hours that the employee will be contactable. The overall policy procedure has to be reported to HR. A weekly/monthly work plan, schedule, and record of achievement has to be reported to the team leader regularly, who will then report it to management and HR.
3. Employees who are required by the Company to work from home should discuss with their team leader if their home circumstances are not conductive for work and should seek other alternatives.

Article 9. Customer Visits

제6장 추가 경비

　재택근무가 회사에 의해 요구되고, 팀장과 경영진의 승인이 있으면, 근로자는 집에서 사무실을 운영함에 따라 야기되는 추가적인 비용, 예를 들어 전화 요금에 대해 회사로부터 상환을 받을 수 있다.

제7장 공간

　근로자들은 사무공간으로 쓰기 위해서 자신의 집안의 적절한 공간을 따로 설치해야 한다. 회사는 근로자의 재택근무를 위해 적절한 장비/가구를 제공함으로써 근로자를 도울 것이다. 그러나 사무실을 만들기 위해 이사를 하거나, 집 확장을 위해 자금을 빌리는 것은 회사의 정책이 아니다.

제8장 근로 형태

1. 팀장들은 재택근무를 하는 근로자와 적절한 연락을 유지하고, 커뮤니케이션 링크(예, 회사 정보 및 통보)가 근로자에게 도달하도록 해야 한다. 근로자들은 적절히 팀 회의 및 교육 과정에 참여하도록 격려하여야 한다.
2. 팀장과 근로자는 근로자의 재택근무로 인해 줄어든 일상적 접촉을 더 상세한 업무 프로그램 및 개정된 직무 목표와 성과 측정방법으로 대체해야 한다. 특히 업무 프로그램(기대된 성과치를 포함)은 부양 가족의 감독, 근무 시간, 연락 가능한 시간 등이 적용되는 조건들에 대해 특정 업무를 명확하게 기술하여 개발 하는 것이 중요하다. 전반적인 정책의 절차는 인사부서에 보고하여야 한다. 주간별/월별 업무계획서, 스케줄, 업무완성표는 팀장에게 정기적으로 보고되어져야 하며, 팀장은 업무진행 상황을 경영진과 인사부로 보고해야 한다.
3. 재택근무가 요구되는 근로자의 집안 환경이 업무에 적합하지 않으면 근로자는 팀장과 상의해서 다른 대안을 찾아야 한다.

제9장 고객의 방문

Chapter 4 Flexible Working Hours

Employees should not invite Company business customers or other business third parties to their home (this does not preclude normal at-home business entertaining). It is not Company policy to conduct interviews (interviewing prospective franchisees for example) within a home office environment. Such activities should be organized, wherever possible, within Company office facilities.

Article 10. Security
1. Employees working from home are covered by the same policies and procedures developed for employees working at the office.
2. Company computers used at an employee's home must have an approved security software product installed and activated to prevent unauthorized access. Advice on and approval for appropriate software will be required via authority from the Company Business Information Manager.
3. All Company computers have a component identification number that resides in a configuration management system. This number must be updated in the system to show the computer's physical location. For further information, contact the Computer Team.
4. Security of Information - Practice, Policies and Procedure (available from the Computer Team) applies to any information/files stored in the employee's home relating to Company business, just as it does in the office. It is the employee's responsibility to comply with this procedure.

This policy will be effective from January 1, 2020, and will be reviewed annually to maintain competitiveness in terms of the Korean market situation.

근로자들은 회사의 사업상 고객이나 기타 제 삼자를 자신의 집으로 초대해서는 안된다 (이는 집에서의 사업상 접대도 포함된다). 자택 사무실에서 인터뷰, 예를 들어 가맹점 후보 인터뷰,를 하는 것은 회사의 정책이 아니다. 그러한 활동들은 가능한 한 회사 사무실 내에서 이루어져야 한다.

제10조 보안
1. 재택근무를 하는 근로자들은 사내근무를 하는 근로자들과 같은 정책 및 절차의 적용을 받는다.
2. 근로자의 집에서 사용되는 컴퓨터는 무단 접근을 막기 위해 승인된 보안 소프트웨어 제품을 설치해야 한다. 적절한 소프트웨어에 대한 조언 및 승인은 회사의 Business Information 팀장의 책임으로 이루어진다.
3. 회사의 모든 컴퓨터는 시스템구성 배치 관리 시스템에 기재된 제품 일련번호를 가지고 있다. 이 번호는 컴퓨터의 물리적 위치를 나타내기 위해 시스템상에 업데이트되어야 한다. 자세한 사항은 전산팀을 통해서 얻을 수 있다.
4. 정보 보안 정책 및 절차 (전산팀에 있음)는 회사 내에서와 마찬가지로 근로자의 집에 저장되어 있는 회사 업무와 관련된 모든 정보/파일에도 적용되며, 이러한 절차를 따르는 것은 근로자의 책임이다.

이 정책은 2020년 1월1일부터 유효하며, 국내 다른 경쟁업체들이나 국내 시장 상황에 비추어 경쟁성을 유지할 수 있도록 매년 재검토 된다.

<Table 4-12> Working from Home Checklist

Employee		Hire Date	
Job Title		Department	
Line Manager		Location	

Induction Checklist		
Action	Date	Person in Charge
Arrange for health and safety assessment of home office		
Arrange basic office training for employee		
Discuss method of recording working days/hours		
Discuss procedure for communicating with line manager and colleagues		
Discuss incident/injury reporting procedures		
Discuss and remedy issues identified during the home office assessment		

Home Office Checklist		
Checklist	Yes/No	Remarks
Are customer file notes kept in a lockable cabinet?		
Are back-ups completed on a regular basis?		
Are electrical items in good condition and are they checked by a qualified electrician?		
Is artificial lighting adequate for reading and computer tasks?		
Is there adequate ventilation / heating & cooling?		
Are PC, printer, internet and internal network connections operational?		
Does the employee have any concerns regarding the home office? (Specify:)		
Has the manager (HR/Line Manager) made any recommendations? (Specify:)		

_____   _____
Employee   Date   Line Manager   Date

_____
HR Manager   Date

<표4-12> 재택근무 체크리스트

재택근로자		입사일	
직급		부서	
직상 상급자		재택지역	

재택 업무 시작 전 체크리스트		
세부 내역	날짜	담당자/담당 책임자
재택사무실의 안전과 보건 상태 평가		
근로자에 대한 재택근무 요령 교육여부		
근무일, 근무시간 기록 방법 교육여부		
직속 상급자나 직장동료와 연락을 취하는 방법 교육여부		
업무 중 사고나 부상 발생시 보고요령 교육여부		
재택근무 중 발생하는 근무여건 개선항목 처리 요령 교육		

재택사무실 체크 리스트		
세부내역	Yes/No	추가 기술 내용
고객 파일은 잠근 장치가 있는 캐비닛에 정리되어 있는가?		
백업 자료는 정규적으로 수행되고 있는가?		
전자 제품 (PC, 프린터, 기타장비)는 기술자에 의해 정규적으로 체크되고 있는지?		
전등은 업무수행과 PC 작업을 위해 적당한가?		
사무실에 난방 및 환기시설은 적절한가?		
PC, 프린터, 인터넷 내부 통신망이 사용 가능한가?		
재택근로자가 재택 사무실에 대해 우려하는 점이 있다면 기술 바랍니다. (상세히 기술)		
직속 상사나 부서장에게 건의하실 사항이 있는지요? (상세히 기술)		

재택근로자   Date   직속 상급자   Date

인사부서장   Date

Chapter 4 Flexible Working Hours

<Table 4-13> Agreement to Protect Security while Working from Home

Agreement to Protect Security while Working from Home

■ Department: ■ Position:
■ Name: ■ Date of Birth:

1. I shall perform my assigned work at a designated work place.
2. I shall not allow any non-Company personnel, including family members, to enter this designated workplace while I am working from home.
3. I shall securely manage the documents that are to be read, written, stored, and printed out while working from home, and shall prevent any leak of such information.
4. I shall securely manage electronic recording media such as USB memory sticks and optical discs that contain documents or information related to my assigned working-from-home tasks, and shall prevent any leak of such information.
5. I shall install and use only the software necessary to perform my telecommuting tasks on a computer provided by the Company.
6. I shall install and run an anti-virus program on the assigned Company computer to prevent viral infection or spread, and shall keep the anti-virus program up to date.
7. I shall set the screen lock on the computer anytime I am away from my designated work place, and ensure that a secure password is required in order to lift the screen lock.
8. I shall securely manage the ID, password, and certificate(s) given to me to prevent any leak of such information while telecommuting.
9. If I recognize that the security of the ID, password, or certificate(s) given me have been compromised, I shall immediately apply for suspension of its usability and receive a replacement.

I pledge to abide by the above.

Date: _____

Position:
Name: Signature:

<표4-13> 재택근무 보안서약서

재택근무 보안서약서

- ■ 소   속 :   　　　　　■ 직   급 :
- ■ 성   명 :   　　　　　■ 생년월일 :

1. 본인은 지정한 근무장소에서 재택근무를 수행한다.
2. 본인은 재택근무 수행 중 근무장소에 가족을 포함한 외부인 출입을 금지한다.
3. 본인은 재택근무 수행 중 열람·작성·저장·출력한 문서는 철저히 관리하고, 이를 외부로 유출하지 아니한다.
4. 본인은 재택근무 수행과 관련된 문서 또는 정보를 수록한 USB메모리, 광디스크 등 전자 기록 매체를 철저히 관리하고, 이를 외부로 유출하지 아니한다.
5. 본인은 재택근무 지원을 위하여 소속기관에서 지급한 컴퓨터에 재택근무 수행에 필요한 소프트웨어만 설치하며 사용한다.
6. 본인은 바이러스 감염이나 유포를 방지하기 위해서, 재택근무 수행용 컴퓨터에 백신 프로그램을 설치·운영하며, 백신 엔진을 최신 상태로 유지한다.
7. 본인은 재택근무 수행용 컴퓨터에 화면보호기능 설정하고, 화면 복귀 시 반드시 비밀번호를 입력하도록 한다.
8. 본인은 재택근무 수행을 위하여 본인에게 부여된 ID, 비밀번호, 인증서가 외부로 유출되지 않도록 철저히 관리한다.
9. 본인에게 부여된 ID, 비밀번호, 인증서가 외부로 유출되었음을 인지한 경우 즉시 사용정지 신청을 하고, 이를 재발급 받도록 한다.

본인은 상기와 같은 사항을 준수할 것을 서약합니다.

　　　　　　　　　　년　　　월　　　일
　　　　서 약 자　직급)　　　　성명)　　　　　(인)

Chapter 4 Flexible Working Hours

VIII. Annual Leave and the Vacation Savings Account System

1. Annual paid leave system under current law

The purpose of the annual paid leave system is to guarantee sufficient leave to workers to help them recharge in the interest of protecting their mental and physical health, while at the same time guaranteeing social and cultural opportunities for workers.[129] ILO Convention No. 132 requires that two weeks of undivided annual leave be secured for each worker. The use of consecutive annual leave is guaranteed in Korea, for civil servants as well. In addition, if an application is made at least three months in advance for the use of consecutive annual leave of more than 10 days, the head of an administrative agency must approve it unless there are special circumstances dictating otherwise.[130]

Under the annual paid leave system, workers with less than 1 year of employment receive 1 paid leave day every month, while workers with at least 1 year of employment receive 15 paid leave days if they attend 80% or more of their work days in 1 year. In addition, one accrued leave day is granted for every 2 years of continuous work, to a maximum of 25 leave days a year. If the vacation is not used within one year after it accrues, it is extinguished and converted into a right to claim monetary compensation (Article 60 of the Labor Standards Act, or LSA).

A system to promote the use of annual paid leave (Article 61 of the LSA) has been introduced so that all leave can be used within one year of the annual leave accruing. Promoting the use of annual paid leave in this way is designed to highlight that the purpose for annual leave is to help maintain employee mental and physical health, and that additional financial compensation is not preferable. Employees shall notify their employers of their vacation plans 6 months prior to the period in which the annual leave can be used and use it. Employers can designate the time of leave for any unused leave for which two months or less remains before expiry. The employee would then have to use his/her unused leave within that period. If the employee still does not use the leave despite these employer measures, the unused leave expires.

---

[129] Kim, Hong-Young, Theory on Improving the System of Annual Leave for Guaranteed Rest, Labor Law Study, 1st half of 2016, No. 40, Seoul National University Labor Law Research Society, p. 165.
[130] Article 16-4 of the National Government Employee Service Regulations (Guaranteed use of at least 10 consecutive annual leave days).

Ⅷ. 연차유급휴가를 이용한 저축휴가제도

1. 현행법의 연차유급휴가제도

연차휴가제도의 취지는 장기간 근로에 지친 근로자에게 충분한 휴가를 보장하여 정신적, 육체적 건강을 회복하도록 하는 동시에, 근로자의 사회적, 문화적 생활을 보장하기 위한 것이라 할 수 있다.[129] ILO의 제132호 협약은 연차휴가기간이 분할되지 않는 2주간의 기간이 확보되도록 하고 있다. 우리나라 공무원의 경우에도 10일 이상 연속된 연가 사용을 보장하고 있으며, 행정기관의 장은 공무원이 3개월 이전에 10일 이상의 연속된 연가 일수 사용을 신청할 경우에는 특별한 사정이 없으면 이를 승인하여야 한다고 규정하고 있다.[130]

연차유급휴가제도는 입사 1년 미만인 근로자는 1월 만근에 1개의 유급휴가가 발생하고, 1년 이상 근무한 근로자는 1년간 80퍼센트 이상 개근한 경우 15개의 유급휴가가 발생한다. 그리고 계속근로 2년차 마다 1개 씩 누적된 휴가가 발생하고 최대 25개까지 부여된다. 이렇게 근로의 대가로 발생한 휴가는 1년간 행사하지 않으면 소멸되고, 금전보상청구권으로 전환된다(근기법 제60조).

연차휴가의 사용유효기간 1년 기간 내에 휴가를 모두 사용할 수 있도록 근로기준법에서 연차 유급휴가의 사용 촉진제도(근기법 제61조)를 도입하고 있다. 이 연차 유급휴가 사용촉진 조치의 목적은 연차휴가의 목적이 휴가 사용을 통해서 근로자의 정신적, 육체적 건강을 유지하는 것이지, 추가 임금보상을 받기 위한 것이 아님을 설명하고 있다. 근로자는 연차휴가 사용가능기간 6개월 전에 휴가 계획을 통보하고, 이를 사용하여야 한다. 그럼에도 불구하고 휴가사용 유효기간 2개월 이내인 휴가에 대해서는 사용하지 못한 휴가에 대해 사용자가 휴가시기를 지정하여 휴가사용을 강제하고 있다. 이러한 사용자의 휴가사용 조치에도 불구하고 근로자가 사용하지 않은 경우, 미사용 휴가는 소멸된다고 규정하고 있다.

---

[129] 김홍영, 휴식보장을 위한 연차휴가의 제도개선론, 노동법연구, 2016 상반기 제40호, 서울대노동법연구회 165면.
[130] 국가공무원 복무규정 제16조의4(10일 이상 연속된 연가 사용의 보장)

2. The vacation savings account system for annual leave

The current period for use of annual paid leave is one year, after which it is converted into monetary compensation. The vacation savings account system would allow unused annual leave to be carried over to the following year. In this regard, the MOEL provides guidelines that allow the use of unused annual leave during the following year. It would be a violation of the law to pay vacation allowance before the right to claim annual paid leave expires, as it would be to fail to grant the earned vacation leave. However, it is legal for two parties (employer and employee) to agree to carry over any unused annual leave instead of converting it to monetary compensation.[131] In addition, the Labor Standards Act stipulates that unused annual leave will expire if the employee comes to work on a designated vacation day and provides work. However, even if an employer has taken measures to promote the use of annual leave, the court holds that the employer has an obligation to compensate for unused annual paid leave if the employer has received the worker's labor provision without any objection related to the unused annual paid leave.[132]

Therefore, according to administrative interpretations and judicial rulings, the vacation savings account system for annual leave is sufficiently possible even under current law. However, in its implementation, individual consent by the employee is required, not a written agreement with the workers' representative. Carried-over unused annual leave is equivalent to an individual worker's wage claim, so the consent of the individual worker is required. At the end of the period of use of annual leave, the annual leave can be converted into wage bonds, which can be accumulated for 3 years and used as long-term leave.

A method that should be taken into consideration when introducing this system is the vacation savings account system for civil servants. In addition to the recommended number of annual leave days, unused annual leave can be deposited in a savings account for up to three years, allowing for long-term vacations. For example, civil servants who have been employed for 6 years or more receive 21 days of annual vacation. If they take the recommended minimum of 10 days as vacation, and then save 11 days a year for 3 years, depositing a total of 33 days over those 3 years, they can go on vacation for more than a month at a time.[133]

---

[131] MOEL Guidelines on Feb. 20, 2009: Labor Condition Dept.-1047.
[132] Supreme Court ruling on Feb. 27, 2020: 2019da279283.
[133] Hwang, Soo-yeon, Civil servants can take more than a month's leave due to 'annual leave savings,' Joongang Ilbo, Sept. 30, 2015.

2. 연차휴가의 저축휴가제도

　현행법에서 연차 휴가에 대해 저축휴가제도로 사용하기 위해서는 현재, 연차 유급휴가 사용기간이 1년이고, 이 사용유효기간이 지나면 금전보상의무로 전환되기 때문에 미사용연차휴가를 이월해서 사용할 수 있는지가 저축휴가제도의 쟁점이다. 이에 대해 행정해석은 미사용 연차휴가를 이월하여 사용하는 것은 가능하다고 해석하고 있다. 여기서 연차유급휴가 청구권이 소멸되기 전에 미리 휴가수당을 지급하고 그 만큼 휴가를 부여하지 않는 것은 법위반이 될 수 있다. 그러나 미사용 연차유급휴가에 대해 금전보상 대신 이월하여 사용하도록 당사자간에 합의하는 것은 무방하다고 보았다.[131] 또한, 연차 유급휴가 사용촉진조치에 있어서 사용자가 연차유급휴가 사용촉진조치를 취하였음에도 근로자가 지정된 휴가일에 출근하여 근로를 제공한 경우, 미사용 연차휴가가 소멸한다는 근로기준법 조항에 대해 엄격한 판단을 하고 있다. 이런 경우 법원은 미사용 연차 유급휴가에 대해 사용자가 별다른 이의 없이 근로자의 노무제공을 수령하였다면 사용자는 미사용 연차휴가에 대한 보상의무가 있다고 판시하고 있다.[132]

　따라서 행정해석과 판례의 내용을 가지고 판단할 때, 현행법 내에서도 연차휴가에 대한 저축휴가제도는 충분히 가능하다고 할 수 있다. 다만, 이 제도의 시행에 있어서는 근로자대표와의 서면합의가 아닌 근로자의 개별동의가 필요하다. 연차유급휴가를 이월하여 휴가로 사용하는 것은 개별근로자의 임금채권과 같으므로 개별근로자의 동의를 전제로 한다. 연차유급휴가 사용기간이 끝나는 시점에서 임금채권으로 변경된 3년 동안 연차휴가를 적립하여 장기휴가로 사용이 가능하다.

　도입 시에 참고할 만한 방식이 공무원 연가 저축제도이다. 이는 권장 연가일수 이외 미사용 연가는 저축계좌에 최대 3년까지 적립해 장기휴가를 갈 수 있게 하는 연가저축제도이다. 예를 들어, 현재 6년 이상 공무원의 연가일수는 21일로 이 가운데 권장 연가일수 10일을 제외하고 매년 11일씩 3년간 총 33일을 저축한다면 한꺼번에 한 달 이상 휴가를 가는 게 가능해진다.[133]

---

[131] 행정해석 2009.2.20. 근로조건지도과-1047.
[132] 대법원 2020.2.27. 선고 2019다279283 판결.
[133] 중앙일보(황수연기자), 공무원 '연가 저축' 생겨 한 달 이상 휴가 가능, 2015.9.30.

Chapter 4 Flexible Working Hours

Because of this attractive outcome, this vacation savings account system has been expanded from government organizations to public institutions and is in wide use.

3. Applications (Agreement and Regulation)

In accordance with Article 57 (Compensatory Leave System) of the Labor Standards Act, the vacation savings account system for working hours can be introduced through a written agreement between labor and management, with the application as follows.

<Table 4-14> Sample Labor-Management Agreement to Introduce a Vacation Savings Account System for Working Hours

Representative Director ○○○ of AA Co., Ltd. and Worker Representative ○○ of AA Co., Ltd. agree to implement the compensatory leave system pursuant to Article 57 of the Labor Standards Act as follows.
1. Scope of eligible workers: All regular employees of the company are covered.
2. Scope of compensatory working hours: Overtime work that exceeds contractual working hours, or holiday work in which work is provided on a statutory holiday or contractual holiday. However, this does not include night work allowances for field workers.
3. Settlement period: The settlement period is from January 1 to December 31, while the period for use of the leave days to be within one year of the year following the date the leave is accumulated. Leave that remains unused after this settlement period shall be converted to financial compensation for the employee by the first month after the end of the settlement period.
4. How compensator leave is to be used: The company guarantees 10 days of summer vacation for workers to ensure a lengthy time away from work. If a request is to be made for other long-term leave, it must be made at least 3 months in advance. In return, the company guarantees the timing of the requested leave unless special circumstances exist otherwise.

April 1, 2022

AA Co., Ltd. CEO 000   / AA Co.,   Ltd. employee representative 000

이 연가 저축휴가제 대상은 정부부처에서 공공기관으로 확대되어 널리 사용되고 있다.

3. 근로시간 저축휴가제 도입 합의서와 규정

근로시간 저축휴가제는 근로기준법 제57조(보상휴가제)에 따라 노사 서면 합의로 도입할 수 있는데, 그 적용사례는 다음과 같다.

<표4-14> 근로시간 저축휴가제 노사합의서

주식회사 AA 대표이사 ○○○와 주식회사 AA 근로자대표 ○○○는 근로기준법 제57조에 따른 보상휴가제 실시에 대하여 다음과 같이 합의한다.

1. 대상 근로자의 범위: 회사의 정규직 근로자 전체를 대상으로 한다.
2. 대상 근로시간의 범위: 소정근로시간을 초과하는 연장근로, 법정휴일이나 약정휴일에 근로를 제공한 휴일근로로 한다. 다만, 현장직 근로자의 야간근로 수당은 여기에 포함되지 않는다.
3. 정산기간: 정산기간은 1월 1일부터 12월 31일까지 적립하고, 휴가의 사용기간은 적립이 끝난 다음해 1년 이내로 한다. 이 사용기간 내에 미사용된 휴가는 휴가사용기간이 끝난 그 다음 해 첫번째 달에 금전으로 보상한다.
4. 보상휴가의 사용방법: 회사는 근로자의 장기 휴가를 보장하기 위해서 10일의 여름휴가를 보장한다. 그 외에의 장기휴가를 신청할 경우에는 적어도 3개월 전에 휴가신청을 하고, 회사는 특별한 사정이 없는 한 휴가를 보장한다.

2022. 4. 1.

주식회사 AA 대표이사 ○○○ / 주식회사 AA 근로자 대표 ○○○

Chapter 4 Flexible Working Hours

<Table 4-15> Introduction through the Rules of Employment

Article 21 (Banking up annual leave) ① Employees may save a portion of their unused annual leave for later use, for up to three years as of the last day of the year it was accumulated.
② Any banked up annual leave shall expire if it is not used within two years after the three-year period in paragraph (1).
③ Annual leave allowance shall not be paid for annual leave saved pursuant to paragraph (1) and annual leave that has expired pursuant to paragraph (2).
④ In addition to the matters stipulated in Paragraphs 1 through 3, matters concerning the procedure for saving up and using annual leave, etc. shall be determined by the company president.

Article 22 (Guaranteed Use of Annual Leave of at least 10 Consecutive Days) If an employee applies for annual leave for 10 or more consecutive days 3 months in advance and shall use the banked up annual leave under Article 21, it shall be approved if doing so will not unduly impede the employee's performance of his or her duties. In this case, the company shall make the necessary efforts to ensure smooth operation and free use of annual leave, such as by designating a business agent to handle the employee's work during his or her use of the annual leave.
② In addition to the matters stipulated in Paragraph 1, the president shall determine any other matters necessary in regards to the application procedure for the use of annual leave for 10 consecutive days or more.

4. Opinion

The ILO's Paid Leave Convention (No. 132) also stipulates that 3 weeks of leave must be guaranteed for a one-year working period, and that at least 2 consecutive weeks must be allowed to be used as leave (Articles 3 and 8). Through long-term leave used in return for work, workers can better maintain their mental and physical health and their dignity as human beings through social and cultural activities. Therefore, it is necessary to recognize that guaranteeing long-term leave is more desirable for workers than monetary compensation in lieu of leave. In addition, guaranteeing long-term leave is virtually impossible unless it is systematically implemented through a company's collective leave policy or introducing the employer's obligation to make such a guarantee through the rules of employment. Therefore, a long-term leave guarantee policy is very much needed, along with a vacation savings account system for working hours and annual paid leave.

<표4-15> 취업규칙을 통한 도입 내용

제21조(연차휴가의 저축)
① 직원은 사용하지 아니하고 남은 연차휴가의 일부를 그 해의 말일을 기준으로 최대 3년까지 저축하여 사용할 수 있다.
② 제1항에 따른 최대 3년의 저축 가능기간이 종료된 후 2년 이내에 사용하지 아니한 저축된 연차휴가는 소멸된다.
③ 제1항에 따라 저축된 연차휴가 및 제2항에 따라 소멸된 연차휴가에 대해서는 연차휴가수당을 지급하지 아니한다.
④ 제1항부터 제3항까지에서 규정한 사항 외에 연차휴가의 저축 및 사용절차 등에 관하여 필요한 사항은 사장이 정한다.

제22조(10일 이상 연속된 연차휴가 사용의 보장)
① 공사는 직원이 제21조의 연차휴가로 저축된 연차휴가를 활용하여 충분한 휴식, 가족화합 또는 자기계발 등을 위하여 3개월 이전에 10일 이상 연속된 연차휴가 사용을 신청한 경우에는 업무 수행에 특별한 지장이 없으면 승인하여야 한다. 이 경우 공사는 연차휴가 사용에 따른 업무대행자 지정, 인력보충 등 원활한 업무수행과 자유로운 연차휴가 사용 보장에 필요한 노력을 하여야 한다.
② 제1항에서 규정한 사항 외에 10일 이상 연속된 연차휴가 사용의 신청절차 등에 관하여 필요한 사항은 사장이 정한다.

4. 시사점

ILO의 유급휴가협약(제132호)에서도 1년 근무기간에 대해 3주의 휴가를 보장하여야 하고, 이 휴가 중 최소 2주는 연속하여 부여하여 한다고 규정하고 있다(제3조, 제8조). 근로의 대가로 사용하는 장기 휴가를 통해 근로자는 정신적, 육체적 건강을 회복하고, 인간으로서의 사회적, 문화적 활동을 통해 인간의 존엄성을 회복할 수 있다. 따라서 장기휴가의 보장은 금전보상보다 더 바람직한 근로자의 복지라는 인식이 필요하다. 또한 이것은 회사의 집단휴가 사용정책이나 취업규칙을 통한 사용자의 보장의무 규정 도입 등을 통해 체계적으로 이루어지지 않으면 사실상 불가능하다. 따라서 근로시간이나 연차유급휴가에 대해 저축휴가제도의 도입과 함께 장기휴가보장 정책의 도입이 절실히 요구된다.

Chapter 5 Statutory and Contractual Holidays

I. Statutory Holidays
II. Contractual Holidays

⟨Case Study 5-1⟩ Petition for Unpaid Weekly Holiday Allowance

⟨Case Study 5-2⟩ Unpaid Wages for Temporary Workers

제5장 법정휴일과 약정휴일

Ⅰ. 법정휴일

Ⅱ. 약정휴일

〈실무사례 5-1〉 주휴수당 미지급 진정사건

〈실무사례 5-2〉 지방의회의 일급직
사무보조자(위촉직)의 임금체불 사례

Chapter 5 Statutory and Contractual Holidays

I. Statutory Holidays

Labor Standards Act: Article 55 (Holidays)
① Employers shall allow workers an average of one or more paid holidays per week.
② Employers shall provide paid holidays for holidays declared by Presidential Decree: Provided, that the holidays can be shifted to other working days upon a written agreement with the workers' representative.[134]

LSA Enforcement Decree: Article 30 (Holidays)
① Paid holidays under Article 55 (1) of the Act shall be granted to a person who has shown perfect attendance for the contractual working days during one week. <Amended by Presidential Decree No. 29010, Jun. 29, 2018>
② "Holidays prescribed by Presidential Decree" in the main sentence of Article 55 (2) of the Act means the holidays under any subparagraphs (excluding subparagraph 1) of Article 2 of the Regulations on Holidays of Government Offices and the alternative statutory holidays under Article 3 of the same Regulations.

Regulations on Holidays of Government Offices
Article 2 (Public Holidays) Statutory holidays of government offices shall be as follows: Provided, that statutory holidays of embassies and legations abroad shall be the statutory holidays among the national holidays of Korea and statutory holidays of residing nations:
1. Sundays;
2. The March 1 Independence Movement Day, Independence Day, National Foundation Day of Korea, and Hangul (Korean alphabet) Day;
3. The first day of January; 4. The day preceding Seollal (Korean New Year's Day), Seollal, and the day following Seollal (the last day of December, and the first and second days of January on the lunar calendar);
5. Deleted; 6. Buddha's Birthday (the eighth day of April on the lunar calendar);
7. The fifth day of May (Children's Day); 8. The sixth day of June (Memorial Day);
9. The day preceding Chuseok (Korean Thanksgiving Day), Chuseok, and the day following Chuseok (14th, 15th, and 16th days of August on the lunar calendar);
10. The 25th day of December (Christmas Day);

Ⅰ. 법정휴일

근로기준법 제55조(휴일)

① 사용자는 근로자에게 1주에 평균 1회 이상의 유급휴일을 보장하여야 한다.

② 사용자는 근로자에게 대통령령으로 정하는 휴일을 유급으로 보장하여야 한다. 다만, 근로자대표와 서면으로 합의한 경우 특정한 근로일로 대체할 수 있다.

근로기준법 시행령 제30조(휴일)

① 법 제55조제1항에 따른 유급휴일은 1주 동안의 소정근로일을 개근한 자에게 주어야 한다.

② 법 제55조제2항 본문에서 "대통령령으로 정하는 휴일"이란 「관공서의 공휴일에 관한 규정」 제2조 각 호(제1호는 제외한다)에 따른 공휴일 및 같은 영 제3조에 따른 대체공휴일을 말한다.

관공서의 공휴일에 관한 규정[134]

제2조(공휴일) 관공서의 공휴일은 다음 각 호와 같다. 다만, 재외공관의 공휴일은 우리나라의 국경일 중 공휴일과 주재국의 공휴일로 한다.

1. 일요일.
2. 국경일 중 3·1절, 광복절, 개천절 및 한글날
3. 1월 1일
4. 설날 전날, 설날, 설날 다음 날(음력 12월 말일, 1월 1일, 2일)
5. 삭제.
6. 부처님오신날 (음력 4월 8일)
7. 5월 5일 (어린이날)
8. 6월 6일 (현충일)
9. 추석 전날, 추석, 추석 다음날 (음력 8월 14일, 15일, 16일)
10. 12월 25일 (기독탄신일)
10의2. 「공직선거법」 제34조에 따른 임기만료에 의한 선거의 선거일

Chapter 5 Statutory and Contractual Holidays

> 10-2. Election days for elections on the termination of terms of office referred to in Article 34 of the Act on Election of Public Officials and the Prevention of Election Malpractices;
> 11. Other days the Government designates from time to time.
>
> Article 3 (Alternative Public Holidays) (1) Where a public holiday specified in any of subparagraphs 2 through 10 of Article 2 falls under any of the following cases, the first non-public holiday following the public holiday (referring to a day other than the public holidays under the subparagraphs of Article 2; hereinafter the same shall apply) shall be an alternative public holiday: <Amended on May 4, 2023>
> 1. Where a public holiday under subparagraph 2, 6, 7 or 10 of Article 2 overlaps with a Saturday or Sunday;
> 2. Where a public holiday under subparagraph 4 or 9 of Article 2 overlaps with a Sunday;
> 3. Where a public holiday under subparagraph 2, 4, 6, 7, 9 or 10 of Article 2 is not a Saturday or Sunday and overlaps with any of the other public holidays listed in subparagraphs 2 through 10 of Article 2.
>
> ② Where the alternative public holiday under paragraph (1) overlaps on the same day, the alternative holidays shall last until the first non-public holiday following such alternative public holiday.
>
> ③ Where the alternative public holiday under paragraphs (1) and (2) falls on a Saturday, the first non-public holiday thereafter shall be an alternative public holiday.

1. Weekly Holidays

An employer shall grant a weekly holiday with pay at least once a week on average, provided that the employee concerned has worked all of the contractual working days (as determined in the rules of employment, etc.) for the preceding week. It is advisable that weekly holidays, which are not necessarily Sundays, should be stated in the rules of employment or other forms of company rules. Once a weekly holiday is fixed on a specific day (for example, Sunday), it is possible that an employee who was absent from work on a working day might use

---

[134] [Enforcement Date] The amendment of Article 55 paragraph (2) shall be effective on a date specified in a pertinent subparagraph:
1. With regard to businesses that employ 300 people or more, public institutions: Jan. 1, 2020
2. With regard to businesses that employ 30 to fewer than 300 people: Jan. 1, 2021
3. With regard to businesses that employ 5 to fewer than 30 people: Jul. 1, 2022

> 11. 기타 정부에서 수시 지정하는 날
>
> 제3조(대체공휴일) ① 제2조제2호부터 제10호까지의 공휴일이 다음 각 호의 어느 하나에 해당하는 경우에는 그 공휴일 다음의 첫 번째 비공휴일(제2조 각 호의 공휴일이 아닌 날을 말한다. 이하 같다)을 대체공휴일로 한다. <개정 2023. 5. 4.>
>   1. 제2조제2호·제6호·제7호 또는 제10호의 공휴일이 토요일이나 일요일과 겹치는 경우
>   2. 제2조제4호 또는 제9호의 공휴일이 일요일과 겹치는 경우
>   3. 제2조제2호·제4호·제6호·제7호·제9호 또는 제10호의 공휴일이 토요일·일요일이 아닌 날에 같은 조 제2호부터 제10호까지의 규정에 따른 다른 공휴일과 겹치는 경우
>
> ② 제1항에 따른 대체공휴일이 같은 날에 겹치는 경우에는 그 대체공휴일 다음의 첫 번째 비공휴일까지 대체공휴일로 한다.
> ③ 제1항 및 제2항에 따른 대체공휴일이 토요일인 경우에는 그 다음의 첫 번째 비공휴일을 대체공휴일로 한다.

1. 주휴일

1주일간 소정근로일수(취업규칙 등에 일하도록 정해진 날)를 개근하면, 1주일에 평균 1회 이상의 유급휴일을 주어야 한다. 휴일은 취업규칙 등에 특정일을 정하여 주는 것이 바람직하며 반드시 일요일일 필요는 없다. 휴일이 특정되어 있는 경우(예 : 일요일) 주중에 결근한 근로자에게는 휴일을 무급으로 줄 수 있다. 주휴일에 근로하면 그날의 근로에 대해 통상임금의 50/100을 가산하여 지급하여야 한다(근로기준법 제56조).

주휴일에서 다음 주휴일까지의 간격은 7일 이내가 바람직하다. 다만, 근로기준법 제18조 규정에 따라 4주간을 평균하여 1주간의 소정근로시간이 15시간

---

134) [시행일] 제55조제2항의 개정규정은 다음 각 호의 구분에 따른 날부터 시행한다.
  1. 상시 300명 이상의 근로자를 사용하는 사업 또는 사업장, 공공기관: 2020년 1월 1일
  2. 상시 30명 이상 300명 미만의 근로자를 사용하는 사업 또는 사업장: 2021년 1월 1일
  3. 상시 5인 이상 30명 미만의 근로자를 사용하는 사업 또는 사업장: 2022년 1월 1일

the weekly holiday without pay. An employee who has worked on a weekly holiday shall be paid an additional 50% of the normal wage for the hours worked (Article 56 of the LSA).

The interval between a weekly off-day and the following weekly off-day shall be ideally within 7 days. However, Article 55 shall not apply to a short-term employee whose weekly average contractual hours for a 4-week period are less than 15.

① Inclusion or non-inclusion of paid weekly holiday[135]

If an employer pays employees according to a monthly wage system, the monthly wage shall be considered to include a paid weekly allowance, barring exceptional situations.[136] If the employee receives fixed allowances along with basic hourly wages every month in a monthly wage system, such fixed allowances shall be interpreted to have similar characteristics as wages for paid weekly holiday allowance.[137]

② The weekly holiday does not normally apply to daily workers, but if a daily worker works for six consecutive days, a paid weekly holiday shall be provided.[138]

Weekly holiday allowance under the Labor Standards Act shall be given to a worker who fulfills his/her weekly contractual working hours. However, in principle, the weekly holiday shall not be given to daily workers because it is not possible to calculate weekly contractual working hours for daily workers, as they engage in daily employment contracts.

The purpose for providing a weekly holiday is to reduce the accumulated fatigue on workers after one week's work, thereby helping to protect their health and to provide time to participate in social and cultural activities. If a daily worker works for 6 consecutive days per week without absence, actual working days (and not contractual working days) shall be applied and weekly holiday shall be granted. The employer shall pay weekly holiday allowance separately from wages for daily workers, unless the affected worker agrees to receive the weekly holiday allowance in advance, with their daily wages.

2. Labor Day

Labor Day is officially May 1st by establishment of the Labor Day Act (Mar.

---

[135] MOEL Guidelines: Kunrokijun-2455, on July 8, 2008.
[136] Supreme Court ruling on May 24, 1994, 93Da32514.
[137] Supreme Court ruling on Apr. 24, 1998, 97Da28421.
[138] MOEL Guidelines: Kungi 68207-424, on Apr. 2, 1997.

미만인 단시간 근로자에게는 같은 법 제55조의 주휴일규정이 적용되지 않는다.

① 유급 주휴일 수당 산정 여부[135]

근로자에 대한 임금을 월급으로 지급할 경우 특별한 사정이 없는 한 월급에는 유급 휴일에 대한 임금도 포함된 것으로 볼 수 있으며,[136] 시급제 사원이 기본 시급과 함께 매월 고정 수당을 월급의 형태로 지급받는 경우, 그 고정 수당 중에는 유급 휴일에 대한 임금의 성격을 갖는 부분도 포함되어 있는 것으로 보는 것[137]이 판례의 입장이다.

② 일용근로자의 경우 주휴일이 적용되지 않지만, 계속해서 1주일에 6일을 근무한 경우 일용근로자에게도 임금과 별도로 주휴일을 유급으로 부여하여야 한다.[138]

근로기준법상의 주휴일은 1주간의 소정근로일수를 개근한 자에게 주도록 되어 있으므로 근로계약이 1일단위로 체결되어 1주간의 소정근로일수를 산정할 수가 없는 일용근로자에게는 원칙적으로 주휴일을 부여할 수 없다.

그러나 주휴일의 부여 목적이 1주간의 근로로 인하여 축적된 근로자의 피로를 풀어주고 건강을 확보하게 하며, 여가의 이용을 가능케 하여 사회적·문화적 생활을 할 수 있도록 하는데 있다. 따라서 일용근로자가 계속적으로 근로를 한다면 이때에는 소정근로일수 대신 실 근로일수를 기준으로 하여 1주일에 6일을 개근하였으면 주휴일을 부여하여야 한다. 한편, 일용근로자의 경우 주휴수당을 포함하여 임금을 지급받기로 사전에 약정하지 않은 한 주휴수당은 임금과는 별도로 지급되는 것이므로 주휴일이 부여된 일용근로자에게는 임금과는 별도로 주휴수당을 지급하여야 한다.

2. 근로자의 날

근로자의 날은 "근로자의 날 제정에 관한 법률(1994.3.9)"에 의해 매년 5월

---

[135] 행정해석: 2008.07.08. 근로조건지도과-2455.
[136] 대법 1994.05.24. 선고 93다32514 판결.
[137] 대법 1998.04.24. 선고 97다28421 판결.
[138] 행정해석: 1997.04.02. 근기 68207-424.

Chapter 5 Statutory and Contractual Holidays

9,1994). This day is counted as a paid holiday according to the Labor Standards Act. The designation of Labor Day as a paid holiday under the Labor Standards Act is an exception for private autonomy. By defining Labor Day as a legal paid holiday, it ensures an additional annual day off for ordinary workers, beyond the regular holidays, contributing to the improvement of their working conditions. Moreover, historically, Labor Day is a product of labor movements where workers, as a concept opposing employers, fought for the enhancement of working conditions.[139]

3. Public Holidays

Public holidays, according to Regulations on Holidays of Government Offices[140] include: Sunday; Independence Movement Day, National Liberation Day, National Foundation Day, Hangul Proclamation Day, New Year's Day (Jan. 1st); Lunar New Year's Day (Dec. 31~Jan. 2 on the lunar calendar), Thanksgiving Day (Aug. 14~16 on the lunar calendar); Buddha's Birthday (Apr. 8 on the lunar calendar), Christmas Day (Dec. 25), Children's Day (May 5), Memorial Day (June 6), and Election Day (designed to elect new officials in accordance with the Act on Election of Public Officials and the Prevention of Election Malpractices), and other particular days specified by the Government.

4. Holiday Work

> Article 56 (Extended, Night or Holiday Work)
> ① An employer shall, in addition to the ordinary wages, pay employees at least 50/100 thereof for extended work (referring to the work during the hours extended pursuant to Articles 53 and 59 and to the proviso to Article 69).
> ② Notwithstanding paragraph (1), an employer shall, in addition to the ordinary wages, pay employees who perform work on a holiday an amount the same as or more than the following amounts:
>   1. Holiday work for up to eight hours: 50/100 of ordinary wages;
>   2. Holiday work exceeding eight hours: 100/100 of ordinary wages

---

[139] Constitutional Court decision on May 28, 2015, 2013Hunma343.
[140] Presidential Decree 24273, Dec. 28, 2012.

1일로 지정되어 있다. 이 날은 근로기준법에 의한 유급휴일이다. 근로자의 날을 근로기준법에 의한 유급휴일로 한다고 규정한 것은 사적 자치의 예외로서 근로자의 날을 법정유급휴일로 정함으로써 일괄근로자에게 법정유급휴일을 주휴일 외에 연간 1일 더 보장하여 그 근로조건을 향상시킨다는 의미를 갖는 것이다. 더욱이 역사적으로 볼 때 근로자의 날은, 사용자에 대항하는 개념으로서의 근로자가 근로조건의 향상을 위해 투쟁하였던 노동운동의 산물이다.[139]

3. 국가 공휴일

관공서의 공휴일에 관한 규정[140]에 따른 공휴일은 일요일; 국경일 중 3.1절, 광복절, 개천절 및 한글날, 1월1일, 설날(음 12.31 ~ 1.2), 추석날(음8.14 ~ 8.16), 석가탄신일(음4.8), 기독탄신일(양12.25), 어린이날(5.5), 현충일(6.6), 공직선거법에 따른 임기만료에 의한 선거의 선거일, 기타 정부에서 수시 지정하는 날이다.

4. 휴일근로

제56조(연장·야간 및 휴일 근로)
① 사용자는 연장근로(제53조·제59조 및 제69조 단서에 따라 연장된 시간의 근로를 말한다)에 대하여는 통상임금의 100분의 50 이상을 가산하여 근로자에게 지급하여야 한다.
② 제1항에도 불구하고 사용자는 휴일근로에 대하여는 다음 각 호의 기준에 따른 금액 이상을 가산하여 근로자에게 지급하여야 한다.
 1. 8시간 이내의 휴일근로: 통상임금의 100분의 50
 2. 8시간을 초과한 휴일근로: 통상임금의 100분의 100

---

[139] 헌법재판소 2015. 5. 28. 선고 2013헌마343 결정
[140] 대통령령 제24273호, 2012.12.28.

Chapter 5 Statutory and Contractual Holidays

1) Additional allowance

An additional allowance is paid for work provided during paid or unpaid holidays. In cases where extended work and holiday work overlap, allowances shall be paid in a combined sum. For the two-shift every-other-day work system, the off-day is differentiated from a holiday without work duty, thus an additional allowance shall not be paid even if the employee works on the off-day.

2) Prior substitution of holiday

Prior substitution of holiday signifies a system in which the employee works on the designated off-days and instead takes another day off from work, through prior arrangement of the parties concerned in the collective agreement or rules of employment. In this case, the original holiday becomes a regular working day. Consequently, neither a holiday allowance nor an additional paid holiday allowance shall be provided.

3) MOEL guidelines and judicial rulings

① For work on paid holidays, the rate of payment shall be 250 percent: 100 percent for paid holiday, 100 percent for actual work, and 50 percent as an additional allowance.[141]

② Weekly holiday and monthly and annual paid leave shall be calculated according to the attendance rate for the total number of days after omitting the period of a justified labor strike.[142]

③ Weekly holidays and monthly and annual paid leave are calculated according to the attendance rate of working days excluding the period of justified labor strikes. Those days of no work due to unjustified labor strike shall be treated as absences.[143]

④ The act of substituting leave with allowances promptly after monthly and annual leave was granted is forfeiting the employee from use of leave.[144]

⑤ Whether the employee maintains perfect attendance or a 80 percent attendance is determined from the first day he/she began working for the company; but the attendance rate can be calculated from January 1st of each year according to collective agreement or rules of employment.[145]

⑥ When extended work and night work overlap, 50 percent or more of ordinary wage shall be paid for each.[146]

---

[141] MOEL Guidelines: Kungi 1455-15569, on May 20, 1981.
[142] MOEL Guidelines: Kungi 01254-4245, on Mar. 20, 1990.
[143] MOEL Guidelines: Kungi 01254-198, on June 16, 1990.
[144] MOEL Guidelines: Kungi 1451-9020, on Apr. 6, 1984.
[145] MOEL Guidelines: Kungi 68207-646, on Apr. 4, 1998.
[146] MOEL Guidelines: Kungi 01254-7592, on May 12, 1987.

1) 가산임금

유급휴일·무급휴일을 구별하지 않고 가산임금을 지급해야 한다. 연장근로와 휴일근로가 겹치는 경우에는 연장근로수당과 휴일근로수당을 함께 지급한다. 격일제 근로형태 하에서의 휴무일은 처음부터 근로의무가 없는 휴일과는 다른 것이므로, 이러한 휴무일에 근로하더라도 가산임금이 적용되지 않는다.

2) 휴일의 사전대체

단체협약이나 취업규칙 등으로 노사가 미리 약정하여 지정된 휴일에 근로를 하고 다른 날에 휴일을 부여하는 제도를 '휴일의 사전대체'라고 한다. 이 경우 원래의 휴일은 평일 근로가 되어 유급휴일 수당과 휴일근로 가산수당을 지급하지 않을 수 있다.

3) 휴일 관련된 판례 및 행정해석

① 유급휴일 근로 시 임금지급률은 유급당연지급분 100% 휴일근로분 100%, 가산임금 50%를 합한 250%이다.[141]

② 주휴일, 연·월차 유급휴가는 정당한 쟁의행위기간을 제외한 나머지 근로일수에 대한 출근율에 따라 산정 지급되어야 한다.[142]

③ 주휴일, 연·월차유급휴가 산정 시 정당한 쟁의행위로 인한 파업기간은 동 기간을 제외한 근로일수에 대한 출근율에 따르고, 불법쟁의행위로 근로를 제공하지 않은 날은 결근으로 처리해도 무방하다.[143]

④ 연·월차휴가 발생 즉시 일방적인 금전 대체지급은 사실상 휴가를 박탈하는 것으로 부당하다.[144]

⑤ 1년간 개근했는지 또는 8할 이상 출근했는지 여부는 근로자가 입사한 날을 기산점으로 하여 계산하는 것이 원칙이나 단체협약, 취업규칙 등에 의해 매년 1월 1일을 기산점으로 계산할 수도 있다.[145]

⑥ 연장근로와 야간근로 중복 시 통상임금의 50/100 이상을 각각 가산하여 지급하여야 한다.[146]

---

141) 행정해석: 1981.5.20. 근기 1455-15569.
142) 행정해석: 1990.3.20. 근기 01254-4245.
143) 행정해석: 1990.6.16. 근기 01254-198.
144) 행정해석: 1984.04.06. 근기 1451-9020.
145) 행정해석: 1998.4.4. 근기 68207-646.
146) 행정해석: 1987.5.12. 근기 01254-7592.

Chapter 5 Statutory and Contractual Holidays

II. Contractual Holidays

Unlike statutory holidays, contractual holidays must be stipulated in the rules of employment or collective agreement in order to be legally recognized as paid or unpaid holidays. Statutory holidays shall be granted on particular dates and if work is done on those days, the company shall pay an additional holiday work allowance. Statutory holidays consist of a weekly holiday (Article 55 of the LSA: An employer shall allow a worker on the average one or more paid holidays per week), Labor Day (Act Concerning Establishment of Labor Day: The day of May 1st shall be proclaimed as Labor Day and is a paid holiday as determined by the National Labor Relations Commission) and public holidays as confirmed by the government. However, contractual holidays are determined exclusively by the employer regarding particular dates and whether the holidays are paid or unpaid. If an employee works on a holiday stipulated as paid, the company shall pay an additional overtime allowance.

	Statutory	Contractual
Holiday	1) Weekly Holidays (Article 55) 2) Labor Day (Establishment of Labor Day on May 1st) 3) Public holidays	Company holidays (e.g. Company foundation day)
Remarks	1) Obligated by law 2) Wage is paid	1) Based upon collective agreement, rules of employment, etc. 2) Issue of payment depends on mutual agreement

Corporate holidays refer to paid off-days, such as Company Foundation Day, Labor Union Day, etc., that the company has designated in the collective agreement and the rules of employment.

In cases where contractual holidays are settled as paid off-days, employees are exempted from providing labor. If they have to work on contractual holidays like paid public holidays, they are entitled to paid wages (100%), which are already included in monthly wages, and additional holiday work allowance (150%) (Article 56 (Extended, Night or Holiday Work) of the LSA).

II. 약정휴일

약정휴일은 법정휴일과 다르게 반드시 취업규칙이나 단체협약으로 정해진 경우에 인정되는 것으로 사용자가 무급휴일 또는 유급휴일로 운용할 수 있다. 법정휴일의 경우에는 해당되는 특정 일자에 반드시 휴일을 부여하거나 근로자가 근무할 경우에는 그에 따른 별도의 휴일근로수당을 지급해야 한다. 법정휴일은 「근로기준법」 제55조에 의한 주휴일(사용자는 근로자에게 1주일에 평균 1회 이상의 유급휴일을 주어야 한다), 「근로자의 날 제정에 관한 법률」에 의한 근로자의날(5월 1일을 근로자의 날로 하고 이 날을 「근로기준법」에 의한 유급휴일로 한다.)과 국가가 인정한 국가 공휴일이 있다. 그러나, 약정휴일은 날짜지정이나 유급 또는 무급을 전적으로 사용자의 판단에 따른다. 약정휴일이 유급으로 정해진 경우에 약정휴일에 근무한 경우에는 휴일근로수당을 지급해야 한다.

구분	법 정	약 정
휴일	1) 주휴일(근로기준법 제55조) 2) 근로자의 날 (근로기준법) 3) 국가공휴일	기업의 휴일 (회사창립일등)
특징	1) 법에 근거하여 의무적으로 부여 2) 임금지급(유급)	1) 부여 여부, 부여 조건 등이 단체협약, 취업규칙 등을 통해 결정됨 2) 임금지급 여부도 결정하는 바에 따름

회사가 정한 회사의 창립일, 노조설립일 등으로 회사가 단체협약이나 취업규칙으로 유급휴일로서 인정하는 경우에 해당된다.

약정휴일을 유급으로 설정한 경우에는 그 약정휴일에는 근로제공의무가 제외되며, 이 약정휴일에 사용자의 지시에 의해 근로를 제공한 경우에는 근로제공이 없더라도 지급받을 수 있었던 임금(100%)과 휴일근로 가산임금(150%: 근로기준법 제56조: 가산임금)을 추가로 지급해야 한다.

Chapter 5 Statutory and Contractual Holidays

〈Case Study 5-1〉 Petition for Unpaid Weekly Holiday Allowance

1. Summary

On September 21, 2009, a Korean cook (hereinafter referred to as "the Employee") who worked at a US Army restaurant based in Korea applied to the Seoul Regional Labor Office for his unpaid weekly holiday allowance. The Employee claimed that his monthly salary was calculated by multiplying his actual working hours by an hourly wage rate and then allowances, like bonuses, were included, but he did not receive anything called a weekly holiday allowance. He therefore asked that the company pay him the unpaid weekly holiday allowance from the previous three years until the present time. The Labor Inspector investigated the claims of both parties related to the case and concluded on January 12, 2010, that the company had not violated any related laws.

2. The Employee's Claim

According to his employment contract, the restaurant Employee received an hourly wage, paid every month, in an amount calculated by multiplying actual working hours by hourly wage rate, plus an amount reflecting the Welfare Benefit allowance & PIK allowance, as well as a monthly bonus calculated by dividing 700% of the annual bonus by 12. The Employee had not received anything called a weekly holiday allowance in his salary. Monthly wages have always varied according to the hours worked each month because the wage structure was not a monthly wage system but an hourly wage system. Accordingly, as the company had not paid a fixed monthly wage, but paid different wages every month according to the number of hours worked, the company should also pay a weekly holiday allowance.

3. The Employer's Claim

When paying wages in an hourly wage system, the company calculated the wages as (working hours × hourly wage rate) and, instead of adding a weekly holiday allowance, included a fixed monthly 'Welfare Benefit' allowance and 'PIK' allowance, which was an amount exceeding the weekly holiday allowance. Given

〈실무사례 5-1〉 주휴수당 미지급 진정사건

1. 사건 개요

주한미군 식당에서 근무한 한국인 요리사(이하 '근로자'라 함)는 2009년 9월 21일 회사를 상대로 주휴수당을 받지 못했다고 주장하면서 서울지방노동청에 진정을 제기하였다. 근로자는 자신이 받는 월급이 실제로 일한 시간에 시간당 임금을 곱한 후 보너스 등 수당을 지급받았으며, 주휴수당 명목으로 받은 것이 없기 때문에 미지급된 주휴수당에 대해 청구 가능한 3년치 수당을 소급하여 추가적으로 지급해야 한다고 주장하였다. 관할 노동사무소에서는 사건을 조사한 후 2010년 1월 12일 회사가 법 위반사항이 없다는 결론을 내리면서 사건을 종결하였다.

2. 근로자 주장

식당 근무자의 근로계약은 개인별로 시급이 있기 때문에 실제로 근로한 시간에 시급을 곱한 금액에, 복지수당과 현물수당(PIK)을 더한 후 상여금 700%를 12분의 1로 나눈 금액을 매월 지급받았다. 급여구성항목 어디에도 주휴수당의 명칭을 가지고 지급된 사실이 없다는 것이다. 임금체계가 월급제가 아니라 시급제로 운영되었기 때문에 월급은 매월 일한 시간에 따라 변동되는 임금을 지급받았다. 따라서 회사가 매월 일정한 월급제로 급여를 지급한 것이 아니라 시급제를 기준으로 매월 변동되는 급여를 지급하면서 주휴수당을 지급하지 않았기 때문에 회사는 추가적으로 지급해야 한다.

3. 사용자 주장

회사는 근로자에게 시급으로 지급할 때, 일한 시간 × 시급으로 계산하면서 일주일 만근한 것에 대한 주휴 유급수당이 별도로 계산되어야 하지만, 월 단위 일정액의 복지수당과 현물수당(PIK)을 고정적으로 지급하여 왔고 이 금액이 주휴수당에 해당되는 금액을 초과하고 있다. 어떤 회사가 법정 주휴수당도

Chapter 5 Statutory and Contractual Holidays

that this is the case, how would it be possible for the company to pay 700% of the annual bonus (divided into 12 months), as well as subsidize middle and high school students' tuition while neglecting to pay the statutory weekly holiday allowance? As the company has paid an amount equivalent to the weekly holiday allowance each month, even though the company did not call it a weekly holiday allowance, this amount can replace the weekly holiday allowance.

4. Related Administrative Guidelines

(1) Inclusion or non-inclusion of paid weekly holiday

If an employer pays employees according to a monthly wage system, the monthly wage shall be considered to include a paid weekly allowance, if there are no exceptional situations (Supreme Court ruling 93 da 32514). If the employee receives fixed allowances along with basic hourly wages every month in a monthly wage system, such fixed allowances shall be interpreted to have similar characteristics as wages for paid weekly holiday allowance (Supreme Court ruling 97 da 28421).[147]

(2) The weekly holiday does not normally apply to daily workers, but if a daily worker works for six consecutive days, a paid weekly holiday shall be provided.

Weekly holiday allowance under the Labor Standards Act shall be given to a worker who fulfills his/her weekly contractual working hours. However, in principle, the weekly holiday shall not be given to daily workers because it is not possible to calculate weekly contractual working hours for daily workers, as they engage in daily employment contracts. The purpose for providing a weekly holiday is to reduce the accumulated fatigue on workers after one week's work, thereby helping to protect their health, and to provide time to participate in social and cultural activities. If a daily worker works for 6 consecutive days per week without absence, actual working days, and not contractual working days, shall be applied and weekly holiday shall be granted. The employer shall pay weekly holiday allowance separately from wages for daily workers, unless the affected worker agrees to receive the weekly holiday allowance in advance, with their daily wages.[148]

---

[147] MOEL Guideline: July 8, 2008; kunrokijun-2455.
[148] MOEL Guideline: Apr. 2, 1997, Gungi 68207-424.

지급하지 않으면서 기본급에 대하여 상여금을 연간 700% 지급하고 있으며, 중 고등학교 자녀에 대하여 학자금까지 지급하겠는가? 회사는 비록 명칭은 주휴수당으로 지급하지 않았지만, 월 단위 주휴수당에 상당하는 금액만큼을 지급하였으므로 이는 주휴수당으로 갈음할 수 있다고 할 수 있다.

4. 관련 행정해석 자료

(1) 유급 주휴일 수당 산정 여부

근로자에 대한 임금을 월급으로 지급할 경우 특별한 사정이 없는 한 월급에는 유급 휴일에 대한 임금도 포함된 것으로 볼 수 있으며(대법 93다32514), 시급제 사원이 기본 시급과 함께 매월 고정 수당을 월급의 형태로 지급받는 경우, 그 고정 수당 중에는 유급 휴일에 대한 임금의 성격을 갖는 부분도 포함되어 있는 것으로 보는 것(대법 97다28421)이 판례의 입장이다.[147]

(2) 일용직 근로자의 경우 주휴일이 적용되지 않지만, 계속해서 일주일에 6일을 근무한 경우라면 일용직 근로자에게는 임금과 별도로 주휴일을 유급으로 부여하여야 한다.

근로기준법상의 주휴일은 1주간의 소정근로일수를 개근한 자에게 주도록 되어 있으므로 근로계약이 1일 단위로 체결되어 1주간의 소정근로일수를 산정할 수가 없는 일용직 근로자에게는 원칙적으로 주휴일을 부여할 수 없다. 그러나 주휴일의 부여 목적이 1주간의 근로로 인하여 축적된 근로자의 피로를 풀어주고 건강을 확보하게 하며, 여가의 이용을 가능하게 하여 사회적·문화적 생활을 할 수 있도록 하는 데 있으므로 일용근로자가 계속적으로 근로를 한다면 이때는 소정근로일수 대신 실 근로일수를 기준으로 하여 1주일에 6일을 개근하였으면 주휴일을 부여하여야 한다. 한편, 일용직 근로자의 경우 주휴수당을 포함하여 임금을 지급받기로 사전에 약정하지 않은 한 주휴수당은 임금과는 별도로 지급되는 것이므로 주휴일이 부여된 일용직 근로자에게는 임금과는 별도로 주휴수당을 지급하여야 한다.[148]

---

[147] 행정해석 2008.07.08, 근로조건지도과-2455

Chapter 5 Statutory and Contractual Holidays

5. Judgment on the Case

The labor inspector in charge of this case concluded that the company had paid a weekly holiday allowance to the employee as the company paid monthly wages based on the hourly wage system and added a regular allowance for each month, which was an amount equivalent to the weekly holiday allowance. If, in this case, the company had paid wages by multiplying the actual working hours by the hourly wage rate without a monthly regular allowance, only adding a monthly bonus calculated for the annual 700% bonus, the company would have to pay all employees, including the employee in this case, all unpaid weekly holiday allowances for the past three years.

〈Case Study 5-2〉 Unpaid Wages for Temporary Workers

1. Introduction

I would like to introduce a recent case regarding claims for unpaid wages against a local council and how it was handled. Since 2016, the local council has been hiring 30 audit assistants for 40 days each year to assist with administrative audits. These assistants worked for KRW 100,000 per day, 5 days a week and 8 hours a day.

An audit assistant sought to claim the weekly holiday allowance and annual paid leave, neither of which had been given, but the local council explained that the assistant would not be regarded as a worker because he was hired for a commissioned position only during the administrative audit period. In response, the audit assistant filed a complaint with the Labor Office on December 9, 2022, stating that the local council owed him unpaid wages. During investigation by the Labor Office on December 28, the local council argued that audit assistants were not workers because they were used for commissioned work only during the administrative audit period in accordance with local ordinances. However, the Labor Office ordered the local council to pay KRW 800,000 in unpaid weekly holiday allowance and unused annual paid leave allowance since the complainant was a worker. The local council paid the amount ordered by the Labor Office. However,

5. 관련 사례 판단

　이번 진정사건에 있어 근로감독관은 시급제로 계산된 월 급여가 지급되면서, 월 단위의 일정한 수당을 지급하였고, 이것이 주휴수당에 상응하는 금액을 지급하였기 때문에 이번 사건의 경우 주휴수당이 지급되었다고 판단하였다. 만약, 이번 사건에서 회사가 월 일정한 수당지급 없이 일한시간만큼 시급을 계산한 후, 연 700%의 보너스를 월 단위로 분배하여 지급하였다면 회사에서는 충분한 급여를 지급하였음에도 불구하고 주휴수당을 미지급한 것이 되고, 이 근로자뿐만 아니라 다른 모든 근로자에 대해서도 3년 동안의 임금에 대해 미지급된 주휴수당을 추가적으로 지급하여야만 한다.

〈실무사례 5-2〉 지방의회의 일급직 사무보조자(위촉직)의 임금체불 사례

1. 사실관계 (문제의 소재)

　최근 모 지방의회에서 발생한 임금체불 사건과 그 처리과정에 대해서 소개하고자 한다. 의회는 행정감사 수행을 위해 2016년부터 매년 30여명 사무보조인을 40여일간 채용하고 있다. 근로조건은 일급 10만 원이고, 주 5일과 하루 8시간 근무하는 조건이었다.
　한 사무보조인은 의회에 대하여 '주휴수당' 미지급과 '연차유급휴가' 미지급 부분에 대해 이의를 제기하였으나, 의회는 행정감사 기간 동안만 '위촉직'으로 채용하고 있기 때문에 근로자로 볼 수 없다고 설명하면서 요구한 금품을 지급하지 않았다. 이에 사무보조인은 2022년 12월 9일, 노동청에 의회가 임금체불을 하였다는 내용으로 진정을 제기하였다. 의회 담당자는 12월 28일 노동청 조사 시 지방조례에 따라 행정감사 기간 동안만 업무지원을 받기 위해 사무보조인들을 위촉직으로 채용하였기 때문에 근로자가 아니라고 주장하였다.
　그러나 노동청은 진정인이 근로자에 해당되기 때문에 미지급된 주휴수당과

---
148) 행정해석 1997.04.02, 근기 68207-424

Chapter 5 Statutory and Contractual Holidays

the complainant requested criminal punishment whether the delayed wages were paid or not. On February 17, 2023, the labor inspector visited the local council and conducted a labor inspection. The labor inspector pointed out 6 violations of the Labor Standards Act during the inspection, and ordered the payment of unpaid wages amounting to KRW 96 million, by March 7, 2023.

 Herein, I would like to review the six violations pointed out by the labor inspectors during the inspection, and look carefully into three major disputed issues that came up: (1) the details on unpaid wages, (2) the retroactive scope of unpaid wages, and (3) criminal penalties against the local council.

2. Major Issues Disputed on during the Labor Inspection

(1) Details on unpaid wages

1) Related details:

An audit assistant who worked from October 11, 2022 to December 2 (39 days) submitted a claim to the Labor Office for unpaid weekly holiday allowance and annual paid leave allowance. The local council attended an investigation hearing of the Labor Office on December 28, 2022 and submitted to an investigation, and agreed the day after the investigation to pay KRW 800,000 for weekly holiday and annual paid leave allowances. On February 17, 2023, the labor inspector visited the local council and conducted a labor inspection on the employment relationship with audit assistants. The labor inspector found that the local council had not paid weekly holiday allowance or unused annual paid leave allowance during employment of its audit assistants. The Labor Office directed the local council to retroactively pay unpaid wages to all audit assistants employed during the last five years.

2) Judgment:

If a worker hired for hourly or daily wage continues to work, an additional weekly holiday allowance shall be paid. If wages are calculated on a monthly basis, the weekly holiday allowance shall be included in the monthly wage. A related precedent states that the hourly or daily wage system does not include weekly holiday pay, which is a statutory allowance under Article 55 of the Labor Standards Act (LSA), paid even if the employees do not actually work on such paid holidays. Therefore, if a worker on the hourly or daily wage system receives a fixed allowance paid for a certain period of time exceeding one

월차수당 80만 원 지급을 지시하였다. 의회는 노동청에서 제시한 금액을 모두 지급하였다. 그러나 진정인은 의회에 대해 임금체불 지급여부와 상관없이 형사처벌을 요구하였다. 이에 근로감독관은 2023년 2월 17일 지방의회를 방문하여 근로감독을 실시하였고 사업장 근로감독을 통해 근로기준법 위반사항 6가지(아래 본문 참조)를 지적하고, 2023년 3월 7일 까지 미지급 수당 9600만 원의 지급을 명하였다.

이번 호에는 노동청 근로감독관이 근로감독을 통해 지적한 6가지 구체적 내용에 대한 판단과 주요 쟁점이 되었던 (ⅰ) 임금체불에 대한 내용, (ⅱ) 임금체불에 대한 소급 범위, 그리고 (ⅲ) 지방의회에 대한 형사 처벌과 관련된 내용에 대해 구체적으로 살펴보고자 한다.

2. 근로감독의 내용 중 주요 쟁점

(1) 임금체불에 대한 쟁점 내용

1) 사실관계

2022년 10월 11일 - 12월 2일 까지(39일)을 근무한 사무보조자 1명이 의회가 주휴수당과 연차유급휴가 수당을 지급하지 않았다고 하여 노동청에 진정을 제기하였다. 의회는 2022년 12월 28일 노동청에 출석하여 조사를 받았고, 해당 의회는 조사받은 다음날 주휴수당과 연차수당 80만 원을 지급하였다. 노동청의 근로감독관은 2023년 2월 17일 해당 의회를 방문하여 사무보조인 고용관계에 대해 근로감독을 실시하였다. 근로감독관은 의회가 사무보조인들을 사용하면서 주휴수당과 연차유급휴가의 미사용 수당을 지급하지 않았다는 사실을 확인하였다. 노동청은 의회에 대하여 공소시효에 해당되는 지난 5년 동안 고용했던 사무보조원 전체에 대해 소급하여 미지급한 수당을 지급하도록 지시하였다.

2) 관련판례:

시급, 일급으로 고용된 근로자가 계속해서 근무하는 경우에는 주휴수당을 별도로 추가하여 지급하여야 하고, 월급으로 계산된 임금의 경우에는 주휴수당이 월 급여에 포함되어 있다. 관련 판례는 시급제 또는 일급제는 근로기준법 제55조에 따라 부여되는 유급휴일에 실제로 근무를 하지 않더라도 근무를 한 것으로 간주하여 지급되는 법정수당인 주휴수당이 포함되어 있지

month, he or she can claim the difference between the weekly holiday pay calculated based on the newly calculated hourly wage and the previously paid fixed allowance, and this is not a duplicated pay for the weekly holiday pay."[149]

(2) Retroactive payment of unpaid wages

1) **Related details:** The labor inspector conducted an on-site audit on February 17, and on February 21, 2023, directed the local council to pay an amount equivalent to KRW 96.1 million, calculated as unpaid weekly holiday allowances of KRW 85.2 million (for 132 persons) and unused annual paid leave allowances of KRW 10.9 million (for 109 persons over the past 5 years between 2018 and 2022.

2) **Judgment:** Extinctive prescription refers to expiration of the period during which an employee with the right to receive compensation may exercise a claim against the employer in the event of a delay in the payment of wages or severance pay. The extinctive prescription for prosecution refers to expiration of the period when prosecution can occur for violating labor law, such as delaying the payment of wages, and begins either on the date the violation occurred or the date a continuing violation ends.

The period before the extinctive prescription kicks in for prosecution of violation of labor-related acts in terms of delayed payment of wages was extended from 3 years to 5 years in 2007. The period before the extinctive prescription for prosecution kicks in shall be deemed to have started 14 days from the date the wages should have been paid or the date the violations terminate.[150] According to Article 49 of the LSA, the extinctive prescription for a wage bond kicks in after 3 years. However, since the extinctive prescription for prosecution is now 5 years, prosecution for delayed payment of wages will continue to be possible.[151] Thus, an employee may file a claim for unpaid wages for a period of 5 years.

(3) Criminal punishment for late payment of wages

1) **Related content :** On December 9, 2022, one audit assistant filed a complaint with the Labor Office that wages were overdue. On December 28, the local council was investigated by the Labor Office, and the next day, it paid KRW 800,000 in unpaid weekly holiday pay and unused annual paid leave. However,

---

[149] Supreme Court ruling on Jan. 28, 2010, 2009da74144; see also Supreme Court ruling on Aug. 20, 2014, 2014da6275
[150] Criminal Procedure Act, Article 249, Paragraph 1, Item 5 (Duration of Criminal Prescription) and Article 252 (Starting Time for Statute of Limitations)
[151] Ministry of Employment and Labor Guide, Guide on Handling Unpaid Wages, 2016, pp. 31-32.

않다. 따라서 시급제 또는 일급제 근로자가 1개월을 초과하는 일정기간마다 지급되는 고정수당을 받았다면 새로이 산정한 시간급 통상임금을 기준으로 계산한 주휴수당액과의 차액을 청구할 수 있고, 이를 주휴수당의 중복 청구라고 할 수 없다. 고 판시하고 있다.[149]

(2) 임금체불에 대한 소급 범위

1) **사실관계** : 노동청은 2023년 2월 17일에 현장조사를 실시하였고, 2월 21일 지난 5년간 2018년부터 2022년 사이 미지급한 주휴수당 85,200,000원(132명)과 연차유급휴가 미사용 수당 10,900,000원(109명) 총합 96,100,000원의 지급을 지시하였다.
2) **관련판례** : 소멸시효는 돈 받을 권리가 있는 근로자가 사용자를 상대로 임금이나 퇴직금의 체불이 있는 경우에 청구권을 행사할 수 있는 기간을 말한다. 이에 대해 공소시효는 임금체불 등 노동법 위반 사용자를 법 위반행위가 있는 날 또는 법 위반행위가 계속되는 경우 종료일로부터 형벌권을 행사할 수 있는 기간을 말한다.

임금체불로 인한 노동관계법령 위반 범죄의 공소시효 기간은 2007년에 기존 3년에서 5년으로 연장되었다. 공소시효 기산점은 범죄행위가 종료된 때부터 임금지급일 또는 퇴직일로부터 14일이 경과한 때까지를 말한다.[150] 이에 반해 임금채권의 소멸시효는 3년이다(근기법 제49조). 임금채권의 소멸시효 3년이 완성되었다 하더라도 공소시효가 아직 남아 있기 때문에 임금체불사업주에 대해 형사처벌이 가능하다.[151] 따라서 공소시효를 근거로 하여 근로자는 체불된 임금에 대해 5년간 청구가 가능하다.

(3) 임금체불에 대한 형사처벌

1) **사실관계** : 2022년 12월 9일 사무보조인 1인은 임금체불이 되었다고 노동청에 진정을 제기하였다. 12월 28일 의회의 담당자가 노동청의 조사를 받았고, 그 다음날 주휴수당과 연차유급휴가 미사용 수당 80만원 지급을 완료하였다. 그러나 진정인은 체불임금 수령과는 별개로 근로

---

[149] 대법원 2010.1.28. 선고 2009다74144 판결, 대법원 2014.8.20. 선고 2014다6275 판결.
[150] 형사소송법 제249조(공소시효의 기간) 제1항 제5호, 제252조(시효의 기산점)
[151] 고용노동부 근로기준정책과, 「체불사건 업무처리 요령」, 2016. 31-32면.

the petitioner requested criminal punishment for violation of the LSA, regardless of whether the unpaid wages were paid.

2) **Judgment** : Late payment of wages is subject to criminal punishment. Workers who have received unpaid wage want their employer to be punished. However, prosecutors did not prosecute the local council as the employer responsible for the late payment of wages. The reason for this is that the local council's violation of the obligation to pay weekly holiday allowance and unused annual leave allowance was not intentional. A related precedent states, If there are grounds to dispute the existence of the obligation to pay wages and severance pay, it should be seen that there is a considerable reason why the employer did not pay the wages and severance pay. It is difficult to reason that the employer intentionally committed the crime of violating Article 36 of the Labor Standards Act (Settlement of Payment). Whether there are grounds for dispute regarding the existence and scope of the obligation to pay wages and severance pay depends on the reason for the employer's refusal to pay and the basis for the payment obligation, and the organization and scale of the company operated by the employer. Also, all matters such as business purpose, and the existence and scope of payment obligations, such as other wages, should be judged in light of the general circumstances at the time of the dispute. Even if the employer's civil liability for payment is recognized retroactively, it should not be immediately concluded that the employer's violation of Article 36 of the Labor Standards Act is recognized intentionally.[152]

3. Opinion

This case is a good example of the characteristics of labor law. Labor law violations do not end with correction of a single person's violation. Through this example of unpaid wages for daily wage workers, the following characteristics of labor law can be understood.

First, even if an administrative agency temporarily hires a commissioned worker, if that worker provides work under the management supervision of the employer and receives wages, employee status is recognized.

Second, a notice of violation of the LSA is applied to all workers in the same category, and unpaid wages can be claimed retroactively for 5 years, which is the statute of limitations for criminal punishment. Thirdly, even if a violation regarding wages occurs, if there was no intentional violation of the law and there exists a legitimate reason for not paying the wages in question, criminal punishment may be avoided.

---

[152] Supreme Court ruling on June 28, 2007, 2007do1539.

기준법 위반에 대해 의회의 형사처벌을 요구하였다.
2) **관련판례** : 임금체불은 형사처벌의 대상이 된다. 임금체불금을 지급받은 근로자가 사용자의 처벌을 원하고 있다. 그러나 검찰은 임금체불을 한 사용자인 의회에 대해 기소하지 않았다. 그 이유는 피진정인인 의회가 임금체불 위반에 대한 고의성이 없다고 판단하였다. 관련 판례는 임금과 퇴직금 지급의무의 존재에 관하여 다툴 만한 근거가 있는 것이라면 사용자가 그 임금과 퇴직금을 지급하지 아니한 데에는 상당한 이유가 있다고 보아야 할 것이다. 사용자에게 근로기준법 제36조 (금품청산)의 위반죄에 고의가 있었다고 인정하기 어렵고, 임금 및 퇴직금 지급의무의 존부 및 범위에 관하여 다툴 만한 근거 여부는 사용자의 지급거절 이유와 그 지급의무의 근거, 그리고 사용자가 운영하는 회사의 조직과 규모, 사업 목적 등 제반 사항, 기타 임금 등 지급의무의 존부 및 범위에 관한 다툼 당시의 제반 정황에 비추어 판단하여야 한다. 사후적으로 사용자의 민사상 지급책임이 인정된다고 하여 곧바로 사용자에 대한 근로기준법 제36조의 위반에 대해 고의가 인정된다고 단정해서는 안 된다.고 판시하고 있다.[152]

3. 시사점

이번 지방의회의 한시적인 일급 위탁직의 임금체불 사건은 노동법의 특징을 잘 설명해 준 사례다. 노동법 위반은 단 한 사람의 위반에 대한 시정으로 끝나지 않는다. 이번 지방의회의 일급직 근로자의 임금체불 사례를 통해서 다음과 같은 노동법의 특징을 이해할 수 있다.

첫째, 행정기관에서 위촉직으로 일시적으로 채용하였다고 하더라도 사용자의 관리감독 하에서 근로를 제공하고 임금을 받았다고 한다면 근로자 신분이 된다.

둘째, 근로기준법의 위반에 대한 지적은 동종 근로자 전체에 적용되고, 공소시효 기간인 5년 동안 소급하여 미지급된 임금을 청구할 수 있다.

셋째로, 임금체불의 위반행위가 발생하였다고 하더라도 법위반의 고의성이 없었고, 지급하지 않았던 이유가 별도로 있었던 경우에는 형사처벌을 면할 수 있다는 사실이다.

---
152) 대법원 2007.6.28 선고 2007도1539 판결

Chapter 6 — Statutory Leave and Contractual Leave

I. Annual Paid Leave
⟨Reference⟩ Annual Paid Leave - Questions and Answers

II. Granting Annual Paid Leave

III. Protective Leave
(Maternity, Paternity, Menstruation Leave, Nursing Hours)
⟨Case Study 6-1⟩ Whether Unused Annual Leave should be Compensated
⟨Table 6-1⟩ Promoting the Use of Annual Leave & Application for Use of Annual Leave

IV. Contractual Leave
⟨Table 6-2⟩ Sick Leave-related Cases in the Rules of Employment
⟨Table 6-3⟩ Congratulatory or Condolence Leave-related Cases in the Rules of Employment

제6장 법정휴가와 약정휴가

Ⅰ. 연차유급휴가
〈참고〉실무자를 위한 연차유급휴가 Q&A

Ⅱ. 연차휴가 부여방식

Ⅲ. 연차유급휴가 사용촉진제도
〈실무사례 6-1〉미사용 연차수당 지급 진정사건

〈표 6-1〉연차 사용 촉진 안내 및 휴가 사용계획 신청서

Ⅳ. 연차유급휴가의 대체

Ⅴ. 약정휴가
〈표 6-2〉병가 관련 취업규칙 사례

〈표 6-3〉경조사 관련 취업규칙 사례

Chapter 6 Statutory Leave and Contractual Leave

I. Annual Paid Leave

1. Concept

> Annual paid leave is intended to provide paid leave (separately from paid weekly holidays) to allow workers the opportunity to pursue good health and relaxation.[153] More specifically, the Constitutional Court stated the purpose for annual leave: "Rest hours or weekly holidays are primarily for the physiological recovery of workers who have accumulated physical or mental fatigue due to daily or weekly work. Annual paid leave is designed to give workers freedom from work for a period of time and to have the opportunity to engage in social and cultural civic life by providing a voluntary leave period without a loss of wages.[154] The Supreme Court also explains, "It is purposed to provide an opportunity for mental and physical recreation and improve cultural access by exempting workers from the obligation to work for a certain period of time."[155] Therefore, the objective of annual leave is to improve the quality of life of workers by providing time for rest and the pursuit of cultural life in terms of relaxation from work.[156]

The international standard for annual paid leave and the Korean standard as per the Labor Standards Act can be compared by dividing them into ① the number of leave days and requirements for the occurrence, ② method of use, ③ the guarantee of annual paid leave, and ④ compensation for unused leave.

The International Labor Organization (ILO) has adopted the Convention concerning Annual Holidays with Pay, 1936 (No. 52) and the Convention concerning Annual Holidays with Pay (Revised), 1970 (No. 132). ① In relation to the number of leave days and the requirements for occurrence, "In any case, a minimum of three weeks must be given for a year (Article 3), and an employee who is less than one year shall be entitled to paid leave in proportion to the period of service for that year" (Article 4). ② Regarding the use of annual leave, "Annual leave shall consist

---

[153] Lim, Jongryul, Labor Law, Park Young Sa, 2016, p. 454.
[154] Supreme Court ruling on May 28, 2015. 2013 hunma 619 (The purpose of annual paid leave).
[155] Supreme Court ruling on Dec. 26, 2003. 2011 da 4629 (The purpose of annual paid leave).
[156] Kim, Hongyoung, "Improvement of System for Annual Paid Leave to Secure Time for Rest," Study on Labor Laws, 2016 Vol. 40, Seoul University's Labor Law Society, p. 165.

Ⅰ. 연차유급휴가

1. 연차휴가의 의의

> 연차휴가는 근로자의 건강하고 문화적인 생활을 실현하기 위하여 유급주휴일과 별도로 유급휴가를 부여하려는 것이다.[153] 좀 더 구체적으로 헌법재판소도 연차휴가의 취지를, "휴게시간이나 주휴일은 하루 또는 일주일의 노동으로 육체적·정신적 피로가 누적된 근로자들의 생리적인 회복을 위한 것이 주목적이라면, 연차유급휴가는 임금 삭감 없이 휴가기간을 스스로 결정할 수 있게 함으로써 근로자들이 노동으로부터 일정기간 해방되고 사회적·문화적 시민생활을 영위할 수 있는 기회를 보장하기 위한 것이다."라고 기술하고 있다.[154] 이에 대해 대법원도 "근로자에게 일정 기간 근로의무를 면제함으로써 정신적·육체적 휴양의 기회를 제공하고 문화적 생활의 향상을 기하려는데 그 취지가 있다."라고 설명한다.[155] 따라서 연차휴가에 대한 설명의 공통점은 근로에 대한 휴식의 측면에 문화적 생활의 측면을 덧붙여 근로자의 생활의 질을 향상시키는 것이라 할 수 있다.[156]

 연차유급휴가 제도에 대한 국제기준과 우리나라의 근로기준법상 기준에 대해서는 ① 휴가일수 및 발생요건, ② 사용방법, ③ 연차유급휴가 보장, ④ 미사용 연차휴가에 대한 보상으로 나누어 비교해 볼 수 있다.

 국제기준으로 ILO(국제노동기구)는 연차휴가에 대해 제52호 연차유급휴가 협약(1936년)과 제132호 연차유급휴가 개정협약(1970년)을 채택하였다. ① 휴가일수 및 발생요건과 관련하여 어떠한 경우라도 1년에 대해 최소 3주 이상을 주어야 하고(제3조), 1년에 미달되는 근로자는 당해 연도에는 당해

---
153) 임종률, 「노동법」, 박영사, 2016, 454면.
154) 헌법재판소 2015.5.28. 선고 2013헌마619 결정 (연차휴가의 취지)
155) 대법원 2003.12.26. 선고 2011다4629 판결 (연차휴가의 취지)
156) 김홍영, "휴식 보장을 위한 연차휴가의 제도개선론", 「노동법연구」, 2016 상반기 제40호, 서울대노동법연구회, 165면.

of at least two weeks to be given without its division, even though it can be used in separate days (Article 8), and annual leave shall be granted within one year after the entitlement of annual paid leave" (Article 9). ③ Annual paid leave should be given as paid during the working day (Article 7). ④ For unused annual leave, "Workers who have worked for the minimum period of six months shall be entitled to paid leave or compensation equivalent to the period of unused annual leave" (Article 11).[157]

The ILO and the EU's annual paid leave regulations, in principle, prohibit the substitution of unused annual leave for benefits and exempt monetary compensation only at the end of employment.[158] Korea still pays for unused annual paid leave because using annual paid leave is not widely accepted. In order to eliminate this monetary compensation, the principle of promoting the use of annual leave is stipulated in Article 61 of the Labor Standards Act. If a worker fails to use the annual leave despite the measures promoting the use of annual paid leave, the annual leave shall expire and the employer shall be exempted from liability for compensation.

Annual paid leave (Article 60) in the Korean Labor Standards Act prescribes the use of leave in principle, but also specifies compensation for unused days. ① As for the number of leave days and the requirements for the occurrence of annual paid leave, "An employer shall grant 15 days' paid leave to a worker who has registered not less than 80 percent of attendance during one year (Article 1). After the first year of service, an employer shall grant one day's paid leave for each two years of consecutive service in addition to the 15 days' paid leave to a worker who has worked consecutively for 3 years or more. In this case, the total number of leave days including the additional leave shall not exceed 25 (Article 4). ② Regarding the use of annual leave, "An employer shall grant paid leave upon request by a worker. However, the leave period concerned may be changed, if granting the leave as requested by the worker might cause serious impediment to the operation of the business (Article 5). Paid leave can be used continuously over a certain day or several days. Here, if a worker requests a leave day by designating a desired date (a claim for leave), the employer can adjust the date of the leave in consideration of the work. ③ In relation to the guarantee of annual paid leave, the annual paid leave shall be granted as paid off-days on the normal working days of the worker (Article 5). Therefore, annual paid leave shall not be

---

[157] Ilhoon Park, 「A Study on the Legal Issues of the Annual Paid Leave System」, MA degree thesis at Korea University Graduate School, December 2014, pp125-140.
[158] ILO Convention (No. 132) Article 5; EU Guide, Number 2003/88/EC Article 7 (2)

연도의 근무기간에 비례하는 유급휴가를 받을 권리를 가진다(제4조). ② 연차휴가의 사용과 관련하여 연차휴가는 분할 사용이 가능하지만 '적어도 중단되지 아니하는 2주'로 구성되어야 하며(제8조), 휴가를 받을 자격이 발생한 시점부터 1년 이내에 주어야 한다(제9조). ③ 연차유급휴가는 근무일 중에 유급으로 주어야 한다(제7조). ④ 미사용 연차휴가에 대해서는 최저 근무기간(6개월)을 근로한 근로자는 고용종료 시에 유급휴가를 받지 않은 근무기간에 비례하는 유급휴가나 이에 갈음하는 보상을 받는다(제11조).라고 규정하고 있다.[157]

ILO나 EU의 연차유급휴가 규정은 미사용 연차휴가에 대한 수당대체를 원칙적으로 금지하고 있고, 고용종료 시에만 예외적으로 금전보상 하도록 하고 있다.[158] 우리나라는 아직 연차유급휴가 사용이 정착되지 않아 미사용 연차유급휴가에 대해 금전보상을 하고 있다. 이러한 금전보상의 폐단을 없애기 위해 연차휴가 사용촉진조치(근로기준법 제61조) 규정을 두고 휴가사용을 원칙으로 하고 있다. 사용자가 휴가사용촉진 조치를 하였음에도 불구하고 연차휴가를 사용하지 못한 경우에는 연차휴가가 소멸되며, 사용자는 이에 대한 보상책임을 면제 받는다.

우리나라 근로기준법 상의 연차유급휴가(제60조)는 휴가사용을 전제로 하지만, 미사용시 금전보상을 명시하고 있다. ① 휴가일수 및 발생요건을 살펴보면 "1년간 80% 이상 출근한 근로자에게 15일의 연차유급휴가를 주어야 한다(제1조). 3년 이상 계속하여 근로한 근로자에게 최초 1년을 초과하는 계속근로연수 매2년에 대해 1일을 가산한 유급휴가를 주어야 하고, 최대 25일을 한도로 한다(제4조)." ② 사용방법을 보면 연차휴가는 근로자가 청구한 시기에 휴가를 주어야 하지만, 근로자가 청구한 시기에 휴가를 주는 것이 사업 운영에 막대한 지장이 있는 경우에는 그 시기를 변경할 수 있다(제5조). 유급휴가는 특정일 또는 여러 날에 걸쳐 연속적으로 사용할 수 있다. 여기서 근로자는 원하는 날짜를 지정하여 휴가를 청구하면(휴가청구권) 사용자는 업무의 상황을 고려하여 휴가 청구일을 조정할 수 있다(시기변경권). ③ 연차유급휴가 보장과 관련하여 연차유급휴가는 근로자의 근무일에 유급으로 보장해 주어야 한다(제5조). 따라서 연차유급휴가는 주휴일이나 무급휴무일, 약정

---

157) 박일훈, 「연차유급휴가제도의 법적 쟁점에 관한 연구」, 고려대학교 대학원 석사논문, 2014.12. 125-140면.
158) ILO 제132호 협약 제5조 및 EU지침 2003/88/EC 제7조 제2항.

Chapter 6 Statutory Leave and Contractual Leave

granted on weekly holidays, unpaid holidays, or other paid holidays. ④ Regarding compensation for unused annual leave, "the annual paid leave will expire if not exercised for one year" (Article 7). This means that in the event that an employee fails to use the annual paid leave, the employer shall pay the employee for the unused paid leave.[159]

2. Annual paid leave

Annual paid leave shall be granted to an employee with perfect attendance for their contractual working hours during one year. This is designed to provide leave to an employee who has served his/her contractual working hours for a long duration, so he/she can recover from fatigue from extended work and refresh his/her mind and body.

LSA Article 60 (Annual Paid Leave):

① An employer shall grant 15 days' paid leave to a worker who has registered not less than 80 percent of attendance during one year.

② An employer shall grant one day's paid leave per month to a worker whose consecutive service period is shorter than one year or whose attendance is less than 80 percent, if the worker has offered work without absence throughout the month.

③ (Deleted)

④ After the first year of service, an employer shall grant one day's paid leave for each two years of consecutive service in addition to the leave prescribed in paragraph (1) to a worker who has worked consecutively for 3 years or more. In this case, the total number of leave days including the additional leave shall not exceed 25.

⑤ An employer shall grant paid leave pursuant to paragraphs (1) through (4) upon request of a worker, and shall pay ordinary wages or average wages prescribed in employment rules or other regulations during the period of leave. However, the leave period concerned may be changed, in case granting the leave as requested by the worker might cause a serious impediment to the operation of the business.

---

[159] Supreme Court ruling on Dec. 26, 2013. 2011 da 4629 (Unused annual leave allowance is regarded as wage.)

휴일에 부여해서는 아니 된다. ④ 미사용 연차휴가에 대한 보상과 관련하여 "연차유급휴가는 1년간 행사하지 아니하면 소멸된다. 다만, 사용자의 귀책사유로 사용하지 못한 경우에는 그러하지 아니하다(제7조)." 이는 근로자가 연차유급휴가를 사용하지 못한 경우에 사용자는 이에 따른 미사용 수당을 지급해야 한다는 것이다.[159]

2. 연차휴가의 발생

연차휴가는 1년 이상 근속한 근로자에게 부여하는 유급휴가로서 장기간 소정의 근로를 한 근로자에게 그에 따른 피로를 회복하고 심신의 재충전을 위하여 부여하는 휴가이다.

근로기준법 제60조【연차 유급휴가】

① 사용자는 1년간 80퍼센트 이상 출근한 근로자에게 15일의 유급휴가를 주어야 한다.

② 사용자는 계속하여 근로한 기간이 1년 미만인 근로자 또는 1년간 80퍼센트 미만 출근한 근로자에게 1개월 개근 시 1일의 유급휴가를 주어야 한다.

③ (삭제)

④ 사용자는 3년 이상 계속하여 근로한 근로자에게는 제1항에 따른 휴가에 최초 1년을 초과하는 계속 근로 연수 매 2년에 대하여 1일을 가산한 유급휴가를 주어야 한다. 이 경우 가산휴가를 포함한 총 휴가 일수는 25일을 한도로 한다.

⑤ 사용자는 제1항부터 제4항까지의 규정에 따른 휴가를 근로자가 청구한 시기에 주어야 하고, 그 기간에 대하여는 취업규칙 등에서 정하는 통상임금 또는 평균임금을 지급하여야 한다. 다만, 근로자가 청구한 시기에 휴가를 주는 것이 사업 운영에 막대한 지장이 있는

---

[159] 대법원 2013.12.26. 선고 2011다4629 판결 (미사용 연차유급휴가 수당은 임금이다.)

Chapter 6 Statutory Leave and Contractual Leave

⑥ In applying paragraphs (1) through (3), a period falling under any of the following subparagraphs shall be considered a period of attendance:
1. A period during which a worker is unable to work due to occupational injuries or diseases;
2. A period during which a pregnant woman does not work on leave taken pursuant to paragraphs (1) through (3) of Article 74;
3. A period during which a worker does not work on parental leave due to article 19 paragraph (1) of the Equal Employment Opportunity and Work-Family Balance Act.
⑦ The leave referred to in paragraphs (1) through (4) shall be forfeited if not used within one year. However, this shall not apply in cases where the worker concerned has been prevented from using the leave due to any cause attributable to the employer.

◐ **Enforcement Decree: Article 33 (Payment Date of Leave Allowance)**
The wages as prescribed in Article 60 (5) of the Act shall be paid on the pay day before or immediately after paid leave is granted.

An employer shall grant 15 days of annual leave with pay to an employee who has recorded 80% or higher in workplace attendance. An employer shall grant 1 holiday with pay per month of full attendance to his/her employees who have worked less than 1 year. The days an employee is absent from work due to an occupational accident, pre- and post-natal leave and childcare leave, shall be treated as days worked.

For an employee who has worked 3 years or longer, the employer shall grant an additional 1 day in paid holiday for every 2 years following the first year, with the number of additional holidays limited to 25. An employer shall grant his/her employee annual leave on the day(s) that the employee wants to use his/her annual leave. However, when the employer believes that allowing the use of annual leave on the desired day(s) would do great harm to his/her business, he/she may reschedule the timing of annual leave. An employer may have his/her employee take a day off on a particular working day in lieu of an annual leave day with pay, as long as he/she and the employee representative have reached a written agreement to do so.

Given that annual leave days may be saved for a year and can be split for use on several occasions, it is advisable that a ledger of leave days saved be recorded and maintained for each individual employee.

경우에는 그 시기를 변경할 수 있다.
⑥ 제1항부터 제3항까지의 규정을 적용하는 경우 다음 각 호의 어느 하나에 해당하는 기간은 출근한 것으로 본다.
  1. 근로자가 업무상의 부상 또는 질병으로 휴업한 기간
  2. 임신 중의 여성이 제74조 제1항 부터 제3항에 따른 보호휴가로 휴업한 기간
  3. 「남녀고용평등과 일·가정 양립 지원에 관한 법률」제19조 제1항에 따른 육아휴직으로 휴업한 기간
⑦ 제1항부터 제4항까지의 규정에 따른 휴가는 1년간 행사하지 아니하면 소멸된다. 다만, 사용자의 귀책사유로 사용하지 못한 경우에는 그러하지 아니하다.

➲ 시행령 제33조【휴가수당의 지급일】
법 제60조 제5항에 따라 지급하여야 하는 임금은 유급휴가를 주기 전이나 준 직후의 임금지급일에 지급하여야 한다.

사용자는 근로자가 1년간 8할 이상 출근 시 15일의 유급휴가를 주어야 한다. 1년 미만의 근속자에 대해서는 1개월간 개근 시 1일의 유급휴가를 주어야 한다. (단, 업무상 재해로 휴업한 기간, 산전·후 휴가기간과 육아휴직기간은 출근한 것으로 보아야 한다)

3년 이상 계속 근로한 근로자에 대하여 최초 1년을 초과하는 매 2년마다 1일을 가산하되 25일을 상한으로 한다. 연차휴가에 대하여 사용자는 근로자의 청구가 있는 시기에 주어야 한다. 다만, 근로자가 청구한 시기에 휴가를 주는 것이 사업운영에 막대한 지장이 있는 경우에는 그 시기를 변경할 수 있다. 근로자대표와 서면합의를 하게 되면 연차 유급휴가일에 갈음하여 특정 근로일에 근로자를 휴무시킬 수 있다.

연차 휴가는 1년간에 걸쳐 분할사용이 가능하므로 휴가 적치대장을 작성하여 개인별로 관리하는 것이 바람직하다.

Chapter 6   Statutory Leave and Contractual Leave

<Example of Calculating Leave Per Service Year>

~1 yr	1~2	2~3	3~4	4~5	5~6	10~11	15~16	20~21	21~22	25~
11 1 per mon	15	15	16	16	17	19	22	24	25	25

(1) A case related to annual leave of retirees[160]

Workers were hired by the Uijeongbu City Facility Management Corporation and retired as street cleaners. In the employment rules it is stipulated that retirement "shall be the last day of December of the year in which the person turns 61." In accordance with the provisions of the collective agreement, 20 days of special paid leave were used for those eligible for mandatory retirement, and the mandatory retirement was on December 31st. The workers said, "The last day of December of the year in which we turned 61 was a special leave period, so the actual retirement date should be considered as January 1 of the following year. The employer is obliged to pay the workers the allowance for the unused annual leave due to their retirement on January 1st, since annual leave was accrued in the year they turned 61 years of age."

Regarding this, the first and second trials agreed to the workers' legal claims, but the Supreme Court ruled "The employment rules set the retirement age as the end of December when they turn 61. The retirement age is reached on December 31, when the person turns 61, and the employment relationship is naturally terminated. Therefore, workers cannot acquire the right to annual leave in return for work in the year in which they turn 61. Therefore, it cannot be seen that their retirement date is postponed to January 1 of the following year."

(2) A case related to annual leave of fixed-term workers[161]

A worker used 15 days of annual leave while working as a caregiver at an aged care welfare facility for one year from August 1, 2017 to July 31, 2018. On May 5, 2018, the Ministry of Employment and Labor distributed the guideline for the revised Labor Standards Act as it related to the expansion of the annual leave guarantee for workers with less than one year of employment. The guideline stated "If the contract period of a one-year fixed-term worker expires, an unused annual leave allowance of up to 26 days must be paid."

---

[160] Supreme Court ruling on June 28, 2018: 2006 da 48297.
[161] Supreme Court ruling on October 14, 2021: 2021 da 227100.

<근속년수별 휴가 산정례>

년 이상 ~ 년 미만	~1년 미만	1~2	2~3	3~4	4~5	5~6	10~ 11	15~ 16	20~ 21	21~ 22	25~
휴가 일수	11 (매월 1일)	15	15	16	16	17	19	22	24	25	25

(1) 정년퇴직자의 연차휴가 사례[160]

근로자들은 의정부시 시설관리공단에 고용되어 가로환경미화원으로 근무하다 정년퇴직을 하였다. 사용자의 고용내규에는 정년에 관해 '만 61세가 되는 해의 12월 말일로 한다.'라고 규정하고 있다. 단체협약 규정에 따라 정년퇴직 대상자들은 특별유급휴가 20일을 사용하고, 12월 31일에 정년퇴직을 하였다. 근로자들은 "만 61세가 되는 해의 12월 말일이 특별유급휴가기간으로 근무를 한 것이고 그에 따라 실제 퇴직일은 다음해 1월 1일로 보아야 한다. 만 61세가 되는 해에 계속 근로한 것에 대한 연차휴가는 발생했으므로 사용자는 근로자들에게 그 다음에 1월 1일 퇴직으로 사용하지 못한 연차휴가에 대한 수당을 지급할 의무가 있다"고 주장했다.

이에 대해 1심과 2심은 근로자들의 입장을 인용하였으나, 상고심인 대법원은 "사용자의 고용내규는 정년을 만 61세가 되는 12월 말일로 정하고 있다. 만 61세가 되는 12월 31일에 정년에 도달하여 근로관계가 당연히 종료된다. 따라서 근로자가 만61세가 되는 해의 근로에 대한 대가로서의 연차휴가에 관한 권리를 취득할 수 없다."라고 판시하면서 "근로자들이 만 61세가 되는 해의 12월 31일 까지 특별유급휴가를 사용하였다고 하여 이들의 퇴직일이 다음해 1월 1일로 미루어진다고 볼 수 없다"고 판단하였다.

(2) 기간제 근로자의 연차휴가 사례[161]

근로자는 2017년 8월 1일부터 2018년 7월 31일까지 1년간 노인요양복지시설에서 요양보호사로 근무하면서 15일의 연차휴가를 사용하였다. 고용노동부는 2018년 5월 "1년 미만 근로자 등에 대한 연차휴가 보장 확대 관련

---

[160] 대법원 2018.6.28. 선고 2016다48297 판결.
[161] 대법원 2021.10.14. 선고 2021다227100 판결

The worker submitted a complaint to the Chungbu Regional Labor Office stating that he had not been paid 11 days' annual leave allowance. With the guidance of the labor inspector, the employer paid 717,150 won to the worker as an annual leave allowance for 11 days.

Later, the employer stated that the information that up to 26 days of annual leave would be granted to workers who signed a one-year fixed-term employment contract was incorrect. Since the worker used all the annual leave granted to him, he could not receive annual leave pay. The employer claimed that the worker is obligated to return the overpaid allowance because the employer paid the additional 11 days' annual leave allowance based on the erroneous guidance of the labor inspector.

In response, the lower court (the second trial) recognized the claim of the employer and issued an order for the worker to pay back the overpaid amount. The worker then appealed to the Supreme Court. The Supreme Court ruled "The right to use annual leave or the right to claim annual leave allowance naturally arises when an employee provides work while meeting the attendance rate in the previous year, and is equivalent to the consideration for work for one year in the preceding year, not the year in which the annual leave is to be used. Paid annual leave as stipulated in Article 60 (1) of the Labor Standards Act is granted to workers who have worked at least 80% of one year, and the worker does not use annual leave within one year after acquiring the right to annual leave, or retires before one year has elapsed. In the event that annual leave can no longer be used due to reasons attributable to the employer, the worker can claim an annual leave allowance, which is a wage corresponding to the number of days of annual leave.[162] However, the right to use a 2nd year's annual leave shall be deemed to occur on the day following completion of work for one year of the preceding year, unless otherwise specified. If the employment relationship is terminated due to retirement before then, no annual leave allowance may be claimed as compensation for the right to use annual leave.[163] Therefore, it was determined that workers who signed a one-year fixed-term employment contract were granted up to 11 days of annual leave.

---

[162] Supreme Court ruling on May 17, 2017: 2014 da 232296.
[163] Supreme Court ruling on June 28, 2018: 2006 da 48297.

개정 근로기준법 설명자료를 배포하였는데, 위 자료에서 "1년 기간제 노동자의 계약기간이 만료되는 경우에는 최대 26일분의 연차휴가 미사용수당을 지급하여야 함"이라고 기재되어 있었다.

근로자는 중부지방노동청에 11일분의 연차휴가수당을 지급받지 못하였다는 내용의 진정서를 제출하였다. 사용자는 근로감독관의 계도에 따라 근로자에게 11일분의 연차휴가수당으로 717,150원을 지급하였다.

이에 사용자는 1년 기간제 근로계약을 체결한 근로자에게 최대 26일의 연차휴가가 발생한다는 취지의 이 사건 설명자료는 잘못되었고, 근로자가 자신에게 부여된 연차휴가를 모두 사용하여 더 이상 연차휴가수당을 청구할 수 없는데도 사용자가 근로감독관의 잘못된 계도에 따라 11일분의 연차휴가 수당을 추가로 지급하였으므로 근로자는 사용자에게 이를 반환할 의무가 있다고 주장한다.

이에 대해 원심(2심)은 사용자의 주장을 인정하여 근로자에게 지급명령을 내렸다. 이에 근로자는 대법원에 상고하였다. 대법원은 "연차휴가를 사용할 권리 또는 연차휴가수당 청구권은 근로자가 전년도에 출근율을 충족하면서 근로를 제공하면 당연히 발생하는 것으로, 연차휴가를 사용할 해당 연도가 아니라 그 전년도 1년간의 근로에 대한 대가에 해당된다. 근로기준법 제60조 제1항이 규정한 유급 연차휴가는 1년간 80퍼센트 이상 출근한 근로자에게 부여되는 것으로, 근로자가 연차휴가에 관한 권리를 취득한 후 1년 이내에 연차휴가를 사용하지 아니하거나 1년이 지나기 전에 퇴직하는 등의 사유로 인하여 더 이상 연차휴가를 사용하지 못하게 될 경우에는 사용자에게 그 연차휴가일수에 상응하는 임금인 연차휴가수당을 청구할 수 있다.[162] 다만, 연차휴가를 사용할 권리는 다른 특별한 정함이 없는 한 그 전년도 1년간 근로를 마친 다음 날 발생한다고 보아야 한다. 그 전에 퇴직으로 근로관계가 종료되는 경우에는 연차휴가를 사용할 권리에 대한 보상으로 연차휴가수당도 청구할 수 없다."고 판단하였다.[163] 따라서 1년 기간제 근로계약을 체결한 근로자에게는 최대 11일의 연차휴가가 부여된다고 보았다.

---

[162] 대법원 2017.5.17. 선고 2014다232296 판결.
[163] 대법원 2018.6.28. 선고 2016다48297 판결.

Chapter 6 Statutory Leave and Contractual Leave

3. Rights related to annual paid leave

(1) Right to request annual paid leave

Annual paid leave is designed to maintain an efficient labor force and provide a balanced life through the spiritual and physical rest of employees who attended work fully during the preceding year. Accordingly, an employer shall grant 15 days of paid leave to an employee who has a workplace attendance rate of 80 percent or higher over the preceding year (Article 60 (1) of the Labor Standards Act). An employee is granted the right to annual paid leave according to his/her workplace attendance rate of the preceding year.

(2) Right to request unused annual paid leave allowance

The right to request unused annual paid leave allowance is the right to ask for an allowance as compensation for the unused annual paid leave days if the employee provided labor service without using the annual paid leave accrued as remuneration for work for the previous year. This right occurs after the right to request annual paid leave expires. There is also the right to ask for an allowance as compensation for unused annual paid leave for the number of unused annual paid leave days due to the termination of an employment contract, for example, upon retirement. However, when the employer takes measures to promote the use of Annual Paid Leave, the right to request an allowance for unused annual paid leave expires (Article of 61 of the LSA).

(3) Whether to include annual paid leave allowance into average wages when calculating severance pay

(ⅰ) Unused annual paid leave allowance already occurring before retirement

By the criteria of attendance rate during the year prior to the retirement year, 3/12 of the unused annual paid leave allowance occurring the year prior to the retirement year shall be included in the basic wage items used to calculate average wage for severance pay.

(ⅱ) Unused annual paid leave allowance occurring only due to retirement

The unused annual paid leave allowance that the employee is granted due to retirement in the retirement year according to the attendance rate of the year before the retirement year shall not be included in the basic wage items used to calculate average wage for severance pay, because the unused annual paid leave allowance is not wages paid during calculation of average wage.

3. 연차휴가의 사용

(1) 연차유급휴가청구권
　연차유급휴가는 전년도에 계속 근로한 근로자에 대해 정신적·육체적 휴양을 통한 노동의 재생산 유지와 문화생활의 기회를 부여하기 위해 마련된 것이다. 따라서 사용자는 근로자가 전년도에 8할 이상 출근한 경우에는 15일의 유급휴가를 부여하여야 하고(근로기준법 제60조), 근로자는 전년도의 출근율에 따라 유급휴가청구권이 발생한다.

(2) 연차유급휴가 미사용수당 청구권
　연차유급휴가 미사용수당 청구권은 근로자가 전전년도의 근로한 대가로 발생한 유급휴가를 전년도에 사용하지 아니하고 근로를 제공한 경우 그 미사용 연차유급휴가일수에 해당하는 연차유급휴가 미사용수당을 사용자에 대하여 청구할 수 있는 권리로 유급휴가 청구권이 소멸된 시점에 발생한다. 또한, 퇴직 등 근로관계가 종료되는 근로자가 이로 인해 사용하지 못하는 미사용 휴가일수에 해당하는 수당을 사용자에 대하여 청구할 수 있는 권리이다. 다만 사용자가 근로기준법에 따른 연차유급휴가 사용촉진을 한 경우 유급휴가 미사용수당 청구권이 소멸된다(근로기준법 제61조).

(3) 연차유급휴가수당의 퇴직금 산정을 위한 평균임금 포함여부
　(i) 퇴직하기 전 이미 발생한 연차유급휴가 미사용수당
　　퇴직 전전년도 출근율에 의하여 퇴직 전년도에 발생한 연차유급휴가 중 사용하지 아니하고 근로한 일수에 대한 연차유급휴가 미사용수당액의 3/12을 "퇴직금 산정을 위한 평균임금 산정 기준임금"에 포함한다.
　(ii) 퇴직으로 인해 비로소 지급사유가 발생한 연차유급휴가 미사용수당
　　퇴직 전년도 출근율에 의하여 퇴직 년도에 발생한 연차유급휴가를 사용하지 아니하고 퇴직함으로써 발생한 연차유급휴가 미사용수당은 평균임금의 정의상 산정사유 발생일 이전에 그 근로자에 대하여 지급된 임금이 아니므로 "퇴직금 산정을 위한 평균임금 산정 기준임금"에 포함되지 아니한다.

Chapter 6 Statutory Leave and Contractual Leave

(4) Generally, absence refers to days that the employee did not, without prior authorization, provide labor on the contractual working day as decided by both labor and management[164]

There is no regulation concerning 'absence' stipulated in the Labor Standards Act, but in general it means that the employee did not, without authorization, provide labor on the contractual working day on which both labor and management decided labor would be provided. However, the day or period to be excluded in calculation of the contractual working days, or deemed as attendance, shall not be deemed an absence pursuant to the following (Labor Standard 68207-709, May 30, 1997, 'Criteria for evaluation of contractual working days and attendance'):

A. **Statutory or contractual holidays (excluded from the calculation of contractual working days)**
  - Weekly holidays under the Labor Standards Act
  - Contractual holidays under the collective bargaining agreement or the rules of employment
  - Holidays or periods regarded as the equivalent of the above.

B. **Day or period suspended for work duty due to special reasons**
  (excluded from the calculation of contractual working days)
  - A period of shutdown due to a cause attributable to the employer
  - A period of justifiable strike
  - A period of childcare leave due to the Equal Employment Opportunity and Work-Family Balance Act
  - Day or period regarded as the equivalent to the above

C. **Day or period deemed as attendance by the laws or its characteristics**
  - A period of suspension of work due to industrial accident or a period of maternity leave
  - A period of training in the reserve forces
  - A period of training in civil defense or a period of mobilization
  - Days off to exercise civil rights
  - Annual and monthly paid leave and menstruation leave
  - Other days or periods regarded as equivalent of the above

(5) Providing Annual and Monthly Paid Leave to Part-time Employees[165]

---

[164] MOEL Guidelines: Labor Standard-4336, on Aug. 18, 2004.
[165] MOEL Guidelines: Labor Standards, Dec. 17, 2002.

(4) 일반적으로 결근일이란 법령의 범위 내에서 노사 당사자가 근로를 제공하기로 정한 날인 '소정근로일'에 근로자가 임의로 근로를 제공하지 아니한 날을 의미한다.[164]

근로기준법상 '결근'의 개념에 관하여 규정한 바는 없으나, 일반적으로 결근일이란 법령의 범위 내에서 노사 당사자가 근로를 제공하기로 정한 날인 '소정근로일'에 근로자가 임의로 근로를 제공하지 아니한 날을 의미한다고 볼 수 있을 것이다. 다만, 소정근로일수 계산에서 제외되거나 출근한 것으로 보아야 하는 다음 각 호의 날 또는 기간에 근로하지 아니한 경우를 결근으로 보아서는 안 된다.

가. 법령이나 약정에 의한 휴일(소정근로일수 계산에서 제외)
 - 근로기준법에 의한 주휴일
 -'근로자의 날 제정에 관한 법률'에 의한 근로자의 날
 - 취업규칙이나 단체협약 등에 의한 약정휴일
 - 기타 이상의 날에 준하여 해석할 수 있는 날 또는 기간

나. 특별한 사유로 근로제공의무가 정지되는 날 또는 기간 (소정근로일수 계산에서 제외)
 - 사용자의 귀책 사유로 인한 휴업기간
 - 적법한 쟁의행위기간
 - 남녀고용평등법에 의한 육아휴직기간
 - 기타 이상의 기간에 준하여 해석할 수 있는 날 또는 기간

다. 법령상 또는 그 성질상 출근한 것으로 보아야 하는 날 또는 기간
 - 업무상 재해로 인한 휴업기간, 산전후휴가기간
 - 예비군 훈련기간
 - 민방위 훈련 또는 동원기간
 - 공민권 행사를 위한 휴무일
 - 연월차유급휴가, 생리휴가 기간
 - 기타 이상의 날 또는 기간에 준하여 해석할 수 있는 날 또는 기간

(5) 단시간 근로자의 연차 휴가 산정방법

---
[164] 행정해석: 2004.08. 18, 근로기준과-4336

Chapter 6 Statutory Leave and Contractual Leave

According to the related Presidential Decree (Table 1-2) to the LSA, annual and monthly paid leave for part-time employees shall be calculated by hourly units (1 hour deemed for periods shorter than 1 hour) by the following method:
Number of annual leave days for full-time employee (Part-time employee contractual working hours/Full-time employee contractual working hours) x8 hours
Contractual working hours of short-term employees or full-time employees shall be the contractual working hours per week. (However, if a part-time employee's contractual working hours are not regular, the contractual working hours shall be averaged for contractual working hours of 4 weeks).
Annual paid leave shall be granted as a one day unit, and use shall be granted according to the amount of contractual working hours.
Example) Part-time employee who works 4 hours per day and 6 days per week
- Annual leave (hours): Number of annual leave days for full-time employee (15 days) × [part-time employee's contractual working hours (24 hours) / full-time employee's contractual working hours (40 hours)] × 8 hours = 72 hours

〈Reference〉 Annual Paid Leave Q&A for Practitioners[166]

Korea's Labor Standards Act defines annual paid leave as a form of compensation for previous work. This means that there are a variety of cases that need to be considered when calculating attendance rate. These cases show that the purpose of annual paid leave is often not met, with employees prioritizing monetary compensation over the original function of rest. As a result, annual paid leave is one of the most frequently asked questions.

<Questions 1> What is the most significant feature of the annual paid leave stipulated by the Korean Labor Standards Act?
A1. The most significant feature of annual paid leave under the Korean Labor Standards Act (LSA) is that it is a form of compensation for past work. This is because annual paid leave is granted to employees on a yearly or monthly basis based on their past attendance rate (Article 60 of the LSA). This feature has led to establishment of the concept of allowance for unused annual paid leave through Supreme Court rulings.
   The Supreme Court has interpreted that if an employee who has acquired the right to paid annual leave does not use the leave within one year from the time the right arises, or if it is confirmed that the employee can no longer use

---
[166] Summarized by Labor Attorney Dongshin Lee

근로기준법시행령 별표1의2에 의거 단시간근로자의 연차휴가는 다음의 방식에 의하여 시간단위로 산정(1시간 미만은 1시간으로 간주) 통상근로자의 연차유급휴가일수 × (단시간근로자의 소정근로시간 / 통상근로자의 소정근로시간) × 8시간 단시간근로자 또는 통상근로자의 소정근로시간은 1주간의 소정근로시간으로 함(단시간근로자의 1주간 소정근로시간이 불규칙한 경우에는 4주간의 소정근로시간을 평균한 시간으로 함). 연차유급휴가는 "1일" 단위로 소정근로일에 부여하되, 동일의 소정근로시간만큼 연차휴가를 사용한 것으로 한다.[165]

예) 1주간 1일 4시간씩 6일 근무하는 근로자의 경우
- 연차휴가(시간) : 통상근로자의 연차휴가일수(15일) × [단시간근로자의 소정근로시간 (24시간) / 통상근로자의 소정근로시간 (40시간)] × 8시간 = 72 시간

〈참고〉 실무자를 위한 연차유급휴가 Q&A[136]

Q1. 우리나라 근로기준법이 규정하는 연차유급휴가의 가장 큰 특징은 무엇인가요?

A1. 과거 출근율을 전제로 1년 또는 1월 단위로 근로자에게 휴가를 부여하는 점(근로기준법 제60조), 즉 과거 근로에 대한 보상의 성격을 갖는다는 점이 가장 큰 특징이다. 이러한 특징 때문에 연차휴가 미사용 수당이라는 개념이 판례를 통해 정립되었다.

대법원은 연차휴가권을 취득한 근로자가 그 휴가권이 발생한 때로부터 1년 이내에 연차휴가를 사용하지 아니하거나, 1년이 경과하기 전에 퇴직 등의 사유로 더 이상 연차휴가를 사용하지 못하는 것으로 확정된 경우에는 그 휴가권이 소멸하는 대신 연차휴가 일수에 상응하는 임금으로서 연차휴가 미사용수당을 청구할 수 있다고 해석하고 있다.[167]

---
165) 행정해석: 2002.12.17, 근기 68207-3373
166) 정리: 이동신 노무사
167) 대법원 2000. 12. 22. 선고 99다10806 판결

the leave due to retirement or other reasons before one year has elapsed, the right to leave expires and the employee may claim unused annual leave allowance corresponding to the number of days of remaining annual leave.[167]

The purpose of the vacation system is to provide employees with time off to rest and relax, to promote labor reproduction, to guarantee the opportunity to engage in cultural activities, and to maintain balance between work and family. Therefore, it is possible to argue that it is desirable to grant vacation rights in advance, along with the labor to be provided through the employment contract, and to check whether labor and vacation are used in a balanced manner after a certain period. However, the LSA grants paid annual leave as compensation for past work and recognizes the right to annual leave allowance for unused leave. As a consequence, many practical questions and disputes arise in operation of the annual leave system.

<Question 2> If someone does not use all of his/her annual leave during the usage period, must that person always be compensated in the form of an unused annual leave allowance? Is it also possible to extend the use period so that the person can use it later?

A2. The Korean Ministry of Employment and Labor (MOEL) has interpreted that it is possible for the parties to agree to carry over unused annual leave. What follows here is a summary of the relevant administrative interpretation.[168]

(Question 1) Our employees asked the company to pay a portion of the annual paid leave that had accrued at the beginning of the year as an allowance in advance and let them use the remaining portion of the leave, and the company agreed. Is this a legal action?

(Answer 1) If an employer pays leave allowance in advance before the right to paid annual leave expires, and agrees not to grant that much annual leave in the future, this could have the effect of restricting the employee's right to request leave, and could violate the regulation of the annual paid leave system under the LSA. However, if the employee's right to request leave is not restricted, such as by ensuring the employee's free use of leave, it will be difficult to see it as a violation of the law.

(Question 2) Can annual leave that has not been used be carried over to the next year? If the carried-over leave cannot be used in the next year either, can it be carried over again to the following year?

(Answer 2) An agreement between an employee and an employer to carry over

---

[167] Supreme Court ruling 99da10806, Dec. 22, 2000.
[168] Labor Conditions Guidance Division 1047, Feb. 20, 2009.

생각해 보면, 휴가제도의 취지는 근로자에게 정신적, 육체적 휴양을 제공해 노동 재생산을 도모하고 문화생활을 보장하며 일과 가정을 양립시킬 수 있도록 여가를 부여하는 것이다. 근로계약을 통해 제공할 근로와 함께 휴가권도 함께 미리 주어지고 일정한 기간 이후에 근로와 휴가가 균형 있게 사용되었는지 정산하는 것이 바람직하다는 견해도 가능하다. 그러나 우리나라 근로기준법은 과거 근로에 대한 보상의 개념으로 연차유급휴가를 부여하고 사용하고 남은 연차휴가에 대해서 미사용수당을 인정하고 있기 때문에 연차휴가 제도 운영에 있어 많은 실무적 질문과 다툼이 발생하는 것 아닌가 생각된다.

Q2. 그러면 사용 기간 중에 연차휴가를 모두 사용하지 않은 경우에는 반드시 수당으로 보상해야 하나요? 사용 기간을 연장하여 다음에 사용하도록 하는 것도 가능한가요?

A2. 고용노동부는 당사자가 합의하여 미사용 연차휴가를 이월하여 사용하는 것이 가능하다고 해석하고 있습니다. 아래에서 관련 행정해석의 내용을 소개한다.[168]

(질의1) 우리 회사의 근로자가 연초에 발생한 연차유급휴가의 일부는 수당으로 미리 지급하고 나머지를 휴가로 사용하게 해 달라고 하여 회사가 이를 수용하였습니다. 합법적인 운영인지요?

(답변1) 연차유급휴가 청구권이 소멸되기 전에 사용자가 미리 휴가수당을 지급하고 향후 그만큼 휴가를 부여하지 않기로 하는 것은 실질적으로 근로자의 휴가청구권을 제한하는 효과를 가져올 수 있어 근로기준법상 휴가제도의 취지에 위반될 수 있다. 그러나 근로자의 자유로운 휴가사용을 보장하는 등 근로자의 휴가청구권을 제한하지 않는다면 그것을 법 위반으로 보기는 어렵다.

(질의2) 연차휴가를 모두 사용하지 못한 경우 다음 해에 사용하기로 이월할 수 있나요? 만일 다음 해에도 이월된 휴가를 모두 사용하지 못하면 또 다시 그 다음 해로 이월하여 사용하도록 할 수 있을까요?

(답변2) 미사용 연차유급휴가에 대한 금전보상 대신 이월하여 사용하도록

---

[168] 근로조건지도과 -1047, 2009.02.20.

Chapter 6 Statutory Leave and Contractual Leave

unused annual paid leave instead of paying allowance in cash is permissible.

(Question 3) If the carry-over of unused annual paid leave is continued, and the annual leave is accumulated for more than 2 years, and then it is claimed as an allowance all at once, the average wage for calculating statutory severance pay will be much higher than normal. Can the average wage be calculated in this way?

(Answer 3) The average wage for calculating statutory severance pay should only include 3/12 of the amount of unused annual leave allowance paid for the number of days worked without including the annual leave accrued in the year before the year of retirement, based on the attendance rate of the year two years before the year of retirement.

Here also we summarize other administrative interpretations on the carry-over of annual paid leave.[169]

(Question) An agreement was made with each employee that remaining annual paid leave could be carried over and used, but a certain employee did not use the annual paid leave again by the deadline. In this case, can an employer carry over the remaining annual leave again as company policy without employee consent but with notification of such carryover?

(Answer) It is possible for the parties to agree to carry over unused leave instead of paying compensation in lieu of an annual paid leave claim that has expired, but the employer cannot unilaterally decide this if it is against the will of the employee.

<Questions 3> My company employs four employees, including myself. However, my company says that we do not have paid annual leave. Paid annual leave is a system stipulated by the LSA, and is it not available to all employees?

A3. The LSA's annual paid leave regulations do not apply to businesses or workplaces with 4 or fewer regular employees (Article 11 (2) of the LSA and Appendix 1 of the Enforcement Decree of the LSA).

In addition, the annual paid leave regulations do not apply to part-time employees whose working hours are less than 15 hours per week on average over a period of 4 weeks (Article 18 (3) of the LSA).

<Question 4> According to the LSA, annual paid leave is calculated individually based on each employee's start date of employment. However, our company

---

[169] Labor Conditions Guidance Division 1046, Feb. 20, 2009.

근로자와 사용자 사이에 합의하는 것은 무방하다.

(질의3) 연차유급휴가 미사용분에 대한 이월이 계속되어 연차휴가를 2년 이상 적치하였다가 이를 한꺼번에 수당으로 청구하면 퇴직금 산정을 위한 평균임금이 정상적인 경우보다 훨씬 많아지는데 이런 형태로 평균임금을 계산할 수 있는지요?

(답변3) 퇴직금 산정을 위한 평균임금에는 퇴직 전전년도 출근율에 의하여 퇴직 전년도에 발생한 연차유급휴가 중 사용하지 않고 근로한 일수에 대하여 지급하는 연차유급휴가 미사용수당액의 3/12만 포함된다.

연차유급휴가 이월에 관한 다른 행정해석의 내용은 아래와 같다.[169]

(질의) 잔여 연차유급휴가에 대해 직원과 개별 동의하여 이월하여 사용하도록 했으나, 이월하여 사용하기로 한 기한까지 직원이 연차유급휴가를 사용하지 않았습니다. 이 경우 직원들의 동의없이 회사의 방침 또는 통보로 다시 한번 더 이월할 수 있는지요?

(답변) 휴가청구권이 소멸된 미사용 휴가에 대해 금전보상 대신 이월하여 사용하도록 당사자간 합의는 가능하지만, 근로자의 의사에 반해 사용자가 일방적으로 강제할 수는 없다.

Q3. 제가 근무하는 회사에는 직원이 저를 포함해서 4명입니다. 그런데 우리 회사에는 연차휴가가 없다고 하네요. 연차휴가는 근로기준법에서 규정한 제도이고 모든 근로자가 사용할 수 있는 것 아닌지요?

A3. 근로기준법의 연차유급휴가 규정은 상시 근로자가 4명 이하인 사업(장)에는 적용되지 않습니다(근로기준법 제11조 제2항 및 근로기준법 시행령 별표1 참조).

또한 소정근로시간이 4주 동안을 평균해 1주 동안 15시간 미만인 초단시간근로자에게도 연차유급휴가 규정이 적용되지 않습니다(근로기준법 제18조 제3항).

Q4. 근로기준법의 규정을 보면 연차유급휴가는 개인별 입사일을 기준으로 개별 산정하는 것으로 보입니다. 그런데 우리회사에서는 회계년도(매년

---

[169] 근로조건지도과-1046, 2009.02.20.

grants and manages annual leave based on the fiscal year (January 1 to December 31 of each year). Isn't this a problem?

A4. The principle is to individually calculate and manage the attendance rate for granting annual paid leave and the period for using it based on the individual employee's start date of employment. However, it is also possible to uniformly grant and manage it based on the fiscal year or other criteria for the convenience of labor management. However, the administrative interpretation,[170] explains that this should not be disadvantageous to the employee. Let us explain the details.

(Question 1) When an employee retires, we compare the employee's employment start date and end date. If the end date is earlier than one year, we do not grant annual paid leave for that year. If the end date is later, we generate annual paid leave and pay unused annual leave allowance. Is our practice legal?

(Answer 1) The starting date of the period for calculating the attendance rate for granting annual paid leave under Article 60 of the LSA should be the employee's employment start date. However, for the convenience of labor management in the workplace, the employer can uniformly set the period on the basis of the fiscal year (January 1 to December 31) for all employees through collective bargaining agreement or the rules of employment, but in this case, it should not be disadvantageous to employees whose employment start date was in the middle of the year.

When calculating annual leave based on the fiscal year, in order to avoid disadvantaging employees whose employment start date was in the middle of the year, annual paid leave should be granted in proportion to the length of service in the year employment relations began for the period of less than one year since they began, and from then on, the number of days of leave should be calculated based on the fiscal year and granted. However, if the number of annual leave days calculated by the employee's start date at the time of retirement is less than the number of days of annual leave calculated based on the fiscal year, the lower number of annual leave days should be paid out.

☞ In summary, the administrative interpretation states that annual paid leave can be uniformly granted and managed based on the fiscal year or other criteria for the convenience of labor management, but at the time of retirement, the amount of annual paid leave granted based on the fiscal year and the amount of annual leave granted based on the individual employee's start date should be compared to ensure that the employee is not disadvantaged.

---

[170] Wage and Working Hours Policy Team 2888, Sept. 11, 2007.

1.1부터 12.31까지)를 기준으로 연차유급휴가를 부여하고 관리하고 있습니다. 문제가 없는지요?

A4. 연차유급휴가 부여를 위해 출근율을 계산하고 연차유급휴가를 사용하는 시기는 개인별 입사일을 기준으로 개별 산정하고 관리하는 것이 원칙이다. 그러나 노무관리 편의를 위하여 회계년도 등을 기준으로 일률적으로 부여하고 관리할 수도 있다. 다만, 그렇게 하는 경우에 근로자에게 불리하지 않게 해야 한다고 행정해석은 설명하고 있다. 그 내용을 소개한다.[170]

(질의1) 직원이 퇴직할 때 입사 월일과 퇴사 월일을 비교하여 퇴사 월일이 빠르면 그 해의 연차유급휴가를 발생시키지 않고, 퇴사 월일이 늦으면 연차유급휴가를 발생시켜 수당을 지급하고 있습니다. 우리가 하는 지급방식이 합당한지요?

(답변1) 근로기준법 제60조의 연차유급휴가를 부여하기 위해 출근율을 산정하는 기간의 기산일은 근로자의 입사일이 기준이 된다. 다만, 사업장의 노무관리 편의를 위하여 단체협약이나 취업규칙 등에 의하여 전체 근로자에 대하여 회계연도(1.1-12.31)를 기준으로 일률적으로 기산일을 정할 수는 있으나, 이 경우 연도 중에 입사한 근로자에게 불리하지 않도록 해야 한다.

회계연도를 기준으로 휴가를 계산하는 경우로써 연도 중 입사한 근로자에게 불리하지 않게 휴가를 부여하려면, 입사한 지 1년이 되지 않은 기간에 대하여는 입사연도의 근속기간에 비례하여 유급휴가를 부여한다. 그 후부터는 회계연도를 기준으로 휴가일수를 산정하여 부여하되 퇴직시점에서 근로자의 입사일을 기준으로 산정한 휴가일수와 비교하여 미달하는 경우에는 그 미달하는 일수만큼 정산해 주어야 한다.

☞ 행정해석의 입장을 요약하면, 노무관리 편의를 위해 회계년도 등을 기준으로 연차유급휴가를 일률적으로 부여하고 관리할 수 있으나, 퇴직 시점에는 회계년도를 기준으로 한 것과 개인별 입사 월일을 기준으로 한 것을 비교하여 해당 근로자에게 불리하지 않도록 해야 한다.

---

170) 임금근로시간정책팀-2888, 2007.09.11.

Chapter 6 Statutory Leave and Contractual Leave

(Question 2) If the company has promoted the use of annual leave, does it not have to pay an annual leave allowance for unused annual leave to employees who have not been able to use all of their annual leave due to early retirement? And for employees who will retire at retirement age, is it okay to promote the use of annual leave based on the date retirement age is reached, not the end of the fiscal year?

(Answer 2) If the employer has taken measures to promote the use of annual paid leave, and an employee leaves the company before the designated period for the use of annual leave, it cannot be considered that the measures promoting use of annual leave have been carried out well, so the unused annual leave should be paid as compensation. In addition, it is considered that measures to promote annual paid leave can be implemented for employees whose date of retirement age is June 30, 6 months earlier than the end of year, in accordance with procedures specified in the law.

☞ The administrative interpretation states that even if the company has promoted the use of annual leave, it must pay annual leave allowance for the number of days of unused annual leave to employees who have retired early, and that the company can promote the use of annual paid leave based on the expected date of retirement age for employees who are scheduled to retire upon reaching retirement age.

<Question 5> I know that annual paid leave must be given at the time specified by the employee (Article 60, Paragraph 5 of the LSA). However, our company's rules of employment require employees to specify the date they will use their annual leave and obtain the company's approval at least one day before their requested leave day(s) would start. Is it legal to require the company's prior approval?

A5. If granting annual leave at the date requested by the employee would cause a significant disruption to business operations, the employer may change the date (Article 60, Paragraph 5, Clause 2 of the LSA). This is called the employer's right to change the time of leave. If the procedures for obtaining approval for the dates requested for annual leave through the company's rules of employment is interpreted as a regulation to properly exercise the employer's reserved right to change the time of annual leave, it cannot be seen as illegal to have such a procedure. The following is a summary of the relevant court decision.[171]

If the rules of employment stipulate that an employee who wishes to take annual leave must apply to their supervisor in advance and obtain approval from the CEO, this is interpreted as a regulation to ensure that the employer can properly exercise its right to change the time of leave, rather than to deprive the

---
[171] Supreme Court ruling 92da7542, June 23, 1992.

(질의2) 연차휴가 사용촉진을 했다면 중도 퇴사로 연차휴가를 모두 사용하지 못한 근로자에 대해서도 미사용 수당을 지급하지 않아도 되는지요? 그리고 정년 퇴직자에 대해서는 회계년도 말이 아니라 정년퇴직일을 기준으로 연차휴가 사용촉진을 하면 되는지요?

(답변2) 사용자가 연차유급휴가 사용촉진 조치를 한 이후 근로자가 휴가 지정일 이전에 퇴직한 경우라면 정상적으로 사용촉진 조치가 이루어졌다고 볼 수 없으므로 미사용 휴가에 대하여는 수당으로 지급하여야 합니다. 또한 정년퇴직일이 6월말인 근로자에 대하여도 법에서 정한 절차에 따라 연차유급휴가 사용촉진조치를 실시할 수 있다.

☞ 행정해석의 입장은, 연차휴가 사용촉진을 했더라도 중도 퇴사자에 대해서는 미사용 연차유급휴가 일수에 해당하는 수당을 지급해야 한다. 정년 퇴직자에 대해서는 정년퇴직 예정일을 기준으로 연차유급휴가 사용촉진을 할 수 있다.

Q5. 연차유급휴가는 근로자가 지정한 시기에 주어야 한다고 알고 있습니다(근로기준법 제60조 제5항). 그런데 우리 회사의 취업규칙은 휴가를 사용하기 원하는 날의 최소 1일 전에 휴가 사용 시기를 지정하여 회사의 승인을 받도록 하고 있습니다. 회사의 사전 승인을 받도록 하는 절차가 적법한 것인지요?

A5. 근로자가 청구한 시기에 휴가를 주는 것이 사업 운영에 막대한 지장이 있는 경우에는 사용자가 그 시기를 변경할 수 있다(근로기준법 제60조 제5항 단서). 이를 사용자의 시기변경권이라고 한다. 회사가 취업규칙을 통해 휴가 승인을 받도록 하는 절차가 사용자에게 유보된 휴가 시기 변경권을 적절하게 행사하기 위한 규정이라고 해석된다면 그 절차를 둔 것을 위법한 것으로 볼 수는 없다. 이와 관련하여 참조할 수 있는 판례의 내용을 소개하면 다음과 같다.[171]

취업규칙에 휴가를 받고자 하는 자는 사전에 소속장에게 신청하여 대표이사의 승인을 득하여야 한다고 규정하고 있는 경우 이는 근로기준법 제48조 제3항(현행 근로기준법 제60조 제5항)이 규정하는 근로자의

---

[171] 대법원 1992. 6. 23. 선고 92다7542 판결

employee of the right to designate the time of leave as stipulated in Article 48, Paragraph 3 of the LSA (Article 60, Paragraph 5 of the current LSA). Therefore, regulations in the rules of employment requiring prior approval of leave will not be considered invalid or violations of the provisions of the LSA.

In the case of a transportation company that operates regular passenger transportation services to an unspecified number of people, a regular and continuous passenger transportation schedule is confirmed, and the vehicle operations scheduled at designated times must be carried out smoothly. Disruptions in operations will cause a significant disruption to the business of the transportation company. Therefore, it can be said that requiring the driver of an operating vehicle to apply for paid leave in advance and obtain approval from the CEO is a necessary measure to properly exercise the employer's right to change the time of annual leave.

<Question 6> If the rules of employment do not specify the procedure for requesting annual paid leave, how should an employee apply for annual leave?

A6. You can specify the type of annual leave you want to use and the dates you want to use it by expressing your intention in a reasonable manner, such as orally or in writing.

According to a court decision,[172] in a company that does not have a procedure for requesting annual leave in its rules of employment, if an employee does not come to work due to injuries sustained in a physical fight with a colleague, and calls the company to ask for the treatment period to be treated as continuous annual leave, this is a valid request for annual leave. If the company does not exercise its right to change the time of annual leave in a lawful manner, the period during which the employee did not come to work cannot be considered as absenteeism.

On the other hand, even if an employee exercises their right to designate the time of leave without specifying what leave they want to use and when they want to use it, this cannot be considered a lawful designation of the time.

According to another court decision,[173] in a case where a union leader submitted an annual leave application without specifying the type or period of leave for the purpose of enforcing a demand for collective bargaining and a meeting, but the employer refused to approve it and instructed the employee to come to work, the employee's refusal to comply and absence from work was considered to be an unauthorized absence and grounds for disciplinary action.

<Question 7> What does "significant disruption to business operations" mean, which

---

[172] Supreme Court ruling 92nu404, Apr. 10, 1992.
[173] Supreme Court ruling 96nu4220, Mar. 28, 1997.

휴가시기 지정권을 박탈하기 위한 것이 아니라 단지 사용자에게 유보된 휴가시기 변경권의 적절한 행사를 위한 규정이라고 해석되므로 휴가를 사전에 승인 받도록 한 취업규칙의 규정을 근로기준법 규정에 위반되는 무효의 규정이라고 할 수 없다. 불특정다수인을 상대로 정기여객운송사업을 경영하는 운수회사의 경우 정기적이고 계속적인 여객운송계획이 확정되어 있고 정해진 시각에 예정된 차량운행이 순조롭게 이루어져야 하며, 만일 그 운행에 차질이 생길 때에는 운송사업 운영에 막대한 지장을 초래하게 된다. 운행차량 운전사로 하여금 미리 유급휴가를 신청하여 대표이사의 승인을 받아 휴가를 실시하도록 한 것은 사용자의 휴가시기 변경권을 적절하게 행사하기 위한 필요한 조치라고 할 것이다.

Q6. <u>그러면 취업규칙 등에 연차유급휴가 청구 절차를 규정하고 있지 않은 경우, 휴가 사용신청은 어떻게 해야 하나요?</u>

A6. 어떤 휴가를 언제부터 언제까지 사용할 것인지에 관하여 구두, 서면 등의 적절한 방법으로 의사표시하여 특정하면 된다. 판례에 따르면,[172] 취업규칙에 연차휴가 청구 절차 규정을 두지 않은 회사에서 근로자가 동료와의 상호 폭행으로 입은 상해 때문에 출근하지 않고 회사에 전화로 치료기간 중 계속 연차휴가를 실시한 것으로 처리해 달라고 하였다면 이는 적법한 연차휴가 청구이고, 회사가 적법한 시기 변경권을 행사하지 않는 한, 출근하지 않은 기간을 결근으로 볼 수 없다.

반대로, 근로자가 어떤 휴가를 언제부터 언제까지 사용할 것인지 특정하지 아니한 채 휴가 시기지정권을 행사하더라도 이는 적법한 시기지정이라 할 수 없다. 판례에 따르면,[173] 노조위원장인 근로자가 단체교섭 및 면담 요구를 관철할 목적으로 종류와 기간이 특정되지 않은 연월차 휴가원을 제출하였으나 사용자가 이를 불허하고 출근을 지시한 경우, 근로자가 이에 불응하고 결근한 것은 무단결근에 해당하여 징계사유가 된다고 판단하였다.

Q7. <u>사용자가 연차유급휴가 시기변경권을 행사할 수 있는 '회사운영에 막대한</u>

---
172) 대법원 1992.04.10. 선고 92누404 판결
173) 대법원 1997.03.28. 선고 96누4220 판결

Chapter 6 Statutory Leave and Contractual Leave

allows the employer to exercise the right to change the time of annual paid leave, and on whom does the onus of proof lie?

A7. The term "significant disruption to business operations" means a case that would significantly hinder or have a major impact on normal business operations. This means that if the employee is given annual leave on the requested date, it will not only be impossible to operate the business unit (department, team, etc.), but it will also be impossible to secure replacement workers for this purpose. The burden of proof for this is on the employer.

There is a lower court decision[174] that is worth referring to. Here, the court ruled that the employer's right to change the time of annual leave is not recognized solely on the general possibility that the number of workers will decrease due to the employee's use of annual leave, resulting in increased workload for the remaining workers.

<Question 8> I understand that annual paid leave is granted as a form of compensation based on attendance rate. If so, how is attendance rate calculated? And there are many complex factors, such as work days missed due to mandatory reserve military training, disciplinary action, and labor disputes. Please explain the complex factors that should be considered when calculating the attendance rate.

A8. The attendance rate is calculated as a percentage of work days in a year fulfilled by an employee of the required number of days, i.e., the annual scheduled working days, to the total number of days actually worked in a year. In other words, it is calculated as "Annual days actually worked / Annual scheduled working days."

The following are examples of periods that are considered as attendance when calculating the attendance rate, even though the employee did not actually provide work (Article 60, Paragraph 6 of the LSA):

- The period of absence of an employee due to occupational injury or illness;
- The period of absence of a pregnant employee due to maternity leave under the LSA;
- The period of absence due to parental leave under the Equal Employment Opportunity and Work-Family Balance Assistance Act.

In addition to the above, the following cases should also be considered as days attended, even if the employee did not provide labor:

---

[174] Seoul High Court ruling 2018nu57171, Apr. 4, 2019.

지장'이란 어떤 경우를 의미하고, 그 입증은 누가 해야 하나요?

A7. '사업운영에 막대한 지장이 있는 경우'라 함은 사업의 정상적인 운영을 현저히 저해하거나 중대한 영향을 주는 경우로서 당해 근로자가 지정한 휴가일에 휴가를 주게 되면 해당 단위(과, 팀 등)의 업무의 운영이 불가능하게 될 뿐만 아니라, 이를 위한 대체 근로자를 확보할 수 없는 경우를 말한다. 이에 대한 입증 책임은 사용자에게 있다.

참조할만한 하급심 판례가 있어 소개한다.[174] 해당 판례는 중에 근로자가 연차휴가를 사용함으로써 근로 인력이 감소되어 남은 근로자들의 업무량이 상대적으로 많아진다는 일반적 가능성만으로는 사용자의 시기변경권이 인정되지 않는다고 판단하였다.

Q8. 연차유급휴가는 출근율에 따라 보상의 개념으로 부여한다고 이해하였습니다. 그러면 출근율은 어떻게 계산하나요? 그리고 예비군 훈련, 징계, 쟁의행위 등으로 출근하지 못한 경우 등 예외적인 경우가 많이 있는데 출근율을 계산할 때 알아야 하는 예외적인 사항에 대해 설명 부탁합니다.

A8. 출근율은 연간 근로의무가 있는 일수, 즉 연간 소정근로일수 중에서 근로자가 현실적으로 근로를 제공한 출근일수의 비율로 계산한다. 공식으로 표현하자면 "연간 출근일수 / 연간 소정근로일수"가 된다.

출근율을 계산할 때 현실적으로 근로를 제공하지 않아도 출근한 것으로 보는 기간이 있는데 해당되는 사례는 다음과 같다(근기법 제60조 제6항).
- 근로자가 업무상 부상 또는 질병으로 휴업한 기간
- 임신 중의 여성이 근로기준법의 규정에 따른 출산전후 휴가로 휴업한 기간
- 남녀고용평등법에 따른 육아휴직으로 휴업한 기간
  이 외에도 다음의 경우와 같이 근로를 제공하지 않은 날도 출근한 날로 보는 것이 옳을 것입니다.
- 예비군/민방위 훈련 기간, 공민권 행사를 위한 휴무일 등 법령에 의해 근로한 것으로 인정된 기간
- 연차유급휴가, 생리휴가 등

---

[174] 서울고법 2019.04.04. 선고 2018누57171 판결

- Periods recognized by law as the employee having worked, such as mandatory reserve military training/civil defense training, and days off for exercising civil rights;
- Annual paid leave, menstrual leave, etc.;
- Days of absence due to the employer's fault, such as management-related difficulties;
- Days on which the employee was unable to come to work due to an illegal lockout;
- Periods of unjust dismissal.[175]

On the other hand, there are periods that should be excluded from the annual scheduled working days when considering the purpose of the annual leave system. These periods are as follows:[176]
- Periods during which the employee did not actually provide work due to a legitimate labor dispute;
- Periods during which the employee did not actually provide work due to the use of sick leave (in accordance with the rules of employment, etc.);
- Periods during which the employee worked as a union leader;
- Periods during which the employee was unable to come to work due to a lawful lockout by the employer.

According to the Supreme Court decision mentioned above, it is reasonable to reduce the number of annual paid leave days in proportion to the reduction in annual scheduled working days. For example, if there are 250 usual annual scheduled working days, but this has been reduced to 150 days due to the use of sick leave, and the attendance rate for the 150 days is 80% or more, then it is reasonable to grant 9 days of annual paid leave, not 15 days [15 (150/250)].

Finally, there are periods that should be considered as absences when calculating the attendance rate. These periods are:
- Days on which the employee went on an illegal strike;
- Periods during which the employee participated in an illegal labor action during the employer's lawful lockout period;
- Periods during which the employee did not work due to disciplinary action, such as suspension or dismissal.[177]

---

[175] Supreme Court ruling 2011da95519, Mar. 13, 2014.
[176] Supreme Court ruling 2015da66052, Feb. 14, 2019.
[177] Supreme Court ruling 2008da41666, Oct. 9, 2008.

- 경영관리상의 장애와 같이 사용자의 귀책사유에 의해 휴업한 날
- 위법한 직장폐쇄로 출근하지 못한 날
- 부당해고 기간[175]

한편, 휴가제도의 취지를 고려할 때 연간 소정근로일수에서 제외하는 것이 타당한 것이 있는데 그에 해당되는 기간은 다음과 같다.[176]
- 근로자가 정당한 쟁의행위로 현실적으로 근로를 제공하지 아니한 기간
- (취업규칙 등에 따른) 병가의 사용으로 현실적으로 근로를 제공하지 아니한 기간
- 노동조합 전임자로 활동한 기간
- 사용자의 적법한 직장폐쇄로 인하여 근로자가 출근하지 못한 기간

이와 같이 연간 소정근로일수가 감소되는 경우에는 연차유급휴가 일수도 그에 비례하여 감소되는 것이 합리적이라는 것이 바로 위에서 소개한 판례의 입장이다. 예를 들어 연간 소정근로일수가 250일인데 병가의 사용 등으로 감소된 연간 소정근로일수가 150일이고, 150일에 대한 출근율이 80% 이상이라면 연차유급휴가 일수는 15일이 아닌 9일 [15 × (150/250)]을 부여하는 것이 합리적이라는 것이다.

마지막으로, 출근율을 계산할 때 결근으로 보아야 하는 기간도 있다. 다음과 같은 경우가 이에 해당된다.
- 근로자가 위법하게 파업한 날
- 사용자의 적법한 직장폐쇄 기간 중 근로자가 위법한 쟁의행위에 참가한 기간
- 정직이나 직위해제 등의 징계로 인해 근로하지 않은 기간[177]

우리 근로기준법이 정하는 연차유급휴가는 기왕의 근로에 대한 보상으로 주어지는 성격을 가지고 있어서 기왕의 근로를 확인하는 과정에서 고려해야 하는 다양한 case가 있다. 판례를 통해 인정된 연차유급휴가 미사용 수당으로 인해 휴가 본연의 기능인 휴식 보다 금전 보상을 우선 시 하는 등 취지에 맞지 않게 운영되는 사례가 많아, 노동법 영역 중에서 실무자의 질문이 가장 많은 규정의 하나입니다.

---
[175] 대법원 2014.03.13. 선고 2011다95519 판결
[176] 대법원 2019.02.14. 선고 2015다66052 판결
[177] 대법원 2008.10.09. 선고 2008다41666 판결

Chapter 6 Statutory Leave and Contractual Leave

II. Granting Annual Paid Leave

'Annual paid leave' in the current Labor Standards Act refers to paid vacations that employees receive in return for work. It was originally designed to provide physical and mental rest to employees tired from hard work, to maintain the continuity of the labor force, and to secure a balance in people's lives. However, human resource (HR) managers are often confused about how to best allow for annual leave and continually ask questions on this subject. According to the Labor Standards Act (LSA), annual leave is to be calculated and provided based on the individual employee's start date. However, for companies with many employees, individual management of annual leave is not easy to calculate due to the different starting dates, and it is also not easy to take advantage of related laws promoting its use.

Although the rules of employment and collective agreements may stipulate that annual leave will follow the LSA, many companies, for the sake of convenient labor management, provide uniformity in annual leave for employees based on a 'calendar year' period, and then recalculate the annual leave based on individual start dates at the time when employment ends. The number of annual leave days can differ in accordance to the various annual leave-provision methods, and individual companies follow different types depending on their HR policy.[178] In this chapter, I would like to review, in detail, the various ways in which annual leave can be calculated:

1. Legal Bases for Calculating Annual Leave

(1) The Labor Standards Act – Start date

Article 60 of the LSA stipulates that annual leave shall be calculated on the basis of the start date of each individual employee.

---

[178] Jung, Bongsoo, The Korean Labor Law Bible, 5th ed., June 17, 2016, p. 168.

II. 연차휴가 부여방식

현행 근로기준법상 '연차유급휴가'는 장기간 근로한 근로자가 유급의 휴가를 받는 것을 말한다. 이는 근로를 통해 지친 육체적/정신적 휴양, 노동의 재생산 유지와 문화적인 생활의 확보를 위하여 마련한 것이다. 그런데 실무상 이러한 '연차휴가 부여방식'에 대하여 기업 인사 담당자들이 혼란을 느끼고 문의해 오는 경우가 종종 있다. 근로기준법에 의하면, 연차휴가는 근로자 '개인별 입사일'을 기준으로 하여 산정·부여하면 된다. 하지만 근로자 수가 많은 사업장의 경우, 근로자 개인별 입사일을 기준으로 개별적으로 연차휴가를 산정해 부여하는 것이 쉽지 않고, 연차휴가의 사용촉진제도를 활용하는 것도 간단하지 않다.

회사의 취업규칙이나 단체협약에 연차휴가는 근로기준법에 따라 지급한다는 규정이 명시되어 있음에도 실제로는 사용자가 노무관리의 편의를 위해 '회계연도 기준'으로 모든 근로자에게 연차휴가를 일률적으로 관리한 후, 퇴직 시 개인별 입사일을 기준으로 재정산하는 경우가 많다. 연차휴가 부여방식에 따라 산정되는 연차휴가일수가 달라질 수 있고, 연차휴가 부여에 대하여 회사마다 조금씩 다른 방식을 취하고 있다.[178]

이하에서는 실무상 '연차휴가 부여방식'에 대하여 구체적으로 검토해 보고자 한다.

1. 연차휴가 부여의 법적근거

(1) 근로기준법-입사일

근로기준법 제60조에서는 근로자 개개인의 '입사일'을 기준으로 연차휴가를 부여하도록 규정하고 있다.

---

[178] 정봉수, 「한국노동법 해설」 5개정판, 2916.6. 168면.

Chapter 6 Statutory Leave and Contractual Leave

> **Article 60 (Annual Paid Leave)**
> ① An employer shall grant 15 days' paid leave to a worker who has registered not less than 80 percent of scheduled attendance in a one year period.
> ② An employer shall provide one day's paid leave per month to a worker whose consecutive service period is shorter than one year or whose attendance is less than 80 percent, if the worker has worked without absence for a full month.
> ③ <deleted on November 28, 2017>
> ④ After the first year of service, an employer shall provide one day's paid leave for each two years of consecutive service in addition to the leave prescribed in paragraph (1) to a worker who has worked consecutively for 3 years or more. In this case, the total number of leave days including the additional leave shall not exceed 25.

(2) Government Guidelines - Calendar year

Government guidelines allow for the management of annual leave based on a calendar year, with the detailed method as follows:

The period for calculation of the attendance rate in order to calculate annual paid leave under Article 60 of the Labor Standards Act shall follow the individual employee's annual service period in principle, but for the sake of efficient labor management, the calculation period may follow a calendar year period (Jan. 1 ~ Dec. 31) in accordance with the rules of employment and/or the collective agreement where applicable. To avoid disadvantaging new employees when calculating by calendar year, in the following year the paid leave shall be calculated in proportion to the start date of the first year for those who have worked for less than one year, after which the company can then provide annual leave on a calendar year basis. Provided, if the total number of annual leave days calculated by calendar year is less than the number of annual leave days calculated by actual start date, the company shall provide the lesser number of additional annual leave days.[179]

2. Rules of employment or collective agreement (sample): start date or calendar year

---

[179] MOEL Guidelines: Labor Improvement Team-5352, issued on Dec. 19, 2011.

> 근로기준법: 제60조(연차 유급휴가)
> ① 사용자는 1년간 80퍼센트 이상 출근한 근로자에게 15일의 유급휴가를 주어야 한다.
> ② 사용자는 계속하여 근로한 기간이 1년 미만인 근로자 또는 1년간 80퍼센트 미만 출근한 근로자에게 1개월 개근 시 1일의 유급휴가를 주어야 한다.
> ③ 삭제 <2017.11.28>
> ④ 사용자는 3년 이상 계속하여 근로한 근로자에게는 제1항에 따른 휴가에 최초 1년을 초과하는 계속 근로 연수 매 2년에 대하여 1일을 가산한 유급휴가를 주어야 한다. 이 경우 가산휴가를 포함한 총 휴가일수는 25일을 한도로 한다

(2) 행정해석-회계연도

행정해석은 회계연도를 기준으로 연차휴가를 관리하는 방식을 인정하고 있으며 구체적인 관리 방식은 다음과 같다.

근로기준법 제60조의 연차유급휴가를 부여하기 위한 출근율 산정대상기간의 기산일은 근로자 개인별로 정함이 원칙이며, 사업장에서 노무관리의 편의를 위하여 단체협약이나 취업규칙으로 회계연도(매년 1월1일 ~ 12월31일) 등을 기준으로 일률적으로 정할 수도 있다. 회계연도를 기준으로 휴가를 계산할 경우, 연중 입사자에게 불리하지 않게 휴가를 부여하려면, 근무기간이 1년이 도래하지 않은 근로자에 대해서도 다음연도에 입사년도의 근속기간에 비례하여 유급휴가를 부여하고, 이후 연도부터는 회계연도를 기준으로 연차유급휴가를 부여하면 된다. 다만, 퇴직 시점에서 총 휴가일수가 근로자의 입사일을 기준으로 산정한 휴가일수에 미달하는 경우에는 그 미달하는 일수에 대하여 연차휴가근로수당으로 정산해야 한다.[179]

2. 취업규칙 및 단체협약(예시) - 입사일 또는 회계연도

---

179) 행정해석: 근로개선정책과-5352, 2011.12.19

Chapter 6 Statutory Leave and Contractual Leave

Annual leave stipulated in the rules of employment is usually provided as follows:

(1) Where annual leave is calculated by the individual employee's start date

> Article ○○ (Annual Paid Leave)
> ① Each employee shall be granted 15 days for a minimum of 80% attendance during the previous one (1) full year;
> ② With respect to an employee who has worked for less than one year or an employee who has an attendance rate of less than 80% in one year, the company shall allow one day of paid leave for perfect attendance for one month; and
> ③ Each employee who has been employed for 3 years or longer shall be allowed one additional day for every two years exceeding the first one year of continuous employment in addition to the days of leave mentioned in Item a. above. However, the total paid leave including the additional days shall not be more than 25 days.

(2) Where annual leave is managed by calendar year

> Rules of Employment: Article ○○ Annual Leave
> Note - Subparagraphs ①, ②, and ③, have the same content as the above ROE.
> ④ The calculation period for annual paid leave shall start January 1 of each year and finish on December 31 of that same year.
> ⑤ As for an employee who started work in the middle of year, the company shall allow on January 1 of the next year, the number of annual leave days calculated in proportion to the employment period of the first year, and beginning the following year, annual leave will be adjusted and provided on a calendar year basis.
> ⑥ At the end of employment, if the number of annual leave days calculated by calendar year is less or more than the number of annual leave days calculated by the individual's start date, the company will provide to the related employee an annual paid leave allowance for the correct number of annual leave days recalculated by his/her joining date.

(3) Where annual leave is managed by calendar year, and granted in advance and later recalculated as of the resigning date

회사의 취업규칙은 연차휴가규정 관리 방식에 따라 보통 다음과 같이 명시한다.

(1) 개인별 입사일 기준으로 연차휴가를 관리하는 경우 (2018.6.1. 이후 개정)

취업규칙 제 ○○ 조 (연차유급휴가)
① 회사는 전년도에 1년간 8할 이상 출근한 직원에 대하여는 15일간의 유급휴가를 준다.
② 계속근무년수가 1년 미만인 직원 또는 1년간 80%미만 출근한 직원에 대해서는 1개월간 개근 시 1일의 유급휴가를 부여한다.
③ 회사는 3년 이상 계속 근무한 직원에 대해서는 위 제1호의 규정에 의한 휴가일에 최초 1년을 초과하는 계속근무년수 매 2년에 대하여 1일을 가산한 유급휴가를 준다. 다만 가산 휴가를 포함한 총 휴가일수는 25일이 넘지 않는다.

(2) 회계연도를 기준으로 연차휴가를 관리하는 경우

취업규칙 제○○조 연차 휴가
①, ②, (3)은 위의 취업규칙 내용과 동일
④ 연차유급휴가의 산정기간은 매 년 1월 1일부터 12월 31일까지로 한다.
⑤ 연중 입사한 직원에게는 입사한 해의 다음 연도의 1월 1일에 제1항의 연차유급휴가를 근속기간에 비례하여 부여하고, 그 다음 연도부터는 회계연도에 따라 연차유급휴가를 산정하여 부여한다.
⑥ 직원 퇴사 시 그동안 부여받은 총 연차유급휴가일수가 입사일을 기준으로 산정한 총 연차유급휴가일수에 미달하는 경우 그 미달하는 일수를 연차휴가근로수당으로 정산한다.

(3) 회계연도를 기준으로, 미리 부여한 뒤 퇴직할 경우 해당연도에 한해 비례지급

> Rules of Employment: Article XX (Annual Leave)
>
> Note - Subparagraphs ①, ②, and ③, have the same content as the above ROE.
>
> ④ The calculation period for annual paid leave shall start January 1st of each year and finish on December 31st of that same year.
>
> ⑤ As for an employee who started work in the middle of year, the company shall provide one monthly paid leave each month until the first day of the following year in addition to monthly leave days of the above paragraph (2). On January 1st of the next year, the company provides 15 days of annual paid leave in advance.
>
> ⑥ At the end of the term of employment (or when resigning), the number of annual leave days that occurs on January 1st of the year in which the employee resigns will be adjusted and settled in proportion to the date of resignation for the period from January 1 to the resigning date.

3. Methods for Calculating Annual Leave

(1) Methods Available (Employees joining before June 2017)

The details for granting annual leave, as stipulated in the Labor Standards Act or the rules of employment, are generally similar, but the actual calculation for that leave varies greatly by company. Three types are shown (A, B, and C), each of which may be used by companies.

※ Annual Leave for a Period from May 15, 2013 to March 31, 2019
(5 Years and 10 Months' Service)

Type A: Based on Employee Start Date	Type B: Start Date + Calendar year	Type C: Prior Payment + Prorated
5/15/2013 hired 5/15/2014 15 days 5/15/2015 15 days 5/15/2016 16 days 5/15/2017 16 days	5/15/2013 hired 1/01/2009 10 days (prorated based on start date) 1/01/2014 15 days 1/01/2015 15 days	5/15/2013 hired (7 days granted as monthly leave in advance) 1/01/2014 15 days 1/01/2015 15 days 1/01/2016 16 days

취업규칙 제○○조 연차 휴가
①, ②, (3)은는 위 취업규칙 내용과 동일
④ 연차유급휴가의 산정기간은 매 년 1월 1일부터 12월 31일까지로 한다.
⑤ 위의 2항의 월차휴가가 1년 미만자에 지급되는 것과 별도로, 연중 입사한 직원에게는 입사한 해에 그 해 예상되는 월차를 미리 지급한다. 다음 년도 1월 1일에 발생하는 연차유급휴가 15일을 미리 지급한다.
⑥ 직원이 해당 년도에 퇴사시 그 해당 년도 1월 1일에 발생한 연차휴가를 퇴직일에 기준하여 비례하여 지급한다.

3. 연차휴가 부여방법

(1) 연차휴가 부여 방법 예시 (2017년 6월 이전 입사자)

일반적으로 근로기준법과 취업 규칙상 동일한 연차휴가 규정을 적용하고 있지만, 실제로 연차휴가 부여 방식은 각 회사별로 다르게 사용하는 경우가 많다. 아래의 A, B, C방식 중 한 가지의 방법으로 사용하고 있다.

※ 5년 10개월 근무 후 퇴사시의 연차휴가
　입사일 : 2013년 5월15, 퇴사일: 2019년3월31일

A방식: 입사일기준 부여	B방식: 입사일+회계연도	C방식: 사전지급+비례정산
2013-05-15 입사 2014-05-15: 15개 2015-05-15: 15개 2016-05-15: 16개	2013-05-15 입사 2014-01-01: 10개 (입사일기준 비례발생) 2015-01-01: 15개	2013-05-15 입사: 7개 (월차 미리 부여) 2014-01-01: 15개 2015-01-01: 15개 2016-01-01: 16개

Chapter 6 Statutory Leave and Contractual Leave

5/15/2018 17 days 3/31/2019 resigned	1/01/2016 16 days 1/01/2017 16 days 1/01/2018 17 days 3/31/2019 resigned (10 days deducted, as adjusted according to start date)	1/01/2017 16 days 1/01/2018 17 days 1-01-2019 17 days 3/31/2019 resigned (17 days x 3/12 = 4 days, as adjusted according to finish date)
79 days	79 days	90 days (11 days paid more)

※ Annual Leave for a Period from May 15, 2013 to October 31, 2019
(6 Years and 5 Months' Service)

Type A: Based on Employee Start Date	Type B: Start Date + Calendar year	Type C: Prior Payment + Prorated
5/15/2013 hired 5/15/2014 15 days 5/15/2015 15 days 5/15/2016 16 days 5/15/2017 16 days 5/15/2018 17 days 5/15/2019 17 days 10/31/2019 resigned	5/15/2013 hired 1/01/2014 10 days (prorated based on start date) 1/01/2015 15 days 1/01/2016 15 days 1/01/2017 16 days 1/01/2018 16 days 1/01/2019 17 days 10/31/2019 resigned (7 days added, as adjusted according to start date)	5/15/2013 hired (7 days granted as monthly leave in advance) 1/01/2014 15 days 1/01/2015 15 days 1/01/2016 16 days 1/01/2017 16 days 1/01/2018 17 days 1/01/2019 17 days 10/31/2019 resigned (17 days x 10/12 = 14 days, as adjusted according to finish date)
96 days	96 days	100 days (extra 4 days)

※ Annual Leave for a Period from June 1, 2017 to March 31, 2020
(2 Years and 10 Months' Service)

2017-05-15: 16개 2018-05-15: 17개 2019-03-31 퇴사	2016-01-01: 15개 2017-01-01: 16개 2018-01-01: 16개 2019-01-01: 17개 2019-03-31: -10개 삭감 (입사일 기준 정산지급)	2017-01-01: 16개 2018-01-01: 17개 2019-01-01: 17개 2014-03-31: 4개 (=17*3/12:퇴사일 기준 정산)
79개 부여	79개 부여(삭감정산)	90개 부여 (초과 11개)

※ 6년 5개월 근무 후 퇴사시의 연차휴가
  입사일 : 2013년 5월15일, 퇴사일: 2019년 10월31일

A방식: 입사일기준 부여	B방식: 입사일+회계연도	C방식: 사전지급+비례정산
2013-05-15 입사 2014-05-15: 15개 2015-05-15: 15개 2016-05-15: 16개 2017-05-15: 16개 2018-05-15: 17개 2019-05-15: 17개 2019-10-31 퇴사	2013-05-15 입사 2014-01-01: 10개(입사일기준 비례발생) 2015-01-01: 15개 2016-01-01: 15개 2017-01-01: 16개 2018-01-01: 16개 2019-01-01: 17개 2019-10-31: +7개 (입사일 기준 정산지급)	2013-05-15입사: 7개 (월차 미리 부여) 2014-01-01: 15개 2015-01-01: 15개 2016-01-01: 16개 2017-01-01: 16개 2018-01-01: 17개 2019-01-01: 17개 2014-10-31: 14개 (=17*10/12:퇴사일 기준 정산)
96개 부여	96개 부여(보전정산)	100개 발생(초과 4개)

※ 2년 10개월 근무 후 퇴사시 연차휴가
  입사일 : 2017년6월1일, 퇴사일: 2020년 3월 31일

Chapter 6 Statutory Leave and Contractual Leave

Type A: Based on Employee Start Date	Type B: Start Date + Calendar year	Type C: Prior Payment + Prorated
6/01/2017 hired 6/01/2018 Monthly Leave 11 days 6/01/2018 15 days 6/01/2019 15 days 6/01/2020 resigned	6/01/2017 hired 6/01/2018 Monthly Leave 11 days 1/01/2018 8 days (prorated based on start date) 1/01/2019 15 days 1/01/2020 15 days 3/31/2020 -9 days deducted (recalculated from starting date)	6/01/2017 hired 6 days (Granting 6 days monthly leave ahead) 6/01/2018 Monthly Leave 11 days 1/01/2018 15 days 1/01/2019 15 days 1-01-2020 16 days 3/31/2020 4 days (4=16*3/12 prorated as of date of resignation
41 days	41 days	51 days (10 extra days)

※ Annual Leave for a Period from June 1, 2017 to October 31, 2020
(3 Years and 5 Months' Service)

Type A: Based on Employee's Start Date	Type B: Start Date + Calendar year-based	Type C: Prior Payment + Prorated
6/01/2017 started 6/01/2018 Monthly Leave 11 days 6/01/2018 15 days 6/01/2019 15 days 6/01/2020 16 days 10/31/2020 resigned	6/01/2017 started 6/01/2018 Monthly Leave 11 days 1/01/2018 9 days (prorated based on start date) 1/01/2019 15 days 1/01/2020 15 days 10/31/2020 +7 days added (recalculated from starting date)	6/01/2017 started 6 days (Granting 6 days monthly leave ahead) 6/01/2018 Monthly Leave 11 days 1/01/2018 15 days 1/01/2019 15 days 2020-01-01 16 days 10/31/2020 13 days (13=16*10/12 prorated as of date of resignation
57 days	57 days	60 days (3 extra days)

A방식: 입사일기준 부여	B방식: 입사일+회계연도	C방식: 사전지급+비례정산
2017-06-01 입사 2018-06-01 월차 11개 2018-06-01: 15개 2019-06-01: 15개 2020-03-31: 퇴사	2017-06-01 입사 2018-06-01 월차 11개 2018-01-01: 9개 (입사일기준 비례발생) 2019-01-01: 15개 2020-01-01: 15개 2020-03-31: -9개 삭감 (입사일 기준 정산지급)	2017-06-01 입사: 6개 (월차 미리 부여) 2018-06-01 월차 11개 2018-01-01: 15개 2019-01-01: 15개 2020-01-01: 16개 2020-03-31: 4개 (4=16*3/12:퇴사일 기준 정산)
41개 부여	41개 부여(삭감정산)	51개 부여 (초과 10개)

※ 3년 5개월 근무 후 퇴사시 연차휴가
　　입사일 : 2017년6월 1일, 퇴사일: 2020년10월31일

A방식: 입사일기준 부여	B방식: 입사일+회계연도	C방식: 사전지급+비례정산
2017-06-01 입사 2018-06-01 월차 11개 2018-06-01: 15개 2019-06-01: 15개 2020-06-01: 16개 2020-10-31: 퇴사	2017-06-01 입사 2018-06-01 월차 11개 2018-01-01: 9개 (입사일기준 비례발생) 2019-01-01: 15개 2020-01-01: 15 2019-10-31: +7개 (입사일 기준 정산지급)	2017-06-01 입사: 6개 (월차 미리 부여) 2018-06-01 월차 11개 2018-01-01: 15개 2019-01-01: 15개 2020-01-01: 16개 2020-10-31: 13개 (=16*10/12:퇴사일 기준 정산)
57개 부여	57개 부여(보전정산)	60개 발생(초과 3개)

Chapter 6   Statutory Leave and Contractual Leave

(2) Methods available (Employees hired after June 2017)

Since the guaranteed paid leave for employees working less than two years is insufficient (15 days granted for the entire two-year period), Article 60 paragraph (3) was deleted in an amendment of the LSA to provide additional paid leave days. It now guarantees 11 annual paid leave days for the first year for employees working less than two years. Thus, a total of 26 paid days are granted over that two-year period: 11 days in the first year and 15 days in the second. Therefore, in calculation of annual leave by calendar year, an additional 11 days shall be added, to maintain the annual management system.

(3) Advantages & disadvantages of each method
1) Type A (based on employee's start date):

The advantage of this method is that annual leave can be accurately calculated in accordance with the Labor Standards Act.

However, the disadvantage is that: 1) it requires a lot of time and effort in that the company needs to calculate each individual employee's annual leave separately; 2) it is difficult to take measures to promote the use of collective annual leave; and 3), employees who intend to leave may "game the system" to find the best time for resignation to maximize their annual leave days.

2) Type B (start date + calendar year): This method is a way of providing annual leave based on calculating 15 days in proportion to the working period of the first year, on January 1 of the following year, and then to deem January 1 of the following year as the start date for calculating annual leave for that year. When employment comes to an end, the number of annual leave days calculated based on calendar year is compared with the number of annual leave days calculated by the start date. If the number of annual leave days based on calendar year is more than the number calculated by start date, it is preferable to stipulate such a reduction of annual leave in the rules of employment.

The advantage of Type B is that a company can easily manage annual leave, effectively use the method to promote its collective use, and be able to calculate annual leave very accurately while still adhering to the Labor Standards Act.

The disadvantage of Type B is that the company needs more time to recalculate individual annual leave. As well, employees may seek to "game the

(2) 연차휴가 부여 방법 예시 (2017년 6월 이후 입사자)

 2년 미만의 재직근로자의 유급휴가 보장이 미흡하기 때문에(15개 사용가능) 이를 시정하고자 국회에서 근로기준법 제60조의 3항을 삭제하였다. 따라서 2년 미만의 재직근로자에 대해 최초 1년에 대해서도 11개의 휴가를 보장해 주고 있다. 다만, 1년을 재직하고 그만 두는 경우에 1년 계속근로연수에 대해 26개의 휴가가 발생할 수 있지만, 계속 근로를 하는 근로자의 경우를 기준으로 볼 때는 첫해의 휴가를 11개 보장해주어 근로자 생활의 질의 향상시킬 수 있다고 하겠다. 따라서 연차휴가의 계산에 있어서도 기존의 방식에 11개를 추가적으로 부여함으로써 연도별 관리체계를 유지할 수 있다.

(3) 연차휴가 부여 방법별 장·단점

1) A방식(입사일기준 부여): 개인별 입사일을 기준으로 연차휴가를 산정하여 부여하는 방식이다. 이 방식의 장점은 근로기준법에 따라 정확하게 연차휴가를 계산한다는 것이다.

 반면, 단점으로는 1) 다수의 인원을 개인별로 관리함에 따라 업무적으로 시간이 많이 소요되고 복잡하며 2) 근로기준법 제61조에 의한 연차휴가 사용촉진조치가 어렵고, 3) 근로자가 연차유급휴가를 부여받기 위하여 인위적으로 퇴직일자를 조정할 수도 있다는 것이다.

2) B방식(입사일 + 회계연도 관리 절충): 입사 년도의 다음 해 1월 1일에 15일의 연차휴가를 근속기간에 비례해서 지급하면서 입사일을 다음 년도 1월 1일로 하여 이후 연차휴가를 부여하고, 퇴사할 때에는 회계연도 관리에 의해 지급된 연차휴가 일수를 개인별 입사 일자를 기준으로 산정한 연차휴가 일수에 맞추어 재정산하는 방식이다. 이 때 회계연도를 기준으로 산정한 연차휴가 일수를 퇴직 시에 개인별 정산 할 때, 회계연도 관리에서 추가로 지급된 휴가를 삭감하기 위해서는 취업규칙에 관련된 규정을 마련해 두는 것이 바람직하다고 본다.

 이 방식의 장점은 회계 연도별로 휴가를 관리함으로써 휴가의 관리와 연차휴가 사용촉진조치를 쉽게 할 수 있고, 근로기준법에 의해 연차휴가를 정확히 정산하여 지급한다는 것이다. 단점은 퇴직 시 연차휴가를 개인별로 계산해야 하므로 많은 시간이 소요되고, 근로자가 연차휴가를 부여받기

system" and select a finishing date which allows for more annual leave days.

3) **Type C (prior payment + prorated):** This method provides monthly leave for each attendance month for the first year of employment, and then allows 15 days of annual leave in advance on January 1 of the following year, which is then continuously granted in advance based upon the calendar year. For the month when employment is ended, the annual leave will be adjusted up to the last working day on a prorated basis.

The advantages of Type C are that: 1) the company can effectively use the measure to promote the use of collective annual leave; 2) the company can adjust annual leave easily as it is calculated on a prorated basis; 3) the method can be seen as beneficial in that the employees receive their annual leave ahead of its actual occurrence; and 4) that an employee will not derive any preference for a finishing date because the annual leave is based upon the actual service period calculated on a prorated basis.

Type C's disadvantage is that the company will always grant more annual leave than what would be provided by the start-date based calculation.

(4) Review of annual leave calculation methods

Companies generally use Type B or C, which are all calendar year-based, when managing their annual leave. Type B (start date + calendar year) takes a recalculation procedure by matching annual leave calculated according to a calendar year with annual leave based on the employee's start date.

Accordingly, in my opinion, the most suitable is Type C (prior payment + prorated). This type provides monthly leave for each attendance month for the first year of employment, then allows for 15 days of advance annual leave the following year, and in the month when employment is ended, allows for an adjusted annual leave prorated according to the last working day. In particular, Type C can be the most desirable method because it takes full advantage of the convenient calculation of annual leave as well as the benefits of calendar year-based management.

4. Conclusion

Annual leave is designed to provide an opportunity for exhausted employees to

위해서 불필요하게 퇴직일자를 조정할 수도 있다는 점이다.
3) C방식(사전 지급 및 비례정산): 입사한 첫 해의 각 월에 월차를 미리 지급하고, 입사년도의 다음 해 1월 1일에 15일의 연차휴가를 전부 미리 부여하고, 이후에는 회계연도를 기준으로 연차휴가를 미리 지급하는 방식으로 관리한다. 퇴직하는 년도에는 퇴직하는 일자를 기준으로 비례해서 연차휴가를 정산하는 방식이다.

장점은 1) 연차휴가 관리와 연차휴가 사용촉진 조치가 용이하며 2) 퇴직하는 경우에는 퇴직연도에 발생한 연차휴가 일수를 퇴직일 기준으로 정산하기 때문에 관리가 용이하다. 3) 근토자들이 연차휴가를 후불제가 아닌 선불제로 부여받기 때문에 더 나은 복지제도로 인정하게 된다. 4) 근로자의 퇴직시점에 상관없이 연차휴가가 정산되어 지급되기 때문에 근로자의 불필요한 퇴직시점을 사전에 예방 할 수 있다. 단점으로는 실제로 회사가 입사일을 기준으로 산정한 연차휴가일수보다 더 많은 연차휴가를 부여하여야 한다는 점이다.

(4) 연차휴가 지급방법에 대한 검토

일반적으로 회사에서는 회계연도를 기준으로 연차휴가를 관리하는 B방식을 사용하고 있다. B방식(입사일+회계연도)의 경우에는 근로자가 퇴직할 때 미리 지급된 연차휴가를 가지고, 개인별 관리의 연차휴가와 일치시켜야 하는 번거로움이 발생한다.

가장 바람직한 방법은 C형(사전지급 + 비례정산) 방식이다. 이 방식은 입사연도에는 월차로 부여하고, 그 다음연도어는 15일의 연차휴가를 미리 지급하며, 퇴직연도에는 근속일수에 비례하여 지급하는 형태이다. 특히, C방식은 계산이 편리할 뿐만이 아니라 회계연도별 연차휴가 관리의 장점을 살리고 근로자들의 수용성이 높기 때문에 가장 바람직한 연차휴가 부여방식이라고 본다.

4. 시사점

연차휴가는 일에 지친 근로자에게 휴식을 제공하여 재충전하는 기회를

Chapter 6 Statutory Leave and Contractual Leave

recharge through the provision of a paid vacation; this should not be considered an expense, but rather an investment in securing a constant workforce. Employers should also consider some basic principles when applying a method for calculating annual leave. Firstly, the employee should be able to understand and anticipate his or her annual leave and the available number of days that can be used in the near future. Secondly, the company should provide for collective annual leave so it can easily manage the annual leave for all employees and also promote its use. Thirdly, when employment is terminated, the company can easily calculate the annual leave and the employee has no reason to consider the date of termination in the expectation of additional annual leave. That is to say, the final annual leave can be easily adjusted based on termination date.

III. Promoting the use of annual paid leave

If an employee has not used the leave days saved within the year, he/she shall be paid for the unused days of leave at average or ordinary wages, as prescribed in the rules of employment. However, if the employees have not used their annual leave despite the employer strongly promoting its use, the employer is exempted from the obligation to provide monetary compensation for the unused annual leave.

> Article 61 (Measures to Urge Employees to Take Annual Paid Leave)
> ① Where any employee's paid leave is terminated by time limitation pursuant to the main sentence of Article 60 (7) because the employee fails to take his/her paid leave although the relevant employer has taken the measures falling under each of the following subparagraphs to urge employees to take their respective annual leave pursuant to Article 60 (1) and (4) (which excludes the monthly leave given for employees who have worked less than one year, in accordance with Article 60(2)), the relevant employer is not obligated to compensate the employee for his/her failure to take the paid leave, and the employee's failure to take the paid leave shall be deemed not to fall under the reasons attributable to the employer provided for in the proviso to Article 60 (7):

보장해주므로, 이를 비용이 아닌 노동력 보전을 위한 투자로 간주할 필요가 있다. 연차휴가 부여방식을 결정할 때에는 다음의 몇 가지 원칙을 고려해야 한다. 첫째, 근로자 스스로 연차휴가 사용 가능 일수를 명확히 이해하고 예상할 수 있어야 한다. 둘째, 회사가 연차휴가를 일괄적으로 관리하면서 휴가 관리 및 휴가사용촉진조치를 용이하게 진행할 수 있어야 한다. 셋째, 근로자가 퇴직할 경우 연차휴가 정산이 쉬워야 하고, 근로자가 연차휴가를 부여받기 위하여 퇴직시점을 조정할 필요가 없어야 한다. 즉, 퇴직 일자에 비례한 연차휴가 일수의 부여 방식이어야 할 것이다.

Ⅲ. 연차유급휴가 사용촉진제도

근로자가 1년 이내에 연차 휴가를 사용하지 않고 근로한 경우에는 그 근로일수(휴가일수)만큼 취업규칙에서 정하는 바에 따라 평균임금 또는 통상임금을 지급하여야 한다. 그러나 다음과 같은 사용자의 적극적인 사용촉진 조치에도 불구하고 근로자가 연차유급휴가를 사용하지 않는 경우 금전보상의무가 면제된다(근로기준법 제61조).

> 제61조(연차 유급휴가의 사용 촉진)
> ① 사용자가 제60조 제1항·제2항 및 제4항에 따른 유급휴가(계속하여 근로한 기간이 1년 미만인 근로자의 제60조 제2항에 따른 유급휴가는 제외한다)의 사용을 촉진하기 위하여 다음 각 호의 조치를 하였음에도 불구하고 근로자가 휴가를 사용하지 아니하여 제60조 제7항 본문에 따라 소멸된 경우에는 사용자는 그 사용하지 아니한 휴가에 대하여 보상할 의무가 없고, 제60조 제7항 단서에 따른 사용자의 귀책사유에 해당하지 아니하는 것으로 본다.
> 1. 제60조제7항 본문에 따른 기간이 끝나기 6개월 전을 기준으로

Chapter 6 Statutory Leave and Contractual Leave

1. Any employer shall notify in writing every employee of the number of days of his/her paid leave that has not been taken, and shall urge every employee to notify the employer of a period he/she is planning for the paid leave after determining on such period within ten days, at the six month point before the period under the main sentence of Article 60 (7) expires;
2. Notwithstanding the encouragement referred to in subparagraph 1, if the employee fails to notify the employer of a period during which he/she is planning to take all of part of his/her remaining paid leave within ten days from the date he/she is urged to take his/her paid leave, the employer shall notify the employee in writing after setting a period for his/her paid leave, by no later than two months before the period under the main sentence of Article 60 (7) expires.

② Where any employee's paid leave is terminated by time limitation pursuant to the main sentence of Article 60 (7) because the employee fails to take his/her paid leave although the relevant employer has taken the measures falling under each of the following subparagraphs to urge employees to take their respective annual leave pursuant to Article 60 (2): the monthly leave given for an employee who has worked less than one year, the relevant employer is not liable to compensate the employee for his/her failure to take the paid leave, and the employee's failure to take the paid leave shall be deemed not to fall under the reasons attributable to the employer provided for in the proviso to Article 60 (7):
1. Any employer shall notify in writing every employee of the number of days of his/her paid leave that has not been taken, and shall urge every employee to notify the employer of a period he/she is planning for the paid leave after determining on such period within ten days, at the three month point prior to one year of his/her service;
2. Notwithstanding the encouragement referred to in subparagraph 1, if the employee fails to notify the employer of a period during which he/she is planning to take all of part of his/her remaining paid leave within ten days from the date he/she is urged to take his/her paid leave, the employer shall notify the employee in writing after setting a period for his/her paid leave, by no later than one month before the end of his/her first year.

10일 이내에 사용자가 근로자별로 사용하지 아니한 휴가 일수를 알려주고, 근로자가 그 사용 시기를 정하여 사용자에게 통보하도록 서면으로 촉구할 것

2. 제1호에 따른 촉구에도 불구하고 근로자가 촉구를 받은 때부터 10일 이내에 사용하지 아니한 휴가의 전부 또는 일부의 사용 시기를 정하여 사용자에게 통보하지 아니하면 제60조 제7항 본문에 따른 기간이 끝나기 2개월 전까지 사용자가 사용하지 아니한 휴가의 사용 시기를 정하여 근로자에게 서면으로 통보할 것

② 사용자가 계속하여 근로한 기간이 1년 미만인 근로자의 제60조 제2항에 따른 유급휴가의 사용을 촉진하기 위하여 다음 각 호의 조치를 하였음에도 불구하고 근로자가 휴가를 사용하지 아니하여 제60조 제7항 본문에 따라 소멸된 경우에는 사용자는 그 사용하지 아니한 휴가에 대하여 보상할 의무가 없고, 같은 항 단서에 따른 사용자의 귀책사유에 해당하지 아니하는 것으로 본다.

1. 최초 1년의 근로기간이 끝나기 3개월 전을 기준으로 10일 이내에 사용자가 근로자별로 사용하지 아니한 휴가 일수를 알려주고, 근로자가 그 사용 시기를 정하여 사용자에게 통보하도록 서면으로 촉구할 것. 다만, 사용자가 서면 촉구한 후 발생한 휴가에 대해서는 최초 1년의 근로기간이 끝나기 1개월 전을 기준으로 5일 이내에 촉구하여야 한다.

2. 제1호에 따른 촉구에도 불구하고 근르자가 촉구를 받은 때부터 10일 이내에 사용하지 아니한 휴가의 전부 또는 일부의 사용 시기를 정하여 사용자에게 통보하지 아니하면 최초 1년의 근로기간이 끝나기 1개월 전까지 사용자가 사용하지 아니한 휴가의 사용 시기를 정하여 근로자에게 서면으로 통보할 것. 다만, 제1호 단서에 따라 촉구한 휴가에 대해서는 최초 1년의 근로기간이 끝나기 10일 전까지 서면으로 통보하여야 한다.

Chapter 6 Statutory Leave and Contractual Leave

① In the means to promote the use of leave, the employer has the right to change the date selected by the employee for the claiming of his/her leave, as the employee's leave rights are restricted since the employer shall only promote the use of leave shortly before the leave expires.

② When an employee specifies the period for using leave upon the employer's request, the specified period shall be admitted in principle, and the leave shall be effective during no other period. If the employer decides on the period instead, because the employee fails to do so, it shall also remain unchanged. However, if the employee specifies the leave period, but it is deemed to seriously impede the operation of the business to allow leave for that specified period, the period concerned may be altered.

③ Regarding promotion of the use of annual leave, it is frequent for companies to take formal measures without assigning annual leave for definite working days to employees and in this way avoid paying allowance for the unused annual leave. That is, companies promote the use of annual leave by informing through email only. In cases where the employees come to work on days designated for annual leave, companies do not pay annual leave allowance for unused annual leave owing to their efforts to promote the use of annual leave. However, as this case shows that the Company did not provide the use of annual leave on the designated days, the fact that employees could not use annual leave was due to reasons attributable to the Employer and the Employer shall pay an unused annual leave allowance.

⊃ MOEL Guidelines

The 'written document' mentioned in Article 61 of the LSA refers to a paper document. Electronic documents are only possible in exceptional cases where the company has handled every operation by means of electronic documents in the process of its drafting, obtaining approval and implementing through equipped electronic work-processing systems.[180] Accordingly, informing by email in the course of promoting the use of annual leave cannot be regarded as notification by written document.[181]

If the employee has submitted a vacation plan with stipulated dates of leave after the employer has promoted the use of annual leave, the stipulated dates of leave shall be regarded as the employee's declaration of intention to use his/her annual leave. In cases where the employee comes to work on the stipulated date of leave,

---

[180] MOEL Guidelines: Kunjung-1128, on Feb. 7, 2012.
[181] MOEL Guidelines: Kunjung-6488, on Nov. 1, 2013.

① 휴가사용촉진조치를 하는 경우에도 근로자의 시기 지정권과 사용자의 시기 변경권은 인정된다. 다만, 휴가사용촉진조치는 휴가사용 기간이 얼마 남지 않은 상태에서 이루어지는 것이므로 동 권리의 행사도 제한을 받는다.
② 근로자가 사용자의 휴가시기 지정 촉구에 따라 휴가 시기를 지정한 경우에는 원칙적으로 그 지정한 시기에 휴가를 사용해야 하며, 다른 시기에 시기 지정권을 행사할 수 없다. 근로자가 휴가시기를 지정하지 않아 사용자가 그 휴가 시기를 지정한 경우에는 사용자는 원칙적으로 그 지정한 시기를 변경할 수 없다. 다만, 사용자가 근로자로부터 휴가사용 시기를 지정받은 경우에 그 지정받은 대로 휴가를 부여하는 것이 사업운영에 막대한 지장을 초래하는 경우에는 휴가 시기를 조정하여 지정할 수 있다.
③ 사용자가 연차휴가 사용촉진조치에 대해 형식적 조치만을 취하고 실질적으로 연차휴가를 부여하지 않으면서도 미사용 연차휴가수당을 지급하지 않는 경우가 많다. 즉, 연차휴가 사용촉진 조치를 이메일로 통보하면서, 휴가일자에 출근하여 근무를 하는 경우 회사가 휴가사용촉진조치를 다하였기 때문에 미사용 연차수당을 지급하지 않아도 된다고 생각하는 경우가 많다. 하지만, 이러한 경우에 사용자가 휴가를 보장하지 않은 것이라 볼 수 있기 때문에 사용자의 귀책 사유로 휴가를 사용하지 못한 것으로 간주하여 미사용 연차휴가수당을 지급해야 한다.

◯ 행정해석

근로기준법 제61조의 서면은 종이로 된 문서를 의미하고 전자문서는 회사가 전자결제체계를 완비해 전자문서로 모든 업무의 기안, 결재, 시행과정을 관리하는 경우에만 예외적으로 가능하다.[180] 이에 연차유급휴가의 사용촉진 조치와 관련해 이메일로 통보하는 것이 근로자 개인별로 서면촉구 또는 통보하는 것에 비해 도달 여부의 확인 등이 불명확한 경우, 서면 촉구 또는 통보하였다고 인정되기 어렵다.[181]

휴가사용 촉진조치에 의하여 근로자가 휴가사용 시기를 정하여 사용자에게 휴가 사용계획서를 제출하였다면 그 지정된 시기에 연차유급휴가를 사용하겠다는

---

180) 행정해석: 2012.2.7. 근정과-1128
181) 행정해석: 2013.11.01 근정과-6488

if the employer received the employee's labor and did not express an objection to his/her coming in to work, it shall be regarded that the employer has approved the labor service on the expected date of leave, and so the employer shall pay an unused leave allowance.[182]

⟨Case Study 6-1⟩ Whether Unused Annual Leave should be Compensated

1. Summary

In the Seoul office of a foreign company (hereinafter referred to as "the Company") that has about 300 employees and is engaged in the apparel business, a labor case occurred due to escalating disputes between directors in April 2015. With two departments of the Company combining into one, the executive managing director told the managing director that it would be not desirable to have two directors in one department, and told the managing director that she needed to resign from the Company. The managing director (hereinafter referred to as "the Employee") told the Company that she would sue it for violating the Labor Standards Act and would also report additional claims of other employees unless the Company paid her a severance bonus of two years' annual wages. The Company responded that it did not order the Employee to resign, rejected her demand for a severance bonus, and explained that the Company had not violated the Labor Standards Act. Just after that, the Employee began a lawsuit against the Company and visited the Gangnam Labor Office to claim the Company had violated the Labor Standards Act, and had not paid annual leave allowance for unused leave or additional allowance for her overtime work.

The main item in these accusations: First, the Company regulated in the Rules of Employment that it would not compensate for unused annual leave and instead would promote its use, which the Company did through individual emails to all personnel. Where the promotion of annual leave use has been done through email, the main point is whether or not the Company must give financial compensation for unused leave. Herein, I would like to look substantially into these two main points of dispute to confirm whether or not the Company had violated the Labor Standards Act.

---

[182] MOEL Guidelines: Limjang-285, on Oct. 21, 2005.

의사표시로 볼 수 있을 것이므로 휴가를 청구한 것으로 볼 수 있다. 다만, 근로자가 휴가사용 시기를 지정하고도 출근한 경우 사용자가 노무수령 거부의 의사표시 없이 근로를 제공받았다면 휴가일 근로를 승낙한 것으로 보아야 하므로 연차유급휴가 근로수당을 지급하여야 한다.[182]

〈실무사례 6-1〉 미사용 연차수당 지급 진정사건

1. 사실관계

서울에 사무소를 두고 직원 300여 명을 고용하여 의류 사업을 하고 있는 한 외국기업에서, 2015년 4월에 임원 간의 갈등이 노동사건으로 확대된 사건이 발생하였다. 부서가 통폐합되면서 한 부서에 전무와 상무가 같이 근무하게 되었는데, 전무가 상무에게 하나의 부서에 임원 둘이 같이 근무하는 것은 바람직하지 않으니, 퇴사할 것을 권유하였다. 이에 상무(이하, "이 사건의 근로자"라 함)는 회사가 근로기준법을 위반하였다고 주장하면서, 2년 치 퇴직위로금을 주지 않을 경우 회사를 고용노동부에 고소하고, 다른 직원들에 대한 위반사항도 고발할 것이라 압박하였다. 이에 대해 회사는 이 사건의 근로자에게 퇴직을 권유하지 않았으며, 근로기준법을 위반한 사실도 없다고 하면서 퇴직위로금의 지급을 거부하였다. 그러자 이 사건의 근로자는 회사가 미사용 연차휴가에 대한 연차수당을 지급하지 않고, 연장근로에 대한 가산임금을 지급하지 않는 등 근로기준법을 위반하였다고 '강남고용지청'에 회사를 고소하였다.

이 고소내용에 대한 주요 쟁점사항을 살펴보면, 회사는 취업규칙 (연차휴가 사용촉진)을 통해 근로자에게 미사용 연차휴가는 보상하지 않는다고 규정하고 있고, 이메일로 개인별 휴가사용을 적극적으로 권장하였다. 눈여겨볼 사항은 이러한 이메일 상 휴가사용촉진조치를 한 경우, 사용자의 금전보상이 면제될 수 있는지의 여부이다. 위의 쟁점사항에 대하여 회사가 근로기준법을 위반했는지 구체적으로 살펴보고자 한다.

---

[182] 행정해석: 2005.10.21. 임장팀-285

2. Company's Measures for Promoting the Use of Annual Leave

The Company regulated in the Rules of Employment that it would not compensate for unused leave, had informed personnel of the number of available annual leave days in the early part of the year, and sent similar emails again after six months to the employees to actively promote their use. In October, it notified each individual employee by email that he or she needed to use his/her remaining annual leave days by the end of the year, and that there would be no financial compensation for unused leave. In reality, the Company had not paid any allowance for unused annual leave so far.

3. The Employer's Countermeasures

The Company has promoted the use of annual leave through email, but has not done so through written documents. Also, the Company did not evidentially reject the provision of the employee's labor when the employee provided work on dates expected to be used as annual leave. Based upon these facts, the employer recognized that it had not taken measures promoting the use of leave as stipulated by the LSA, and then paid unused annual leave allowance for the past three years in the salary payment for June 2015.

4. Conclusion

The labor case herein is a very common one that can occur easily for companies. Regarding promotion of the use of annual leave, it is frequent for companies to take formal measures without assigning annual leave for definite working days to employees and in this way avoid paying allowance for the unused annual leave. That is, companies promote the use of annual leave by informing through email only. In cases where the employees come to work on days designated for annual leave, companies do not pay annual leave allowance for unused annual leave owing to their efforts to promote the use of annual leave. However, as this case shows, the Company did not provide the use of annual leave on the designated days, so the fact that employees could not use annual leave was due to reasons attributable to the Employer. The Employer therefore had to pay an unused annual leave allowance.

2. 회사의 연차휴가 사용촉진조치

취업규칙에 '연차휴가 사용촉진' 규정을 두어 미사용 연차휴가는 보상을 하지 않는다고 명시하고 있고, 회사는 이메일을 통해 연초에 휴가 일수를 알려주었으며, 6개월이 지난 후에는 잔여일수를 알려주고 휴가사용을 적극 권장하였다. 그리고 매월 10월에는 휴가사용에 대해 개인별로 미사용휴가 일수를 이메일로 알려주었고, 휴가를 사용하지 않을 시에는 금전보상이 없음을 이미 통지하였다. 또한 실제로 휴가사용을 권장하는 등 수차례의 관련 이메일을 발송하였다. 실제로 회사는 미사용 연차휴가에 대한 수당을 한 번도 지급한 사례가 없었다.

3. 회사의 대응 및 처리결과

회사는 이메일로 연차휴가 사용촉진조치를 하였지, 근로기준법에 따른 서면에 의한 사용촉진 조치를 하지 않았다. 또한 근로자가 휴가신청을 한 경우에도 불구하고 휴가신청기간에 근로를 제공한 경우에 근로거부 표시를 명확히 하지 않았다. 이러한 사실에 대해 회사는 근로기준법에서 정한 휴가 사용촉진조치를 하지 않았다는 것을 인정하고, 2015년 6월 급여에서 전 직원의 최근 3년 기간의 미사용 연차휴가수당을 모두 지급하였다.

4. 시사점

위에서 다루었던 사례는 기업에서 일상적으로 일어날 수 있는 사건이다. 사용자가 연차휴가 사용촉진조치에 대해 형식적 조치 만을 취하고 실질적으로 연차휴가를 부여하지 않으면서도 미사용 연차휴가수당을 지급하지 않는 경우가 많다. 즉, 연차휴가 사용촉진 조치를 이메일로 통보하면서, 휴가일자에 출근하여 근무를 하는 경우에 회사가 휴가사용촉진조치를 다하였기 때문에 미사용 연차수당을 지급하지 않아도 된다고 생각하는 경우가 많다. 하지만, 이러한 경우에 사용자가 휴가를 보장하지 않은 것이라 볼 수 있기 때문에 사용자의 귀책사유로 휴가를 사용하지 못한 것으로 간주하여 미사용 연차휴가수당을 지급해야 한다.

Chapter 6 Statutory Leave and Contractual Leave

<Table 6-1> Promoting the Use of Annual Leave & Application for Use of Annual Leave

Department		Name	
Co-worker ID		Hire Date	

We want 00000Korea to be a great place to work. We care as much about our co-workers as the development of our business. This is why the Company encourages you to take the annual leave and why any remaining annual leave at the end of 2020 will not be compensated. You can read more about annual leave in our current co-worker handbook.

Please be informed that you have _____ days of unused annual leave as of the 1st of June 2020. This annual leave balance can be adjusted according to any contract changes.

This form is only for planning the use of annual leave. You should talk with your manager to use your annual leave, then request use via 0000000.

I confirm the number of unused leave hours contained in this document hereto, and have stated my plan below to take annual leave in 2020.

Month	Planned leave (date/hours)	Month	Planned leave (date/hours)
Jun	Please fill out your plan after the 1st of June)	Oct	
Jul		Dec	
Aug		Dec	
Sep			

If there is a problem with your balance on paper, please confirm with your manager.

Co-worker's Signature: _____   Manager's signature: _____
Co-worker's Name: _____   Manager's Name: _____
Date: _____   Date: _____

<표 6-1> 연차 사용 촉진 안내 및 휴가 사용계획 신청서

부서		이름	
사번		입사일	

　○○○○회사는 직원들이 즐겁게 일할 수 있는 환경을 만들고자 연차촉진제도를 도입하고 있습니다. 해당연도에 발생된 연차를 반드시 소진할 수 있도록 회사가 직원을 독려하는 제도로, 사용하지 않은 연차는 돈으로 보상되지 않습니다. 자세한 내용은 취업규칙을 확인해 주시기 바랍니다.

　귀하의 2020년 6월 1일 기준, 사용하지 않은 연차는 _____ 일 입니다. 위의 제시된 잔여 연차는 계약변경 상황에 따라서 조정 될 수 있음을 알려드립니다.

　아래의 연차사용계획서는 본인이 사용하고자 하는 "계획"을 의미하는 것으로 연차신청과는 별개입니다. 아래의 내용을 바탕으로 귀하의 매니저와 협의 후 ○○○○를 통해 연차신청을 해주시기 바랍니다.

　본인은 아래와 같이 2020년도 잔여 연차를 사용할 계획입니다.

월	연차사용계획	월	연차사용계획
7월	(7월 1일 이후 사용예정인 연차휴가를 기재하기 바랍니다.	10월	
8월		11월	
9월		12월	

* 위의 잔여 연차기간에 이상이 있으신 분들은 팀 리더 또는 매니저에게 반드시 확인 부탁드립니다

직원서명 _____　　매니저서명 _____
직원이름 _____　　매니저이름 _____
날짜 _____　　　　　　날짜 _____

Chapter 6 Statutory Leave and Contractual Leave

IV. Substitution of Annual Paid Leave

The employer may, through a written agreement with the labor representative, have employees take a paid leave on a particular working day in substitution of annual paid leave (Article 62 of the LSA). The particular working day means a particular day among contractual working days required for labor duty. Accordingly, the employer cannot, pursuant to Article 62 of the LSA, substitute a paid leave day with contractual holiday and leave, nor with statutory holiday and leave.

⊃ **MOEL Guidelines and Judicial Rulings**

1. If an employment contract expires before the employee uses their annual paid leave, how much can he/she receive as annual paid leave allowance?

The right to use annual leave as paid days off is acquired definitely as remuneration for labor when the employee has worked for a one-year period. As soon as the employee acquired the right to annual paid leave, his employment was terminated due to retirement, etc. before using his annual paid leave. In this case, while the right to use annual paid leave requires continuous labor service, this cannot be granted due to retirement. However, the right to request annual paid leave allowance does not require continuous labor service and so shall be compensated as a paid allowance. Accordingly, the employee can request the annual paid leave allowance equivalent to the whole number of annual paid leave days unused up to the employment termination date.[183]

V. Contractual Leave

1. Concept

Contractual leave refers to paid vacation, free of the obligation to provide labor

---

[183] Supreme Court ruling on May 27, 2005, 2003Da48549, 2003Da48556.

Ⅳ. 연차유급휴가의 대체

사용자는 근로자대표와의 서면합의에 의하여 연차유급휴가일에 갈음하여 특정 근로일에 근로자를 휴무시킬 수 있다(근로기준법 제62조). 여기서 특정 근로일이라 함은 근로의무가 있는 '소정근로일' 중의 특정일을 의미한다. 따라서 사용자는 법정 휴일·휴가뿐만 아니라 약정 휴일·휴가로 근로기준법 62조의 규정에 의한 휴가를 대체할 수 없다.

➲ 연차휴가와 관련된 주요 판례 및 행정해석

1. 연차유급휴가를 사용하기 전 근로관계가 종료된 경우 받을 수 있는 연차휴가수당의 범위

유급(연차휴가수당)으로 연차휴가를 사용할 권리는 근로자가 1년간 소정의 근로를 마친 대가이며 확정적으로 취득하는 것이므로, 근로자가 연차유급휴가권을 취득한 후 연차유급휴가를 사용하기 전에 퇴직 등의 사유로 근로관계가 종료된 경우, 근로관계의 존속을 전제로 하는 연차휴가를 사용할 권리는 소멸한다 할지라도 근로관계의 존속을 전제로 하지 않는 연차휴가수당을 청구할 권리는 그대로 잔존하는 것이어서, 근로자는 근로관계 종료 시까지 사용하지 못한 연차휴가일수 전부에 상응하는 연차휴가수당을 사용자에게 청구할 수 있는 것이다.[183]

Ⅴ. 약정휴가

1 개 념

약정휴가는 사용자의 승인, 단체협약이나 취업규칙으로 유급휴가를 제공함

---
[183] 대법원 2005.05.27. 선고 2003다48549, 2003다48556 판결

Chapter 6 Statutory Leave and Contractual Leave

in accordance with employer approval, a collective agreement or the rules of employment. Such leave includes congratulatory and condolence leave, sick leave, summer vacation, and other special leave, etc. Contractual leaves are not statutory like annual paid leave, or maternity/paternity leave, but were introduced to maintain traditional Korean values and improve employee wellbeing, and can be stipulated as paid, partially paid, or unpaid leave. A company that does not stipulate these contractual leaves is not in violation of the Labor Standards Act.

2. Types of Contractual Leave

(1) Congratulatory and condolence leave

Many companies provide congratulatory and condolence leave for wedding and funeral services in accordance with traditional Korean rituals. Although the coverage and number of leaves vary from company to company, such leave is granted in addition to annual paid leave. A maximum of five leave days are given for an employee's wedding as congratulatory leave, five days as condolence leave in the event of the death of an employee's direct family member, and one day for a parent's 60th birthday.

(2) Sick leave

Should an employee be unable to carry out his/her duties due to non-occupational injury or illness, the employee shall use annual paid leave to receive medical treatment and shall bear the medical expenses him/herself as there is no statutory sick leave. Government employees can use up to 60 days per year as sick leave according to Article 18 of the Government Employee Service Regulations (Sick Leave). In the private sector, if an employee has used up all his/her annual leave days, he/she may request unpaid leave to take care of illness or injury. If the employee has to continually be absent in order to receive treatment for his/her illness or injury, the company can dismiss the employee for reasons attributable to the employee. Many companies have some restricted types of sick leave, such as follows.

으로써 근로제공의무를 면제해주는 휴가로 경조휴가, 병가, 하계휴가, 특별휴가 등이 있다. 약정휴가는 연차유급휴가, 산전산후휴가, 배우자출산휴가와 같이 근로기준법으로 보장된 것이 아니라 한국의 전통적 가치를 존중하고 근로자들의 복지차원에서 도입된 휴가라 할 수 있다. 이러한 약정휴가를 설정해놓지 않았다고 하여 근로기준법을 위반한 것이 아니며, 회사의 재량에 따라 유급, 부분적 유급, 또는 무급으로 설정하여 운용할 수 있다.

2 약정휴가의 유형

(1) 경조휴가

많은 회사들이 한국의 오래된 관혼상제의 전통에 따라 혼례와 상례에 관련하여 경조휴가를 부여하고 있다. 그 대상범위나 부여일수가 다를 수 있지만, 일반적으로 연차유급휴가와 별개로 추가적으로 유급휴가를 부여한다. 본인 결혼의 경우 5일 이내, 직계가족의 사망 시에 5일 이내, 부모님의 환갑의 경우 1일을 부여한다.

(2) 병가

근로자가 업무 외에 발생한 개인적 질병이나 부상으로 인하여 직무를 수행할 수 없을 때에는 법정 병가가 인정되지 않기 때문에 본인의 연차유급휴가를 사용하여 요양을 해야 하고 또는 치료비 일체도 근로자 개인이 부담해야 한다. 다만, 공무원인 경우에는 국가공무원 복무규정 제18조(병가) 규정에 의해 연 60일까지 유급병가를 사용할 수 있다. 따라서 병가 규정이 없는 일반 회사의 경우에 근로자는 병가를 신청할 수 없기 때문에 자신에게 주어진 잔여 연차유급휴가를 사용하여 치료하여야 하고, 연차유급휴가를 모두 사용한 경우에는 무급휴직을 청구하게 된다. 근로자가 질병 또는 부상 치료를 위해 계속해서 결근하는 경우에는 회사는 근로자의 귀책 사유로 인한 통상해고를 할 수 있다. 많은 회사들이 취업규칙에 제한적인 유급 병가규정을 설정하고 있는데 그 유형은 다음과 같다.

Type 1	No regulation for sick leave days. Annual paid leave shall be used instead.
Type 2	"The company may grant unpaid sick leave of up to 90 days per calendar year."
Type 3	"If an employee requires an extended time of absence due to accident or illness unrelated to his/her duties, he/she may request to use paid leave. The period shall not exceed 14 calendar days, provided that the accrued annual leave has been used up already
Type 4	"In case of a leave of absence due to non work-related injury or illness, 90% of monthly ordinary wage shall be paid for the first month, 70% for the second month and 50% for the third to sixth months."

(3) Summer vacation

Summer vacation refers to contractual leave of a maximum one week besides annual paid leave during the heat of the summer in order to promote employee morale. This summer leave is used collectively by production companies, while smaller companies generally use annual paid leave days as summer vacation.

3. Relationship between Labor Law and Contractual Leave

(1) It is impossible to change the date for congratulatory or condolence leave or to apply for it retroactively[184]

Congratulatory and condolence leave refers to paid leaves granted on particular days or for a particular period to the corresponding employee in accordance with the collective agreement or rules of employment so that the employee can participate in congratulatory or condolence events. It is not possible to change the period of leave nor apply for them retroactively.

(2) Congratulatory and condolence leave not granted during labor strikes[185]

According to the Labor Standards Act (LSA), holiday refers to a day when the employee is exempted from the obligation to provide labor to the employer, while leave refers to days exempted from the obligation to provide work even though the employer is available to receive the labor service. While contractual holidays or

---

[184] MOEL Guidelines: Kungi 68207-1452, on Sept. 14, 1994.
[185] MOEL Guidelines: Kungi 68207-883, on Dec. 15, 1999.

유형1	병가규정 없음. 이 경우 연차휴가로 사용하여야 함
유형2	"회사는 역년으로 90일까지의 병가를 지급할 수 있다. 병가는 무급으로 한다."
유형3	"직원이 업무 외의 사고나 질병으로 장기간 결근해야 할 경우, 연차휴가를 모두 사용하고 휴일을 포함하여 14일을 초과하지 않는 범위 안에서 유급 병가를 신청할 수 있다."
유형4	"개인상병에 의한 휴직일 경우에는 최초1개월: 월 통상급여의 90%; 2개월 차: 월 통상급여의 70%; 3~6개월차: 월 통상급여의 50%를 지급한다."

(3) 여름휴가

여름휴가는 연차유급휴가와 별도로 직원들의 사기진작을 위해 한 여름에 1주일 이내에서 지급하는 약정휴가제도이다. 주로 제조업체에서 집단적으로 사용하고, 소규모 사업장의 경우에는 연차휴가를 대체해서 여름휴가로 사용하기도 한다.

3 노동법과 약정휴가와의 관계

(1) 경조휴가 시기변경권 불가능 및 소급 불가[184]

경조휴가는 노사가 단체협약이나 취업규칙 등으로 경조일의 기념이나 경조사 참여를 보장하기 위해 해당 근로자에게 특정일 또는 특정기간에 유급으로 부여하는 휴가로서 사용자의 휴가시기에 따른 변경권 행사가 불가능하고 또한 그 기일이 경과하면 휴가 사용목적이 소멸되어 휴가청구권 또한 소멸한다.

(2) 쟁의행위기간 중 경조유급휴가는 발생하지 않음[185]

근로기준법상 휴일이라 함은 근로자가 사용자에 대하여 근로제공의무가 없는 날을 말하며, 근로기준법상 휴가라 함은 사용자가 근로자의 노무수령을

---

[184] 행정해석: 근기68207-1452, 1994.09.14.
[185] 행정해석: 근기68207-883, 1999.12.15.

Chapter 6   Statutory Leave and Contractual Leave

contractual leave stipulated by a collective agreement or rules of employment are not statutory holidays where workers are exempted from the obligation to provide labor according to the Labor Standards Act (LSA), workers are to be so exempted from work on working days due to special agreement between employer and employees. Accordingly, if there is a certain condition where the employer, in reality, can neither receive the employee's labor nor exempt him/her from providing labor, then the contractual holiday or contractual leave cannot occur. However, for those who did not participate in strikes during labor disputes, whether a contractual holiday or contractual leave occurred should be judged according to whether the employer could receive the employee's labor or not.

(3) Calculation of average wages during periods of leave[186]

Average wages where an employee came to resign after a period of leave from work that the employee took with approval from the employer due to non-occupational injury, illness or other reason shall be calculated as follows: average wages to calculate severance pay refer to the amount calculated by dividing the total amount of wages paid to the relevant employee during three calendar months prior to the date of calculation by the total number of calendar days during those three calendar months (Article 2 of the LSA). If the amount calculated by this method is lower than the ordinary wages of the employee concerned, the amount of the ordinary wages shall be deemed as average wages. In cases where the period of average wage calculation includes a period during leave from work with approval from the employer caused by non-occupational injury, illness, or other reason, the period and wages paid for that period shall be deducted respectively from the basis period for the calculation of average wages and the total amount of average wage (Article 2 of the Enforcement Decree to the LSA). Therefore, in cases where an employee took a leave of absence for non-occupational injury, illness or other reason in accordance with Article 2 (8) of the Enforcement Decree to the LSA (with approval from the employer), the remaining period and wages excluding the period mentioned above shall be used for the calculation of average wages. If the leave of absence exceeds three months, the first day of the leave of absence shall be the date for calculating average wages based on the previous three months. In any case, if the amount calculated above is lower than the ordinary wages of the employee concerned, the amount of the ordinary wages shall be deemed as average wages.

(4) In cases where changes to contractual leave in the rules of employment is considered disadvantageous[187]

---

[186] MOEL Guidelines: Retirement Pension Dept-518, on Oct. 21, 2008.
[187] MOEL Guidelines: Working Conditions Inspection Team-1774, on Mar. 25, 2009.

할 수 있는 상태임에도 사용자가 그날의 근로제공의무를 면제시켜 주는 것을 말한다. 노사 간 단체협약 또는 취업규칙에서 정한 이른바 약정휴일 또는 약정휴가의 경우는 근로제공의무가 없는 근로기준법상 휴일과는 달리 근로제공의무가 있는 날임에도 노사 간 특약에 의하여 사용자가 근로자의 근로제공의무를 면제시켜 준 것으로 보아야 할 것이다. 따라서 사용자가 사실상 근로자의 노무제공을 수령할 수 없고 사용자의 면제행위도 행사할 수 없는 상태였다면 약정휴일 또는 약정휴가 자체가 발생하지 아니한다. 다만 파업기간 중 파업 미참석자의 경우에는 사용자가 근로자의 노무제공을 수령할 수 있는 상태인지의 여부에 따라 판단해야 한다.

(3) 휴직기간의 평균임금 산정방법[186]

업무 외 부상이나 질병, 그 밖의 사유로 사용자의 승인을 받아 휴업한 후 퇴직하게 된 경우에 평균임금을 다음과 같이 계산한다. 퇴직금산정을 위한 평균임금은 이를 산정하여야 할 사유가 발생한 날 이전 3개월 동안에 그 근로자에게 지급된 임금의 총액을 그 기간의 총일수로 나눈 금액을 말하며(「근로기준법」 제2조), 이러한 방법으로 산출된 평균임금액이 당해 근로자의 통상임금보다 저액일 경우에는 그 통상임금을 평균임금으로 하도록 정하고 있다. 평균임금 산정기간 중에 업무 외 부상 또는 질병으로 사용자의 승인을 받아 휴업한 경우에는 그 기간과 그 기간에 지불된 임금은 평균임금 산정기준이 되는 기간과 임금의 총액에서 각각 공제하도록 규정하고 있다 (근로기준법시행령 제2조). 따라서 근로자가 업무 외 부상이나 질병, 그 밖의 사유로 사용자의 승인을 받아 휴업한 기간일 경우에는 동기간을 제외한 나머지 일수 및 임금을 대상으로 평균임금으로 산정하여야 하며, 휴직한 기간이 3개월을 초과하여 평균임금 산정기준기간이 없게 되는 경우에는 휴직한 첫 날을 평균임금산정 사유발생일로 보아 이전 3월간을 대상으로 평균임금을 산정하여야 한다. 아울러, 위와 같은 방법으로 산출된 평균임금액이 당해 근로자의 통상임금보다 저액일 경우에는 그 통상임금액을 평균임금으로 하여야 한다.

(4) 약정휴가 사용변경은 취업규칙 불이익변경[187]

---

[186] 행정해석: 퇴직연금복지과-518, 2008.10.21.

Chapter 6 Statutory Leave and Contractual Leave

A particular company has provided 5 to 10 days of 'health vacation' per year according to rank and length of service, but did not set any restrictions on the time of use. If it were to later decide to allow its use only after annual paid leave is used up, this would be restricting free use of the contractual leave. It would be acceptable and applicable after consent is received according to the appropriate procedures (Article 94 of the LSA).

4. Comments

Contractual holidays and contractual leaves are only effective if they are regulated by a collective agreement, rules of employment or the employment contract. Generally speaking, public holidays are treated as paid holidays, but in legal actuality are considered contractual holidays. If smaller workplaces such as small private institutes (hagwon) have workers take paid leave on particular public holidays in lieu of annual paid leave, they would be free of any liability in a legal claim for compensation of unused annual paid leave. Also, as sick leave is widely accepted by many countries as statutory leave, many foreign employees assume sick leave is statutory in Korea too, but as explained earlier, it is considered contractual leave. Accordingly, by taking advantage of these contractual holidays and contractual leaves, healthy medium-sized companies can use these holidays and leaves to improve employee morale, while small companies can use them to adjust their working conditions.

<Table 6-2> Sick Leave-related Cases in Rules of Employment

<#1: IT Company>
Article 00 (Sick Leave)
1. Generally, sick leave shall be deducted from annual leave. Provided, that employees who require intensive medical treatment through hospitalization shall be granted up to 7 days' (including holidays) sick leave per year.
2. Employees shall submit to the Company a medical certificate from a clinic or general hospital recognized by the Company.

회사에서는 직급, 근속년수에 따라 1년에 5~10일의 건강휴가를 부여하고 있고 그 사용 시기에 관하여는 별도의 제한을 두고 있지 않았다. 그러나, 종전에는 건강휴가의 사용시기에 대하여 아무런 조건 없이 허용하다가 이를 연차유급휴가 소진 이후에만 사용할 수 있도록 변경하는 것은 결과적으로 자유로운 사용이 제약되는 것으로, 이는 불이익한 변경에 해당하고 따라서 소정의 동의절차(근로기준법 제94조제1항)를 거쳐야 유효하게 적용될 수 있다.

4. 시사점

약정휴일과 약정휴가는 전적으로 단체협약, 취업규칙 또는 근로계약에 규정된 경우에 한해서 사용할 수 있다. 일반적으로 국공휴일의 경우에는 유급휴일로 간주하여 사용하는 경우가 많지만, 이는 실제로는 약정휴일에 해당된다. 소규모학원 등 열악한 사업장의 경우에 국공휴일을 연차휴가 대체 사용일로 지정하여 사용하도록 하면, 차후 근로자가 연차휴가 미지급으로 인한 임금체불 진정사건으로부터 자유로울 수 있다. 또한 병가도 법정휴가로 인정하는 국가가 많은 관계로 외국인 근로자들이 당연히 병가를 받을 수 있다고 생각하지만, 상기한 바와 같이 한국에서는 아직까지 병가는 약정휴가에 해당된다. 따라서 이러한 약정휴일이나 약정휴가를 잘 이해함으로써 중견기업에서는 휴일 및 휴가를 직원들의 사기진작을 위한 방향으로 사용할 수 있고, 소규모 열악한 사업장의 경우에는 사업장의 수준에 맞는 근로조건을 설정하는데 사용할 수 있다.

<표 6-2> 병가 관련 취업규칙 사례

<규정 #1: IT 회사>
제 ○○ 조 (병가)
1. 일반적인 병가는 연차휴가에서 공제한다. 다만 입원을 요하는 환자의 경우에는 공휴일 포함 최대 7일까지 유급으로 보상한다.
2. 직원은 회사에서 인정한 개인병원이나 종합병원 의사가 서명한 진단서를 회사에 제출하여야 한다.

---

187) 행정해석: 근로조건지도과-1774, 2009.03.25.

Chapter 6   Statutory Leave and Contractual Leave

<#2: Pharmacy Sales Company>

Article 00 (Sick Leave)

If an employee requires an extended time of absence due to accidents or illness not related to his/her duties, he/she may request paid leave. Such a period shall not exceed 14 calendar days, provided that the accrued annual leave has been used up already. The employee shall present a certificate of treatment and condition of health signed by a doctor at a clinic or hospital accepted by the Company.

<#3: Pharmacy Production and Sales Company>

Article 8 (Sick Leave)

1. An employee with an injury or disease can request sick leave up to 6 months. The sick leave period can be extended only one time, if the Company agrees.
2. In the above case, 80% of the basic salary shall be paid.
3. Those seeking to take sick leave must obtain the Company's approval with a medical certificate from a second-level hospital or higher.
4. The period for sick leave shall be included in the length of service.

<#4: Large-scale Retail Company>

1. Article 00. Sick leave (Long-term and Short-term)
1. If you are sick and unable to work, you should report to your manager in advance.
2. There are 2 kinds of sick leave: long-term and short-term.
 - Short-term: Up to 10 days a year with 50% of wages paid; a doctor's prescription is required after the 3rd day in a row.
 - Long-term: 50% of wages paid for the first 90 days, 30% paid from 91 to 180 days, an no wages paid after 180 days.
3. The Company may withhold the paid sick leave if your manager feels it is inappropriate, e.g. you do not follow the absence reporting procedures, you do not submit the verification document, your leave of absence is at an unacceptable level, or the Company has a reasonable doubt of the validity.

<규정 #2: 제약 판매 회사>
제 ○○ 조 (병가)

　직원이 업무 외의 사고나 질병으로 장기간 결근해야 할 경우, 연차휴가를 모두 사용하고 휴일을 포함하여 14일을 초과하지 않는 범위 안에서 유급 병가를 신청할 수 있다. 직원은 회사에서 인정한 개인병원이나 종합병원 의사가 서명한 진단서를 회사에 제출하여야 한다.

<규정 #3: 제약 제조 및 판매 회사>
제 ○○ 조　(병가)
1. 직원은 질병 혹은 부상이 있는 경우 6개월 이내의 병가를 신청할 수 있다. 단, 회사의 동의가 있을 때에는 1회에 한하여 동 기간의 연장을 인정한다.
2. 병가기간중의 임금은 기본급의 80%를 지급한다.
3. 병가 신청 시에는 반드시 2차 진료기관 이상의 의료기관에서 의사의 진단서를 첨부하고 회사의 승인을 받아야 한다.
4. 병가는 근무 연수에 포함한다.

<규정 #4: 대형매장 판매회사>
제 ○○ 조: 병가 (단기/장기)
1. 건강 문제로 인해 근무를 할 수 없을 경우, 근무 시작시간 이전에 직속상사에게 보고하고 병가를 신청할 수 있다.
2. 병가는 단기병가와 장기병가가 있으며 각각의 내용은 아래와 같다.
   - 단기병가 : 년 10일 한도이며 기본급의 50%가 지급 된다. 3일이상 연속으로 신청하는 경우 의사의 진단서를 제출하여야 한다.
   - 장기병가 : 총 180일 내에서 유급으로 부여되며 첫날부터 90일 까지는 기본급의 50%, 91일부터 180일 까지는 기본급의 30%, 그 이후에는 무급으로 부여된다. 최초 신청시기부터 의사의 진단서를 제출하여야 한다.
3. 직속 상사가 적절치 않다고 판단하는 경우에는 승인을 받을 수 없다. 예를 들어, 결근 보고 절차를 따르지 않은 경우, 증명서를 작성하지 않은 경우, 병가를 수용할 수 없는 수준이거나, 회사가 질병으로 인한 휴가의 타당성을 의심할 만한 이유가 있는 경우 등이 이에 속한다.

Chapter 6 Statutory Leave and Contractual Leave

<#5: Production Company>
Article 00. Sick Leave
  If an employee asks for sick leave due to an illness, injury, etc. unrelated to work, approval shall be based upon a doctor's written diagnosis. Before taking sick leave, the employee shall use annual leave first.
  An employee who has been absent from work for one week or more due to an injury or illness shall provide a doctor's written diagnosis. The following list is for the length of sick leave:
  - 30 days or less: 100% of ordinary wages paid
  - 31 ~ 90 days: 50% of ordinary wages paid
  2. - More than 90 days: no wages paid
  If an employee takes more than 90 days of sick leave, the company may adjust that employee's work duties or compensation.

<Table 6-3> Congratulatory or Condolence Leave-related Cases in Rules of Employment

<#1: IT Company>
Article 00 (Special Leave)
1. The Company shall grant congratulatory or condolence leave on the working date for the following occasions:

Congratulatory & Condolence Events	Leave
Marriage of employee	5 days
Death of parents/spouse's parents/spouse	5 days

2. When paid leave by the congratulatory or condolence leave falls on the same day(s) as a holiday (excluding Saturday and Sunday), additional leave shall not be given. Congratulatory or condolence paid leave shall not be accumulated or compensated in cash.
3. Employees claiming special leave shall use it one week before or after the actual occasion takes place and submit a Leave Request Form with documentary evidence verifying the occasion to the HR Dept one week in advance.

<#2: Pharmacy Company>
Article 00. Special Leave
  1. The Company shall grant special leave with pay to the Employee as follows:
  (1) Marriage of Employee: 3 days;
  (2) Death of Employee's parent or spouse, or a parent of the Employee's

<규정 #5: 제조업 회사>
제 ○○ 조: 병가휴직
직원은 허가 받은 전문의의 진단서에 근거하여 병가휴직을 신청하고 회사의 승인을 득하여야 한다. 병가휴직은 사용 전 신청하여야 하며, 해당 종업원은 휴직시점에서의 잔여연차일수를 먼저 소진하여야 한다. 병가휴직기간 및 처우는 다음과 같다.
- 30일 이내   : 월 통상임금100 %
- 31일 ~ 90일   : 월 통상임금의 50%
- 90일이상   : 무급

병가휴직이 90일 이상 지속되는 경우 회사는 해당 직원의 업무 또는 기타 보상등을 조정할 수 있다.

<표 6-3> 경조사 관련 취업규칙 사례

<규정 #1: IT 회사>
제 ○○ 조 (특별휴가)
1. 사원의 경조사 발생시 경조 휴가를 다음과 같다.
         경조사   경조휴가
         본인의 결혼   5일
         부모/배우자 부모/배우자/ 사망   5일
2. 경조휴가는 유급휴일 (토요일과 일요일 저외) 과 중복될 경우에는 추가적으로 주어지지 않는다. 또한 경조휴가는 적치하여 사용하거나 금전보상이 되지 않는다.
3. 경조휴가는 사유가 발생하는 경우에는 본인 또는 소속 부서장이 휴가신청서 및 증빙서류를 인사팀에 제출하여야 한다.

<규정 #2: 제약 판매 회사>
제 ○○ 조 (특별휴가)
1. 회사는 직원에게 다음과 같이 특별 유급휴가를 준다.
(1) 직원의 결혼   3일
(2) 직원의 부모, 직원 배우자의 부모, 배우자의 사망   5일
(3) 직원자녀의 사망   5일

spouse: 5 days;
(3) Death of Employee's child: 5 days;
(4) Death of sibling or grandparent of Employee: 2 days
(5) Exercising the rights of citizenship or performing public duties or military reserve service training: necessary number of hours or days; and
(6) When the Employee cannot work due to serious disaster such as flood or fire: necessary number of hours or days.

<#3: Large-scale Retail Company>
Article 00. Special Leave
1. Co-workers are entitled to paid leave for any situation falling under the following categories: (Calendar Days)
- Marriage of co-worker: 3 days (Working Days)
- Marriage of co-worker's child: 1 day
- Death of co-worker's spouse or co-worker's child: 5 days
- Death of parent of co-worker or co-worker's spouse: 3 days
- Relocation (Mobility) 1 day

<#4: Production Company>
Article 00 (Leave for Congratulations and Condolence)
The Company shall grant special leave with pay in the following circumstances: (The leave period for the marriage of an employee means five consecutive business days excluding holidays.)

1. Marriage of employee	5
2. Marriage of son or daughter	1
3. Marriage of brother or sister	1
4. Marriage of brother or sister of his/her spouse	1
5. 60th or 70th birthday of parent or parent-in-law (optional)	1
6. Funeral of parent or parent-in-law	5
7. Funeral of spouse	5
8. Funeral of son or daughter	5
9. Funeral of grandparent or grandparent-in-law	3
10. Funeral of brother or sister	3
11. Funeral of brother or sister of his/her spouse	3

(4) 직원의 형제, 자매, 조부모의 사망 － 2일
(5) 공민권 행사, 공적의무수행 또는 예비군 훈련 － 필요한 시간 또는 일수
(6) 홍수, 화재 등 중대한 재난으로 근무할 수 없을 때 － 필요한 시간 또는 일수

<규정 #3: 대형 유통 회사>
제 ○○ 조 (특별휴가)
1. 직원들은 다음과 같은 경우에 유급 휴가를 받을 수 있습니다. (발생일 기준)

본인의 결혼	3일
본인 자녀의 결혼	1일
본인의 배우자, 혹은 자녀 상	5일
본인 또는 배우자의 부모 상	3일
전근 휴일 (Relocation)	1일

<규정 #4: 제조업 회사>
제 ○○ 조 (경조휴가)
　회사는 다음과 같은 경우 휴일을 포함한 유급 휴가를 준다. 단, 직원 본인의 결혼 시에는 휴일을 제외한 연속 5일을 적용한다.

1. 본인의 결혼	5
2. 자녀의 결혼	1
3. 형제, 자매의 결혼	1
4. 배우자의 형제, 자매의 결혼	1
5. 부모 및 배우자 부모의 회갑/칠순(선택)	1
6. 부모 및 배우자부모 사망	5
7. 배우자의 사망	5
8. 자녀의 사망	5
9. 조부모 또는 배우자 조부모의 사망	3
10. 형제, 자매의 사망	3
11. 배우자의 형제, 자매의 사망	3

Chapter 7 Protection of Motherhood

Ⅰ. Protection of Maternal Employees
Ⅱ. Protection leave for maternal employees
Ⅲ. Childcare Leave and Reduced Working Hours for the Childcare Period
Ⅳ. Menstruation Leave

제7장　모성보호

- Ⅰ. 임산부 보호
- Ⅱ. 임산부의 보호휴가
- Ⅲ. 육아휴직과 육아기 근로시간 단축
- Ⅳ. 생리휴가

Chapter 7 Protection of Motherhood

Ⅰ. Protection of Maternal Employees

A maternal employee refers to a woman who is pregnant or is within her first year after childbirth, and is therefore provided special protection under the various laws so designed.

The Korean government is taking steps to protect motherhood through specific provisions stipulated by the Constitution of the Republic of Korea[188] as well as other practical provisions stipulated by various labor laws. Despite these protection laws, the birthrate has decreased to an average of just 0.72 persons per couple as of 2023, and the government has strengthened its efforts in response towards revising labor laws designed to promote workforce participation by women and also increase the birthrate.

1. Employment in hazardous/dangerous work prohibited

Employers shall not assign maternal employees to mentally and physically hazardous work. In addition, they shall not assign women aged 18 or older who are not pregnant to work that is hazardous to their possible future pregnancy and/or childbirth. Occupations that are prohibited are described in the attached Table 4 of the Presidential Decree(Article 65 of the LSA).

2. Restrictions on extended work, night work and holiday work

(1) Extended work

Employers shall not place pregnant female employees on overtime duty or flexible work, and, in the event of such a request from the employee, she shall be assigned light duties. Employers shall not permit women for whom less than one year has passed since childbirth to work more than 2 hours in overtime per 8-hour work day, and 6 hours per work week of 40 hours, even if so agreed in a collective agreement(Article 51, 71, 74 of the LSA).

(2) Night work and holiday work (Article 70 of the LSA)

Employers shall not assign maternal employees to work at night(from 10 P.M to 6 A.M.) or on holidays. However, exception to such restrictions on night work and holiday work are possible in cases where the employer obtains permission in

---

[188] Constitution of the Republic of Korea (Article 36, Subparagraph 2): The State shall endeavor to protect mothers.

제7장 모성 보호

I. 임산부 보호

 임산부는 임신 중이거나 산후 1년이 지나지 아니한 여성을 말하며, 이 기간 동안 모성보호를 위한 각종 보호 규정을 통해 특별한 보호를 받는다.
 우리나라는 모성과 관련하여 헌법에 의한 명시적 보호규정[188]과 노동법에 의한 실천적 보호규정을 두고 엄격하게 모성을 보호하고 있다. 이러한 법률적 보호규정에도 불구하고 출산율이 계속 떨어져 2023년에는 0.72명에 까지 하락함에 따라 여성근로를 장려하고 출산율을 높이기 위한 노력이 노동법에 반영되고 있다.

1. 유해·위험한 사업에 사용금지

 사용자는 임산부를 도덕상 또는 보건 상 유해.위험한 사업에 사용하지 못한다. 특히, 임산부가 아닌 18세 이상의 여성을 보건 상 유해.위험한 사업 중 임신 또는 출산에 관한 기능에 유해.위험한 사업에 사용하지 못한다. 이와 관련 임산부의 금지직종은 근로기준법시행령 별표 4호에 명시하고 있다(근기법 제65조).

2. 연장근로, 야간근로, 휴일근로의 제한

(1) 연장근로(근로기준법 제51조, 제71조, 제74조)
 사용자는 임신 중의 여성 근로자에게 연장근로 및 탄력적 근로를 하게 하여서는 아니 되며, 그 근로자의 요구가 있는 경우에는 쉬운 종류의 근로로 전환하여야 한다. 사용자는 산후 1년이 지나지 아니한 여성에 대하여는 단체협약이 있는 경우라도 1일의 8시간 근무에 2시간, 1주일 40시간 근무에 6시간을 초과하는 연장근로를 시키지 못한다.

(2) 야간근로 및 휴일근로(근기법 제70조)
 사용자는 임산부를 야간근로(오후 10시부터 으전 6시까지)와 휴일 근로를

---
[188] 헌법 제36조 제2항: 국가는 모성의 보호를 위하여 노력하여야 한다.

advance from the Minister of Employment and Labor and ① there is consent from the employee for whom less than one year has passed since childbirth; or ② a pregnant woman makes such a request.

II. Protection leave for maternal employees

1. Maternity leave

Employers shall grant pregnant female employees 90 days of maternity leave(120 days if a woman is pregnant with two or more babies), to be used before and after childbirth. In such cases, a minimum of 45 days(60 days for multiple babies) shall be allocated after childbirth. At the end of the maternity leave, the employer shall allow the female employee to return to the same work, or other work at the same rate of pay as before the leave. The first 60 days(75 days for multiple babies) of leave shall be paid. The remaining 30 days(or 45 days for multiple babies) qualify for reimbursement of up to 2 million won through employment insurance, provided, that for companies[189] eligible for preferential support, the employee concerned will receive the first 60 days' maternity leave allowance(up to 2 million won per month) from employment insurance. In this case, the employer will pay the amount of the ordinary wage exceeding the government subsidy(Article 74 of the LSA).

Employers shall not dismiss any female employee during a period of temporary interruption of work before or after childbirth as provided herein and within 30 days thereafter. For the purpose of calculating annual paid leave, the maternity leave shall be regarded as attended days. Also, in calculating the average wage for

---

[189] Preferentially Supported Companies (Article 12 of the Presidential Decree to the LSA)

Type of Industry (Classification Code)	Number of Employees
1. Manufacturing (C);	Up to 500 persons
2. Mining (B); 3. Construction (F); 4. Transportation (H); 5. Publishing, filming, broadcasting, and IT services (J); 6. Facility management and company support services (N); 7. Professional, science and technology services (M); 8. Health and social security insurance services (Q).	Up to 300 persons
9. Wholesale and retail services (G); 10. Hotel and restaurant services (I); 11. Finance and insurance (K); 12. Art, sports, and other leisure-related services (R);	Up to 200 persons
13. Other businesses	Up to 100 persons

근로시키지 못한다. 다만, 예외적으로 사용자가 노동부장관의 인가를 받고, ① 산후 1년이 지나지 아니한 여성의 동의가 있는 경우와 ② 임신 중의 여성이 명시적으로 청구하는 경우에는 야간근로와 휴일근로가 가능하다.

II. 임산부의 보호휴가

1. 출산휴가

사용자는 임신 중의 여성에게 출산 전과 출산 후를 통하여 90일(한 번에 둘 이상 자녀를 임신한 경우에는 120일)의 출산전후휴가를 주어야 한다. 이 경우 휴가 기간의 배정은 출산 후에 45일(한 번에 둘 이상 자녀를 임신한 경우에는 60일) 이상이 되어야 한다. 사용자는 출산전후휴가 종료 후에는 휴가 전과 동일한 업무 또는 동등한 수준의 임금을 지급하는 직무에 복귀시켜야 한다. 사용자는 출산휴가 중 최초 60일(한 번에 둘 이상 자녀를 임신한 경우에는 75일)은 통상임금을 지급해야 한다. 나머지 30일은 고용보험에서 최대 200만 원까지 통상임금을 보전해 준다. 다만, 우선지원 대상기업[189]은 국가로부터 최초 60일에 대해서도 매월 200만 원까지 지원을 받을 수 있는데, 이 경우에는 정부지원금을 초과하는 통상임금에 대해서만 유급으로 지급하면 된다(근기법 제74조).

출산휴가는 해고 제한에 해당되어 사용자는 근로자가 산전.산후의 여성이 이 법에 따라 휴업한 기간과 그 후 30일 동안은 해고하지 못한다. 연차유급휴가 계산에 있어 출산휴가는 출근한 것으로 본다. 퇴직금 계산을 위한 평균

---

[189] 우선지원 대상기업의 상시 사용하는 근로자 기준(고용보험법시 행령 제12조 관련)

산업분류(분류기호)	상시 근로자 수
1. 제조업(C);	500명 이하
2. 광업(B), 3.건설업(F), 4.운수업(H), 5.출판, 영상, 방송통신 및 정보서비스업(J), 6.사업시설관리및사업지원서비스업(N), 7.전문,과학및기술서비스업(M), 8.보건업및사회복지서비스업(Q)	300명 이하
9. 매매소매업(G), 10.숙박및음식점업(I), 11.금융및보험업(K), 12.예술,스포츠및여가관련서비스업(R)	200명 이하
13. 그 밖의 업종	100명 이하

Chapter 7 Protection of Motherhood

purposes of severance payment, the period of maternity leave and the wage paid during the maternity period shall be deducted from the calculation of average wage required to be included in the period and wage.

Labor Standards Act: Article 74 (Protection for Maternity)

① An employer shall grant a pregnant woman a total of a 90-day maternity leave (120-day maternity leave, if she is pregnant with at least two children at a time) before and after childbirth. In such cases, at least 45 days (60 days, if she is pregnant with two or more children at a time) of the leave period after childbirth shall be allowed.

② Where a pregnant female employee requests the leave under paragraph (1) due to her experience of miscarriage or other reasons prescribed by Presidential Decree, an employer shall allow her to use the leave at multiple times any time before her childbirth. In such cases, the period of leave after the childbirth shall be at least 45 days (60 days, if she is pregnant with at least two children at a time) consecutively.

③ Where a pregnant woman has a miscarriage or stillbirth, an employer shall, upon the relevant employee's request, grant her a miscarriage/stillbirth leave, as prescribed by Presidential Decree: Provided, That the same shall not apply to any abortion carried out by artificial termination of pregnancy (excluding cases under Article 14 (1) of the Mother and Child Health Act).

④ The first 60 days (75 days, if she is pregnant with at least two children at a time) in the period of leave under paragraphs (1) through (3) shall be stipendiary: Provided, That when the leave allowances before and after childbirth, etc. have been paid under Article 18 of the Equal Employment Opportunity and Work-Family Balance Assistance Act, the payment responsibility shall be exempted within the limit of the relevant amount.

⑤ No employer shall order a female employee in pregnancy to engage in overtime work, and if there exists a request from the relevant employee, he or she shall transfer her to an easy type of work.

⑥ A business owner shall reinstate her to the same work or to the work for which wages of the same level as before leave are paid after the end of

임금 산정에 있어서도 출산휴가 기간과 그 기간 중에 지급된 임금은 평균임금 산정기준이 되는 기간과 임금의 총액에서 뺀다.

> **근로기준법: 제74조(임산부의 보호)**
>
> ① 사용자는 임신 중의 여성에게 출산 전과 출산 후를 통하여 90일(한 번에 둘 이상 자녀를 임신한 경우에는 120일)의 출산전후휴가를 주어야 한다. 이 경우 휴가 기간의 배정은 출산 후에 45일(한 번에 둘 이상 자녀를 임신한 경우에는 60일) 이상이 되어야 한다.
>
> ② 사용자는 임신 중인 여성 근로자가 유산의 경험 등 대통령령으로 정하는 사유로 제1항의 휴가를 청구하는 경우 출산 전 어느 때라도 휴가를 나누어 사용할 수 있도록 하여야 한다. 이 경우 출산 후의 휴가 기간은 연속하여 45일(한 번에 둘 이상 자녀를 임신한 경우에는 60일) 이상이 되어야 한다.
>
> ③ 사용자는 임신 중인 여성이 유산 또는 사산한 경우로서 그 근로자가 청구하면 대통령령으로 정하는 바에 따라 유산·사산 휴가를 주어야 한다. 다만, 인공 임신중절 수술(「모자보건법」 제14조제1항에 따른 경우는 제외한다)에 따른 유산의 경우는 그러하지 아니하다.
>
> ④ 제1항부터 제3항까지의 규정에 따른 휴가 중 최초 60일(한 번에 둘 이상 자녀를 임신한 경우에는 75일)은 유급으로 한다. 다만, 「남녀고용평등과 일·가정 양립 지원에 관한 법률」 제18조에 따라 출산전후휴가급여 등이 지급된 경우에는 그 금액의 한도에서 지급의 책임을 면한다.
>
> ⑤ 사용자는 임신 중의 여성 근로자에게 시간외근로를 하게 하여서는 아니 되며, 그 근로자의 요구가 있는 경우에는 쉬운 종류의 근로로 전환하여야 한다.
>
> ⑥ 사업주는 제1항에 따른 출산전후휴가 종료 후에는 휴가 전과 동일한 업무 또는 동등한 수준의 임금을 지급하는 직무에 복귀

Chapter 7 Protection of Motherhood

a maternity leave under paragraph (1).

⑦ Where a female employee who has been pregnant for not more than 12 weeks or for not less than 36 weeks requests the reduction of her work hours by two hours a day, the employer shall permit it: Provided, That he or she may permit to reduce her work hours to six hours if her work hours are shorter than eight hours a day.

⑧ No employer shall reduce an employee's wages for reason of reduction of work hours under paragraph (7).

⑨ Where a pregnant female employee requests to modify the start and end time of work hours while maintaining the contractual daily work hours, the employer shall permit such modification: Provided, That the same shall not apply to cases prescribed by Presidential Decree, such as where the normal operation of business can be significantly impeded.

⑩ Matters necessary for the methods and procedures for requesting a reduction of working hours under paragraph (7) and the methods, procedures, etc. for requesting the modification of the start and end time of work hours under paragraph (9) shall be prescribed by Presidential Decree.

Article 74-2 (Permission for Time for Medical Examination of Unborn Child)

① Where a pregnant employee claims time necessary for a periodical medical examination of pregnant women under Article 10 of the Mother and Child Health Act, an employer shall grant permission for such time.

② The employer shall not cut wages of such employee by reason of time for medical examination under paragraph (1).

LSA Presidential Decree: Article 43 (Request for Miscarriage or Stillbirth Leave)

① "Reasons prescribed by Presidential Decree" in the former part of Article 74 (2) of the Act means any of the following cases:
  1. Where a pregnant employee has an experience of miscarriage / stillbirth;
  2. Where a pregnant employee is at the age of 40 or more when she applies for a maternity leave;
  3. Where a pregnant employee submits a report prepared by a medical institution stating that she has the risk of miscarriage/stillbirth.

시켜야 한다.
⑦ 사용자는 임신 후 12주 이내 또는 36주 이후에 있는 여성 근로자가 1일 2시간의 근로시간 단축을 신청하는 경우 이를 허용하여야 한다. 다만, 1일 근로시간이 8시간 미만인 근로자에 대하여는 1일 근로시간이 6시간이 되도록 근로시간 단축을 허용할 수 있다.
⑧ 사용자는 제7항에 따른 근로시간 단축을 이유로 해당 근로자의 임금을 삭감하여서는 아니 된다.
⑨ 사용자는 임신 중인 여성 근로자가 1일 소정근로시간을 유지하면서 업무의 시작 및 종료 시각의 변경을 신청하는 경우 이를 허용하여야 한다. 다만, 정상적인 사업 운영에 중대한 지장을 초래하는 경우 등 대통령령으로 정하는 경우에는 그러하지 아니하다.
⑩ 제7항에 따른 근로시간 단축의 신청방법 및 절차, 제9항에 따른 업무의 시작 및 종료 시각 변경의 신청방법 및 절차 등에 관하여 필요한 사항은 대통령령으로 정한다.

제74조의2(태아검진 시간의 허용 등)
① 사용자는 임신한 여성근로자가 「모자보건법」 제10조에 따른 임산부 정기건강진단을 받는데 필요한 시간을 청구하는 경우 이를 허용하여 주어야 한다.
② 사용자는 제1항에 따른 건강진단 시간을 이유로 그 근로자의 임금을 삭감하여서는 아니 된다.

<근로기준법 시행령> 제43조(유산·사산휴가의 청구 등)
① 법 제74조제2항 전단에서 "대통령령으로 정하는 사유"란 다음 각 호의 어느 하나에 해당하는 경우를 말한다.
 1. 임신한 근로자에게 유산·사산의 경험이 있는 경우
 2. 임신한 근로자가 출산전후휴가를 청구할 당시 연령이 만 40세 이상인 경우
 3. 임신한 근로자가 유산·사산의 위험이 있다는 의료기관의 진단서를 제출한 경우

Chapter 7 Protection of Motherhood

② Where an employee who suffers from miscarriage or stillbirth requests the miscarriage or stillbirth leave pursuant to Article 74 (3) of the Act, she shall submit to the business owner an application for miscarriage or stillbirth leave, stating the reason for requesting the leave, the date on which miscarriage or stillbirth occurred, the pregnancy period, etc., along with a medical certificate issued by a medical institution.

③ The the business owner shall give a miscarriage or stillbirth leave according to the following guidelines to any employee who requests a miscarriage or stillbirth leave pursuant to paragraph (2):
1. Where a pregnancy period of the employee who suffers from miscarriage or stillbirth (hereinafter referred to as the "pregnancy period") is not more than 11 weeks: up to five days from the date of miscarriage or stillbirth;
2. Where the pregnancy period is not less than 12 weeks but not more than 15 weeks: up to 10 days from the date of miscarriage or stillbirth;
3. Where the pregnancy period is not less than 16 weeks but not more than 21 weeks: up to 30 days from the date of miscarriage or stillbirth;
4. Where the pregnancy period is not less than 22 weeks but not more than 27 weeks: up to 60 days from the date of miscarriage or stillbirth;
5. Where the pregnancy period is not less than 28 weeks: up to 90 days from the date of miscarriage or stillbirth.

Article 43-2 (Requests for Reduction of Work Hours during Pregnancy Period) A female employee who intends to request a reduction of her work hours under Article 74 (7) of the Act shall submit a document (including electronic documents) in which her pregnancy period, the expected date of the commencement and termination of the reduction of work hours, the time to start and finish her work, etc. are specified by no later than three days before the expected commencement of reduction of work hours to an employer, appending a doctor's medical certificate (excluding cases where a reduction of work hours is requested again for the same pregnancy).

Article 43-3 (Modification of Start and End Time of Work Hours for Pregnancy Period)
① A female employee who intends to request to modify the start and end time of work hours pursuant to the main clause of Article 74 (9) of the Act shall submit to the employer a document (including electronic documents) stating the pregnancy period, the scheduled period for the modification of the start and end time of work hours, the start and end time of work hours, etc., along with a medical certificate issued by a doctor verifying the fact of pregnancy (excluding cases where a request is made again to modify the start and end time of work hours for the same pregnancy) no

② 법 제74조제3항에 따라 유산 또는 사산한 근로자가 유산·사산휴가를 청구하는 경우에는 휴가 청구 사유, 유산·사산 발생일 및 임신기간 등을 적은 유산·사산휴가 신청서에 의료기관의 진단서를 첨부하여 사업주에게 제출하여야 한다.

③ 사업주는 제2항에 따라 유산·사산휴가를 청구한 근로자에게 다음 각 호의 기준에 따라 유산·사산휴가를 주어야 한다.

1. 유산 또는 사산한 근로자의 임신기간(이하 "임신기간"이라 한다)이 11주 이내인 경우: 유산 또는 사산한 날부터 5일까지
2. 임신기간이 12주 이상 15주 이내인 경우: 유산 또는 사산한 날부터 10일까지
3. 임신기간이 16주 이상 21주 이내인 경우: 유산 또는 사산한 날부터 30일까지
4. 임신기간이 22주 이상 27주 이내인 경우: 유산 또는 사산한 날부터 60일까지
5. 임신기간이 28주 이상인 경우 : 유산 또는 사산한 날부터 90일까지

제43조의2(임신기간 근로시간 단축의 신청) 법 제74조제7항에 따라 근로시간 단축을 신청하려는 여성 근로자는 근로시간 단축 개시 예정일의 3일 전까지 임신기간, 근로시간 단축 개시 예정일 및 종료 예정일, 근무 개시 시각 및 종료 시각 등을 적은 문서(전자문서를 포함한다)에 의사의 진단서(같은 임신에 대하여 근로시간 단축을 다시 신청하는 경우는 제외한다)를 첨부하여 사용자에게 제출하여야 한다.

제43조의3(임신기간 업무의 시작 및 종료 시각의 변경)

① 법 제74조제9항 본문에 따라 업무의 시작 및 종료 시각의 변경을 신청하려는 여성 근로자는 그 변경 예정일의 3일 전까지 임신기간, 업무의 시작 및 종료 시각의 변경 예정 기간, 업무의 시작 및 종료 시각 등을 적은 문서(전자문서를 포함한다)에 임신 사실을 증명하는 의사의 진단서(같은 임신에 대해 업무의 시작 및 종료 시각 변경을 다시 신청하는 경우는 제외한다)를 첨부하여 사용자에게 제출해야

Chapter 7 Protection of Motherhood

> later than three days prior to the scheduled date of modification.
> ② "Cases prescribed by Presidential Decree, such as where the normal operation of business can be significantly impeded" in the proviso of Article 74 (9) of the Act means any of the following cases:
> 1. Where the normal operation of business can be significantly impeded;
> 2. Where the modification of the start and end time of work hours violates the relevant statutes or regulations concerning the safety and health of pregnant female employees.

<Maternity Leave Benefits>

> * Amount of maternity leave benefits for companies eligible for priority support
> 1) Maximum amount: 6 million won (2 million won per month) in cases where the amount of ordinary wage corresponding to 90 days of maternity leave or miscarriage/stillbirth leave exceeds 6 million won, provided that in cases where the period of payment of maternity leave benefits, etc., is less than 90 days, the amount shall be calculated based on the number of actual leave days; and
> 2) Minimum amount: an amount equivalent to ordinary wage for the period of payment of the maternity leave benefits, etc., calculated using the hourly minimum wage as the hourly ordinary wage of the employee in cases where the hourly ordinary wage of the employee is lower than the hourly minimum wage applied on the beginning date of maternity leave or miscarriage/stillbirth leave in accordance with the Minimum Wage Act

2. Advance maternity leave

In cases where an employee who is or was recently pregnant requests leave due to a miscarriage or other pregnancy-related reason, the employer shall allow her to take leave at any time prior to the expected due date. In any case, 45 or more continuous days(60 days for multiple babies) shall be provided after childbirth or miscarriage. Reasons for advance maternity leave are as follows(Article 74 of the LSA).

> 한다.
> ② 법 제74조제9항 단서에서 "정상적인 사업 운영에 중대한 지장을 초래하는 경우 등 대통령령으로 정하는 경우"란 다음 각 호의 어느 하나에 해당하는 경우를 말한다.
>   1. 정상적인 사업 운영에 중대한 지장을 초래하는 경우
>   2. 업무의 시작 및 종료 시각을 변경하게 되면 임신 중인 여성 근로자의 안전과 건강에 관한 관계 법령을 위반하게 되는 경우

<출산휴가 급여지원>

> * 출산휴가 급여지원
> 1) 상한액: 출산전후휴가기간 또는 유산·사산휴가기간 90일에 대한 통상임금에 상당하는 금액이 600만 원(월 200만 원)을 초과하는 경우에는 600만 원. 다만, 출산전후휴가 급여등의 지급기간이 90일 미만인 경우에는 일수로 계산한 금액으로 한다.
> 2) 하한액: 출산전후휴가 또는 유산·사산휴가기간 시작일 당시 적용되던 「최저임금법」에 따른 시간 단위에 해당하는 최저임금액보다 그 근로자의 시간급 통상임금이 낮은 경우에는 시간급 최저임금액을 시간급 통상임금으로 하여 산정된 출산전후휴가 급여등의 지원기간 중 통상임금에 상당하는 금액

2. 조기출산휴가

　사용자는 임신 중인 여성 근로자가 유산의 경험 등 사유로 출산휴가를 청구하는 경우 출산 전 어느 때라도 휴가를 나누어 사용할 수 있도록 하여야 한다. 이 경우 출산 후의 휴가 기간은 연속하여 45일(한 번에 둘 이상 자녀를 임신한 경우에는 60일) 이상이 되어야 한다(근기법 제74조, 시행령 제43조).
여기서 조기 출산휴가의 사유는 다음과 같다.

① In cases where a pregnant employee went through a miscarriage or stillbirth in the past;
② In cases where a pregnant employee is over 40 years of age at the time of the request for maternity leave; and
③ In cases where a pregnant employee submits a medical document issued by a hospital that describes the danger of miscarriage or stillbirth.

3. Maternity leave for miscarriage or stillbirth

At the request of a female employee who has suffered a miscarriage or stillbirth, the employer shall grant her leave for miscarriage or stillbirth, except where the miscarriage is the result of an artificially-induced abortion. If a female employee who has had a miscarriage or stillbirth asks for maternity leave, she must submit to the employer an application for miscarriage or stillbirth leave, providing the reason for the request for leave, the date of the miscarriage or stillbirth and the pregnancy period, along with a medical certificate issued by a medical organization. In cases of miscarriage or stillbirth, the employer shall pay the ordinary wage for the period given for maternity leave, just as with a normal maternity leave, as follows:
① A pregnancy period of 11 weeks or less: five days from the date of miscarriage or stillbirth;
② A pregnancy period of 12 weeks or more but less than 15 weeks: ten days from the date of miscarriage or stillbirth;
③ A pregnancy period of 16 weeks or more but less than 21 weeks: thirty days from the date of miscarriage or stillbirth;
④ A pregnancy period of 22 weeks or more but less than 27 weeks: sixty days from the date of miscarriage or stillbirth; and
⑤ A pregnancy period of 28 weeks or more: ninety days from the date of miscarriage or stillbirth.

4. Reduced working hours during the pregnancy period

In cases where a female employee who is pregnant for 12 weeks or less or 36 weeks or more applies for reduced working hours, the employer shall allow it. Provided that the pregnant employee's current working hours are fewer than 8 per day, the employer may reduce her working hours to 6 hours per day. The employer cannot reduce the wage of the employee due to the reduced working hours(Article 74 of the LSA).

① 임신한 근로자에게 유산·사산의 경험이 있는 경우
② 임신한 근로자가 출산전후휴가를 청구할 당시 연령이 만 40세 이상인 경우
③ 임신한 근로자가 유산·사산의 위험이 있다는 의료기관의 진단서를 제출한 경우

3. 유산 · 사산휴가

사용자는 임신 중인 여성이 유산 또는 사산한 경우로서 그 근로자가 청구하면 유산.사산 휴가를 주어야 한다. 다만, 인공 임신중절 수술에 따른 유산의 경우는 그러하지 아니하다. 이 경우, 유산 또는 사산한 근로자가 유산.사산휴가를 청구하는 경우에는 휴가 청구 사유, 유산.사산 발생일 및 임신기간 등을 적은 유산.사산휴가 신청서에 의료기관의 진단서를 첨부하여 사용자에게 제출하여야 한다. 사용자는 유산.사산휴가도 출산휴가와 같이 주어진 휴가범위 내에서 통상임금을 지급해야 한다(근기법 제74조, 시행령 제43조).

① 임신기간이 11주 이내인 경우: 유산 또는 사산한 날부터 5일까지
② 임신기간이 12주 이상 15주 이내인 경우: 유산 또는 사산한 날부터 10일까지
③ 임신기간이 16주 이상 21주 이내인 경우: 유산 또는 사산한 날부터 30일까지
④ 임신기간이 22주 이상 27주 이내인 경우: 유산 또는 사산한 날부터 60일까지
⑤ 임신기간이 28주 이상인 경우: 유산 또는 사산한 날부터 90일까지

4. 임신기간 중 단축근로

사용자는 임신 후 12주 이내 또는 36주 이후에 있는 여성 근로자가 1일 2시간의 근로시간 단축을 신청하는 경우 이를 허용하여야 한다. 다만, 1일 근로시간이 8시간 미만인 근로자에 대하여는 1일 근로시간이 6시간이 되도록 근로시간 단축을 허용할 수 있다. 사용자는 근로시간 단축을 이유로 해당 근로자의 임금을 삭감하여서는 아니 된다(근기법 제74조 제7항, 제8항).

Chapter 7 Protection of Motherhood

* Reference: Shortening of working hours during pregnancy (Labor Standards Act revised March 24, 2014)
- Target workers: Female workers within 12 weeks of conception or after 36 weeks
- Description: If a target worker applies for a reduction of 2 working hours a day, the employer must allow it. Failure to do so will result in a fine of 5 million won.
- Method: (ⅰ) She will start 1 hour later and leave the workplace 1 hour earlier; (ⅱ) She will start 2 hours later or leave the workplace 2 hours earlier.
- Procedure: She shall submit to the employer a doctor's medical certificate that includes the pregnancy period, the expected date and time the reduction of working hours should start, and the recommend work start and end time, 3 days prior to the expected starting time of the reduction of working hours.

5. Allowing paid time off for prenatal examinations

If a pregnant female employee requests time off from work to receive a regular prenatal health checkup, the employer shall allow her to do so. An employer shall not reduce an employee's wage on the grounds that she took time off for the relevant health checkup. The paid time off allowance for prenatal examinations is as follows: ① one time every two months up to the 7th month of pregnancy; ② one time per month during the 8th and 9th months; ③ one time every two weeks during the 10th month or later(Article 74-2 of the LSA, Article 10 of the Protection of Motherhood Act).

6. Paternity Leave

If an employee requests leave on the grounds of his spouse giving birth, the employer shall grant him paid leave of up to 10 days. The leave may not be requested after a lapse of 90 days from the date when the employee's spouse gave birth(Article 18-2 of the Equal Employment Opportunity and Work-Family Balance Act). Paternity leave will also be usable on two separate periods if desired.

To reduce the burden on SMEs of this extended period of paid leave, the government will pay for 5 days of those paternity leave benefits(100% of normal wage) for SME workers.

> * 참고자료: 임신기간 근로시간 단축제도 (근로기준법 개정 - 2014.03.24)
> - 대상 근로자 : 임신 12주 이내 또는 36주 이후의 여성 근로자
> - 내용: 대상이 되는 근로자가 1일 2시간의 근로시간 단축을 신청하면 사용자는 허용 하여야 하고, 위반 시 500만 원의 과태료 부과
> - 방법: 출근시간을 1시간 늦추고 퇴근시간을 1시간 당기는 방식 or 출근시간을 2시간 늦추는 방식 or 퇴근시간을 2시간 당기는 방식 등
> - 절차: 근로시간 단축개시 예정일의 3일 전까지 임신기간, 근로시간 단축개시 예정일 및 종료 예정일, 근무개시 시각 및 종료시각 등을 적은 문서에 의사의 진단서를 첨부하여 사용자에게 제출

5. 태아건강 검진시간 보장

사용자는 임신한 여성 근로자가 정기건강진단을 받는데 필요한 시간을 청구하는 경우 이를 허용하여 주어야 한다. 사용자는 건강진단 시간을 이유로 그 근로자의 임금을 삭감하여서는 아니 된다. 정기건강검진 실시기준은 ① 임신 7월까지는 매 2월에 1회 ② 임신 8월에서 9월까지는 매 1월에 1회 ③ 임신 10월 이후에는 매 2주에 1회이다(근기법 제74조의 2, 모자보건법 제10조).

6. 배우자 출산휴가

사용자는 근로자가 배우자의 출산을 이유로 휴가를 청구하는 경우에 10일의 유급휴가를 주어야 한다. 배우자 출산휴가는 근로자의 배우자가 출산한 날부터 90일이 지나면 청구할 수 없다(고평법 제18조의 2). 배우자 출산휴가는 1회에 한해서 분할하여 사용할 수 있다.
휴가기간 확대에 따른 중소기업의 부담을 덜어주기 위해 정부는 중소기업(우선지원 대상기업) 근로자의 유급 5일분에 대해서는 배우자 출산휴가급여(통상임금의 100%)를 지급한다.

Chapter 7 Protection of Motherhood

7. Nursing hours

A female employee who has an infant under twelve months of age shall be allowed to take paid nursing recesses, twice per day for at least 30 minutes each(Article 75 of the LSA).

III. Childcare Leave and Reduced Working Hours for the Childcare Period

1. Childcare Leave

Employers shall grant childcare leave if an employee asks for it to take care of his/her child(including an adopted child) aged 8 or under who is attending up to the 2nd grade of elementary school. This shall not apply in such cases where an employee has offered continuous services in the business concerned for less than 6 months prior to the scheduled date of childcare leave. An employee who intends to apply for childcare leave shall submit to his/her employer an application with documentation verifying the birth date of the infant to be cared for, not less than 30 days prior to the scheduled start date of leave.[190]

The period of childcare leave shall be one year or less. The childcare leave can be used all at once or at two different times, up to a total period of one year. The period of childcare leave shall be included in the employee's continuous service period. Employers shall not dismiss or give any other unfavorable treatment to a employee on account of taking childcare leave, nor dismiss the employee concerned during the childcare-leave period; provided that this shall not apply if the employer is not able to continue operating his/her business. After the end of the childcare leave, the employer shall restore the employee to the same work as before the leave, or any other work paying the same level of wage. In calculating the attendance rate for the annual paid leave, the period of childcare leave shall be included for the contractual working hours, which means that the annual paid leave is granted for the period of actual work. The period of childcare leave for a fixed-term employee or a dispatched employee shall not be included in the employment period or the dispatched period.

---

[190] Article 19 of the Equal Employment Act: Article 10 and 11 of its Presidential Decree, Article 70 of the Employment Insurance Act

7. 육아시간

생후 1년 미만의 유아를 가진 여성 근로자가 청구하면 1일 2회 각각 30분 이상의 유급 수유 시간을 주어야 한다(근기법 제75조).

Ⅲ. 육아휴직과 육아기 근로시간 단축

1. 육아휴직

사용자는 근로자가 만 8세 이하 또는 초등학교 2학년 이하의 자녀(입양한 자녀를 포함한다)를 양육하기 위하여 육아휴직을 신청하는 경우에 이를 허용하여야 한다. 다만, 육아휴직을 시작하려는 날의 전날까지 해당 사업에서 계속 근로한 기간이 6월 미만인 근로자는 제외된다. 육아휴직을 신청하려는 근로자는 휴직개시예정일의 30일전까지 해당 자녀의 출생 등을 증명할 수 있는 서류를 첨부하여 육아휴직신청서를 사용자에게 제출하여야 한다.[190]

육아휴직의 기간은 1년 이내로 하며, 1회에 1년간 사용하든지 총 사용기간 1년 이내에서 1회에 한하여 분할 사용할 수 있다. 육아휴직 기간은 근속기간에 포함한다. 사용자는 육아휴직을 이유로 해고나 그 밖의 불리한 처우를 하여서는 아니 되며, 육아휴직 기간에는 그 근로자를 해고하지 못한다. 다만, 사업을 계속할 수 없는 경우에는 그러하지 아니하다. 사용자는 육아휴직을 마친 후에는 휴직 전과 같은 업무 또는 같은 수준의 임금을 지급하는 직무에 복귀시켜야 한다. 연차유급휴가의 개근여부 계산에 있어 육아휴직기간은 소정근로일수계산에서 포함되기 때문에 육아휴직기간에 대해서 연차유급휴가가 발생한다. 기간제 근로자 또는 파견 근로자의 육아휴직 기간은 사용기간 또는 근로자파견기간에 산입하지 아니한다.

---

[190] 고평법 제19조, 시행령 제10조, 제11조, 고용보험법 제70조

EQUAL EMPLOYMENT OPPORTUNITY AND WORK-FAMILY BALANCE ASSISTANCE ACT (Equal Employment Act):

Article 19 (Childcare Leave)

① Where a pregnant female employee or an employee applies for a leave of absence (hereinafter referred to as "childcare leave") in order to enjoy maternity protection or to raise his or her children (including adopted children; hereinafter the same shall apply) aged eight years or younger or in the second grade or lower of elementary school, respectively, their employer shall grant permission therefor: Provided, That the same shall not apply to cases prescribed by Presidential Decree.

② The period of childcare leave shall not exceed one year.

③ No employer shall dismiss, or take any other disadvantageous measure against, an employee on account of childcare leave, or dismiss the relevant employee during the period of childcare leave: Provided, That this shall not apply where the employer is unable to continue his or her business.

④ After an employee uses childcare leave, the employer shall reinstate the relevant employee in the same work as before the leave, or any other work paying the same level of wages. The period of childcare leave under paragraph (2) shall be included in the period of his or her continuous service.

⑤ The period of childcare leave of fixed-term employees or temporary agency workers shall not be included in the employment period prescribed in Article 4 of the Act on the Protection, etc. of Fixed-Term and Part-Time Employees or in the period of temporary employment prescribed in Article 6 of the Act on the Protection, etc. of Temporary Agency Workers.

⑥ Matters necessary for methods and procedures for application for childcare leave and other matters shall be prescribed by Presidential Decree.

Article 19-2 (Reduction of Working Hours for Period of Childcare)

① Where any employee applies for a reduction of working hours to rear his or her children aged eight years or younger or in the second grade or lower of elementary school (hereinafter referred to as "reduction of working hours for a period of childcare"), his or her employer shall grant it: Provided, That this shall not apply to cases prescribed by Presidential Decree, such as where it is impossible to employ his or her substitute or where the normal operation of business is significantly impeded.

② Where the employer does not grant a reduction of working hours for a period of childcare under the proviso of paragraph (1), he or she shall notify the relevant employee of the ground therefor in writing and have him or her use childcare leave, or consult with the relevant employee as to whether to support him or her through other measures, such as the adjustment of commuting time.

남녀고용평등과 일, 가정 양립 지원에 관한 법률 (남녀고용평등법):
제19조(육아휴직)

① 사업주는 임신 중인 여성 근로자가 모성을 보호하거나 근로자가 만 8세 이하 또는 초등학교 2학년 이하의 자녀(입양한 자녀를 포함한다. 이하 같다)를 양육하기 위하여 휴직(이하 "육아휴직"이라 한다)을 신청하는 경우에 이를 허용하여야 한다. 다만, 대통령령으로 정하는 경우에는 그러하지 아니하다.

② 육아휴직의 기간은 1년 이내로 한다.

③ 사업주는 육아휴직을 이유로 해고나 그 밖의 불리한 처우를 하여서는 아니 되며, 육아휴직 기간에는 그 근로자를 해고하지 못한다. 다만, 사업을 계속할 수 없는 경우에는 그러하지 아니하다.

④ 사업주는 육아휴직을 마친 후에는 휴직 전과 같은 업무 또는 같은 수준의 임금을 지급하는 직무에 복귀시켜야 한다. 또한 제2항의 육아휴직 기간은 근속기간에 포함한다.

⑤ 기간제근로자 또는 파견근로자의 육아휴직 기간은 「기간제 및 단시간근로자 보호 등에 관한 법률」 제4조에 따른 사용기간 또는 「파견근로자 보호 등에 관한 법률」 제6조에 따른 근로자파견기간에서 제외한다.

⑥ 육아휴직의 신청방법 및 절차 등에 관하여 필요한 사항은 대통령령으로 정한다.

제19조의2(육아기 근로시간 단축)

① 사업주는 근로자가 만 8세 이하 또는 초등학교 2학년 이하의 자녀를 양육하기 위하여 근로시간의 단축(이하 "육아기 근로시간 단축"이라 한다)을 신청하는 경우에 이를 허용하여야 한다. 다만, 대체인력 채용이 불가능한 경우, 정상적인 사업 운영에 중대한 지장을 초래하는 경우 등 대통령령으로 정하는 경우에는 그러하지 아니하다.

② 제1항 단서에 따라 사업주가 육아기 근로시간 단축을 허용하지 아니하는 경우에는 해당 근로자에게 그 사유를 서면으로 통보하고

Chapter 7 Protection of Motherhood

③ Where the employer grants a reduction of working hours for a period of childcare to the relevant employee under paragraph (1), the working hours after reduction shall be at least 15 hours a week, but shall not exceed 35 hours a week.

④ A reduction of working hours for a period of childcare shall be granted for up to one year: Provided, That where an employee who is eligible to apply for childcare leave pursuant to Article 19 (1) have not fully used such leave for a period of childcare leave under Article 19 (2), the remaining period shall be added to the period for reduction of working hours.

⑤ No employer shall dismiss, or take any disadvantageous measures against, an employee on grounds of a reduction of working hours for a period of childcare.

⑥ After an employee completes a reduction period of working hours for a period of childcare, the employer shall reinstate him or her in the same work as before a reduction of working hours, or any other work paying the same level of wages.

⑦ Matters necessary for methods and procedures for filing an application for a reduction of working hours for a period of childcare and other matters shall be prescribed by Presidential Decree.

Article 19-3 (Working Conditions under Reduction of Working Hours for Period of Childcare)

① No employer shall apply unfavorable working conditions to an employee on reduced hours for a period of childcare under Article 19-2, except for applying them in proportion to working hours, on grounds of a reduction of working hours for a period of childcare.

② Working conditions of an employee on reduced hours for a period of childcare under Article 19-2 (including working hours after the reduction of working hours for a period of childcare) shall be determined in writing between the employer and the relevant employee.

③ No employer may request an employee on reduced hours under Article 19-2 to work overtime: Provided, That where the relevant employee requests such overtime work specifically, the employer may have him or her work overtime up to 12 hours a week.

④ Where average wages are calculated under subparagraph 6 of Article 2 of the Labor Standards Act with regard to an employee on reduced hours for a period of childcare, the period during which the working hours for a period of childcare of the relevant employee are reduced shall be excluded in calculating the period of average wages.

육아휴직을 사용하게 하거나 출근 및 퇴근 시간 조정 등 다른 조치를 통하여 지원할 수 있는지를 해당 근로자와 협의하여야 한다.
③ 사업주가 제1항에 따라 해당 근로자에게 육아기 근로시간 단축을 허용하는 경우 단축 후 근로시간은 주당 15시간 이상이어야 하고 35시간을 넘어서는 아니 된다.
④ 육아기 근로시간 단축의 기간은 1년 이내로 한다. 다만, 제19조제1항에 따라 육아휴직을 신청할 수 있는 근로자가 제19조제2항에 따른 육아휴직 기간 중 사용하지 아니한 기간이 있으면 그 기간을 가산한 기간 이내로 한다.
⑤ 사업주는 육아기 근로시간 단축을 이유로 해당 근로자에게 해고나 그 밖의 불리한 처우를 하여서는 아니 된다.
⑥ 사업주는 근로자의 육아기 근로시간 단축기간이 끝난 후에 그 근로자를 육아기 근로시간 단축 전과 같은 업무 또는 같은 수준의 임금을 지급하는 직무에 복귀시켜야 한다.
⑦ 육아기 근로시간 단축의 신청방법 및 절차 등에 관하여 필요한 사항은 대통령령으로 정한다.

제19조의3(육아기 근로시간 단축 중 근로조건 등)
① 사업주는 제19조의2에 따라 육아기 근로시간 단축을 하고 있는 근로자에 대하여 근로시간에 비례하여 적용하는 경우 외에는 육아기 근로시간 단축을 이유로 그 근로조건을 불리하게 하여서는 아니 된다.
② 제19조의2에 따라 육아기 근로시간 단축을 한 근로자의 근로조건(육아기 근로시간 단축 후 근로시간을 포함한다)은 사업주와 그 근로자 간에 서면으로 정한다.
③ 사업주는 제19조의2에 따라 육아기 근로시간 단축을 하고 있는 근로자에게 단축된 근로시간 외에 연장근로를 요구할 수 없다. 다만, 그 근로자가 명시적으로 청구하는 경우에는 사업주는 주 12시간 이내에서 연장근로를 시킬 수 있다.
④ 육아기 근로시간 단축을 한 근로자에 대하여 「근로기준법」 제2조

Chapter 7 Protection of Motherhood

Article 19-4 (Types of Using Childcare Leave and Reduction of Working Hours for Period of Childcare)
① An employee may use childcare leave over several occasions, split into a maximum of two periods. In such cases, the number of childcare leave used by a pregnant female employee for maternity protection shall not be included in the number of split use of the child care leave.
② An employee may reduce working hours for a period of childcare over several occasions. In such cases, each period of use shall be at least three months (in cases of fixed-term employees who cannot reduce working hours for at least three months due to the termination of the contract period, referring to the remaining contract period).

Article 19-5 (Other Measures to Support Childcare)
① The employer shall endeavor to take any of the following measures in order to support childcare of an employee who rears children aged eight years or younger or in the second grade or lower of elementary school:
  1. To adjust time to start and finish work;
  2. To restrict overtime work;
  3. To adjust working hours, such as reduction or flexible operation of working hours;
  4. Other measures necessary to support childcare of the relevant employee.
② The Minister of Employment and Labor may provide necessary support, in consideration of effects on employment, etc., where the employer takes measures under paragraph (1).

Article 19-5 (Other Measures to Support Childcare)
① The employer shall endeavor to take any of the following measures in order to support childcare of an employee who rears children aged eight years or younger or in the second grade or lower of elementary school:
  1. To adjust time to start and finish work;
  2. To restrict overtime work;
  3. To adjust working hours, such as reduction or flexible operation of working hours;
  4. Other measures necessary to support childcare of the relevant employee.
② The Minister of Employment and Labor may provide necessary support, in consideration of effects on employment, etc., where the employer takes measures under paragraph (1).

2. Reduction of working hours for the childcare period

If an employee eligible to ask for childcare leave requests a reduction of working hours instead of childcare leave, the employer shall grant it. However, the employer is not required to grant it in cases where it is not possible to hire replacement personnel, and where it causes a considerable difficulty for the normal operation of

> 제6호에 따른 평균임금을 산정하는 경우에는 그 근로자의 육아기 근로시간 단축 기간을 평균임금 산정기간에서 제외한다.
>
> **제19조의4(육아휴직과 육아기 근로시간 단축의 사용형태)**
> ① 근로자는 육아휴직을 2회에 한정하여 나누어 사용할 수 있다. 이 경우 임신 중인 여성 근로자가 모성보호를 위하여 육아휴직을 사용한 횟수는 육아휴직을 나누어 사용한 횟수에 포함하지 아니한다.
> ② 근로자는 육아기 근로시간 단축을 나누어 사용할 수 있다. 이 경우 나누어 사용하는 1회의 기간은 3개월(근르계약기간의 만료로 3개월 이상 근로시간 단축을 사용할 수 없는 기간제근로자에 대해서는 남은 근로계약기간을 말한다) 이상이 되어야 한다.
>
> **제19조의5(육아지원을 위한 그 밖의 조치)**
> ① 사업주는 만 8세 이하 또는 초등학교 2학년 이하의 자녀를 양육하는 근로자의 육아를 지원하기 위하여 다음 각 호의 어느 하나에 해당하는 조치를 하도록 노력하여야 한다.
> 1. 업무를 시작하고 마치는 시간 조정
> 2. 연장근로의 제한
> 3. 근로시간의 단축, 탄력적 운영 등 근로시간 조정
> 4. 그 밖에 소속 근로자의 육아를 지원하기 위하여 필요한 조치
> ② 고용노동부장관은 사업주가 제1항에 따른 조치를 할 경우 고용효과 등을 고려하여 필요한 지원을 할 수 있다.

2. 육아기 근로시간 단축

 사용자는 육아휴직을 신청할 수 있는 근로자가 육아휴직 대신 육아기 근로시간 단축을 신청하는 경우에 이를 허용하여야 한다. 다만, 대체인력 채용이 불가능한 경우, 정상적인 사업 운영에 중대한 지장을 초래하는 경우 등의 경우에는 그러하지 아니하다. 사업주가 육아기 근로시간 단축을 허용하지 아니하는 경우에는 해당 근로자에게 그 사유를 서면으로 통보하고 육아휴직을 사용하게 하거나 그 밖의 조치를 통하여 지원할 수 있는지를 해당 근로자와

business If the employer does not grant the reduction of working hours for the childcare period, the employer shall notify the employee in writing of the reason for such decision, and have the employee take normal childcare leave or else consult with the employee as to whether to support him/her through other measures. Employers shall not apply unfavorable working conditions to an employee who works reduced working hours for the childcare period on grounds of the working hour reduction, except when applying them in proportion to the usual working hours.[191]

The period of working hour reduction for the childcare period shall be two years or less. If the employer grants a reduction of working hours for the childcare period to the relevant employee, the working hours after reduction shall be a minimum of 15 hours per week but shall not exceed 35 hours per week. Employers shall not dismiss or give any other disadvantageous treatment to the employee on account of the working hour reduction. After the period of working hour reduction is over, the employer shall restore the employee to the original work or to other work paying the same level of wage as before the reduction of working hours.

IV. Menstruation Leave

> An employer shall, if requested by a female worker, grant her one day's menstruation leave per month (Article 73).

Menstruation leave is given to female employees who suffer from physical and/or mental difficulties at work due to her menstruation. The leave shall be granted to an employee who requests it, regardless of whether or not she has come to work for all the contractual working days of the given month. On the basis of the revised law that now recognizes menstruation leave as unpaid leave, the employer does not have to pay an allowance for the use of the leave, if requested. However, allowance shall be paid if both parties agree differently in the collective agreement, rules of employment or labor contract. Though menstruation leave is now considered unpaid, it is permitted by law to consider it paid so as to have no effect on attendance in calculating the number of contractual working days and rate of attendance for weekly holiday, annual paid leave, etc.

---

[191] Article 19 of the Equal Employment Act, Article 73-2 of the Employment Insurance Act

협의하여야 한다. 고용보험으로부터 근로자가 수령하는 육아기 근로시간 단축급여는 정상적인 육아휴직 급여를 기준으로 단축된 근로시간에 비례한 금액으로 한다. 사업주는 육아기 근로시간 단축을 하고 있는 근로자에 대하여 근로시간에 비례하여 적용하는 경우 외에는 육아기 근로시간 단축을 이유로 그 근로조건을 불리하게 하여서는 아니 된다.[191]

육아기 근로시간 단축기간은 2년 이내로 한다. 사용자가 해당 근로자에게 육아기 근로시간 단축을 허용하는 경우 단축 후 근로시간은 주당 15시간 이상이어야 하고 35시간을 넘어서는 아니 된다. 사용자는 육아기 근로시간 단축을 이유로 해당 근로자에게 해고나 그 밖의 불리한 처우를 하여서는 아니 된다. 사용자는 근로자의 육아기 근로시간 단축기간이 끝난 후에 그 근로자를 육아기 근로시간 단축 전과 같은 업무 또는 같은 수준의 임금을 지급하는 직무에 복귀시켜야 한다.

Ⅳ. 생리휴가

> 사용자는 여성인 근로자가 청구하는 때에는 월 1일의 생리휴가를 주어야 한다(근기법 제73조, 생리휴가)

생리휴가는 여성근로자가 생리로 인하여 신체적·정신적으로 근로에 어려움을 겪지 않도록 생리 사실에 기하여 본인이 청구할 경우에 부여하여야 한다. 또한 생리휴가는 1월간 소정근로일수 만근 여부와 관계없이 근로자가 청구하면 부여하여야 한다. 생리휴가가 유급에서 무급으로 개정됨에 따라 생리휴가를 청구 시 휴가사용에 대하여 임금지급의무가 없다. 다만, 단체협약, 취업규칙, 근로계약 등에 의거 당사자간에 달리 약정한 바가 있으면 그에 따라야 할 것이다. 생리휴가가 무급으로 개정되었더라도 법에 의하여 부여되는 휴가이므로 주휴일, 연차휴가 등을 부여하기 위한 소정근로일수 및 출근율 산정 시 소정근로일수에 포함하고 그 날은 출근한 것으로 보아야 한다.

---
[191] 고평법 제19조의 2, 고용보험법제73조의 2

Chapter 8 Other Related References

I. Rules of Employment regarding Working Hours, Holidays, and Leaves (Standard Sample)

⟨Table 7-1⟩ Form: Application for Leave

제8장 기타 근로시간 관련 참고자료

Ⅰ. 근로시간, 휴일, 휴가에 대한 취업규칙(표준샘플)

〈표 7-1〉 휴가신청서 서식

Chapter 8 Other Related References

Ⅰ. Rules of Employment regarding Working Hours, Holidays, and Leaves (Standard Sample)

CHAPTER ○. WORKING HOURS, REST PERIODS, AND HOLIDAYS

Article 14. Working Hours and Rest Period

1. Employees' working hours per week shall not exceed forty hours (40) excluding recess hours.
2. If an employee works outside of his or her office for a business trip or other similar reasons, his/her working hours will be deemed equivalent to the regular working hours unless there is clear documentation to demonstrate that his/her working hours differed from his/her normal working hours. However, if an employee exceeds his/her regular working hours in performing a specific work, the hours needed to perform the task are added to his/her working hours.

Article 14-2. Flexible working hours

1. The Company shall allow employees to work more than 8 hours on a certain day and 40 hours in a certain week as long as the average weekly working hours in 2 weeks do not exceed 40 hours. But working hours in a certain week shall not be more than 48 hours.
2. In cases below as decided upon according to a written agreement with the employees' representative, the Company shall allow employees to work for more than 8 hours on a certain day and 40 hours on a certain week as long as the average weekly working hours during 3 months do not exceed 40 hours. But working hours on certain weeks and on a certain day shall not be more than 52 hours and 12 hours, respectively.
   ① Scope of work of relevant employees
   ② Period (A certain time period within 3 months shall be made.)
   ③ Working days and working hours for each working day during the relevant periods
   ④ Validity for the written agreement

Ⅰ. 근로시간, 휴일, 휴가에 대한 취업규칙(표준샘플)

제○장 근무시간, 휴게 및 휴일

제14조【근무시간 및 휴게시간】

1. 모든 사원의 근로시간은 휴게시간을 제외하고 1일에 8시간, 1주일에 40시간으로 한다.
2. 사원이 출장 또는 그와 유사한 사유로 근로시간의 전부 또는 일부를 사업장 밖에서 근로하여 근로시간을 산정하기 어려운 때에는 소정근로시간을 근로한 것으로 본다. 다만, 당해 업무를 수행하기 위하여 통상적으로 소정근로시간을 초과하여 근로할 필요가 있는 경우에는 그 업무의 수행에 통상 필요한 시간을 근로한 것으로 본다.

제14조의2【탄력적 근로시간제】

1. 회사는 교대제 기타 방식으로 2주 이내의 일정한 단위기간을 평균하여 1주간의 근로시간이 40시간을 초과하지 아니하는 범위 안에서 특정주에 40시간을, 특정일에 8시간을 초과하여 근로하게 할 수 있다. 다만 특정주의 근로시간은 48시간을 초과 할 수 없다.
2. 회사는 사원 대표와 서면합의에 따라 다음 각 호의 사항을 정한 때에는 3월 이내의 단위기간을 평균하여 1주간의 근로시간이 40시간을 초과하지 아니하는 범위 안에서 특정 주에 40시간을, 특정일에 8시간을 초과하여 근로하게 할 수 있다. 다만, 특정주의 근로시간은 52시간을, 특정일의 근로시간은 12시간을 초과 할 수 없다.
   ① 대상근로자의 범위
   ② 단위기간(3월 이내의 일정한 기간으로 정하여야 한다)
   ③ 단위기간에 있어서의 근로일 및 당해 근로일별 근로시간
   ④ 서면합의의 유효기간

Chapter 8 Other Related References

Article 15. Time of Arrival and Leaving

1. An employee shall come to the workplace and prepare for work before working hours.
2. An employee shall not prepare to leave before the end of the working hours. An employee shall leave the office after arranging and fixing office supplies, documents, tools, etc.
3. During working hours, except in the case of an emergency, an employee shall not leave the Company without obtaining permission from the appropriate supervisor.

Article 16. Late Arrival and Early Departure

An employee opting to arrive late or depart early shall request permission in advance from the appropriate supervisor. In case of an emergency, when it is impossible to obtain such permission, the employee shall report as soon as possible, or at the latest, immediately upon his/her return to work, the reason for the late arrival or early departure and inability to obtain prior permission.

Article 17. Change in Working Hours

The working days and hours, starting time, finishing time, and rest time may be modified by the Company in accordance with the Labor Standards Act, work requirements, traffic conditions, and other factors.

Article 18. Holidays

Unless otherwise provided in the relevant laws, paid off-days shall be as follows:
1. Weekly off-days (every Sunday);
2. Labor Day (May 1st);
3. Company Foundation Anniversary; and
4. Public holidays designated by the Korean Government (subject to change).

Article 19. Work beyond Regular Working Hours and on Holidays

According to work requirements, employees may be requested to work at times other than the regular working hours or on holidays based upon mutual

제15조【출퇴근】

1. 사원은 시업시각 이전에 출근하여 근무를 개시할 수 있도록 하여야 한다.
2. 사원은 종업시각 이전에 종업의 준비를 하지 아니하며 사무비품, 서류, 공구 등의 정리, 정돈, 정비를 마친 후 퇴근하여야 한다.
3. 긴급을 요하는 경우를 제외하고, 사원은 관련 상사의 허락을 받지 아니하고는 통상적 근무시간 중에 회사를 이탈하여서는 안 된다.

제16조【지각 및 조퇴】

지각이나 조퇴를 하고자 하는 사원은 사전에 회사의 승인을 득하여야 한다. 긴급한 사태로 사전 승인을 취득하기가 불가능할 때에는 사원은 가능한 한 빨리, 늦어도 업무복귀 후 즉시 지각이나 조퇴의 이유 및 사전승인을 취득할 수 없었던 사유를 보고하여야 한다.

제17조【근무시간의 변경】

회사는 근로기준법, 업무상의 필요, 교통상황 또는 그 밖의 사유에 따라 근무일, 근무시간, 시업시간, 종업시간 및 휴게시간을 변경할 수 있다.

제18조【휴 일】

회사는 법률이 달리 정하지 않는 한 다음의 날들을 유급휴일(주휴일 및 기타 휴일)로 한다.
1. 주휴일(매주 일요일)
2. 근로자의 날
3. 회사창립일
4. 대한민국 정부가 공휴일로 지정한 날 (단, 변경이 있을 때에는 그에 따른다).

제19조【정규근무시간 이외의 근무 및 휴일근무】

회사업무상 필요한 경우, 당사자와의 합의에 의하여 회사는 사원에게

Chapter 8 Other Related References

agreement of the parties concerned.

Article 20. Exemption

The provisions concerning working hours, rest periods, and holidays set forth in Chapter 4 shall not apply to any of the following employees:

1. An employee engaged in supervisory or managerial work and/or an employee dealing with company secrets as prescribed in Article 34 of the Enforcement Decree of the Labor Standards Act.

2. An employee engaged in watching or intermittent work as set forth in Article 63 of the Labor Standards Act (e.g., drivers or guards).

CHAPTER ○. LEAVE

Article 21. Types of Leave

1. Annual paid leave;
2. Maternity leave (Paternity leave);
3. Menstruation leave;
4. Special leave; and
5. Sub-fertility treatment leave.

Article 22. Procedures for Taking Leave

1. Any employee wishing to take leave shall obtain prior permission from the appropriate supervisor one week in advance by submitting a written request in the form designated by the Company (in exceptional circumstances, he/she may obtain permission less than one week in advance). With respect to annual and monthly paid leave, the Company may alter the period of an employee's leave in accordance with the Company's workload and needs, provided that the Company shall, to the utmost extent, try to respect the time appointed by the employee.

2. If an employee, for inevitable reasons, is unable to submit a prior request as provided for in the preceding paragraph, the employee shall report as soon as possible, or, at the latest, immediately upon resuming work, any absence, clearly stating the reasons therefore.

정규근무시간 이외의 시간이나 휴일에 근무할 것을 명할 수 있다.

제20조【적용의 제외】

본 제4장에 규정된 근로시간, 휴게시간 및 휴일에 관한 규정은 다음 각 호의 사원에게는 적용되지 않는다.

1. 근로기준법 시행령 제34조에 규정된 감독이나 관리의 지위에 있는 사원 또는 기밀 사무를 취급하는 사원
2. 근로기준법 제63조에 규정된 감시적 및 단속적 근로에 종사하는 사원 (예컨대 운전기사나 경비업무에 종사하는 사원)

제○장 휴 가

제21조【휴가의 종류】

1. 연차유급휴가
2. 출산휴가 (배우자 출산휴가)
3. 생리휴가
4. 경조휴가
5. 난임휴가

제22조【휴가의 절차】

1. 휴가를 받고자 하는 사원은 회사 소정양식에 의거한 서면 신청서를 1주일 전에 회사에 제출함으로써 관련 감독 간부사원의 사전승인을 얻어야 한다.(회사가 인정하는 예외적인 경우에는 1주일 이내). 연차 유급휴가에 관하여 회사는 업무량 및 업무상의 필요에 따라 휴가 시기를 변경할 수 있다. 단, 회사는 가능한 한 사원이 선택한 시기를 존중하여야 한다.
2. 사원이 불가피한 사정으로 전항에 규정된 사전 신청을 할 수 없는 경우에는 업무복귀 즉시 그 이유를 명시하여 신청서를 제출하여야 한다.

Chapter 8 Other Related References

Article 23. Annual Paid Leave
The Company shall grant employees annual paid leave as follows:
1. Employees who have more than an eighty (80) percent or higher attendance rate in the given year shall acquire fifteen (15) days of annual paid leave.
2. Employees whose consecutive service years are less than one (1) year or whose attendance is less than 80 percent shall acquire 1 day of annual paid leave for every one month of perfect attendance.
3. Employees shall acquire fifteen (15) days of annual paid leave as stated in Clause 1 for their initial one-year working period. Additionally, the Company shall grant monthly paid leave as stated in Clause 2.
4. Employees who have consecutively worked for more than three (3) years shall acquire one (1) additional day of annual paid leave for every two (2) years exceeding an initial one working year stated in Clause 1. However, the maximum number of paid annual leave shall be limited to twenty five (25) days.
5. The Company shall grant annual paid leave to employees on their requested dates. However, the dates for annual paid leave requested by employees may be adjusted when the Company thinks the timing is inappropriate (e.g., due to heavy workload period or busy working season).
6. Annual leave days may be used by an employee at his/her own discretion, by accumulating or dividing them within one (1) year.
7. Claims for paid leave days shall be extinguished if not used within one (1) year; Provided that this shall not apply in cases where the worker concerned has been prevented from using them due to any cause attributable to the Company.

Article 24. Calculation Criteria of Annual Paid Leave
1. The calculation period of annual paid leave starts January 1st and ends December 31st; provided that if the consecutive service period of a newly hired employee is less than one year, monthly paid leave at each service month shall be obtained up to the end of that first year in advance. Then, on January 1st of the following year, the company provides 15 days of annual paid leave in advance.
2. At the end of the term of employment (or when resigning), the number of annual leave days that occurs on January 1st of the year in which the employee resigns will be adjusted and settled in proportion to the date of resignation for the period from January 1 to the resigning date.
3. Such holidays as holidays to exercise civil rights, weekly holidays, and

제23조【연차유급휴가】

회사는 사원에게 연도의초에 다음과 같이 연차를 부여한다.
1. 사원은 1년간 8할 이상 출근한 경우 15일의 유급휴가를 취득한다.
2. 계속근로연수가 1년 미만인 사원 또는 1년간 8할 이상 근무하지 못한 경우에 대하여는 1월간 개근 시 1일의 유급휴가를 부여한다.
3. 사원의 최초 1년간의 근로에 대하여 유급휴가를 주는 경우에는 제1항의 규정에 의한 15일의 휴가를 부여하되, 제2항의 휴가는 제1항의 휴가와 별도로 추가적으로 지급한다.
4. 3년 이상 계속 근로한 사원에 대하여는 제1항의 휴가에 최초 1년을 초과하는 계속근로연수 매 2년에 대하여 1일을 가산한 유급휴가를 부여하되, 가산휴가를 포함한 총 휴가일수는 25일을 한도로 한다.
5. 연차휴가는 사원의 청구가 있는 시기에 주어야 하며, 사원이 청구한 시기에 유급휴가를 주는 것이 사업운영에 막대한 지장이 있는 경우에는 그 시기를 변경할 수 있다.
6. 연차휴가는 사원의 자유의사에 의하여 1년간에 한하여 적치 또는 분할하여 사용할 수 있다.
7. 연차휴가를 1년간 사용하지 아니할 때에는 휴가청구권은 소멸한다. 다만, 회사의 귀책사유로 사용하지 못한 경우에는 제외한다.

제24조【연차휴가의 산출기준】

1. 연차유급휴가의 계산기간은 당해 년 1월1일부터 12월 31일까지로 한다. 단, 신규채용직원 또는 휴직 후 복직될 사원의 근속기간이 12월 31일 현재 만 1년에 미달할 경우 기산일을 기준으로 예상되는 월차 유급휴가를 미리 지급한다. 다음 년도의 1월 1일에 연차유급휴가 15일을 미리 지급한다.
2. 사원이 해당 년도에 퇴사 시에 그 해당 년도 1월 1일에 발생한 연차유급휴가를 퇴직일에 기준하여 비례하여 지급한다.
3. 공민권 행사를 위한 휴일, 주휴일, 법정 공휴일 및 기타의 휴일은

Chapter 8 Other Related References

public holidays shall be included as working days.
4. The period during which an employee cannot work due to occupational injuries or diseases, the period of maternity leave and child-care leave shall be regarded as a period of attendance.

Article 24-2. Promoting the Use of Annual Paid Leave
1. If an employee does not use leave notwithstanding the fact that the Company takes measures falling under any of the following subparagraphs to promote the use of paid leave prescribed in Article 23 (1) to (4), their leave will be forfeited; the Company shall have no obligation to compensate the employee for unused leave, unless the cause is attributable to the Company.
   (1) Within the first ten (10) days of the six (6) months before the unused leave is to be forfeited, the Company shall notify each worker of the number of their unused leave days and urge them in writing to decide when they would prefer to claim the leave and to inform the Company of their decided leave period.
   (2) Notwithstanding the notification prescribed in Subparagraph (1), if an employee fails to decide when to use the whole or part of the unused leave and inform the Company of the decided leave period within ten (10) days after the notice, the Company shall decide for the employee when they should use the unused leave and notify the employee of the decided leave period in writing no later than two (2) months before the unused leave is forfeited.
2. Where any employee's paid leave is terminated by time limitation pursuant to the main sentence of Article 23 (2) because the employee fails to take his/her paid leave although the relevant employer has taken the measures falling under each of the following subparagraphs to urge employees to take their respective annual leave pursuant to Article 60 (2): the monthly leave given for an employee who has worked less than one year, the relevant employer is not liable to compensate the employee for his/her failure to take the paid leave, and the employee's failure to take the paid leave shall be deemed not to fall under the reasons attributable to the

이를 각각 근무일수에 산입한다.
4. 사원이 업무상 상병으로 인하여 요양 휴직하는 기간, 여사원의 산전후 휴가와 육아휴직 기간은 연차휴가 적용에 있어서는 출근한 것으로 간주한다.

제24-2조【연차유급휴가 사용촉진】

1. 회사는 제23조 제1항내지 제4항의 규정에 의한 유급휴가의 사용을 촉진하기 위하여 다음 각호의 조치를 하였음에도 불구하고 사원이 휴가를 사용하지 아니하여 연차휴가가 소멸된 경우에는 회사는 미사용휴가에 대하여 보상할 의무가 없으며, 회사의 귀책사유에 해당하지 아니하는 것으로 본다.

    (1) 연차휴가가 소멸하기 6월 전을 기준으로 10일 이내에 회사가 사원별로 미사용휴가일수를 알려주고, 직원이 그 사용시기를 정하여 회사에게 통보하도록 서면으로 촉구한다.

    (2) 1호의 규정에 의한 촉구에 불구하고 사원이 촉구를 받은 때부터 10일 이내에 미사용휴가의 전부 또는 일부의 사용시기를 정하여 회사에 통보하지 않은 경우에는 연차휴가가 소멸하기 2월 전까지 회사가 미사용휴가의 사용시기를 정하여 사원에게 서면으로 통보한다.

2. 사용자가 계속하여 근로한 기간이 1년 미만인 근로자의 제23조 제2항에 따른 유급휴가의 사용을 촉진하기 위하여 다음 각 호의 조치를 하였음에도 불구하고 근로자가 휴가를 사용하지 아니하여 제23조 제7항 본문에 따라 소멸된 경우에는 사용자는 그 사용하지 아니한 휴가에 대하여 보상할 의무가 없고, 같은 항 단서에 따른 사용자의 귀책 사유에 해당하지 아니하는 것으로 본다.

    (1) 최초 1년의 근로기간이 끝나기 3개월 전을 기준으로 10일 이내에 사용자가 근로자별로 사용하지 아니한 휴가 일수를 알려주고, 근로자가 그 사용 시기를 정하여 사용자에게 통보하도록 서면으로

employer provided for in the proviso to Article 23 (7):

(1) Any employer shall notify in writing every employee of the number of days of his/her paid leave that has not been taken, and shall urge every employee to notify the employer of a period he/she is planning for the paid leave after determining on such period within ten days, at the three month point prior to one year of his/her service;

(2) Notwithstanding the encouragement referred to in subparagraph 1, if the employee fails to notify the employer of a period during which he/she is planning to take all of part of his/her remaining paid leave within ten days from the date he/she is urged to take his/her paid leave, the employer shall notify the employee in writing after setting a period for his/her paid leave, by no later than one month before the end of his/her first year.

Article 25. Replacement of Paid Leave

1. In cases where the Company has an employee on leave, it will replace his/her annual paid leave with a specific work day through a written agreement with the employee representative.
2. In cases where the employee has not used all leave by the end of the following calendar year, the Company shall compensate the employee for all of the unused annual paid leave.

Article 26. Special Leave

Congratulatory and Condolence Leave In the event that an employee falls under any of the following categories, the Company shall grant prescribed special leave with pay.

1. Marriage of employee : 5 days
2. Marriage of child : 2 days
3. 60th and 70th birthday of employee's or his/her spouse's parents : 1 day
4. Death of spouse, child, employee's or his/her spouse's parents : 5 days
5. Death of employee's or his/her spouse's siblings or grandparents : 2 day

CHAPTER 0. LEAVE OF ABSENCE

촉구할 것. 다만, 사용자가 서면 촉구한 후 발생한 휴가에 대해서는 최초 1년의 근로기간이 끝나기 1개월 전을 기준으로 5일 이내에 촉구하여야 한다.

(2) 제1호에 따른 촉구에도 불구하고 근로자가 촉구를 받은 때부터 10일 이내에 사용하지 아니한 휴가의 전부 또는 일부의 사용 시기를 정하여 사용자에게 통보하지 아니하면 최초 1년의 근로기간이 끝나기 1개월 전까지 사용자가 사용하지 아니한 휴가의 사용 시기를 정하여 근로자에게 서면으로 통보할 것. 다만, 제1호 단서에 따라 촉구한 휴가에 대해서는 최초 1년의 근로기간이 끝나기 10일 전까지 서면으로 통보하여야 한다.

제25조【유급휴가 대체 및 보상】

1. 회사는 사원대표와 서면합의에 의하여 연차유급휴가일을 특정 근무일로 대체하여 근로자를 휴무시킬 수 있다.
2. 회사는 업무상의 이유로 익년도 말까지 사용하지 못한 미사용 휴가일에 대하여 차익년도 1월에 사원에게 미사용 휴가에 대하여 연차유급휴가 근로수당을 지급한다.

제26조【경조휴가】

회사는 사원이 다음 각 호에 해당하는 경조사가 있을 경우에는 증빙서류를 제출한 자에 한하여 해당일수의 유급 경조휴가를 지급한다.

1. 본인결혼	5일
2. 자녀결혼	2일
3. 본인과 배우자의 부모 회갑, 칠순	1일
4. 배우자, 자녀, 본인과 배우자의 부모 사망	5일
5. 본인과 배우자의 형제, 자매, 조부모 사망	2일

제6장 휴 직

Article 27. Reasons for and Period of Leave of Absence

The Company may, on its judgment or discretion, order an employee falling under any of the following categories to take a leave of absence for the period concerned:

1. When the employee receives an order of draft or call under the Military Service Act for a period of at least one (1) month: for the period of draft or call;
2. When the employee is absent for fourteen (14) days or longer due to personal reasons: for up to two (2) months;
3. When it is deemed that the employee is unable to perform his/her duty due to physical or mental disorder: for up to six (6) months; provided, however, that, in unavoidable cases, this period may be extended up to three (3) months, one time only;
4. When the employee falls in the category where employment is restricted in accordance with Paragraph 1 of Article 45 of the Industrial Safety and Health Act: for up to six (6) months;
5. When the employee is under arrest or prosecuted under a criminal case: until the final verdict;
6. When the employee wishes to take a leave of absence in order to care for his/her infant of eight (8) years old or less or less than second grade in elementary school; or
7. In other unavoidable cases related to the Company's business and work requirements, provided that the Company shall decide after consultation with the employee representative.

Article 28. Treatment of Employees on Leave of Absence

1. The employee who is on leave shall maintain his/her status as an employee of the Company, but shall not perform his/her duties.
2. The employee who is on leave due to suspension from working or enlistment shall not be paid for the period from the day he/she receives the order of leave of absence to the preceding day of reinstatement.

Article 29. Reinstatement

1. The employee on leave shall submit an application for reinstatement within fourteen (14) days after the completion of the period of leave of absence, or after the cessation of the cause of such leave of absence, whichever is sooner.

제27조【휴직의 사유】

회사는 회사의 판단 및 재량에 따라 사원이 다음 각 항에 해당하는 사원에 대하여 규정된 기간 동안 휴직을 명할 수 있다.

1. 병역법에 의하여 1월 이상 징·소집 명령을 받았을 때 : 그 기간
2. 일신상 사정으로 14일 이상 결근을 요할 때 : 2개월 이내
3. 신체상 또는 정신상 장애로 인하여 업무수행이 곤란하다고 판정되었을 때 : 6개월 이내 단, 부득이한 경우에는 1회에 한하여 3개월 이내에서 연장할 수 있다.
4. 산업안전보건법 제45조 제1항에 의거 근로금지 제한사항에 해당할 때 : 6개월 이내
5. 형사사건으로 구속 또는 기소되었을 때 : 확정 판결시까지
6. 만 8세 이하 또는 초등학교 2학년 이하의 자녀를 양육하기 위해 휴직을 원할 때
7. 기타 회사경영 및 업무상 부득이한 사유가 있을 경우
   (단, 이 경우에는 사원대표와 협의 후 결정한다)

제28조【휴직자 처우】

1. 휴직된 자는 사원의 신분은 보장되나 직무에 종사하지 못한다.
2. 휴직자에 대하여는 본 규칙에서 별도로 정하지 않는 한 휴직 발령일로부터 복직 발령 전일까지 급여를 지급하지 아니한다.

제29조【복 직】

1. 휴직자는 휴직기간 만료 후 또는 휴직사유 소멸 후 먼저 도래하는 날 14일 이내에 복직원을 제출해야 한다.
2. 휴직기간이 만료되거나 휴직기간 만료 전이라도 휴직 사유가 소멸되어 휴직자가 복직하고자 할 때 회사는 즉시 원직에 복직시켜야 한다. 단, 원직의 소멸 또는 3개월 이상의 휴직으로 원직 복귀가 어려울 때는 본인과의 협의 하에 동등 직급, 또는 유사직무, 또는 다른

2. If the period of leave of absence expires or the employee desires to be reinstated prior to the expiration of leave of absence because the reason for the leave of absence has ceased to exist, the Company shall immediately reinstate him/her to his/her former position; provided, however, that in the event it is difficult to reinstate him/her to the former position due to closure of the former position or due to a period of leave of absence for three (3) months or longer, the Company shall reinstate him/her to a corresponding position, similar position or another position after discussion with the employee concerned.
3. Concerning the employee who has been on a leave of absence for six (6) months or more, the Company may assign the employee to different duties as required by business necessity.

Chapter 7. Maternity Protection Rules

Article 30 [Maternity leave]
1. The Company shall grant 90 days including before and after childbirth (120 days in the event of carrying two or more babies at once) of paid maternity leave to pregnant employees and maternity leave can be used in parts even before childbirth according to the relevant laws when there is a miscarriage, etc. But post-natal holidays shall be more than 45 days (60 days in the event of carrying two or more babies at once).
2. The first 60 days (75 days in the event of carrying two or more babies at once) of the leave in the preceding article are paid (based on ordinary wages) but if there is any pre or post-natal holiday pay according to the relevant law, the amount paid shall be excluded.

Article 31 [Leave for miscarriage and stillbirth]
Company shall grant the following to female employees who request for leave with a medical certificate for miscarriage or stillbirth. But abortion is an exception.
1. If the pregnancy of an employee with miscarriage or stillbirth (hereinafter called pregnancy) is within 11 weeks: Up to 5 days from the day of miscarriage or stillbirth
2. When pregnancy is more than 12 weeks and less than 15 weeks Up to 10 days from the day of miscarriage or stillbirth
3. When pregnancy is more than 16 weeks and less than 21 weeks Up to

직무로 복직시킨다.
3. 6개월 이상의 휴직 이후 복직을 하게 되는 경우에는 해당 사원에게 회사 업무상 필요에 따라 다른 직무를 부여할 수 있다.

제7장 모성보호규정

제30조【출산전후휴가】

1. 회사는 임신 중인 여사원에 대해 출산·전후를 통하여 휴일을 포함한 90일간(한 번에 둘 이상 자녀를 임신한 경우에는 120일)의 유급휴가를 부여하며, 유산경험 등 관계법령이 정한 사유에 해당하는 경우에는 출산 전 어느 때라도 휴가를 나누어 사용할 수 있도록 한다. 다만, 휴가는 출산 후에 45일 이상(한 번에 둘 이상 자녀를 임신한 경우에는 60일)을 보장하여야 한다.
2. 전항의 휴가 중 최초 60일(한 번에 둘 이상 자녀를 임신한 경우에는 75일)은 유급(통상임금 기준)으로 하며, 다만 관계법령에 따라 출산전후휴가급여 등이 지원된 경우에는 그 금액의 한도에서 지급책임을 면한다.

제31조【유산·사산휴가】

회사는 의료기관의 진단서를 첨부하여 유산·사산휴가를 청구한 여사원에 대하여 각 호의 기준에 따라 이를 부여한다. 다만, 인공임신중절수술에 의한 유산의 경우는 그러하지 아니하다.
1. 유산·사산한 사원의 임신기간(이하 '임신기간'이라 한다)이 11주 이내인 경우 : 유산 또는 사산한 날로부터 5일까지
2. 임신기간이 12주 이상 15주 이내인 경우 : 유산 또는 사산한 날로부터 10일까지
3. 임신기간이 16주 이상 21주 이내인 경우 : 유산 또는 사산한 날로부터 30일까지

Chapter 8 Other Related References

30 days from the day of miscarriage or stillbirth
4. When pregnancy is more than 22 weeks and less than 27 weeks: Up to 60 days from the day of miscarriage or stillbirth
5. When pregnancy is more than 28 weeks: Up to 90 days from the day of miscarriage or stillbirth

Article 32 [Time allowed for prenatal checkups]
1. The Company shall accept a request by a pregnant female employee for the time necessary for regular prenatal checkups according to relevant laws.
2. The Company shall not reduce the pay of an employee in paragraph 1 for the time spent obtaining prenatal checkups.

Article 33 [Menstrual leave]
   One day of unpaid monthly leave shall be given to a female employee at request.

Article 34 [Paternity leave]
1. The Company shall grant 10 days paid paternity leave for each confinement of his spouse.
2. Paternity Leave can't be requested 90 days after the childbirth of the spouse.
3. The Leave referred to in paragraph (1) may divided use only once
4. The company shall not dismiss or give any other unfavorable treatment to an employee on account of taking paternity leave.

Article34-2[Sub-fertility treatment leave]
1. The company provide the sub fertility treatment leave (3 days per year) for employees who wish to receive medical fertility treatment, such as artificial insemination and IVF(In vitro fertilization).with the first day paid: Provided, That the company and employee can arrange a different date if the requested one will likely result in significant disruptions to the business.
2. The company shall not dismiss, penalize, or take any other disadvantageous action against an employee for taking a sub-fertility

4. 임신기간이 22주 이상 27주 이내인 경우 : 유산 또는 사산한 날로부터 60일까지
5. 임신기간이 28주 이상인 경우 : 유산 또는 사산한 날로부터 90일까지

제32조【태아검진 시간의 허용】
1. 회사는 임신한 여성근로자 관계법령에 따른 임산부 정기건강진단을 받는데 필요한 시간을 청구하는 경우 이를 허용하여야 한다.
2. 회사는 제1항에 따른 건강진단 시간을 이유로 그 근로자의 임금을 삭감하여서는 아니된다.

제33조【생리휴가】
여사원이 생리일에 휴가를 청구한 경우에는 월 1일의 무급휴가를 부여한다.

제34조【배우자 출산휴가】
1. 회사는 사원의 배우자가 출산하는 경우 10일의 유급휴가를 준다.
2. 배우자 출산휴가는 사원의 배우자가 출산한 날부터 90일이 지나면 청구할 수 없다.
3. 전 항의 배우자 출산휴가는 1회 분할하여 사용할 수 있다
4. 회사는 배우자 출산휴가를 이유로 사원을 해고하거나 그 밖의 불리한 처우를 하여서는 아니된다.

제34-2조【난임휴가】
1. 회사는 사원이 인공수정 또는 체외수정 등 난임치료를 받기 위하여 휴가 (이하 '난임치료휴가'라 한다) 를 청구하는 경우 연간 3일 이내 휴가를 주어야 하며, 이 경우 최초 1일은 유급으로 한다. 다만, 사원이 청구한 시기에 휴가를 주는 것이 정상적인 사업운영에 중대한 지장을 초래하는 경우에는 사원과 협의하여 그 시기를 변경할 수 있다.

treatment leave.

Article 35 [Childcare leave]
1. Childcare leave shall be given at an employee's request in pursuit of taking care of children of less than 8 years old and less than second grade in elementary school.
2. Childcare leave shall be within 1 year.
3. The Company shall not give unfavorable treatment involving dismissal due to childcare.
4. The Company shall actively cooperate with an employee for childcare benefits based on the relevant laws by providing evidentiary documents.

Article 36 [Reduction of Working Hours for Childcare Period]
1. The company shall grant 'Reduction of Working Hours for childcare, if an employee asks for reduction of working hour to take care of his/her child(including an adopted child) aged 8 and under or in the second year of elementary school or lower (hereinafter referred to as 'working hour reduction for childcare period') However, in cases where it is not possible to hire his/her replacement personnel, where it cause a considerable difficulty for normal business operation, and where there are other cases stipulated in the enforcement decree.
2. If the company does not grant working hour reduction for childcare period under exceptional conditions of paragraph (1), he/she shall notify the employee of the reason in writing and have him/her take childcare leave or consult with the employee as to whether to support him/her through other measures such as adjusting the hours of working time
3. If the company grants working hour reduction for childcare period to the relevant employee under paragraph (1), the working hours after reduction shall be 15 hours or more a week but shall not exceed 35 hours a week.
4. The period of working hour reduction for childcare period shall be one year or less. However, if an employee who is entitled to childcare leave does not use the entire period of childcare leave (1 year), the employee can apply for a working hour reduction for childcare period by summing up with the remaining period.
5. The company shall not dismiss or give any other disadvantageous

2. 회사는 난임치료휴가 사용을 이유로 해고, 징계 등 사원에게 불리한 처우를 하여서는 아니 된다.

제35조【육아휴직】
1. 육아휴직은 만 8세 이하 또는 초등학교 2학년 이하의 자녀를 양육하기 위해 사원이 신청할 경우 이를 부여한다.
2. 육아휴직기간은 1년 이내로 한다.
3. 회사는 육아휴직을 이유로 해고 기타 불리한 처우를 하지 아니한다.
4. 회사는 사원이 육아휴직을 사용할 경우 관계법령이 육아휴직급여를 받을 수 있도록 증빙서류를 제공하는 등 적극 협조한다.

제36조【육아기 근로시간 단축】
1. 회사는 사원이 만 8세 이하 또는 초등학교 2학년 이하의 자녀를 양육하기 위하여 근로시간의 단축(이하 "육아기 근로시간 단축"이라 한다)을 신청하는 경우에 이를 허용하여야 한다. 다만, 대체인력 채용이 불가능한 경우, 정상적인 사업 운영에 중대한 지장을 초래하는 경우 등 대통령령으로 정하는 경우에는 그러하지 아니하다.
2. 제1항 단서에 따라 회사가 육아기 근로시간 단축을 허용하지 아니하는 경우에는 해당 사원에게 그 사유를 서면으로 통보하고 육아휴직을 사용하게 하거나 출근 및 퇴근 시간 조정 등 다른 조치를 통하여 지원할 수 있는지를 해당 사원과 협의하여야 한다.
3. 회사는 제 1항에 따라 해당 사원에게 육아기 근로시간 단축을 허용하는 경우 단축 후 근로시간은 주단 15시간 이상이어야 하고 35시간을 넘어서는 아니 된다.
4. 육아기 근로시간 단축 기간은 1년 이내로 한다. 다만, 육아휴직을 신청할 수 있는 사원이 육아휴직 기간 중 사용하지 아니한 기간이 있으면 그 기간을 가산하여 육아기 근로시간 단축을 사용할 수 있다.
5. 회사는 육아기 근로시간 단축을 이유로 해당 사원에게 해고나 그 밖의

Chapter 8 Other Related References

treatment to the relevant employee on account of working hour reduction for childcare period.

Article 37 [Childcare time]
Feeding time shall be granted 2 times a day for more than 30 minutes each at the request of a female employee with an infant of less than 1 year old.

Article 38. Family Care Leave
1. If an Employee applies for family care leave ("Family Care Leave") in order to take care of his/her parents, spouse, children, or the parents of his/her spouse having a disease, accident, or old age, the Company shall grant permission therefor as unpaid leave. However, in the cases stipulated under the Presidential Decree of the Equal Employment Opportunity and Work-Family Balance Assistance Act, for example where it is not possible to employ substitute workers, or material interference is caused to the normal operation of the business, etc., then the Company may refuse.
2. Where the Company does not allow Family Care Leave according to the last sentence of paragraph 1 above, the Company shall notify the relevant employee of the reasons therefor in writing, and exert efforts to take any of the following measures:
   (1) Adjustment of the starting and ending times;
   (2) Restrictions on overtime work;
   (3) Adjustment of working hours, such as reduction or flexible operation of working hours; or
   (4) Other supportive measures appropriate to the relevant workplace conditions.
3. Family Care Leave shall be granted for up to ninety (90) days and may be divided for use. In such case, each period must be at least thirty (30) days. However, 10 days out of 90 days can be used daily.
4. The Company shall not dismiss or disadvantage an employee by such means as worsening the working conditions for an employee, due to the use of Family Care Leave.
5. The Family Care Leave period shall be included in the years of continuous service. However, such period shall not be included in the base period for calculation of average wages.

불리한 처우를 하여서 아니된다.

제37조 【육아시간】

생후 1년 미만의 유아를 가진 여성 근로자의 청구가 있는 경우에는 1일 2회 각각 30분이상의 유급수유시간을 주어야 한다.

제 38 조 (가족돌봄휴직)

1. 회사는 근로자가 부모, 배우자, 자녀 또는 배우자의 부모의 질병, 사고, 노령으로 인하여 그 가족을 돌보기 위한 휴직("가족돌봄휴직")을 신청하는 경우 무급휴가를 허용하여야 한다. 다만, 대체인력 채용이 불가능한 경우, 정상적인 사업 운영에 중대한 지장을 초래하는 경우 등 남녀고용평등과 일·가정 양립 지원에 관한 법률, 시행령으로 규정하는 경우에는 회사는 거부할 수 있다.
2. 회사는 전항 단서 조항 따라 가족돌봄휴직을 허용하지 아니하는 경우에는 해당 근로자에게 그 사유를 서면으로 통보하고, 다음 각 호의 어느 하나에 해당하는 조치를 하도록 노력하여야 한다.
   (1) 출퇴근 시간 조정
   (2) 연장근로의 제한
   (3) 단축근무, 탄력적 운영 등 근무시간 조정 또는
   (4) 그 밖에 사업장 사정에 맞는 지원조치
3. 가족돌봄휴직 기간은 연간 최장 90일로 하며, 이를 나누어 사용할 수 있다. 이 경우 나누어 사용하는 1회의 기간은 최소 30일 이상이 되어야 한다. 다만, 90일 중 10일은 하루 단위로 사용할 수 있다.
4. 회사는 가족돌봄휴직을 이유로 해당 근로자를 해고하거나 근로조건을 악화시키는 등 불리한 처우를 하여서는 아니된다.
5. 가족돌봄휴직 기간은 근속기간에 포함한다. 다만, 이 기간은 평균임금 산정을 위한 기준기간에서는 제외된다.

Chapter 8 Other Related References

<Table 8-1> Form: Application for Leave

APPLICATION for LEAVE
휴가 신청서

Dept. 부 서			Name 이 름			
Job title 직 위			Company ID No. 사 번			
Type of leave 휴가의 종류		Estimated period		2.1. Actual Period		Remarks
		From / To / days		From / To / Days		
Annual Leave	연 차					
Congratulatory /Condolence	경 조					
Sick Leave	병 가					
Reserve Forces Training	향 군					
Leaving Early	조 퇴					
Maternity Leave	출 산					
Other	기 타					
Reason for leave 사 유:						

1. This application must be submitted and approved in advance.
   본 신청서는 사전에 제출 승인 되어야 한다.
2. Reserve training and sick leave must be summated with relevant certificates.
   향토 예비군 및 병가등의 휴가 신청시에는 관련 증빙서류를 제출해야 한다.

APPROVAL 승 인

Prepared by
신청자   Signature   /   /   Date

Approved by Dept. Manager
승인자   Signature   /   /   Date

Original to HR Team
                      Signature   /   /   Date

<표 8-1> 서식: 휴가 신청서

APPLICATION of LEAVE
휴가 신청서

Dep't 부서		Name 이름	
Job title 직위		Company ID No. 사번	

Type of leave 휴가의 종류		Estimated period			Actual Period			Remarks
		From	To	days	From	To	Days	
Annual Leave	연차							
Congratulatory /Condolence	경조							
Sick Leave	병가							
Reserve Forces Training	향군							
Leaving Early	조퇴							
Maternity Leave	출산							
Others	기타							

Reason 사유:

1. This application must be submitted and approval in advance.
   본 신청서는 사전에 제출 승인 되어야 한다.
2. Reserve training and sick leave must be summated with relevant certificates.
   향토 예비군 및 병가등의 휴가 신청시에는 관련 증빙서류를 제출해야 한다.

APPROVAL 승 인

Prepared 신청자	_____ Signature	___/___/___ Date
Approved by Dept. Manager 승인자	_____ Signature	___/___/___ Date
Original to HR Team	_____ Signature	___/___/___ Date

Manual on Working Hours, Holidays and Leaves
근로시간, 휴일, 휴가 매뉴얼(제2개정판)

발 행 일 : 2020년 5월 13일 초판발행

발 행 일 : 2024년 1월 12일 2개정판

지 은 이 : 정 봉 수

펴 낸 이 : 정 봉 수

펴 낸 곳 : 강남노무법인 출판부 (K-Labor Press)

편집·디자인 : 정 영 철

주   소 : 서울시 강남구 대치동 테헤란로 406 A-1501 (대치동, 샹제리제센터)

전   화 : 02-539-0098

팩   스 : 02-539-4167

홈페이지 : www.k-labor.com

출판등록 : 강남, 바00177

I S B N : 979-11-85290-28-7

정   가 : 30,000원

■ 이 책자는 저작권법에 따라 보호받는 저작물이므로 무단전재와 복제를 금합니다.